SUPPORT GROUPS FOR CHILDREN

Kathleen O'Rourke, Ed.D.
John C. Worzbyt, Ed.D.

ACCELERATED DEVELOPMENT
A member of the Taylor & Francis Group

USA	Publishing Office:	ACCELERATED DEVELOPMENT *A member of the Taylor & Francis Group* 325 Chestnut Street, Suite 800 Philadelphia, PA 19106 Tel: (215) 625-8900 Fax: (215) 625-2940
	Distribution Center:	ACCELERATED DEVELOPMENT *A member of the Taylor & Francis Group* 47 Runway Road, Suite G Levittown, PA 19057 Tel: (215) 269-0400 Fax: (215) 269-0363
UK		Taylor & Francis Ltd. 1 Gunpowder Square London EC4A 3DE Tel: 0171 583 0490 Fax: 0171 583 0581

SUPPORT GROUPS FOR CHILDREN

2 3 4 5 6 7 8 9 0   B R B R   9

This book was set in Times Roman by Sandra F. Watts. Edited by Judith L. Aymond. Technical development by Cynthia Long. Cover design by Michelle Fleitz. Printing and binding by Braun-Brumfield, Inc.

A CIP catalog record for this book is available from the British Library.
⊗ The paper in this publication meets the requirements of the ANSI Standard Z39.48-1984 (Permanence of Paper)

Library of Congress Cataloging-in-Publication Data

O'Rourke, Kathleen
  Support groups for children / Kathleen O'Rourke, John C. Worzbyt.
    p. cm.
  Includes bibliographical references and index.
  1. Group counseling for children. I. Worzbyt, John C. II. Title.
RJ505.G7076   1996
362.2'04256'083—dc20   96-11202
                                                               CIP

ISBN 1-56032-395-7

TABLE OF CONTENTS

Part I
VALUES, GOALS, AND FACILITATIVE CONCERNS

Part II
SUPPORT GROUPS AND RELATED ACTIVITIES

CHAPTER 6
CHILDREN IN STEPFAMILIES   **133**

CHAPTER 7
LATCHKEY CHILDREN   **181**

CHAPTER 8
ANGER MANAGEMENT   **215**

CHAPTER 9
CONFLICT MANAGEMENT   **259**

CHAPTER 13
STRESS MANAGEMENT   437

CHAPTER 14
DIVERSITY GROUPS   493

LIST OF FIGURES

LIST OF ACTIVITY SHEETS

PREFACE

Support Groups for Children is a practical, easy-to-use handbook for teachers, counselors, psychologists, and social workers interested in helping children cope with *family* (alcoholism, divorce, and stepfamily living); *personal* (stress, anger, and low self-esteem); and *social* (peer acceptance, conflict, and loss) problems in their day-to-day lives.

In the chapters that follow, the reader will be provided with useful background information; a sound, educationally based teaching-learning model; and appropriate suggestions and activities for helping children achieve personal success in

- living in an alcoholic family;
- coping with divorce;
- coping with stepfamily living;
- being home alone (latchkey children);
- managing anger responsibly;
- resolving conflict peacefully;
- coping with death, loss, and grief;
- enhancing self-esteem;
- developing interpersonal skills and peer relationships;
- managing stress in healthy ways; and
- living, learning, and growing through diversity.

Support Groups for Children upholds the premise that most children possess the seed of resiliency necessary for turning life's setbacks into comebacks;

however, this seed must be nurtured if children are to beat the odds in the face of adversity. They need love; support from family, friends, and peers; and guidance from caring adults who can help them meet their needs. Support groups can provide children with a safe and secure climate in which to risk and to work in acquiring the necessary information, skills, and self-confidence to turn adversity into opportunity.

HOW THE BOOK IS ORGANIZED

Support Groups for Children is a 14-chapter text. Chapters 1 through 3 provide an overview of support groups and what makes them successful. The three main goals of support groups are presented, and the curriculum design forming the foundation for the 11 support groups is explained. The reader also is presented with detailed management guidelines to follow in planning, organizing, implementing, and monitoring the support groups presented in this book.

Chapters 4 through 14 present 11 support group topics that can help children better understand their current life situations, develop more effective coping strategies and how to use them, and learn how to make responsible life choices in responding to their dilemmas. The support groups presented in this handbook are listed here.

Chapter 4, Children of Alcoholics
Chapter 5, Children of Divorce
Chapter 6, Stepfamilies
Chapter 7, Latchkey Children
Chapter 8, Anger Management
Chapter 9, Conflict Management
Chapter 10, Coping with Death, Grief, and Loss
Chapter 11, Children and Self-esteem
Chapter 12, Social Skills Training
Chapter 13, Stress Management
Chapter 14, Diversity Groups

The reader is provided with background information on each group, suggestions for facilitating the group experience, detailed session guidelines and activities, homework assignments, and lists of resources containing useful supplemental information and materials that can be used for enrichment.

WHO MAY PARTICIPATE

The support group curriculum is geared for children ages 8 through 11. With some modifications in content and delivery, however, most children ages 5 through 13 can benefit from the support group experiences presented in this book.

EDUCATIONAL SETTINGS

Support Groups for Children can be implemented in a variety of educational settings. While school settings are most attractive due to the availability of children and needed resources (i.e., people, space, material, and equipment), child support groups can be conducted in community and religious settings as well.

Many youth oriented organizations such as the YMCA, Boy Scouts and Girl Scouts of America, 4-H groups, and the Parent-Teacher Association facilitate support groups and would find this text a useful addition to their program libraries.

CURRICULUM DESIGN

Support Groups for Children was designed with ease of use and flexibility in mind. The support groups are not arranged in any particular order and therefore can be introduced in any sequence deemed appropriate.

The support group sessions are designed to meet the needs of all children not just those experiencing adversity in their lives. All children can benefit from learning how to self-manage more effectively in such areas as self-esteem enhancement; anger, conflict, and stress management; and social skills development.

Although support groups are presented as distinct units, they do overlap in many respects. For example, the children of alcoholics support group can be enhanced, depending upon children's needs, by using group sessions and activities from the self-esteem, anger management, stress management, and loss support groups. The curriculum is designed so that group facilitators can organize support group sessions around their own ideas and those featured in this book.

FACILITATOR TRAINING

Readers having a background in teaching and working with children in small groups should do well in facilitating support groups. By following the format and suggestions provided, facilitators are guided in helping children talk about their concerns, express their feelings, and develop a sense of security and belonging while learning new ways to cope with their problems.

The primary purpose of *Support Groups for Children* is to meet the needs of well-adjusted children who are experiencing some difficulty in coping with recent life changes. The support group curriculum is designed to meet those ends.

We strongly encourage anyone planning to use this curriculum *in mental health settings*, as opposed to educational settings, to be properly credentialed to offer therapy. With this caution in mind, graduate students and practicing professionals in counseling, psychology, and social work will find this book particularly useful in working with at-risk children.

We sincerely hope you find *Support Groups for Children* informative and practical in your quest to help children live satisfying and productive lives.

ACKNOWLEDGEMENTS

Writing *Support Groups for Children* has been a labor of love. We have learned the value of patience and persistence in staying with our plan to create a book that will guide educators in their quest to help children find meaning and purpose in adversity. We are especially grateful to all those children who have taught us that life's setbacks and challenges can be full of opportunity to those who have the courage and determination to keep striving forward.

Just as we have sought to nurture and support educators in their efforts to support children, we likewise have received support from many people who have helped us find the courage and determination to keep striving forward as well. These are the people to whom we owe a debt of gratitude and to whom we dedicate this book.

To Linda Butler for her coordination of student worker efforts, personally typing and editing many drafts of the manuscript, and for her cheerful and "always ready to help" disposition.

To Corena Stefanik, our principal typist, we thank you for many hours of typing and reworking the manuscript and for your invaluable assistance in developing graphics and worksheets.

To Michele Smith, Sarah Azille, and Cally Scott for their typing assistance, trips to the library to check references, and securing of needed resources.

To Michelle Hainesworth, our principal research assistant, we owe much. Michelle assumed major responsibility for researching book chapters, reviewing resource materials, and securing needed articles, monographs, and books used in developing the manuscript.

To Linda Woleslagle for her assistance and significant contribution in helping to develop Chapter 14, Diversity Groups.

To Dr. Joseph Hollis, founder of Accelerated Development, a member of the Taylor & Francis Group, we owe many thanks. His belief in us and our ideas, and his tireless assistance and useful suggestions have significantly enhanced the quality and useability of this text.

To Cindy Long, our contact person, manuscript reviewer, and personal manager at Accelerated Development, we extend our appreciation. Cindy has been there to answer our questions and to improve the quality of our manuscript, and has kept our writing efforts moving forward in a timely manner.

To our colleagues and former graduate students for their support in our writing efforts and whose suggestions and questions about child support groups have helped shape the value and content of this book.

To the many children who have taught us about the value of support groups through their resilience, courage, and forward movement in the face of adversity.

To our families we are especially appreciative. For they have given us love, support, and understanding during those times when we have needed it most.

To each and every person who has contributed to the quality and useability of *Support Groups for Children*, many thanks. Each of you has validated your purpose for being, to pass on to others the very best of what you have to give so that others may in turn do the same. For your efforts, children will be forever indebted.

PART I
VALUES, GOALS,
AND
FACILITATIVE CONCERNS

Chapter 1

UNDERSTANDING SUPPORT GROUPS

Family groups, peer groups, and social groups shape the lives of our children for better or worse. Children learn about themselves and others; address their needs; and formulate their thoughts, feelings, and actions as members of various groups. Because the socialization process so significantly impacts the lives of our children in shaping their successes and how they handle life's adversities, it only makes sense to utilize groups in helping children turn life's set-backs into come-backs.

Support Groups for Children was designed to help facilitators assist children in becoming winners in life despite the daily challenges, set-backs, or barriers they will face. As children experience challenges, what really matters is not where they start, but how they finish in response to them. Their potential can never be fully realized if they back down from or are absorbed by adversity.

Support Groups for Children emphasizes that when children receive constructive support from their peers and professionally trained, caring adults, success is just one step beyond defeat. Most children today want to be winners in life, to self-manage in a responsible manner, and to feel good about themselves. Many children, however, lack the necessary information, skills, self-confidence, and opportunity to turn life's adversities into successes. *Support Groups for Children* provides a plan for facilitators that will assist them in helping children support themselves and each other in the face of family (alcoholism, divorce,

3

stepfamilies), personal (stress, anger, self-esteem), and social (peer pressure, conflict, and loss) challenges.

WHAT SUPPORT GROUPS ARE
AND WHAT THEY ARE NOT

A support group consists of a small group of children (5 to 10 in number) who are experiencing similar life challenges. These children are brought together by a trained facilitator to help them explore their feelings, thoughts, and actions and to achieve new levels of understanding about their dilemmas, which will lead to more effective and responsible methods of self-management.

Most children are motivated by the need to manage their lives successfully and to feel good about themselves while in the process of doing so. Support groups provide the physical and psychological climate necessary for the fulfillment of these needs.

Support groups are not a cure-all for all problems nor are they the answer for all children. Some life challenges may be so unique or of such crisis proportion that they need to be handled via individual counseling. Likewise some children may not be acceptable candidates for support groups. They may not be prepared (physically, socially, and/or emotionally) to benefit from this medium (support groups). Support groups do not seem to work well with children whose personalities, social skill deficits, or current life conditions place them or others potentially at risk.

The key to successful support groups is the bonding and emotional connectiveness that takes place among children as they learn from each other and share positive and responsible ways to self-manage in the face of adversity. Support groups work because they instill camaraderie and hope. They demonstrate that success comes to those with patience, persistence, and a plan. Support groups provide for these three important ingredients.

VALUE OF SUPPORT GROUPS

As previously mentioned, child support groups are composed of children who share a common status (children of alcoholics) or predicament (conflict) that generates some degree of stress. *The goal of child support groups is to help minimize stress through mutual support and sharing of coping strategies, information, and confidence.* The group facilitator does not attempt to change the status of members but rather accepts their situation and helps them carry on with their lives and grow in their understanding of self and others.

Child support groups provide children with support, emotional nurturance, and a sense of identity at a time in their lives when such conditions are missing. They facilitate changes in self-perception and teach children how to empower themselves in light of new information and skills. Child support groups thus provide a cooperative climate for growth, frequent interaction among participants, and an opportunity to learn from each other's successes and mistakes.

SUCCESSFUL SUPPORT GROUPS

Successful child support groups work best when children

- feel safe and secure within their group;
- share a common understanding of their problem (situation/condition);
- learn new and more effective ways to manage their situation;
- express their feelings, thoughts, and diverse points of view;
- experience constructive and nonjudgmental feedback throughout the change process;
- experience a positive self-image and personal pride;
- support and encourage each other in trying new ways of thinking, feeling, and acting as they discover self-qualities and abilities previously unknown;
- participate in group tasks of graduated difficulty and experience personal power that comes from risking and succeeding;
- advance to a status within the group where they not only receive help but also provide assistance to others commensurate with their abilities; and
- apply what they are learning to their life situations and experience the freedom that comes with new choices.

Child support groups make a positive difference in helping children succeed in the face of adversity. They learn to turn adversity into opportunity. Child support group facilitators play a significant role in helping to achieve this reality. They are the catalysts that foster personal growth in children by creating and supporting the necessary climatic conditions for change to occur.

Chapter 2

SUPPORT GROUPS: A BLUEPRINT FOR SUCCESS

Child support groups are designed to accomplish three goals. These goals are to help children:

- understand their current life situations;
- develop coping strengths that will enable them to do better; and
- make effective life decisions based on Right, Reality, and Responsibility.

Although this text is not a facilitator training manual, it does provide an effective teaching-learning model to follow when processing support group sessions. The support group curriculum consists of four interrelated dimensions:

- The Tripartite,
- Strengths Training,
- The Keystone Learning Model, and
- 3 R's Decision Making

These four dimensions contribute to the development of a sound educational curriculum that will assist children in accomplishing the three mentioned goals.

THE TRIPARTITE

Child support groups are like three-legged stools (Figure 2.1). They require three elements to make them productive. The "Tripartite" consists of children's

7

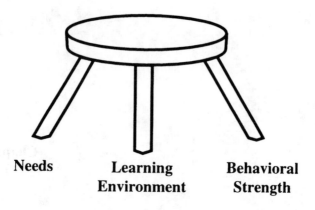

Needs   **Learning**   **Behavioral**
            Environment   **Strength**

Figure 2.1.   The Tripartite.

needs, behavioral strengths, and the learning environment. Together these elements will determine the level of success attained by children participating in support group experiences (Worzbyt & O'Rourke, 1989).

Child Needs

Children have a strong need to manage their lives effectively and to feel good about themselves as they are doing so. As described throughout this book, however, children's needs are constantly being assaulted and challenged (Maslow, 1970). When children's needs are threatened and are in danger of not being fulfilled, they experience a loss of self. Feeling alone and powerless, they are motivated to maintain stability in their lives but often are at a loss as to how to accomplish this end.

Children facing the divorce of their parents, loss of a loved one, low self-esteem, or conflict and peer pressure are in search of ways to feel better about themselves and to manage the adversity in their lives successfully. Children who participate in support groups are looking for ways to satisfy their needs in socially acceptable and responsible ways.

If child support groups are to succeed, facilitators first must identify and then respond to the unfulfilled needs of the children they serve. In *Support Groups for Children*, we identify some of the common needs experienced by children in each support group presented. Only by addressing these needs and others will children benefit from a support group experience.

Strengths to be Learned

What children desire most is to learn those strengths that will best satisfy their needs. As children participate in support groups, they will learn that while they cannot change others to get what they need, they can change themselves and how they respond to life's adversities. Support groups teach children new ways of thinking, feeling, and acting in the face of disruption. *Support Groups for Children* suggests specific strengths to teach children in response to their needs. In addition to the strengths that we have identified for each support group, facilitators are encouraged to monitor their groups closely and to teach additional strengths when appropriate.

Conditions of the Learning Environment

Teaching children what they need to learn only can be accomplished in a supportive learning climate. Such a climate fosters self-confidence, accepts mistakes, is safe, supports risk-taking, and provides opportunities for children to practice what they have learned.

Child support group facilitators must develop sound physical and psychological teaching-learning climates. *Helping children connect with each other, feel unique in a positive way, and experience personal power in meeting their needs are key components of the curriculum.*

Child support groups function best when they address specific needs of children, teach behavioral strengths in addressing their needs, and do so in a climate that fosters positive self-worth and a "can do" state of mind.

STRENGTHS TRAINING

A strength is any learned set of behaviors that will help children satisfy a need. Strengths represent complex processes frequently consisting of a chain of behaviors that, when learned, give children the power to influence their lives in a positive direction. For example, when children have a need to know something, that need can be fulfilled through asking questions. The ability to ask effective questions is a strength requiring the mastery of several subskills to include understanding the benefits of questions, identifying distinguishable characteristics of an effective question, discriminating effective questions from those less effective and applying the steps to create useful questions.

"Strengths Training" is a four-part process consisting of information, skills, confidence building, and opportunity. Strengths Training teaches children how to develop needed behavioral strengths as characterized in the tripartite (Worzbyt, 1991).

Information

Children need to understand the benefits of learning a particular strength and the pitfalls they are likely to incur if they do not master the strength in question. They likewise will learn how their counterproductive behaviors have been contributing to the adverse consequences they have been experiencing. When children identify with and realize that alternative actions are more likely to produce the desired results, they become more receptive to instruction.

Stories, videos, role-plays, and games can be used to help children explore and understand the value of the strength that they will be learning. Through a story, for example, children of divorce can learn the value of sharing their honest feelings with those they trust rather than hiding or communicating false feelings. Teaching children how to talk about their true feelings is a valuable strength with tangible benefits for themselves and others who are helping them respond to their life challenges.

Skills

Every strength (sharing feelings) has subskills (chain of behaviors) that must be learned. In this part of Strength Training, facilitators first must identify the specific subskills that make up the strength. Observing people who have developed a desired strength is a helpful way of identifying the needed subskills. Facilitators should conduct a strength analysis in which they identify and sequence subskills.

After the strength analysis has been completed, the stage must be set for teaching the strength. Children will need information on how to perform each subskill. Likewise, they will need to observe and to model the required subskills in sequence while receiving feedback and positive reinforcement from the facilitator.

Confidence

Strengths are learned more readily when children have confidence in themselves, in their facilitator, and in what they are learning. These outcomes can be achieved when the facilitator helps children

- connect with the benefits to be derived from what they are learning;
- develop and practice strengths in a safe environment;
- move slowly and deliberately when learning strengths;
- accept setbacks as a normal condition of success; and
- develop patience, persistence, and a plan when applying their strengths.

Opportunity

Children are more likely to value their strengths when they discover that they really do get results. Facilitators need to help children identify times and places when they can use their strengths. Helping children set goals in using their newly developed strengths is a must. Once a goal has been identified, facilitators can help children visualize and role-play themselves using their newly developed strengths. With appropriate coaching from peers and facilitators, children will be prepared to use what they have learned.

Children who use their strengths recognize that the true source of their power comes from within. They will exhibit a positive sense of self-worth, address life challenges with confidence, and will be more comfortable accepting personal responsibility in their own self-management.

KEYSTONE LEARNING MODEL

The "Keystone Learning Model" (Figure 2.2) provides structure to the teaching-learning process (Worzbyt & O'Rourke, 1989). The various support group activities described in Part II of this book are designed around this model.

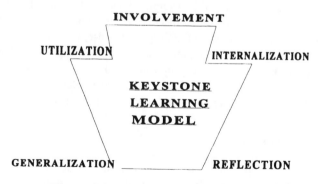

Figure 2.2. Keystone Learning Model.

Keystone Learning focuses on the Tripartite in teaching children personal strengths through a variety of sequenced activities created to address support group objectives. The "key" to successful learning can be described in five sequenced phases of purposeful activity as presented in the model.

Phase 1: Involvement

The involvement phase places children in specifically designed activities in which they experience the objective(s) being taught. For example, most children who have experienced the loss of a family member have a need to express their feelings and to talk about the experience; however, they may not possess or know how to utilize personal strengths that can help them. These children could observe a video or listen to a story (involvement) in which they connect with role models expressing their feelings and talking about their loss experience. *The involvement phase provides the experience from which learning can be extracted in the remaining phases of the Keystone Learning Model.*

Phase 2: Internalization

The internalization phase, with facilitator guidance, helps children focus on what they just have experienced. They are encouraged to share their feelings, thoughts, concerns, and observations. This phase helps children reflect on the activity or experience they have just shared together. Although this phase is usually not very lengthy, it does help children connect with their experience, themselves, and each other.

Phase 3: Reflection

The reflection phase challenges children to find meaning in the activity they have experienced. Using the example of family loss, children observed a video tape of their contemporaries discussing their various feelings regarding the death of a family member. In the reflection phase, the facilitator helps children connect with the video role models and how they expressed their feelings and talked about their loss. The children then should be encouraged to discuss what they personally learned from watching the video presentation and the benefits derived from learning to share feelings in times of loss.

Phase 4: Generalization

While the reflection phase focuses on deriving meaning from the activity itself, generalization helps children see how they can learn and apply the same strengths to their own life experiences. Children, participating in a loss, death, and grief support group, would now be ready to learn how to share their feelings with others.

Phase 5: Utilization

The utilization phase of learning helps children set goals in using their newly acquired strengths. In this phase, children, with the support of their peers and facilitator, can plan and practice the steps in achieving their goals prior to their actual implementation. Referring to our previous example, children are now ready to practice sharing their feelings with those they trust, knowing that such actions will help them through the grieving process.

And so, the learning process continues in a never ending cycle. Each time the cycle is completed, the breadth and depth of learning expands. Children are encouraged to discuss their goal outcomes and how what they have learned and applied have helped them become more effective in responding to life's challenges.

3 R'S DECISION MAKING

The fourth dimension of our success blueprint is "3 R's Decision Making" (Worzbyt, 1991). If children are to become successful self-managers, child support groups must prepare children to eventually function independently. They need an internal guidance system that will help them meet their needs responsibly while keeping them out of harm's way. That internal guidance system is decision making.

Decision making, as with any strength, must be taught and practiced if it is to be used effectively. Researchers suggest that those children who are good at making decisions have the ability to identify their wants, to generate relevant choices, and to rank them according to their benefits and drawbacks. When these steps are taken, skilled decision makers choose what are seemingly the best courses of action and then act.

In contrast, the less effective decision makers either do not possess the requisite skills needed or, possessing them, are inhibited or are thwarted in some way from acting. A failure on the part of children either to *think* or to *do* (act) in response to any decision reduces the odds for success regardless of the situation.

Children who are not required to apply newly acquired information, skills, and attitudes in the context of a fluid environment are not likely to benefit from what they have learned. Decision making, therefore, must become a central factor in all support group activities. After all, it is not how much children know that counts, but rather it is counting on what they know to make effective life decisions based on Right, Reality, and Responsibility.

Support Groups for Children utilizes a risk assessment decision making model known as the 3 R's (Worzbyt, 1991). The model is designed to enhance the practical application of support group learning to actual life challenges that children must address. The three-step decision making model (Figure 2.3) works like a traffic signal light. Children are taught how to make safe, STOP-THINK-and-GO decisions by learning to assess and to reduce personal risk to themselves and others while pursuing their goals.

The 3 R's model first instructs children to STOP and to verbalize the problem or challenge before them. They then are instructed to proceed with caution and to THINK about the various options open to them in solving their dilemma. With those choices in mind, children are taught how to filter each (Right, Reality, and Responsibility) in search of safe choices designed to address their challenge. The last step in the process requires children to GO with choices that are based on Right, Reality, and Responsibility, processing the one(s) they most favor with respect to goal attainment.

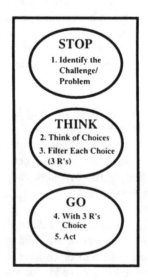

Figure 2.3.   A winning signal.

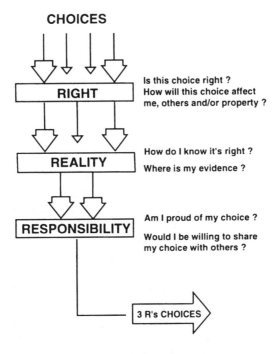

Figure 2.4. The 3 R's filters.

3 R's Filters

The filters of Right, Reality, and Responsibility are key components of the THINK stage of decision making. They work in the same manner as coffee, fuel, and human body filters. Their purpose is to protect children from making harmful choices by removing them from further consideration. In Figure 2.4 is illustrated how the three filters function.

When presented with a life decision, children are taught that their goal is to achieve a safe resolution to their dilemma. During the THINK stage of the Model, children are to brainstorm possible choices that could help them address their challenge. They then filter their choices eliminating those that fail to pass through all three filters. The filters of *Right, Reality,* and *Responsibility* are applied as described in the following paragraphs.

Right Filter. Helpful choices that are based on Right (not wrong) will pass through this filter. Children are asked to consider whether or not each choice being reviewed to solve their dilemma is *legal* (based on law), *ethical* (meets acceptable societal standards of conduct), and *moral* (meets personal rules of conduct and basic goodness). Children also are asked to consider how their choices will effect themselves, others, and/or personal property (help or hurt). If a choice is believed to be legal, ethical, and moral and will be helpful to themselves, others, and property, the choice moves to the next filter. When working with young children, the Right Filter can be examined in terms of helpful versus hurtful in determining the suitability of the choice being filtered.

Reality Filter. In the second filter is emphasized the importance of reality testing. Children must provide evidence (facts, proof, truth) to validate the "Rightness" of their choice. Only by challenging the accuracy and reasonableness of their choice can children legitimately endorse their choice. If after a review of the evidence their choice fails the "Reality check," that choice should be discarded from further consideration.

Responsibility Filter. In the third and final filter, children consider the potential consequences of their choice (benefits vs. pitfalls). When children are proud of their choice and are willing to publicly affirm it in the presence of knowledgeable people who can attest to its soundness, the choice will pass through the Responsibility Filter. Some children, when asked to share their choice openly, may refuse to do so because they know it is not the *right* thing to do and that there is no evidence (reality) to support it. Occasionally some children will believe so strongly in a potentially questionable choice that they should be encouraged to discuss it with qualified people. Arrange for them to do so. Talking with a third party will provide children with additional information with which to review their choice more critically before deciding to commit it to action.

USING 3 R'S DECISION MAKING

We advocate the use of 3 R's Decision Making in support groups to give children an opportunity to apply the new information, skills, and attitudes they have learned. With practice, children can become quite adept at 3 R's Decision Making and its application to their own life situations.

Now that the 3 R's Decision Making model has been explained, the following case situation illustrates its use in support groups. Children are given a copy of "Bobby's Dilemma" to read and then are asked to discuss the case using the "3 R's Decision Making Guide" (Figure 2.5).

STOP

A. State the problem/challenge. _____
_____

Note: Keep in mind that your goal must always be to solve the problem with safety for self and others as the motivating force.

THINK

B. State your choices.

_____
_____

C. Filter each choice.

RIGHT:
1. Is this choice right (legal, ethical, moral)?___ YES___ NO
2. How will this choice effect me, others, and/or property?__ HELP__HURT

REALITY:
3. How do I know it's right? Is my evidence based on fact, truth, and probable?__ YES__ NO

RESPONSIBILITY:
4. Am I proud of my choice?__ YES__ NO
5. Am I willing to share my choices with knowledgeable others?
   __ YES__ NO

GO

D. Go with your best 3 R's choice.
E. Act on your choice.

Figure 2.5.   3 R's Decision Making Guide.

Bobby's Dilemma

Bobby is a 10-year-old boy whose mother died one year ago after a long illness. Bobby is still feeling lonely and sad and speaks of recurring thoughts about his mother and how much he misses her. Bobby wonders when he will start feeling better again. What are some 3 R's choices that Bobby can make that will help him cope with his loss?

Facilitators either can present group members with a list of choices open to Bobby for his consideration or ask the children to generate their own list of choices to be filtered. Prior to reviewing the choices, group members should be asked to state Bobby's problem or challenge and his goal. The choices to be reviewed then can be filtered separately through the 3 R's. Bobby's challenge is to decide how best to handle his feelings of loneliness and sadness in regard to missing his mother.

The value of 3 R's Decision Making comes from the discussion generated by group members and the fact that children are free to make their own filtering decisions. For example, one of Bobby's choices to solve his problem might be to share his feeling with his school counselor or with a trusted family member. The children then can discuss this choice in response to the Right Filter. Following the discussion, children must decide for themselves if this choice should pass through the Right Filter or be eliminated from further discussion. Those electing to eliminate this option may do so whereas others may elect to take it to the Reality Filter.

The Reality Filter discussion continues as the remaining children attempt to provide evidence that supports the "sharing of feelings" as a healing choice for those in grief. Those children who believe that they have solid evidence to support this choice will move it onto the Responsibility Filter. Children can refer to information, activities, and personal observations made in their support group as evidence to support or to refute various choices being considered.

A choice may pass through all three filters for some children but not for others. Based on the reasoning of their peers and compelling evidence to do so, however, children may change their minds about a particular choice. Freedom of choice is a valuable benefit of 3 R's Decision Making and is worth preserving at all costs.

In addition to being provided with choices to examine, children can be asked to generate their own choices and to discuss each in response to the filters. The 3 R's Decision Making Model works to the extent that children work it. The THINK stage of decision making forces children to pause long enough between STOP and GO to consider whether their choices are *Right* versus wrong, based on *Reality* versus myth, and are *Responsible* versus hurtful to self and others.

SUMMARY

A support group curriculum that is developed around life situations and 3 R's Decision Making places new knowledge, skills, and attitudes in their proper perspective as tools to be used in making STOP-THINK-and-GO decisions based on Right, Reality, and Responsibility.

Thus, our blueprint for success emphasizes the importance of meeting children's needs (The Tripartite) through the teaching of strengths (Strengths Training) in a teaching-learning environment (The Keystone Learning Model) that foster independence and effective self-management (3 R's Decision Making). *Support Groups for Children* prepares children for successful living in a challenging world that demands nothing less than their full participation.

REFERENCES

Maslow, A. (1970). *Motivation and personality* (2nd ed.). New York: Harper and Row.

Worzbyt, J. C. (1991). *Beating the odds.* Altoona, PA: R.J.S. Films.

Worzbyt, J. C., & O'Rourke, K. (1989). *Elementary school counseling: A blueprint for today and tomorrow.* Muncie, IN: Accelerated Development.

Chapter 3

GETTING STARTED

Managing support groups for children is both a rewarding and a challenging experience; that is, rewarding in that children's lives are impacted in some very positive ways and challenging in that there is no crystal ball for facilitators to consult in their quest to help children do better. Some of the guess work, however, can be reduced greatly if facilitators view support groups from a managerial perspective consisting of a manager (facilitator) and a process (steps) to be managed.

The support group process starts long before the first session begins and continues after the last session ends. Facilitators who give consideration to the following process (steps) will be well on their way to managing successful group experiences.

Plan

- Identify needed support groups.
- Develop support group proposals.
- Implement strategies for acceptance.

Organize

- Advertise the support group.
- Determine support group logistics.
- Interview perspective children.
- Select group members.

Implement

- Review why we are here.
- State group rules.
- Practice facilitator discussion rules.
- Conduct group sessions.
- Manage unpredictable group dynamics.

Monitor/Evaluate

- Measure group performance.
- Implement corrective actions.

PLAN

The first phase of support group management is planning. Facilitators must determine what support groups are needed, develop written proposals for selected support groups, and create strategies for their acceptance.

Needs Assessment

Child support groups are appropriate for many different settings. Although they are most conducive to school environments because of the availability of children and trained facilitators, they can be initiated in community and religious settings as well. Regardless of the setting, support groups are more likely to be received with favor if there is a perceived need.

Any environmental disruptions or personal challenges that threaten children's emotional stability and their ability to manage their lives responsibly represent children's needs to be addressed. Typical life conditions that can challenge the stability of children's lives are low self-esteem, divorce of loved ones, conflict with peers or family members, personal or family illness, academic failure, anger, and the inability to maintain peer relationships. Although this list is not all inclusive, it does suggest a need for child support groups.

In order to ascertain the need for various support groups, facilitators should survey those groups of people who work most closely with children, namely parents, teachers, administrators, community supporters, and religious volunteers. Ask them to identify potential environmental disruptions prevalent within their own community and, equally important, any evidence that would imply children's lives are being impacted in a negative manner. In addition to surveying adults, children themselves can provide valuable data regarding their perceptions of their own needs for assistance in coping with life's adversities.

The key to collecting useful data is in the design of the survey instrument. Keep the instrument simple, short, and easy to complete. Children's surveys should meet the same criteria with special emphasis on readability and understanding of the instrument. Two sample survey instruments are provided in Figures 3.1 and 3.2.

Needs assessments are important not only because they ascertain need but also because they sensitize survey participants to the value of support groups in helping children respond more effectively to life challenges. The need is there for facilitators to identify and to address children's concerns through well planned support groups.

Support Group Proposal

Once you have established that there is a need for a particular support group, the next step is to develop a plan that details what you are going to do and how you are going to do it. Your proposal should contain the following:

- purpose of the support group,
- students' needs to be addressed,
- goals to be met,
- strengths to be developed, and
- expected outcomes to be attained.

The support group proposal will help you instill confidence in those to whom you must "sell" the proposal and in answering questions of parents, teachers, community supporters, religious leaders, and children about the support group experience. Everyone having a vested interest in your support group needs to be kept informed from conception to inception.

Strategies for Acceptance

Although there are many things that you can do to promote acceptance of your support groups, success is mainly determined by your ability to promote confidence in the support group concept. Confidence building requires that you provide people with accurate information (verbally and in writing) about support group participation by explaining

CHILD SURVEY INSTRUMENT

Dear Student,

This year we would like to offer a series of support groups aimed at helping you and other children better meet your needs at home and in school. Some of the topics that we plan to cover in our support groups include: feeling better about yourself, dealing with stress, dealing with conflict, surviving family problems and getting along better with others. The groups will last for eight weeks and will meet during different periods so that you will not miss the same class each week. Please use the checklist below to tell us if you would be interested in participating in any of these groups. *If you indicate that you are interested in a particular group, your counselor will talk with you on an individual basis about the possibility of being included in a group.*

I would like to be considered for the following support groups:

_____ Feeling better about myself
_____ Dealing with divorce
_____ Taking care of myself at home before & after school
_____ Dealing with stress
_____ Handling conflict more effectively
_____ Making friends
_____ Dealing with alcohol/drug abuse of a family member
_____ Appreciating & accepting differences in others
_____ Dealing with loss and grief (death of parent, friend, pet)
_____ Handling anger more appropriately

Comments or concerns:

Please sign your name if you want to be contacted for a group.

Name _____ **Date**_____

Figure 3.1. Child survey instrument.

ADULT SURVEY INSTRUMENT

Dear Parent/Faculty Member,

This year we would like to offer a series of support groups for children aimed at helping them better deal with the kinds of needs many children seem to be experiencing. Some of the topics that we plan to cover in our support groups include: feeling better about yourself, dealing with stress, dealing with conflict, surviving family problems and getting along better with others. The groups will last for eight weeks and will meet during different periods so that children will not miss the same class each week. Please use the checklist below to tell us which of the groups you feel would be most beneficial to our children.

Thank you for your assistance.

The following support group topics would be most helpful:

_____ Self-esteem
_____ Dealing with divorce
_____ Latchkey and Self-care Issues
_____ Stress Management
_____ Conflict Resolution
_____ Making friends
_____ Dealing with alcohol/drug abuse of a family member
_____ Appreciating & accepting differences in others
_____ Loss/Grief
_____ Anger Management

Comments/Concerns:

Name _____ **Date**_____

Figure 3.2. Adult survey instrument.

- the benefits to children;
- the probability of any risks involved and how they will be addressed;
- how support groups work with respect to goals, content and process;
- what changes parents can expect in their children;
- the availability of the support group curriculum for review by interested parties;
- your availability to answer questions about the support group;
- children's and parents' rights and how they will be protected; and
- your training and skills in managing support groups.

In actuality, you will be providing interested people with a full disclosure statement on each of the various support groups that you plan to facilitate. Important support group disclosure information can be disseminated via

- brochures,
- posters,
- letters,
- information meetings,
- personal contacts with interested parents or guardians, and
- telephone.

Although providing this information may seem unnecessary, the advanced preparation and openness reduce people's fears and increase the odds for support group success. After all, most parents (guardians) recognize their own vulnerability and that of their children and will be reluctant to increase those risks by allowing their children to participate in the realm of the unknown. Anything that you can do to curb their fears should be done so that their children can benefit from your support groups.

ORGANIZE

The next phase of support group management is organizing. The organizing phase provides the necessary structure for support group success. Before a puzzle can be assembled, all of the pieces first must be identified and arranged for assembly. Support groups are like puzzles consisting of many tasks that must be assembled into a meaningful whole. When the following tasks have been completed, you will be ready for your first support group session with the children:

1. Advertise the support group.
2. Determine support group logistics.

3. Interview perspective group members.
4. Select group members.

Advertise

Getting the word out about your support group is a must. You need to provide the following information in order to generate interest and confidence in those who will entrust their children to your care:

- name of the support group and sponsoring group or organization,
- purpose of the support group,
- who should attend,
- number of participants to be selected,
- number of anticipated sessions,
- length of each session,
- time and location of the support group sessions,
- name and office telephone number of the support group facilitator,
- how to obtain additional information if desired, and
- a tear off portion with return address for those wishing to be considered.

Be sure to note in your advertising that group members will be selected by the group facilitator following personal interviews with perspective candidates. Children not selected for participation should be provided with alternatives in receiving the help that they or their parents (guardian) desire for them.

Flyers and/or brochures can be distributed to children, parents, teachers, administrators, community members, and religious leaders. Those people receiving flyers or brochures should be encouraged to share the information with families they believe could benefit from support group involvement. In addition to flyers and brochures, you may consider using the local newspaper (feature article), radio (public spots), and presentations to school, religious, and community groups.

You may wish to restrict your advertising to the most immediate populations that you serve. The more you advertise, the greater the likelihood that you will generate a level of interest far beyond what you can serve. *Remember, most facilitators do not suffer from generating too few participants but too many.*

Logistics

Make sure that you have responded to the following questions and have a plan for addressing each before you advertise your support group to the public.

Are you sufficiently trained to run a support group?

Have you researched your support group?

Did you develop a support group proposal?

Does your group proposal provide the necessary details?

How will you select group members (methods and criteria)?

How many members will be selected?

When will the group meet (time of day)?

How will you address the needs of those not selected?

Will the group be opened or closed to new members once the group process begins?

How often will the group meet (once a week)?

How many sessions are planned?

Have you prepared an interview outline to be used with the candidates?

What do you want children to know about the support group?

Will you alone decide who gets to participate or will you involve each child in the decision making process?

Have you discussed and received clearance from the key people whose permission you must obtain before you begin advertising?

Facilitators have a number of things to think about and decisions to make regarding their support groups. Although we have provided a list of the more obvious questions, our list is by no means all inclusive. And although we believe that facilitators must assume the responsibility for making their own logistical decisions, we would like to comment on group size, group composition, scheduling sessions, and environmental settings, as they can make or break a group's success.

Group Size.   From our experience, support groups numbering from five to ten children are ideal. If the group is too small, the range of discussion is limited as are the availability of effective role models. Groups larger than ten in size reduce participation time for each member and may be intimidating for some shy children, thus stifling their level of involvement.

Group Composition.   As we have indicated, there needs to be a degree of heterogeneity in your homogeneous group. For example, children in a divorce support group should be around the same age and should consist of boys and girls from a variety of backgrounds and experiences. They also should be at different stages regarding the divorce of their parents and should possess a range of responsible strengths (coping skills) that they have used in meeting their needs. Such diversity provides for a climate of hope, optimism, and role models who have responded successfully and responsibly to adversity.

Scheduling Sessions. The availability of children and the success of your support groups will be impacted by the schedule you provide. Most parents and teachers do not want their children taken out of academic classes for fear of having their school work suffer. Most parents and legal guardians do not want their own lives disrupted by having to make special arrangements for transportation, baby-sitters for younger siblings, and managing conflicts with their own schedules.

If you are planning to facilitate groups in a school setting, preplanning is a must. Teachers and administrators who favor the support group concept will be motivated in developing a workable time schedule. Talking with other schools that have support groups and studying your current school schedule are places to begin in establishing an acceptable meeting time. Also, keeping support group meeting times to once a week, for no more than 45 minutes in length, and limited to eight to ten sessions in duration will help provide the parameters for a manageable plan.

Environmental Setting. In order to help children connect with each other and their surroundings, a permanent meeting place is most desirable. The room should be easily accessible, capable of maintaining privacy, free from disruption (noise, telephone calls, etc.), appropriately lighted and heated, large enough in size to accommodate group activities, and comfortably furnished. Confidentiality and personal comfort and security are central issues to support group success.

Informed Consent. Because you will be working with children, an absolute necessity is to obtain written consent from each child's parent(s) or legal guardian as well as from the child. The question that many facilitators ask is, "At what point in the process should consent be obtained?" Should it be prior to the individual interviews or after you have selected the candidates?

Probably the best time to secure informed consent is at the point of final group selection. In this way, you need only contact the parent(s) (guardian) of those children selected for a support group experience. If, however, you feel more comfortable or are required by your organization to obtain written consent from all parents (legal guardians) whose children will be interviewed, by all means do so.

You will need to provide sufficient and accurate information about your support group so that parents and children can make an informed decision regarding their participation. Accompany a formal information statement with the informed consent document. That statement should contain the following information:

- a brief description of the support group and its purpose;
- a description of the group's goals;
- a description of expected benefits to children;
- a description of the facilitator's role;
- a description of the child's role;
- an overview of the kind of activities to be used;
- details regarding session dates, location, meeting time, and length of sessions;
- facilitator's training (professional disclosure);
- offer to answer questions and view the curriculum if desired;
- a synopsis of children's rights to participate, decline involvement in any activity, or drop out of the group at any time;
- a description of possible risks or discomforts;
- other available options to group participation; and
- parent's (legal guardian's) responsibility to support and not pressure their children for group information that they might choose not to share.

The information statement, while covering a number of points, should be concise and written in nontechnical language. Although preparing a statement of such specificity is time consuming, so is answering the same parental questions many times over, or worse yet, having your support group fail for lack of parental support. A "Sample Support Group Information/Consent Letter" is provided in Figure 3.3.

Interview

The pregroup interview is designed to provide the facilitator an opportunity to accomplish the following:

- provide information to children about the support group and its purpose,
- explain participant involvement,
- ask children questions regarding their interest in joining this support group, and
- decide which children to select for group participation.

A sample interview checklist is provided in Figure 3.4. The checklist format provides a degree of standardization to the selection process. Using such a format will help insure that useful data will be collected in a timely manner and will aid you in identifying those children who can most benefit from a support group experience. The pregroup interview is a rough screening tool at best;

SAMPLE SUPPORT GROUP INFORMATION/CONSENT LETTER

To the Parents/Guardians of_____,

Support groups for children provide a confidential setting for children to discuss concerns and issues regarding such topics as self-esteem, handling anger responsibly, resolving conflict, reducing stress and responding to family issues (death, divorce, chemical abuse and stepfamily living). Your son or daughter has expressed an interest in participating in a support group dealing with_____. Groups will meet on alternating periods during school time so as not to interfere with academic progress. The group will run for eight weeks and each meeting will last approximately 45 minutes. The group will be facilitated by _____.

If you would like your child to participate in this support group, please sign the permission slip below and return it to me by _____. Support groups provide children with a wonderful opportunity to share concerns, issues, needs, and experiences while learning to address life challenges responsibly. If you have questions, please contact the guidance office (phone: _____).

Sincerely,

I give permission for my child to participate in the support group on _____.

_____
Parent Signature

_____
Date

Figure 3.3.   A sample Support Group Information/Consent Letter.

CHILD INTERVIEW CHECKLIST

In interviewing children as potential group members, there are several areas that should be covered during the individual interview. This checklist can serve as a reminder to the facilitator.

Student Name: _____ Age: _____ Grade: _____

Information about Group and Group Process
_____Goals/purpose
_____Meeting dates/times
_____Group facilitators
_____Parent permission slips
_____In group, members will share attitudes, feelings and concerns

Information about Confidentiality and Group Rules
_____ The rule is "What we say in group, stays there." We cannot guarantee that every child will keep confidentiality, but most children develop trust in the group and want to keep things confidential.
_____The facilitator would have to break confidentiality if someone talks about harming self or others or someone talks about being harmed by others.
_____No put-downs
_____One person talks at a time. Listening to others is important.

Attendance
_____Children should attend every session.
_____A child may drop out of group but must tell the leader why he or she is choosing to do so.
_____All members should be on time for each meeting.

Other Issues
_____Homework will be assigned with each group (often it is just "thinking" homework).
_____Benefits of being in a group are. . . .
_____Risks of being in a group are. . . .

Questions to ask Potential Group Member
_____Are you receiving any outside counseling?
_____Do you have any questions about group?
_____Would you like to be considered for inclusion in the group?
_____If selected for the group, what goals do you want to work on?

_____Selected for group   _____ Not selected for group

Figure 3.4.   A child interview checklist.

however, it does provide you with an opportunity to meet with children and to ascertain their level of interest.

Prior to beginning the formal part of the interview, it is best to engage in "small talk" with the child. Your goal must be to help the child feel comfortable with you and the setting. Explain to the child that you are going to be bringing a small group of children together that will meet once a week to talk about their feelings regarding the loss of a loved one (support group topic). "Your teacher (referral source) gave me your name as someone who might like to join this new group. I would like to tell you more about this group, ask you a few questions, and then you and I can decide together if joining this group would be something you would like to do."

At the close of the interview, if both you and the child think that joining this group would be beneficial, you should tell the child that you would like to talk with his or her parent(s) and to obtain their written permission at which point group membership will be secured. The same process should be followed for those children making self-referrals.

Select Group Members

Selecting children for participation in a support group is a major responsibility. Your first concern must be to select children whom you believe can benefit from a group experience and not be harmed by it. You must ask yourself as each group member is selected for participation, "What evidence do I have that supports my decision for including this child in the group?" Remember that a support group relies on the interaction of its membership for individual and group growth to occur. The wrong mix of youngsters can foster destructive group dynamics. Therefore, as you make your individual selections, be mindful of the total group makeup.

We have found that the most successful child support groups consist of members that meet the following criteria.

> **Group members who are positive role models from whom others can learn.** Children should be at various stages in understanding their life situation and in their ability to self-manage. Some degree of heterogeneity needs to be in your homogeneous group if children are to experience positive role models who can offer encouragement, optimism, and demonstrate personal strengths.
>
> **Group members who are near the same age.** When children are more than two years apart in age, often a significant developmental gap exists that

inhibits the building of community among the membership, an essential ingredient to support group effectiveness.

Group members who share a similar degree of maturity (personally, socially, emotionally, physically, and intellectually) sufficient for group interaction. Children who are unlikely to contribute to or benefit from a group experience should not be placed in a support group.

Group members who have demonstrated their ability to function well in other group situations. A support group by its very nature works because the members, despite their present adversity, are supportive individuals who have benefited from the support of others in other groups.

Group members who share a similar life setback. Children will more readily connect with each other when they understand that they are experiencing a similar life challenge.

A group membership that promotes diversity. Racial, ethnic, cultural, and socioeconomic diversity are to be encouraged to the extent that such diversity contributes to rather than inhibits group process.

Children who should not be considered for a support group experience in an educational setting include those who

- have parents who do not favor their involvement,
- are hyperactive or easily agitated,
- are suicidal,
- are distracted easily,
- are unsociable—aggressive (verbally and/or physically abusive),
- are experiencing multiple crises in their lives,
- are being seen by a mental health specialist, and
- do not want to be in a support group.

Although we have indicated that some children are not strong candidates for a support group experience, they nevertheless may need professional follow-up. These children may benefit from individual counseling, family therapy, consultation with parents and teachers, or referral to an agency or specialist qualified to provide needed services.

As we have indicated, not all children will be selected for participation in a support group. You will need to take particular care in communicating this message so that these children do not experience a sense of adult rejection. Let them know that you are pleased with the response you have received and their interest in being a group member. Tell them that for now your group is full but that you would like to talk with them (individually) in order to explore other avenues of assistance (individual counseling, referral, other support groups, etc.).

Hopefully the number of children who have to be informed that they have not been selected for your support group will be very small. Needs assessment information and controlled advertising of support groups will no doubt help you estimate the number of children who need assistance so that you can plan accordingly.

IMPLEMENT

The third phase of support group management is implementation. You are now ready to conduct your first session with children. You need to consider six elements that are connected directly to facilitating support group sessions. Implement as many of these ideas as seem appropriate and you will be well on your way to helping children help themselves to be winners in a climate of adversity. The six elements are as follows:

1. develop a supportive teaching-learning climate,
2. review *Support Groups for Children* session format,
3. use effective teaching methods,
4. lead an effective group discussion,
5. apply the Teaching Do's, and
6. manage unpredictable group dynamics.

Develop a Supportive Teaching-Learning Climate

The success of *Support Groups for Children* is dependent upon developing a motivating teaching-learning climate. As a facilitator, your first goal must be to put children at ease, and second, to peak their interest in your support group to the extent that they want to become involved. The four catalytic elements of desire play a major role in establishing motivational teaching-learning climates. The four elements are connectiveness, uniqueness, power, and models (Clemes & Bean, 1981).

Connectiveness. Children need to feel safe, secure, and able to trust you and others throughout the support group experience. When children feel connected to you and each other, they will start to open up and take moderate risks in exploring their life situations. They will reach new levels of understanding that will lead to responsible actions in their quest to "do better." Some examples of connectiveness building responses that you and the children can apply in the group are smiling; using praise and positive feedback; eye contact; showing respect; using names; following group rules; sharing feelings; and being involved (voice inflection, thoughts and ideas, hand gestures).

Uniqueness.   Children need to feel special about themselves and their contributions. They need to feel that they count for something, have net worth, and
are held in high esteem by people they respect. Children possess many unique
attributes (strengths) and will learn new ones in their support group. Help them
understand, value, and use their unique assets (personal characteristics, skills,
thoughts, and feelings) to benefit themselves and others in pursuit of their dreams.
You can help children feel unique (in positive ways) by

- structuring learning experiences so that children will experience success;
- encouraging children to express diverse points of view;
- increasing opportunities for children to express themselves in creative
  ways;
- providing plenty of constructive, nonjudgmental feedback; and
- teaching children new ways of thinking, feeling, and acting that will up
  their net worth and empower them in the face of adversity.

Power.   Children need to believe that they have a significant role to play
in shaping their own destinies. Children with personal power are self-confident,
goal-oriented, and live their lives with direction and purpose. Children need to
experience a sense of power as they participate in support groups. Some things
that you can do to help children experience power are the following:

- move from the simple to the complex when presenting new material,
- move slowly so that everyone can comprehend what is being taught,
- manage activities in ways that allow children to experience success,
- treat failure as a step toward success,
- teach children how to use their strengths in nonviolent and responsible
  ways, and
- be ever conscious of your own presence in the helping relationship and
  how you affect children's lives.

Models.   A model is any action (verbal and nonverbal) observed by others
that results in that action being copied by them. Models represent "how to's" in
life and living. People, philosophical sayings, and the actions of others can serve
as models. Positive models can help children establish ethical and moral standards. Such standards help children exercise self-control, discern right from wrong,
and formulate goals that are responsible to self and society. You can have a
guiding influence in helping children develop a responsible internal guidance
system by encouraging them to

- talk about their beliefs and the standards of right and wrong that they
  apply to their own lives;

- set achievable goals that are ethically, morally, and legally sound;
- search for models (people, sayings, actions) that will guide them in setting responsible life standards; and
- apply helpful models taught through the *Support Groups for Children* curriculum to their own lives.

Understand the Support Group Format

Each support group presented in this book is formatted in the same manner for ease of understanding and application. A brief explanation of the format is provided.

Background Information.   Background information is provided on each support group theme so that you will better understand the children entering your group, some of the counterproductive coping behaviors they may have developed, and the environmental conditions that have contributed to that learning.

Children's Needs.   Following the background information, children's needs have been discussed as they pertain to each support group topic. These needs can be met by teaching children the appropriate strengths that, when applied, will lead to more effective self-management.

Strengths to be Learned.   For each of the needs that children must satisfy, accompanying strengths have been identified and are explained and later taught in the support group sessions that follow.

Message to Facilitator.   Prior to introducing the support group sessions, facilitators are provided with specific ideas and tips to consider when managing the support group in question. Facilitators will find the information useful in meeting the children's needs.

Sessions.   Each session is identified by a title followed by a brief overview of the session identifying the strength(s) to be taught. Next the session goals are presented, materials needed, procedure for managing the activity, information on how to evaluate, and a homework assignment that gives children the opportunity to practice what they have learned from each session. The sessions are designed using the Keystone Learning Model presented in Chapter 2.

Resources.   A variety of supplemental resources have been provided. As much as possible, these resources have been included in the respective chapters where most applicable. These resources will enhance your support group efforts. These resources include the following:

Child and adult survey instruments (Figures 3.1 and 3.2): These survey instruments can be used to help you determine the need for various support group offerings in your community.

Support group information and consent letter (Figure 3.3): This is a sample letter that can be mailed to parents (caregivers) informing them of their child's interest in a support group. The letter provides useful information about the group and asks for caregiver's consent granting permission for their child to participate in the group experience.

Child interview checklist (Figure 3.4): You will want to interview children interested in participating in your support group in order to determine their suitability for inclusion. A child interview checklist can help standardize the selection process.

Tips for caregivers (Figures 4.1, 5.1, 6.1, 7.1, 8.1, 9.1, 10.1, 11.1, 12.1, 13.1, and 14.1): Children seem to gain more from support groups when they can benefit from the active support of their parents (caregivers). Therefore, we have provided *Tips for Caregivers* for each support group that can help parents work with their children at home.

Suggested readings (Figures 4.2, 5.2, 6.2, 7.2, 8.2, 9.2, 10.2, 11.2, 12.2, 13.2, and 14.2): We have provided a separate list of age-appropriate children's books for each support group. These book titles can be shared with parents and can provide supplemental reading for children at home or in the support group.

Use of Effective Teaching Methods

Several teaching methods are used throughout *Support Groups for Children*. Using a variety of techniques will heighten children's interests in what they are learning. A brief description of each method has been provided for your review.

Lecture.   A lecture is a structured presentation of information on a particular topic. The lecture method provides for the quick dissemination of needed information. Lectures should be well prepared, of short duration, and introduce the points to be made in an interesting, clear, and precise manner. Used sparingly and with purpose, mini-lectures (five minutes) can be a powerful tool to facilitate understanding of new material.

Discussion.   Discussion is a guided verbal exchange between and among children. Group discussion provides children with an opportunity to share their thoughts, feelings, and ideas on those topics in question. Discussions are particularly helpful in that they enable children to use their skills, expand on their ideas, and hear the varying opinions of others.

Brainstorming.   Brainstorming is a popular involvement activity that encourages the rapid free flow of ideas in generating choices to life challenges. Children are encouraged to be nonevaluative, creative, and even zany in their exchange. Only after the brainstorming session has ended should participants begin to sort through the many ideas in search of possible solutions.

Role-playing.   Role-playing involves acting out possible solutions to various life challenges. Each role-play lasts for just a few minutes as a variety of options are generated. Role-playing helps children express their feelings, thoughts, and actions in response to a particular life situation or event in a safe environment. Children are given the opportunity to try out new ways of behaving in search of acceptable solutions that are right for them. Role-playing should be a nonthreatening, fun experience.

Structured Activities.   A structured activity is any experience that has been planned to facilitate the learning process. Such activities may be designed to teach new strengths, challenge irrational thoughts, or simulate a life event in a controlled environment so that it can be observed and discussed.

You are encouraged to use a variety of methods and techniques to help children explore, understand, and act in responsible ways in the face of life challenges.

Lead an Effective Discussion

Although leading an effective group discussion is contingent upon many factors, two stand out above the rest. Group members must agree to support a uniform code of conduct, and facilitators must apply their group processing skills if children are to profit from group interaction.

Code of Conduct.   Group discussions and related activities run more smoothly when children practice basic ground rules that govern their interactions with each other. Some examples of useful ground rules are those discussed below.

Listen to One Another. Children are encouraged to maintain eye contact with those speaking and to summarize mentally, in a nonjudgmental manner, what has been said before they speak. You can ask group members, at various points in the discussion, to share what they believe the speaker has said. This helps reinforce the importance of listening.

Speak One at a Time. Children are expected to speak one at a time and are to refrain from engaging in side discussions while a group member is speaking. Listening and speaking one at a time are two rules that reinforce each other and are imperative to group sharing.

Stay on the Topic. Children are encouraged to maintain their focus on what is being discussed. When a discussion gets side-tracked, you may intervene by saying, "I'm not sure how this relates to what we are discussing now. Can someone help me?" This lead provides children with an opportunity to clarify the point being made or to recognize that the discussion is not "on target."

Everyone's Ideas Are Important. All children have value as human beings and should feel free to express themselves in the group. Encourage full participation and let children know that you value their involvement. If incorrect information is provided by children, you can respond by saying, "Many people would agree with you. However, we know that. . . ." In this way, you can correct the response without embarrassing the child.

Right to Pass. Although you should always encourage participation, there will be times when various children, for whatever reason(s), may choose to pass. Let them know that this is their right and that they should feel comfortable using it.

No Put-downs. While it is okay to disagree with another child's point of view, it is not acceptable behavior to judge or to ridicule others for their ideas. If this behavior is allowed to occur, it will eventually destroy openness and risk-taking in the group.

All Questions Have Value. There are no "dumb" questions. Asking questions is to be encouraged and those who ask them are to be respected for their courage and eagerness to learn.

Confidentiality. Explain to the children the importance of respecting each other's privacy and confining their discussion to the group.

Facilitator Discussion Skills. You can enhance your ability to lead effective group discussions by practicing five interpersonal communication skills that, when applied, will help you facilitate effective interactions between and among children. These skills are listening, reflecting, clarifying, questioning, and seeking examples.

Listening is an action-oriented activity that requires the collective utilization of your senses. You can improve your listening skills by focusing on all verbal and nonverbal cues of the group in response to such variables as association of ideas, shifts in conversation, opening and closing remarks, recurrent references, inconsistencies and gaps in conversation, and concealed meaning.

Reflecting is a process of repeating back almost verbatim what another child has said. While reflection should be used sparingly, it can provide the child with an opportunity to validate or correct the message that you have received. Reflection is also a helpful way of letting children know that you did hear their message.

Clarifying goes beyond the process of reflecting. In clarification, you connect a number of related thoughts provided by a child (group) and form a new idea or concept. In so doing, you (facilitator) might say, "During our session, you made the following points. . . . Could it be that you mean . . . ?" The child now has a chance to agree or to disagree with the new idea or thought that has been advanced. As new thoughts and ideas are created, the child (group) is challenged with a newly formed perception to consider.

Questioning is a very useful skill in helping children develop their thoughts and ideas about what is being discussed. When questions are used, they should be used sparingly and with caution. Your role always must be that of a facilitator and not an interrogator. The following tips will help you use questions effectively:

a Ask open-ended questions. "Could you tell me more?" "How did you feel?" "Is there anything else that you wish to say?

b Ask one question at a time. Avoid stringing a series of questions together. Allow the questions to be answered as they are asked.

c Provide adequate time for responses. If a question is worth asking, give time for the answer rather than "jumping in" and answering your own question.

d Validate responses. Acknowledge all responses by thanking the children for their input. If incorrect information is provided, be supportive and then introduce the correct information.

e Give children an out. When asking questions, watch for signs of agitation, fear, or inability to respond. Intervene after a few minutes of silence and say, "You seem to be giving a lot of thought to my question. Would you like more time to think about it and I'll come back to you later?"

f End on a positive note. Let the children know that your questions have been challenging and that they have been doing a great job in sharing their ideas and thoughts.

Seeking examples from children can help them illustrate or describe abstract concepts. Merely asking, "Could you give me an example of what you are trying to say?" will help children advance their thoughts.

All five interpersonal communication skills, used collectively, are designed to help children develop and expand their ideas and keep the discussion flowing smoothly.

Apply the Teaching Do's

Throughout *Support Groups for Children*, you will be planning sessions, presenting information, teaching strengths (skills), building confidence in children, and helping them identify opportunities to apply what they have learned. As you make preparation for engaging children in a support group experience, review the Teaching Do's shown here:

Step 1: Planning Session

DO review each session a day in advance.
DO study the goals for each session.
DO use props, games, and handouts to catch the children's attention.
DO have materials prepared ahead of time.
DO remember to present the sessions in a clear, organized and friendly manner.

Step 2: Presenting Information

DO start with the goal of the lesson. "Today we are going to learn about. . . ."
DO end the session with a review of the goal and what has been learned.
DO speak clearly, slowly, and with sufficient volume so as to be heard.
DO communicate enthusiasm when teaching children.
DO stop periodically and review what you have been teaching.
DO ask children what questions they have.
DO engage children's senses when conducting a session.
DO create a learning climate that is physically and psychologically stimulating.

Step 3: Teaching Strengths

DO explain to children what strengths they will be learning.
DO model each strength for children to see.
DO have children practice each strength under supervision.
DO structure strength practice sessions using small, sequenced steps so as to enhance the likelihood of success.
DO verbalize each step as it is demonstrated.

Step 4: Building Confidence

DO provide immediate, positive, and continuous reinforcement when the correct or approximate behaviors are displayed.

DO teach children how to self-reinforce their correct behaviors (self-affirmation).

DO break down complex strengths into smaller steps and shape the desired responses if necessary.

DO provide for numerous practice sessions.

DO provide continuous and corrective feedback as the strength is being learned.

DO give lots of praise, smiles, and positive feedback for successive approximations of correct behaviors while they are being learned.

DO give homework assignments using new strengths.

Step 5: Providing Opportunities

DO have children use the newly acquired strengths.

DO ask children to identify new ways in which they can use the learned strengths.

DO allow children to initiate some of their own variations in using the learned strengths.

DO continue to provide homework assignments in which the learned strengths are used.

DO have children share with each other their applications of the newly acquired strengths.

Manage Unpredictable Group Dynamics

Whenever children come together in a group experience, certain dynamics can arise that have the potential for interrupting group process. We have tried to anticipate some of those dynamics so, if they do occur, you will be prepared to address them before they become a problem.

Development of Subgroups.   Subgroups represent small cliques of children who share a common bond. Your goal is to create a sense of family in the group. If you do divide children into pairs or triads for activities, be sure to change the membership of these small groups often so that the children will have a chance to interact with each other. Doing this also will reduce the risk of subgroups.

Polarization.   When children divide into opposing factions based on varying values, attitudes, or beliefs, the group has become polarized. Because you will want children to feel free to discuss their varying feelings and beliefs, you will need to create an atmosphere that encourages a diversity of thoughts and actions. Guarding against put-downs and peer pressure and emphasizing freedom of choice (within group guidelines) will help minimize polarization.

Scapegoating.   Scapegoating occurs when children openly blame others for problems within the group. Children also may engage in blaming others outside the group for their troubles as well. Scapegoating can be very divisive in that it destroys trust, impedes discussion, and isolates individuals. Do not allow scapegoating to occur. Stop the group process and have children focus on what is happening. Ask them if these actions are helping or hurting the group and specific members in the group. Ask them to provide evidence that suggests this is the best way to handle their crisis. Engage in 3 R's Decision Making to resolve the conflict.

The Monopolizer.   Some children are so eager to participate that they "take over" the session. When this happens, acknowledge the contributions of this child, but also be direct and indicate that you want to give everyone a chance to participate.

Inappropriate Sharing.   If children, in their eagerness to share, begin to discuss very personal or sensitive material about themselves or family members that you believe should be discussed privately, you should step in immediately. Do so in a kind way and offer the child an opportunity to discuss the matter privately if he or she chooses to do so.

Silent Members.   Many children tend to be quiet; however, just because group members remain silent does not necessarily mean they are not learning or are uninterested in what is taking place. Be ready to reach out to these youngsters, but also acknowledge their right to be quiet if that is what they choose.

Side Conversations.   During group discussion, a small number of children may carry on their own conversation while the group is talking. Stop the process. Let them know that the group is unable to benefit from their ideas and they are unable to hear what others are saying. Review the ground rules for group discussion and move on.

Failure to Stick with the Topic.   Occasionally a group member has something to express that is not related to what is being discussed in the group. Again, stop the process and ask the child how what he or she is saying relates to the topic being discussed by the group. This gives the child an opportunity to re-explain or to acknowledge that the topic is not related to the current discussion. Tell the child either to discuss the point with you privately or to bring it up again when the present discussion comes to a close. Facilitators who are sensitive to group needs enhance the conditions of the learning environment and make it easier for children to address their needs while learning what is being taught.

Group Discomfort. You may sense some discomfort in your group but are unable to identify what may be happening. When this occurs, you should acknowledge your feelings and ask for their input. For example, you could say, "The group seems very quiet today. Can you help me understand what is happening?" Keeping a pulse on group dynamics is as important as the content to be covered.

EVALUATE

Evaluation is an important function of support group management. You have taken time to plan and to organize your support group and are now ready to implement what you have created; however, despite all of your efforts to ensure for a successful support group experience, you have no way to assess that experience in the absence of controls.

Evaluation (a planned ongoing tracking process) provides you with the opportunity to detect and to correct significant deviations that may occur between support group goals and actual outcomes in a timely fashion. You will be able to monitor the progress of your group and make effective decisions regarding its management.

Evaluation Process

Every support group session consists of resources (materials, equipment, people), activities, and goals. The resources must be sufficient in quality and quantity to support the activity. The selected activity must support goal attainment for that session. Finally, the selected goal must be in keeping with meeting the children's needs. Goals may not be met because of problems associated with resources, activities, or the goals themselves. Each link in the chain of success, starting with resources, represents a separate decision point to be evaluated in determining the degree to which children's needs are being served by the support group.

Whereas the support group topics in this book have been thoroughly researched and the individual sessions and their activities field tested, each group that you facilitate will be different. The children will differ as will their needs and current life situations. Consequently, you will no doubt want to adjust some session goals and activities to fit the needs of your group. For this reason we are providing you with five general criteria to consider when making support group session adjustments. The criteria are appropriateness, adequacy, effectiveness, efficiency, and side effects (Craig, 1978).

Appropriateness. How suitable are the chosen resources, activities, and goals in meeting the children's needs? Do qualified people with expertise in the support group topic believe that your goals and methods of attainment are appropriate in helping children meet their needs?

Adequacy. Support group sessions are successful to the extent that resources, activities, and goals accomplish the desired outcomes. If your goals and methods of attainment are appropriate and yet children's needs are not being met, be sure to examine how adequate your resources and activities are in achieving success. Also examine your goals to make sure that they are realistic, attainable, clearly written, and contain the criteria by which attainment will be judged.

Effectiveness. Support group sessions may be Appropriate (supportable) and Adequate (possess the necessary potential for success) and yet not be Effective. The resources, activities, and goals may be judged to be incapable of producing the desired results. When this happens, you may need to substitute resources, rewrite some activities while removing others, and alter or eliminate those support group goals that are not working.

Efficiency. Do the achieved results justify the expenditure of resources (time, money, people)? How cost effective are your support groups? Are you making the kind of difference that you hoped to achieve or is there a more cost effective way of meeting your goals?

Side Effects. In addition to attaining desired outcomes, support group sessions may also produce unexpected results. These side effects, while unplanned, may be helpful or hurtful to children. You must decide if the side effects are positive, or at the very least, can be tolerated. Depending on your evaluation, some adjustments may be required. By incorporating the five mentioned criteria into the planning and evaluating phases of support group management, you will be able to monitor and fine tune group sessions as they unfold. You should also utilize session evaluations and homework assignments in helping you assess child understandings, strengths, and their utilization in addressing their current life situation(s).

Post-group Follow-up and Evaluation

Whenever possible, we recommend meeting support groups approximately one month after the last session. This session should be devoted to assessing the support group experience. The children are now in a position to share their

- personal successes and insights in their use of what they have learned,
- current life challenges and how they are addressing them,
- thoughts concerning the value of their group experience, and
- suggestions for improving future support groups.

For those of you who are interested in formalizing your evaluation efforts, we recommend administering pretest and post-test follow-ups in those areas where you wish to measure growth.

You may wish to design checklists, rating scales, and open-ended stories to assess children's ideas, beliefs, attitudes, feelings, and behaviors in response to each support group that you facilitate.

During your post-session follow-up, you should readminister the same instrument in order to track possible changes that may have resulted during the support group experience. We are cautious in our wording about your results because they are meant only to provide you with an estimate of change and in no way suggest that change was entirely due to support group activities. The results are helpful, however, in improving your support groups and in justifying their continuation based on the evidence.

We hope that this information (Chapters 1 through 3) has provided you with an overview of the curriculum, the skills necessary to teach it, and the confidence necessary to feel comfortable with it. Good luck with your support groups and much success in helping children help themselves turn adversity into opportunity.

REFERENCES

Clemes, H., & Bean, R. (1981). *Self esteem: The key to your child's well-being.* New York: Kensington Publishing.

Craig, D. P. (1978). *Hip pocket guide to planning and evaluation.* San Diego, CA: Learning Concepts.

PART II
SUPPORT GROUPS
AND
RELATED ACTIVITIES

Chapter 4

CHILDREN OF ALCOHOLICS

Children of alcoholics are children who "live in chemically dependent and co-dependent families or families molded around the pain, denial, and confusion of that disease" (Woll, 1990, p. 1). Chemically dependent refers to people who are addicted to alcohol and/or other drugs.

BACKGROUND INFORMATION

An estimated 43% of American adults have been exposed to family alcoholism (Schoenborn, 1991). Seven million children under the age of 18 currently live with an alcoholic parent (Robinson, 1989). Approximately one in every five children of alcoholics occupy classrooms across the United States (Brake, 1988; Woll, 1990). While these statistics certainly give cause for alarm, they only tell part of the story. Many family members who abuse alcohol are also dependent on other drugs (Children of Alcoholics Foundation, 1992). When all forms of chemical dependency are accounted for, the data provided underestimates the number of children living with parents who abuse drugs other than alcohol or in combination with alcohol. Although the exact numbers are unavailable, Austin and Pendergast (1991) estimated that these numbers are rising.

Family Environment

Regardless of the exact numbers of children living in chemically dependent homes, there is sufficient cause for concern regarding the health and wel-

51

fare of these children. Schall (1986) described life with an alcoholic parent as the most widespread cause of severe stress for school-aged children in the United States. Children living in chemically dependent home environments are likely to experience some or all of the following potentially stress-producing situations (Vail-Smith, Knight & White, 1995; Wilson & Blocher, 1990).

> **Family conflict.** Parental quarreling is a central concern of children. Children worry about their parents, disruption of their home life, violent fights, fights with siblings, and the inescapable tension that they must endure.
>
> **Abuse and neglect.** Children of alcoholics (COAs), when compared with other children, are more likely to experience physical and sexual abuse. Naiditch and Learner (1987) reported that as high as 90% of child abuse cases are related to alcoholism. These children are also the victims of personal neglect. Because their parents are generally consumed by their own problems, the needs of their children often go unmet.
>
> **Inconsistent discipline and inadequate structure.** Children need stability and predictability in their lives. COAs find little of either. They often live in households with few concrete guidelines and behavioral limits. Their behavior may go uncensured one day only to be severely reprimanded the next day for doing the same thing. The lack of stability and predictability is cause for stress, anxiety, and depression.
>
> **Disruption of family rituals.** Whereas most children look forward to family birthdays, holidays, and family celebrations, COAs may come to dread such events. The alcoholic parent may use such events to become intoxicated thus embarrassing family members and guests. On other occasions, children must live with broken promises related to family celebrations because a chemically dependent parent is unable to follow through on a promise.
>
> **Role reversal and parentification.** COAs may find themselves in the parenting role putting their own needs aside so that they can take care of a chemically dependent parent, the nonchemically dependent parent, and siblings. They take over household duties and serve as confidants, listening to parental problems and concerns.
>
> **Distortion and denial of reality.** In order to keep the family secret, children and other family members learn to distort and deny the reality around them so that they can "live with the lie" that everything is fine despite the hopelessness. They learn not to feel, trust, or think in reality oriented terms. Distortion and denial protect and perpetuate the lie. They protect the alcoholic and family members from the pain of their existence and perpetuate the very conditions that prevent healthy love and trust.

Isolation. COAs live in families that create isolation by virtue of the very rules by which they "live." They perpetuate an air of secrecy in which family members learn not to discuss alcoholism in or outside of the home for fear of making matters worse. The family secret is kept and maintained at the expense of all family members who live in a shadow of fear that someone will discover what they have been hiding.

As a result of living in chemically dependent homes, many children are left with a number of feelings and thoughts that affect their life coping strategies (Gibson, Mitchell, & Basile, 1993).

They are responsible either directly or indirectly for their parent's drinking.
Their parent's drinking equates with their not being loved.
They are angry with the parent who does not drink for not changing the situation and providing safety for them.
They are afraid of harm coming to the alcoholic as a result of drinking.
They are confused by the differences in behavior when the parent is drinking versus when the parent is not drinking.
They are afraid to bring friends home because it is hard to know what to expect at home.
They are ashamed and embarrassed about the parent's behavior.

COA FAMILY ROLES

Many contemporary writers (Black, 1981; Glover, 1994; Muro & Kottman, 1995; Thompson & Rudolph, 1992; Webb, 1992, 1993) have cited the dysfunction roles that COAs acquire. They are the family hero, the scapegoat, the lost child, the placating child, and the family mascot. These roles provide some insight into the varying coping styles that children have developed in response to living in a chemically dependent household.

Family hero. The family hero is usually a role characteristic of the eldest child in the family. The hero is seen as being self-reliant, capable, overly responsible, and confident. The hero displays positive behavior in and out of school. Heroes tend to be popular, perfectionistic, compulsive, and highly achievement oriented. They believe that they are responsible for curing their family ills and are equally responsible for preventing negative family happenings. The facade of being capable in all respects is a heavy burden to carry for the family hero.

Scapegoat. The scapegoat is the child that everyone unjustifiably holds responsible for the family's difficulties. Scapegoats are always getting into trouble. They may appear withdrawn, hostile, angry, and defiant. Scapegoats draw negative attention to themselves and away from the family's problems. These children find it difficult to trust others, may have few friends in school, and feel totally rejected by family and peers. These hurting children are often argumentative, do not get along with teachers, and are academic underachievers.

Lost child. They are usually the middle children in the family. Lost children are often lonely, isolated, scared, and confused. They receive little attention from other family members and are often kept uninformed about family matters. Withdrawn and ignored, these children do not know how to reach out to others for help. They cope with life's stresses by keeping to themselves. These are the very children who often go unnoticed in school. Their quiet, reserved, and unassuming nature leaves them with few friends and marginal academic success.

Placaters. These children sacrifice themselves and their needs for the family. They often experience feelings of disappointment and hurt in their attempts to please others. Rarely do they accomplish their goals and seldom achieve their own personal wants and needs. These same behaviors carry over into the school environment. Placaters are quiet children who function in the following mode. They strive to please others often investing more of their energy in peer relationships than in their school work.

Mascot. The younger children assume the role of family mascot. These children are sheltered from family problems brought on by substance abuse. They are often immature, overprotected, and fearful children who respond to personal and family stress by clowning around. These children, growing up in a distorted sense of reality, provide comic relief for the family through humor and amusing antics. These same behaviors carry over into the classroom. Mascots are the class clowns whose antics are often poorly timed causing major class disruptions and negatively impacting their academic success.

CHARACTERISTICS OF CHILDREN OF ALCOHOLICS

The adverse side effects of parental chemical dependency in grade school children are most likely to surface in school settings with academic performance, peer relationships, self-esteem, and mood regulation being the prime indicators (Berlin & Davis, 1989). Clinicians and researchers have identified a range of indicators that may prove helpful in identifying COAs in school and related settings (Ackerman, 1983; American Academy of Child & Adolescent Psychiatry, 1991; Knight, 1994; Muro & Kottman, 1995; Robinson, 1989; Wilson & Blocher, 1990).

Absenteeism. School attendance in COAs can be irregular. Children may miss Mondays and Fridays, days before and after vacations, arrive late to school, and be consistently dropped off early.

Academic difficulty. COAs may exhibit low grades or an ebb and flow of academic performance that may coincide with home fluctuations in family problems and stress.

Physical appearance. COAs may show signs of physical abuse and neglect. Cuts, bruises, and other physical marks may indicate abuse. Neglect is most often evidenced in poor hygiene, improper clothing for outside climatic conditions, complaints of hunger, and falling asleep in class.

Peer relationships. Some COAs isolate themselves from their peers, seem withdrawn, and exhibit ineffective interpersonal skills. While some COAs have friends, they often resist bringing them home to their families.

Physical symptoms. More than average physical complaints, stomach aches, headaches, and other health problems are reported by COAs. They make more frequent visits to the health room and school nurse and are more likely to have a higher number of school absences than their counterparts.

Psychological symptoms. Some children may exhibit fears, mood swings, anxiety, nervous tics, low self-esteem, are easily upset, display regressive behaviors, are neurotic, and engage in thumb sucking and nail biting. While not all COAs will exhibit these symptoms, some will experience a variety of them.

Tiredness. Depending on the day of the week, time of the day, and fluctuation in home stresses, some COAs will appear tired and listless.

Problems with emotions and behaviors. Whereas some COAs actively avoid conflict at all costs to avoid situations that might provoke anger, hostility, and arguments, other children are easily provoked to anger, displaying sudden and sometimes uncontrollable emotional outbursts of aggression toward peers and people in authority. They exhibit temper tantrums and other disruptive behaviors (class clown) to gain the attention that they seek.

People pleasing behaviors. Some children are overly concerned by how they are viewed by others. They are preoccupied with doing things right. They often request a lot of direction and feedback in how they are doing. They strive to be perfect in all that they think, feel, and do. Some children may have a strong need to control others and what goes on around them so that they can be viewed in a positive light by those in authority.

Inability to concentrate. Daydreaming, short attention span, hyperactivity, and inability to concentrate are all examples of attention problems experienced by some COAs. In some cases, the cause of attention problems may be related to attention deficit disorder.

Parental actions. Some children may appear to be upset with their parents because they do not attend school functions, whereas other children are just as pleased that their parents do not attend. Some children may go out of their way to block any parental interest and participation. The parents may offer excuses why they can't attend PTA meetings, parent-teacher conferences, and assist their children with schoolwork. Those same parents may drop their children off at school long before school begins and may be late in picking them up. These erratic displays of behavior and seeming lack of interest in their children may represent parental coping behaviors in response to family stress.

In addition to the characteristics mentioned, counselors and teachers should be sensitive to how children respond to classroom programs and educational lessons about drugs and alcohol. Knight (1994) has indicated that COAs may

- react negatively to all alcohol use,
- equate drinking with intoxication,
- express negative feelings about alcoholism,
- be familiar with a wide range of alcoholic beverages and drugs,
- be familiar with what specific drugs look like and how to obtain and use them,
- share stories about parental drinking or other drug use,
- be concerned with whether or not alcoholism can be inherited, and
- exhibit changes in attendance patterns during those days when alcohol education programs are conducted.

Children who appear to experience uneasiness and discomfort or who are unusually attentive during drug education programs may be children who can personally relate to the information being presented. Teachers and counselors need to inform children that they are available to answer questions, discuss feelings, and generally be supportive of them whenever they feel the need to talk with someone.

IDENTIFICATION OF COAs:
METHODS, PROBLEMS, AND CONSEQUENCES

Identification of COAs of elementary school age is not as easy as it may seem. Robinson (1989) has estimated that approximately 95% of these children are never identified.

Methods

Currently there are few, if any, accurate methods for identifying COAs. Although some self-report instruments do exist, they do not work well for a variety of reasons (Knight, 1994).

Current questionnaires tend to focus on alcohol dependency rather than on the full range of chemical dependency in families.

Many of the self-report instruments are designed for use with adolescents and adults rather than with children.

Even if such instruments could be adapted for use with children, reading and writing skills may not be sufficiently developed for very young children (ages 5-8).

The validity of self-report devices to identify COAs (4th, 5th, and 6th grade youngsters) have been seriously questioned (Shell, Groppenbacher, Rossa, & Gensheimer, 1992). They have not proven successful in discriminating COAs from non-COAs.

Ethical and legal issues of collecting identifiable data from children for the purpose of labeling them as COAs or non-COAs represents a potential invasion of privacy and would need to be discussed thoroughly in terms of data collection guidelines and use.

Other informal identification methods relate specifically to

- families and/or children coming forward on their own. Parents and/ or children may discuss their home situation with a caring teacher or counselor.
- parents and/or children being contacted via the school to publicize a variety of available support groups. Some parents and/or children may come forward seeking assistance once they recognize that their school or community conducts a variety of support groups that meet their (COAs') needs.
- teachers and counselors relying on clues, behavior patterns, and intuition. Informed teachers and counselors are ones who have become trained observers in response to identifying some of the roles, behavioral characteristics, and other telltale signs that may be indicative of family problems such as parental chemical dependency.

Problems

Despite the formal and informal methods of identifying COAs, there are many good reasons why as many as 95% of them go undetected (Crews &

Sher, 1992; Knight, 1994; Robinson, 1989; Roosa, Gensheimer, Ayers, & Short, 1990).

- "Many COAs say nothing and exhibit only subtle or little-recognized behavioral clues" (Knight, 1994, p. 276).
- Many COAs come from seemingly well functioning families, the pillars of their communities.
- A high percentage of COAs appear to be healthy, normal, and well adjusted youngsters who may excel in school, are quiet and compliant, and generally are well behaved (Woll, 1990).
- COAs are very effective at keeping their problems hidden. They have developed numerous coping skills that make their detection seemingly impossible except in a very small percentage of cases when telltale cues cannot be ignored easily.

In addition to the fact that many COAs blend easily into their respective classrooms, high emphasis for their detection rests on the application of identifiable characteristics and family roles of COAs. While recognizing family roles is beneficial to helping adults understand how COAs accommodate to trauma, environmental situations and family pathology, we also must recognize that these roles are not unique to COAs. Secondly, there also is the danger of oversimplification when using generalizable characteristics and applying them to one population. Such characteristics (defense mechanisms) are used to one degree or another, by all children who are motivated by self-maintenance and personal preservation. Therefore, there is some danger in jumping to conclusions when identifying COAs.

Consequences

Probably of greatest concern regarding the identification of COAs are the potential consequences to the children and their families once they have been labeled (Roosa et al., 1990). On the one hand, children and their families can benefit from individual and support group counselling services as a result of their being identified. Blume (1984) has indicated that children in support groups are often relieved to know that they are not alone in their situation and benefit from understanding the dynamics in chemically dependent families.

Aside from the benefits of identifying COAs for therapeutic assistance, there are a number of concerns associated with labeling this population, the consequences of which are not fully known (Burk & Sher, 1990). Children from chemically dependent families keep their problems hidden because (Knight, 1994)

- they may not recognize a parent's problem as chemical dependency;
- they are unable or unwilling to admit their parent(s) has a drug problem;
- they may not recognize or understand the connection between their feelings and experiences and their chemically dependent parent(s);
- they deny that a known chemical dependency problem exists;
- they feel ashamed, embarrassed, and confused about their family's drug problem;
- they believe that the family drug problem is their fault and they feel guilty about what they have done;
- they are experiencing strong family pressure to keep the secret;
- they recognize the stigma associated with chemical dependency and the potential legal consequences for using illicit drugs;
- they have learned to distance themselves from the problem and rarely, if ever, discuss their feelings, problems, and thoughts about family drug use;
- they comply with family rules of "don't talk, don't feel, and don't trust" (Black, 1981);
- they remain silent because they do not want to be stigmatized by peers, teachers, counselors, and society in general;
- they have developed socially acceptable and compliant behaviors and masquerade as normal; and
- they are reluctant to draw attention to themselves by requesting personal or family assistance.

This is only a partial list of why COAs maintain secrecy. COAs also are assisted by their parents who are equally motivated to keep the family secret. Parents do this by forbidding their children from seeking help, denying that their children are affected, and distancing themselves and their children from others who might get too close.

Is it any wonder then that children and parents, who will go to almost any extreme to keep others from knowing about the family's chemical dependency, might also be deeply and adversely affected by the disclosure? The stigma associated with carrying a COA label could have dire repercussions for the whole family and especially the children with respect to diminished self-esteem, destroyed peer relationships, and lost coping mechanisms (Burk & Sher, 1990; Woodside, 1991). Sher (1991), in response to the potentially negative side effects of labels, has argued for the use of extreme caution when assessing or promoting services for COAs especially for children who are not experiencing major psychological problems.

POINTS TO CONSIDER

With all that has be said about COAs, few would disagree that children can benefit from receiving individual and support group services. The big question to be resolved, however, is how best to meet these children's needs without causing them more pain via irresponsible labeling.

The following eight points should be kept in mind when addressing the needs of children living in chemically dependent families (Woll, 1990).

The amount of trouble children are causing for adults does not tell how troubled they are. This statement is especially true for COAs, the majority of whom are not children with noticeable behavior problems. To identify children for special services purely on the basis of visibility is to miss many children who could benefit from assistance plus running the risk of reinforcing a child's sense of hurt and shame by focusing on identifying characteristics that further set this child apart from his or her peers.

All children need age-appropriate information about chemically dependent families. All children can benefit from information on chemical abuse and how it affects family members. These children are receiving important drug information they can apply to their own lives. They also are better able to understand and to comfort those classmates whose lives have been touched by a chemically dependent parent. A general audience program approach reaches all children rather than missing up to 95% of the unidentifiable COAs, which is what happens when COA support groups are targeted to receive the same information. Following a classroom- or community-based program, children can be told that those wishing more information may join a support group on the topic.

Words need to be screened to avoid reinforcing shame. Just as we must be concerned about how we identify COAs, we must be equally sensitive about the words we use in helping children learn about chemical dependency in families. For example, rather than using the term alcoholic when describing a parent addicted to alcohol, we could say, "There are lots of children in this school and in the country whose moms or dads may drink too much or use too many drugs. Let me share with you some of the concerns and things that happen to some of their families." Children have a need to go on loving themselves and their parents versus feeling the need to label either themselves or their parents as bad people. Our purpose should not be to bring more shame into their lives but rather to help them understand their situation and how to cope with it more effectively.

Denial and other survival systems are necessary for children's well-being. For children living in chemically dependent households, denial may be their only defense against "truths" that are too difficult to accept. To strip children of their defenses and related survival tactics before they are ready to give them up might well cause more damage to them. Children need support and understanding. They need to be accepted along with their defenses while they learn how to talk, feel, and trust—behaviors that may take a long time to develop.

Support systems need to be in place. Most children learning about chemically dependent families in general audience programs will be able to use denial and other defense mechanisms to screen out truths too difficult to bear; however, some children may find their defense mechanisms breaking down in light of new information. Their safety nets may develop holes leaving them vulnerable to psychological stress and personal conflict. Safety support systems need to be in place for large and small group educational sessions. Children can be helped in identifying "safe people" who they can talk to when the need arises. They also can receive "safety messages" that provide them with options regarding group participation. Children can benefit from receiving information that gives them permission to protect themselves in group. For example, they can be given permission to

- express a full range of feelings,
- leave the group momentarily if they are feeling uncomfortable,
- participate when they feel like doing so, and
- discuss only those thoughts and ideas that they wish to share.

Other safety nets include the inservicing of teachers regarding how to answer children's questions, providing appropriate versus inappropriate responses, and knowing when it is and is not necessary to involve other people in making decisions. Children want to know that they have a safe place to talk and that what they say not only will be respected but also will be held in confidence. Only in cases involving "clear and imminent danger" to children must a confidence be broken, and, even in those instances, there is some latitude regarding disclosure.

All prevention programs should respect the realities in which children live. Children need to receive clear, accurate, and truthful information presented in a sensitive manner. Some of the children in general audience programs will be COAs. If they are to relate to these programs, they must be able to connect with the same message that other children are hearing. The big issue for many COAs is a personal loss of control. They want to know how to cope in a world that seems to have limited choices.

In addition to COAs, you will have children dealing with multiple family issues such as divorce, mental illness, physical and sexual abuse, and chemical dependency. Children confronted with multiple family issues can, if the material is presented properly, relate to such things as

- difficult feelings,
- self-blame,
- denial,
- I'm all alone,
- It's my fault,
- I'm responsible for fixing the problem,
- enabling,
- is there some light at the end of the tunnel,
- family secrets,
- nobody cares about me, and
- I don't know what to do or where to turn.

Every child, whether living in a healthy or unhealthy household, can relate to some of the same issues, but on different levels, since all families must resolve a variety of family living problems.

Information about core issues can strengthen self-esteem. Self-esteem is central to life and living. Children and adults can have a more enjoyable and meaningful life if they can learn to view themselves with kind eyes, respect themselves, and generally like what they see. Children need to develop a sense of self that is separate from others. They must learn to do all that they can to function in a healthy manner. By teaching children how to love, respect, and value themselves, we will help them learn gradually how to detach themselves from demeaning, shameful, and hurtful messages that render them powerless. Unfortunately, chemically dependent family systems rely on manipulation, control, and distorted perceptions to solidify their family unit.

It is important to focus on strengths, resources, and resiliencies. Children of chemically dependent families are victims of negative messages as previously discussed. If these messages are to be challenged, and they must, focusing on children's strengths is a good place to begin. While children have become experts when it comes to identifying their weaknesses, they have had little practice in looking at their positive qualities, and they have many. Children do not survive under adverse family conditions without developing resiliency. These strengths are often their greatest weaknesses because they have been taken to excess. Perfectionism, excessive acts of responsibility, and assuming adult care giving roles are all examples of positive qualities taken to the extreme. Helping children identify and achieve a proper balance with respect to their strengths will add to their sense of personal power and well-being.

CHILDREN'S NEEDS

COAs have a variety of needs to be met as they face the challenges of living in a chemically dependent household. While the needs they must fulfill are not much different from those of other children, the pathological family environment in which COAs live greatly compromises that process. Based on research and the experience of practitioners who work with this population, the following needs surface as the most critical to be addressed in a support group experience:

- information,
- self-understanding,
- cognitive restructuring,
- self-expression, and
- self-care.

Information

COAs are in need of accurate and truthful information about family chemical dependency presented in an understandable and sensitive manner. Information helps children understand what is happening, dispels myths, and reduces fears and anxieties that are often exacerbated in chemically dependent homes. O'Rourke (1990) identified ten key points that many child support groups cover concerning parental abuse of alcohol.

> Alcoholism is a disease.
> Everybody gets hurt in an alcoholic family.
> Children whose parents drink too much are not alone.
> Children cannot cause, control, or cure parents' alcoholism.
> There are many good ways for children to take care of themselves.
> It is healthy to identify and express feelings.
> It is okay to talk about parental drinking to a special group or friend.
> Kids of alcoholics are at a high risk of substance abuse themselves.
> It is important for children to identify and to use a trusted support system outside of the family.
> There are many ways of problem solving and coping with parental alcoholism. (p. 111)

Self-understanding

Children have a need to understand their personal needs, rights, and current strengths. Helping children understand their physiological, safety and security, belonging and love, and self-esteem needs is a first step toward helping children secure what is rightfully theirs. Children will also learn to recognize what happens to them when they respond to unmet needs in an irresponsible manner. Armed with these new revelations, children can be taught how to meet their needs in a responsible manner.

COAs also have many strengths that they may not recognize. They may perceive themselves to be powerless and unique but for all of the wrong reasons. Children need assistance in identifying their current strengths and to perceive themselves as having value and worth based on the assets that contribute to their positive sense of self.

Cognitive Restructuring

Children have a need to examine myths, irrational thoughts, and false assumptions that they have internalized regarding themselves, family members, and life itself. Such cognitive distortions are the root cause of distressful emotions, unsupported attitudes, and illogical coping strategies. With help, children can learn to identify, to challenge, and to replace their illogical thoughts with more rational ones. Cognitive restructuring can help children manage their feelings more effectively and support the application of responsible coping strategies.

Self-expression

Addressing one's wants and needs through feelings, thoughts, and behaviors are basic self-expression responses; however, many COAs have been taught not to talk, feel, or trust. Children have a need to understand themselves fully and to express their feelings, thoughts, and beliefs in ways that will enhance their sense of wellness (physically, socially, emotionally, and spiritually).

Self-care

COAs have a need to develop a variety of strengths that will help them self-manage in their home and school environments. Many COAs have felt powerless at home and in school because all of their energies have been spent sustaining a family secret. Children can learn to energize themselves when they recognize that they must seek a responsible balance between their own self-care and care for their families. Children have a need to learn a variety of self-care strengths that will help them secure accurate and truthful information, understand themselves and their families, think rationally, express their wants and needs effectively, and manage their lives responsibly.

STRENGTHS TO BE LEARNED

If COAs are to develop an understanding of their home situation and learn responsible coping strategies, then support groups must help children address the "don't talk," "don't trust," and "don't feel" rules that have governed their lives. Children of alcoholics need assistance in learning to

- build trusting relationships,
- express themselves, and
- fully experience and share their emotions with others.

If these three goals are to be realized, then children's needs must be met through strength building experiences that are addressed in the sessions and activities that follow. The strengths to be developed in the COA Support Group are

- information acquisition,
- connectiveness building,
- feelings management,
- strengths identification,
- stress management,
- problem solving, and
- self-care.

Information Acquisition

Children will have an opportunity to explore their thoughts and beliefs about living in a chemically dependent home. They will have an opportunity to explore myths, negative labels, and misperceptions about chemical dependency and how misinformation and cognitive distortions can affect their feelings about themselves, their family, and chemical dependency. Children will learn accurate information about themselves, chemical dependency in families, and the notion that unhealthy attitudes and patterns can be changed.

Connectiveness Building

COAs need an opportunity to participate in a positive community building experience. Support groups, above all else, must be designed and managed in ways that will allow children to reach out to one another. This can be accomplished by

- developing group rules that support connectiveness building,
- involving children in noncompetitive activities,
- teaching children how to give compliments and positive feedback,
- providing children with opportunities to explore and use connectiveness building strengths (smiling, listening, sharing ideas and feelings),
- giving children opportunities to exercise personal power in groups, and
- promoting a safe climate that gives children the opportunity to take risks without retribution,

This is only a partial list of community building ideas that can be implemented. Helping children build connections with each other is a necessary condition for personal growth.

Feelings Management

Many COAs have been taught not to feel so that they will not get hurt. When children deny their feelings and fail to share them with significant others, their needs and wants often go unmet. They jeopardize their self-care by holding back or distorting their feelings, thereby sacrificing their needs for the family's needs. The COA support group helps children understand the importance that emotions play in their lives. They are taught a feelings vocabulary, what feelings are, how they affect their lives, responsible ways to communicate their feelings, and how to manage their feelings from a wellness perspective.

Strengths Identification

COAs have developed many strengths that can benefit them in positive ways. Unfortunately, many COAs have learned to devalue themselves by creating a negative identity from the labels that they and others have hung on them. COAs are resilient individuals who have learned to live with adversity. They have developed a number of positive strengths that they can continue to use in addition to the new ones that they will be learning. The COA support group helps children identify and utilize their strengths in developing positive self-identities, enhancing self-esteem, and empowering themselves to manage their lives based on Right, Reality, and Responsibility (the 3 R's). The COA support group encourages children to focus on their positive qualities and teaches them to create, package, and market themselves as winners.

Stress Management

COAs live in stressful environments. One goal of the COA support group is to help children understand what stress is, how it develops, and what they can do to make minimal changes in their own lives to manage their stress more effectively. They will understand that accurate information, feelings management, personal strengths, and problem solving skills will help them plan self-care strategies that will enhance their personal safety and reduce stress in their lives.

Problem Solving

Children need opportunities to practice applying their strengths in response to those life situations that they will encounter. The COA support group experience will help them explore various life problems and how those problems might be addressed through 3 R's decision making. Providing children with a problem-solving format and useful strengths empowers children to explore choices and identify solutions that are based on Right, Reality, and Responsibility.

Self-care

The last strength to be developed is a culmination of all the preceding strengths. Children are encouraged to explore some of their own special needs and how they can take care of themselves by responding to them. Group members are encouraged to identify their strengths and support systems and then to develop their own self-care action plan for "Taking Care of Me."

MESSAGE TO FACILITATORS

Although living in a chemically dependent family is never easy, the vast majority of COAs are responsible and well adjusted (Calder & Kostyniuk, 1989). Many have developed effective coping mechanisms and possess a number of positive strengths. Keeping these points in mind, children can benefit from a support group experience that communicates understanding, establishes a network of support, and offers a glimmer of hope. You can provide a safe, warm, and gentle environment in which children can learn to talk, feel, and trust.

Identifying Participants

We have found that all children can benefit from learning about difficult family issues that many children will face (e.g., divorce, alcoholism, abuse, violence, emotional problems, stepfamilies). We therefore support running classroom size or large group guidance sessions that address the needs of all children in responding to family issues. Following these sessions, you then can introduce specific support groups that children can join that focus on different family issues. Topics to be covered in your general sessions could include

- all families have problems;
- you are not alone;
- family problems are not your fault;
- you cannot fix family problems, but you can learn to help yourself;
- enabling sometimes helps, but often hurts;
- there is light at the end of the tunnel;
- understanding family secrets;
- learning to work it out;
- your rights; and
- help is available.

By covering topics such as these in large group sessions, children may be less apprehensive about joining specific support groups. Children can be told that support groups can benefit everyone. Some children will join a support group because they are living with a specific family issue; others may join because they would like to learn more about that issue; whereas others may join because they have friends living with that particular family problem and would like to be better able to support them.

Anything that you can do to support children in their decision to join a support group such as "Children Growing Up in a Family Troubled with Alcohol" should be done. Large group guidance sessions help. It also is helpful to pick a title for a support group that does not label participants negatively or create a stigma that would repel child participation.

Selecting Group Members

In addition to following the guidelines for selecting group members as provided in Chapter 3, we strongly urge you to interview each child prior to joining a COA support group. You will want to review the group's purpose and what will be covered while at the same time discussing with each child his or her reasons for joining. While difficult to ascertain in one interview, children who you believe would not benefit from a group experience should be considered for alternative forms of assistance.

We also strongly encourage you, with the child's knowledge, to obtain written parental consent (sample form is shown in Figure 3.4) for the child to participate in your COA support group. Provide the parents with information and answer their questions so that they can make an informed decision. Be sure to let them know that your group is open to all children, because some parents may be apprehensive about having their child or their family labeled by joining this group. Share with parents and/or guardians Figure 4.1 so that they will have suggestions on how they can help their children.

Group Process

We cannot overemphasize the importance of developing a sense of family within your group. Trust is an important issue for COAs. Building trust occurs through action and not words. Be consistent, predictable, and congruent in your behaviors. Be genuine, empathetic, and caring. You must set a stage that encourages the building of connections between you and every group member and between and among the members themselves. Establish a set routine, time table, and a positive working climate so that children can feel safe, secure, and connected to your support group experience.

Also remember that group activities are designed to encourage interaction that will lead to discussion and children learning about themselves and chemically dependent families. The activities are the catalysts that stimulate group process. Do not let the activities take precedence over the process. If this happens, children are likely to enjoy the activities but may not connect with their real purpose, of addressing the session's objectives.

Another important point is to remember that the ultimate purpose of the COA support group is to teach children how to self-manage more effectively in a chemically dependent family. Help children get in touch with their emotions, challenge their irrational beliefs, and provide them with lots of opportunities to make 3 R's decisions. Children need practice making life choices based on what they have learned in group. The more decisions they can make in response to "real life" family issues, the more confident they will become in terms of their own self-management.

You are now ready to meet your COA group. These children will surely benefit from this experience because you are there to make a difference in their lives. And that difference comes from providing children with accurate information, useful skills, and an opportunity to care for themselves and others.

Resources

In Figure 4.1 are provided "Tips for Caregivers" in order to strenghen the healing process at home. In Figure 4.2 are provided lists of resources to be used with and by children in the Children of Alcoholics Support Group. The resource materials are grouped according to age of child.

CHILDREN OF ALCOHOLICS GUIDE
Tips for Caregivers

Your child soon will be participating in a Children of Alcoholics Support Group. The goal of this personal growth support group is to help children understand the nature of alcoholism and its impact on the family and how they can learn to feel better about themselves and attend to their own needs. This support group experience will help your child develop friendships, share his or her feelings, build self-esteem, manage stress, and learn other self-help skills that will help make life more complete and hopeful. Your child will need support at home while participating in this group experience. We therefore offer a number of tips that we encourage you to use with your child that also will make his or her group experience more satisfying.

1. Help your child understand that

    a   alcoholism is a disease;
    b   other children are living in alcoholic families (you're not alone);
    c   children can't cause, control, or change a parent's alcoholism;
    d   alcohol is a harmful chemical and that when consumed in large amounts can cause a parent to act in strange and unpredictable ways;

    e   he or she is loved and wanted but that the alcoholic parent is not able to always show that love;

    f   alcohol abuse affects the whole family;

    g   talking about his or her feelings can help; and

    h   you support his or her participation in the support group.

2. Make time each day to be with and talk to your child.

3. Participate in activities with your child.

4. Encourage and support your child's participation in activities with other children.

5. Provide opportunities for your child to interact with other adult role models.

6. Be sure to meet your child's everyday needs for rest, clothing, food, and shelter.

7. Try to provide a consistent and positive home routine reducing as much chaos as possible.

8. Follow through on what you say you will do as often as possible. Your child counts on you to be there and to be dependable and predictable.

9. Be emotionally available for your child. Be there to provide your child with love, comfort, touch, a listening ear, and to sooth hurt feelings.

10. Give your child permission to talk about family matters and personal stress in group.

11. Allow your child the freedom to talk about group experiences, but don't pry or pressure him or her into sharing experiences that he or she wishes not to divulge.

12. Build trust with your child. Only share conversations between the two of you with others with his or her permission to do so.

    Living in a home with an adult caregiver who abuses alcohol is a difficult burden to bear. The 12 tips that have been provided are especially difficult to practice under such circumstances. Do the very best that you can in applying as many of these tips as you can. Seek assistance from professionals (e.g., counselors, clergy, psychologists, support groups) with your questions and ask for assistance from others when needed. You can make a positive difference in your child's life even under the most difficult circumstances.

Figure 4.1. Tips for caregivers to be given to parents and/or guardians. Permission to photocopy is granted.

RESOURCES FOR CHILDREN
Children of Alcoholics

Ages 3 to 7

Jones, P. (1983). *The brown bottle.* Minneapolis: Hazelden. (a story about addiction)

Kenny, K., & Krull, H. (1980). *Sometimes my mom drinks too much.* Milwaukee: Raintree Publications. (alcoholism of mother)

Super, G. (1990). *Drugs and our world.* New York: Troll Books. (outlines the negative aspects of drug and alcohol use)

Vigna, J. (1988). *I wish Daddy didn't drink so much.* Morton Grove, IL: Albert Whitman & Co. (father's alcoholism)

Vigna, J. (1990). *My big sister takes drugs.* New York: Albert Whitman, Co. (an older sibling's drug/alcohol involvement)

Ages 8 to 12

Hall, L., & Cohn, L. (1988). *Dear kids of alcoholics.* Carlsbad, CA: Gurze Books. (alcoholism and recovery)

Hamilton, D. (1984). *Joel's other mother.* Scottdale, PA: Herald Press. (mother's alcoholism, communication)

Hill, K. (1990). *Toughboy and sister.* New York: Margaret K. McElderry Books. (alcoholism of father, death)

Hastings, J., & Typpo, M. (1984). *An elephant in the living room.* Minneapolis: Hazelden. (living with an alcoholic)

Holland, I. (1980). *Now is not too late.* West Caldwell, NJ: Lothrop, Lee and Shepard. (alcoholism of mother)

Holz, L. M. (1984). *Foster child.* New York: Julian Messner. (change, parental neglect)

Mearian, J.F. (1980). *Someone slightly different.* New York: The Dial Press. (single parent, live in grandparent)

Reuter, B. (1989). *Buster's world.* New York: Dutton Children's Books. (alcoholism of father, being bullied)

Rock, G. (1975). *Dream for Addie.* New York: Alfred A. Knopf. (friendship, meaning of alcoholism)

Tapp, K. (1986). *Smoke from the chimney.* New York: Atheneum Publishers. (father's alcoholism, anxiety)

Wood, M. (1989). *The search for Jim McGwynn.* New York: Atheneum Publishers. (parental unreliability, auto accidents)

Ages 12 and Up

Barr, L. (1990). *The wrong way out.* Pinellas Park, FL: Willowisp Press. (father's alcoholism, friendship)

Bell, W. (1986). *Crabbe's journey.* New York: Little Brown and Co. (adolescent alcoholism, running away)

Bunting, E. (1988). *A sudden silence.* San Diego: Harcourt Brace Jovanovich. (mother's alcoholism, accident)

Butterworth, W. E. (1979). *Under the influence.* New York: Four Winds Press. (adolescent alcoholism, auto accident)

Carter, A. R. (1989). *Up country.* New York: Putnam & Grossett Group. (maturation, mother's alcoholism)

Greene, S. M. (1979). *The boy who drank too much.* New York: Viking Press. (adolescent alcoholism, alcoholism of father)

Holland, I. (1985). *Jenny kiss'd me.* New York: Ballantine Books. (alcoholism of father, boy-girl relationships)

Rabinowich, E. (1979). *Rock fever.* New York: Franklin Watts. (alcoholism of mother)

Rattray, J. (1984). *Kids and alcohol: Facts and ideas about drinking and not drinking.* Health Communications. (information for children about the effects of alcohol)

Wersba, B. (1986). *Crazy vanilla.* New York: Harper & Row Publishers. (mother's alcoholism, boy-girl relationships)

Figure 4.2. Resources for use with and by children in Children of Alcoholics Support Group.

SESSION I—NOT MY BAGGAGE, JUST MY BAG

BRIEF OVERVIEW OF SESSION

This session will afford children the opportunity to begin to get to know each other, understand group ground rules, and have a bit of fun together. It also will introduce the purpose of the group and remind children that this group is intended to provide support and assistance to them in dealing with their concern of chemical dependence of a family member.

GOALS

1. To assist children in understanding the reason for their presence in the group.
2. To develop group ground rules.
3. To allow children to become acquainted with other group members.
4. To provide an opportunity for children to begin to talk about chemical dependence.

MATERIALS NEEDED

1. Chart paper
2. Crayons or markers
3. White paper bags

PROCEDURE

1. Introduce self and have each of the children in the group introduce himself or herself by first name. Mention that everyone in the group is here because they are dealing with similar situations in their life. During the course of the session we will be talking about chemical dependency and how it affects all family members. We also will begin to talk about ways each person can have some control over his or her life.

2. Begin to set the stage for the group by inviting a brainstorming session on group rules. (List the rules on a piece of chart paper for future reference and review in subsequent group sessions.) Examples of possible group ground rules may include

    a What is said in the group stays there (confidentiality).
    b No put-downs are allowed.

c   Only one person talks at a time.

d   It is important to attend all sessions.

Note: If children do not suggest these group rules, you as facilitator should bring them up as part of the brainstorming session.

3.   Give each child a white bag. Inform the children that, in some of the future sessions, we will talk about "baggage," but for today, we are just going to have fun. Allow about 5 to 10 minutes for the children to decorate the outside of their bag in any way they want. The outside of the bag should, in some way, describe a little bit about them. For example, a child who enjoys sports may draw a football, baseball, etc. on his or her bag.

4.   After the bags are decorated, inform the children that they are to think about five things that might be in their bag if they were going to describe what is important to them. (It may be helpful to model for the children by telling them what is in your bag (e.g., family, job, time for fun, books, car).

5.   Allow sufficient time for each group member to talk about the five things that would be in his or her bag.

CLOSURE

To conclude this session, it may be helpful to review briefly the ground rules and to praise the group members for their participation in the session. Comment on connections and similarities you observed as the children shared the "contents" of their bag.

HOMEWORK

For homework, ask children to think about at least four different feelings and identify something that makes them feel that way. Remind them that next week the group will focus on feelings.

SESSION II—MY FEELINGS

BRIEF OVERVIEW OF SESSION

In this session the children will have the opportunity to identify a wide variety of feelings, discuss personal feelings, and learn what can happen when feelings are held all bottled up inside.

GOALS

1. To assist children in identifying the wide variety of feelings that one may experience.
2. To provide an opportunity for children to identify times they have felt a variety of ways.
3. To encourage children to identify how they are feeling at that current time.
4. To discuss what happens when feelings are held inside for long periods of time.

MATERIALS NEEDED

1. Feelings chart (A wide variety of feelings charts are currently on the market—any would be suitable.)
2. 3" × 5" cards with feeling words written on them
3. Balloon
4. Post-it notes (cut into small strips—one strip for each child)

PROCEDURE

1. Take just a moment to encourage children to talk about anything that happened in the first group and to review ground rules.

2. Show the feelings chart to the children. Talk about the kinds of things that make people have different types of feelings—choose three or four for further elaboration.

3. Encourage each child to choose one feeling from the chart and tell the group about a time he or she felt that way.

4. Give each child a 3" × 5" card with a feeling word written on it. Remind the children not to show their card to anyone. Ask them to think of what a person might say or do if they were having the feeling written on the card.

5. Allow a few minutes for role-plays of the feelings. Encourage the other group members to try to identify the feeling.

6. Discuss with the group what happens when people keep feelings all bottled up. (Use a balloon to show how the pressure continues to mount and grow as more air is put into the balloon.) Talk about what would happen if no air were left out. Compare this to talking about feelings—if we keep them all inside, sooner or later something will pop (in the form of anger, tears, etc.). Also demonstrate how you can let a little bit of air out of the balloon at a time, thus reducing tension. Again, remind children that we can do the same thing with our feelings when we talk about them.

7. Provide time for examples if children wish to share.

8. Give each child a post-it note strip and ask the group to write their names on the nonsticky side. When they have completed this, encourage them to put their strip on the feelings chart to show how they are feeling right now and tell the group why. Provide much positive reinforcement for sharing feelings.

CLOSURE

Bring closure to the session by asking each child to complete any one of the following unfinished sentence stems:

1. I am afraid of . . .
2. I am happiest when . . .
3. One thing that worries me is . . .
4. One thing I really feel proud of is . . .
5. Something that embarrasses me is . . .

HOMEWORK

To prepare for the next session, encourage the children to think abut masks they may wear to keep people from getting to know the real person inside them.

SESSION III—SOMETIMES I WEAR A MASK

BRIEF OVERVIEW OF SESSION

This session will acquaint the children with the defenses many children use when they do not want anyone to see their true feelings. This is particularly evident in children who grow up in homes affected by a parent's use of alcohol or other drugs.

GOALS

1. To assist children in beginning to identify and discuss their defenses.
2. To promote an understanding of the fact that there is a relationship between feelings, defenses, and wellness.
3. To assist children in finding more appropriate ways to lower their defenses and discuss their feelings and concerns.

MATERIALS NEEDED

1. Several masks
2. 12" × 18" construction paper for each child
3. Feelings poster (from session 2)
4. Crayons or markers

PROCEDURE

1. Show the masks and talk about why people wear masks. Most often the discussion will center around Halloween when people wear masks to "trick" others. Discuss the following questions:

    a   Why do people wear masks?
    b   Do people treat you differently when you wear a mask?
    c   Can you wear a mask without really looking any different?
    d   Do you ever wear an "invisible" mask?

2. Discuss the fact that sometimes people use defenses or "masks" to hide their true feelings. This often is done when Mom or Dad is drinking and we are afraid to tell them how we really feel or when we want to hide the family problems from our neighbors or friends.

3. Brainstorm with the group some of the most common masks children sometimes wear. (Make sure these include smiling, pretending to be sick, blaming others, and hiding.)

4. Discuss whether or not any of the group members have used any of the above mentioned defenses in their lives. Ask the following questions to promote discussion:

a   Which defenses do you use most often?
b   How do others act when you use your defense?
c   What do you think would happen if they knew how you really feel?

5. Give each child a sheet of paper and ask them to draw two large circles (side by side) on the paper. Below the first circle, write the word INSIDE, below the second circle write the word OUTSIDE.

6. Encourage each child to draw a picture of a way they may be feeling on the inside in the first circle and how they look on the outside because they are using their defense so no one will know how they really feel. Discuss how it makes them feel when they do this.

7. Allow time for discussion and sharing.

CLOSURE

Bring closure to this session by reminding children that all of us at one time or another mask our feelings but that it is okay to tell how we really feel. Reinforce that anger is okay as long as we do not hurt ourselves or others when we feel angry.

HOMEWORK

As a homework assignment, remind the children to practice showing and telling their real feelings rather than using their defenses during the next week. Tell them we will talk about how it worked at the beginning of next week's session.

SESSION IV—CHEMICAL DEPENDENCY IS A FAMILY DISEASE

BRIEF OVERVIEW OF SESSION

This session will reinforce the concept that chemical dependency effects everyone in the family and truly is a family disease. Children also will learn that their parent's drinking or drug use is not the child's fault, the dependency was not caused by the child, and the child cannot make the parent stop drinking or using. They also will learn some basic information about chemical dependency.

GOALS

1. To help children understand that chemical dependency is a family disease.
2. To inform children about the progress of the disease of chemical dependency.
3. To help children understand that they are not in control of their parent's chemical dependency.

MATERIALS NEEDED

1. Chart paper
2. Markers

PROCEDURE

1. Introduce the concept of "drug" as a substance that changes the way we act or the way our body works. Discuss the fact that drugs can be very positive as in the case of medicines, which help our body to heal. On the other hand, however, drugs are sometimes misused and, when this happens, often cause the person who is using to act very differently. This can be very frightening.

2. Talk briefly about the kinds of things people do when they have used too much of a substance. Answers may include stagger, fall down, be mean or violent, fall asleep, act crazy, yell, etc.

3. Stress the idea that, when persons regularly overuse chemicals or alcohol, they have the disease of chemical dependency. This means that they are

addicted to the substance and cannot quit on their own. They usually need help to quit drinking or using. (At this point, the children may want to share information about times when their chemically dependent parent quit drinking or using for a long time.) Allow time for sharing if children wish to do so.

4. Reinforce the point that alcoholics are usually regular people who have jobs, families and lives—they are not the stereotypic "street person" whom most people associate with chemical dependency.

5. Point out that no one knows for sure what causes chemical dependency, but it does tend to happen more often in some families. Scientists are still trying to find out why this is so.

6. Make certain to stress to the children that they cannot cause someone to start drinking or using and that it is not their fault.

7. Encourage the children to share ideas about how they take care of themselves when their parent is drinking or using. If you have access to a book or video about chemical dependency, it may be helpful to use it at this point. Some videos that cover the subject at an elementary level are "Elephant in the Living Room" (Carpenteria, CA: F.M.S. Productions) and "Lots of Kids Like Us" (Skokie, IL: Gerald T. Rogers Productions).

8. Allow time for discussion or questions.

CLOSURE

As a way of bringing closure to this session, remind children that there are lots of kids who have parents who drink or use. AGAIN REINFORCE THAT THEY CANNOT CONTROL THEIR PARENTS' DRINKING OR USE.

HOMEWORK

Encourage children to think of ways they can take care of themselves and continue to have a happy life while living in a chemically dependent family. Ask them to try one of the ideas before next week's session.

SESSION V—FAMILY ROLES

BRIEF OVERVIEW OF SESSION

In this session, children will begin to look at the types of roles sometimes played by family members. They will learn that "role-playing" frequently happens in families effected by chemical dependency and that these roles have been studied and are named in books about chemical dependency. The children also will learn that not all roles are played in all families and that sometimes one person will play more than one role based on the situation.

GOALS

1. To present information on the roles identified in families effected by chemical dependency.
2. To allow children an opportunity to discuss each of the roles as they relate to their particular situation.

MATERIALS NEEDED

1. Chart with the roles listed on it (Roberts & Fitzmohan, 1987) (See procedure #4 below.)

PROCEDURE

1. Review briefly the information from the past two sessions. Remind the children that the information they gain today may help them see a little more clearly how the information they dealt with in the past two sessions fits into the "big picture."

2. Introduce the idea of a "role." Sometimes, people on TV or in the movies are playing roles. Their roles are not the way they really are (or really feel).

3. Suggest the idea that in families affected by chemical dependency, family members also play roles and that these have been identified and are described in many books about chemical dependency.

4. Present the information about the "roles" (condensed from "Here's Looking at You, 2000" [Roberts & Fitzmohan, 1987]).

a   Chemically Dependent Person—this person may frequently change his or her behavior. Sometimes he or she is charming, friendly, and loving; at other times he or she is blaming, rigid, self-pitying, hostile, or angry. This person may act this way because he or she feels shame, guilt, or fear.

b   Chief Enabler—this person is the one who provides the family with stability and is usually the spouse of the chemically dependent person. Some behaviors that the enabler may show are: self-blame, self-pity, super responsibility, manipulation, and control. This person may feel self-doubt, helpless, and inadequate.

c   Hero—this person provides the family with self-worth. The hero is a leader, may be a workaholic, is often seeking approval and focuses on tasks that need to be done. The hero may be feeling confusion, loneliness, or inadequacy.

d   Scapegoat—this person provides the family with a target for blame. The scapegoat may show behaviors of defiance, confrontation, early chemical abuse, and rebelliousness. This person may be feeling rejection, resentment, and loneliness.

e   Mascot—this person provides the family with an emotional relief. He or she is often the caregiver who is warm, sensitive, a good listener, and often a joker or clown. The mascot often feels anger, inadequacy, insecurity, and loneliness.

f   Lost Child—this person provides the family with flexibility. He or she often feels isolated, unworthy, powerless, and inadequate.

4.   Spend some time discussing each of these roles and asking the children if they can identify any of these roles in themselves or in their family members. Allow opportunities for sharing from all who wish to contribute.

CLOSURE

To bring closure to the session, it may be helpful to do a very brief review of the roles and talk about why people play roles (because they are afraid to share how they really feel). Relate this to the previous session when we talked about feelings being okay.

HOMEWORK

To prepare for next week's session, the children should be encouraged to think about something positive about every other group member (or a strength that they see in the person).

SESSION VI—SUPER KIDS CAPE

BRIEF OVERVIEW OF SESSION

Because many children who come from homes where chemical abuse is a problem receive little positive feedback, this session will provide an opportunity for children to receive feedback on their strengths as seen by others in the group. The children also will be able to identify strengths in others.

GOALS

1. To assist children in understanding the importance of self-esteem.
2. To provide an opportunity for children to practice giving and receiving positive strokes.
3. To encourage children to begin to value themselves.

MATERIALS NEEDED

1. One 12" × 18" sheet of construction paper for each child
2. Yarn to attach "Super Kid Cape" to each child's back (See Activity Sheet 4.1 for directions on how to make capes.)
3. Super Kid logo for each cape (See Activity Sheet 4.1.)
4. Markers or crayons for each child

PROCEDURE

1. Begin by talking with the children about self-esteem. Ask the following questions:

    a   What are some things others have said that made you feel good?
    b   What can you say about yourself that makes you feel good?
    c   What are some positive things your teacher says that make you feel good?

2. Provide each child with a "Super Kid Cape" and have him or her tie the yarn around his or her neck so that the cape hangs down his or her back. (A "Super Kid" logo already should be placed in the middle of each child's cape.)

3. Instruct the children to think about something they like or see as a strength of each of the other members of the group. Tell them that they will have the opportunity to write these positive statements on each person's cape.

4. Give a marker to each child and allow them to move around the room writing positive comments on the back of the capes of every other group member.

5.   When all children have had the opportunity to write something positive on every other child's cape, ask them to come again to the group for sharing.

6.   Have children remove their cape, read the comments that have been written, and share feelings about what they have read.

7.   Allow time for children to enjoy the positive feedback they have received and to talk about how it feels to give and receive positive feedback.

CLOSURE

As this session comes to an end, it may be helpful to remind the children of the good feelings that occur as a result of giving and receiving positive feedback. Remind them that they, too, can sometimes give themselves a "pat on the back." At the conclusion of this session, it may be particularly important to allow children to discuss how they felt about this activity.

HOMEWORK

For the next session, encourage children to begin to make a list of what they see as their own personal strengths. Each child should think of at least three personal strengths for next session.

Yarn should be long enough to tie around the neck, allowing the "cape" to rest on the child's back.

← Holes for yarn

Write "Super Kid" comments here:

Activity Sheet 4.1.   Directions for "Super Kid Cape" and "Super Kid Logo."

SESSION VII—TOWER OF POWER

BRIEF OVERVIEW OF SESSION

In this session, children will be encouraged to identify as many sources of personal strength or power as they can. They will also discuss ways they can use these strengths to assist them in dealing with their parent's chemical dependency.

GOALS

1. To assist each child in identifying at least four personal strengths.
2. To help children recognize that they have control over their own actions.
3. To encourage children to utilize their power to deal effectively with the day-to-day trials of living with a chemically dependent person.

MATERIALS NEEDED

1. Construction paper for building the "Tower of Power"
2. Scissors, markers, crayons, tape
3. Pictures of famous towers (e.g., Washington Monument, Leaning Tower of Pisa, Tower of London)

PROCEDURE

1. Spend a few moments talking about the homework assignment. Allow children to brainstorm some of the strengths they were able to identify. Encourage them to think of all types of strengths, not just physical or academic. If they seem "stuck" in these areas, point out that often children have different strengths such as

   a   very dependable,
   b   good with little children,
   c   a loyal friend,
   d   helpful around the house, and
   e   keeps a neat room.

2. Show pictures of some famous towers. Ask children to describe the towers in terms of their characteristics. Sooner or later the word "strong" should

be brought into the discussion. The towers are strong because of the materials that were used to construct them—the building blocks.

3. Give each child a piece of construction paper and ask them to draw their own tower. On the building blocks, they will need to write some of their own personal strengths that help build their "Tower of Power." (If you are particularly creative or artistic, it might be fun to develop the towers out of more durable materials and make them three dimensional. This really could have a neat effect when arranged all together as a show of group power.)

4. Allow sufficient time for children to share the information from their towers and display them in the room, if possible.

5. Encourage children to make use of these "powers" to assist them each day.

CLOSURE

Close this session by reminding the children that there are certain things in their life over which they have no control (parent's drug use or drinking) but that there are many things over which they do have control. Encourage them to use their powers to deal with the areas under their control.

HOMEWORK

For a homework assignment, ask the children to begin to identify areas that they need to work on to take better care of their own needs. Ask them to think about these things for their final group session.

SESSION VIII—TAKING CARE OF ME

BRIEF OVERVIEW OF SESSION

In this final group session, the children will begin to identify some special needs they have and how they can take care of themselves physically as well as emotionally. The session will end on a positive note with children having an opportunity to form "friendship links" for the future.

GOALS

1. To assist children in finding a variety of ways to take care of themselves.
2. To encourage children to make a list of positive coping mechanisms they can use.
3. To bring closure to the group.
4. To provide an opportunity for children to develop friendship links for the future.

MATERIALS NEEDED

1. Chart paper
2. Crayons or markers
3. 12" × 18" construction paper for each child
4. Construction paper strips (1½" × 6")
5. Stapler or tape

PROCEDURE

1. Spend a few minutes discussing the homework assignment. As the children share the ideas they have thought of, write these ideas on the chart paper for all to see. (Compliment children for all the positive coping mechanisms they have thought of.) Some of the suggestions they may have thought of may include

    a go visit a friend when parent drinking or using starts,
    b stay in my room,
    c talk to a school counselor or special teacher,
    d talk about feelings with a friend who cares,
    e read a book,

f   watch a favorite TV program, and

g   know whom to call if I feel I am not safe.

2. Provide each child with a sheet of construction paper and ask them to develop their personal action plan for "Taking Care of Me." Ask each child to choose at least five items from the list (or add others they have thought of) and list them on his or her chart. Encourage the children to take the charts home and keep them in their room for further reference.

3. Allow time for children to share their coping mechanisms with the group. Compare and contrast the different choices among group members.

4. Give five strips of 1½" × 6" construction paper (various colors) to each child. Ask them to list the names of at least five people who provide support to them in one way or another (one name on each strip of paper). When they have listed all of the names, instruct them to put their five names together in chain form to make their friendship link. (Use tape or staples to make the chain.) Again encourage them to take this home and keep it in their room as a "visible" reminder of their personal support systems. When things get tough, encourage them to "use these support persons to help you feel better."

5. If children wish to do so, allow them to share the names of the people on their friendship link.

CLOSURE

To bring closure to this group, provide at least 5 to 10 minutes for children to share feelings—both positive and negative—about the group and to complete the written evaluation. Encourage group members to stay in touch if possible to continue to support each other.

EVALUATION

1. Do you feel that participation in the Chemical Dependency group was helpful to you? Why or why not?

2. What part of the group did you like best?

3. What part of the group did you like least?

4. If you had a friend who experienced a chemical dependency in his or her family, would you recommend that he or she participate in a similar group? Why or why not?

5. Did you attend all eight group sessions?

_____ Yes   _____ No

If no, how many did you attend? _____

6. Comments, suggestions, etc.:

REFERENCES

Ackerman, R. (1987). *Children of alcoholics: A guide for parents, educators, and therapists.* New York: Simon & Shuster.

Ackerman, R. J. (1983). *Children of alcoholics: A guidebook for educators, therapists, and parents* (2nd ed.). Holmes Beach, FL: Learning Publications.

American Academy of Child & Adolescent Psychiatry. (1991). Children of alcoholics. *Facts for Families, 17,* 9–10.

American Psychiatric Association. (1994). *Diagnostic and statistical manual of mental disorders* (4th ed.). Washington, DC: Author.

Austin, G., & Pendergast, M. (1991). Young children of substance abusers. *Prevention Research Update,* No. 8. Louisville, KY: Southeast Regional Center for Drug-Free Schools & Communities.

Berlin, R., & Davis, R. B. (1989). Children from alcoholic families: Vulnerability and resilience. In T. F. Dugan & R. Coles (Eds.), *The child in our times: Studies in the development of resiliency* (pp. 81–105). New York: Brunner/Mazel.

Black, C. (1981). Innocent bystanders at risk: The children of alcoholics. *Alcoholism: The National Magazine, 1*(3), 22–26.

Blume, S. B. (1984, December 5). *Report of the Conference on Prevention Research.* New York: Children of Alcoholics Foundation.

Brake, K. (1988). Counseling young children of alcoholics. *Elementary School Guidance and Counseling, 23,* 106–111.

Burk, J. P., & Sher, K. J. (1990). Labeling the child of an alcoholic: Negative stereotyping by mental health professionals and peers. *Journal of Studies on Alcoholics, 51,* 156–163.

Calder, P., & Kostyniuk, A. (1989). Personality profiles of children of alcoholics. *Professional Psychology: Research and Practice, 20*(6), 417–418.

Children of Alcoholics Foundations. (1992). *Help for inner-city children of addicted parents (1992).* New York: Author.

Crews, T. M., & Sher, K. J. (1992). Using adapted. Short masts for assessing parental alcoholism: Reliability and validity. *Alcoholism: Clinical & Experimental Research, 16*(3), 576–584.

Gibson, R. L., Mitchell, M. H., & Basile, K. S. (1993). *Counseling in the elementary school: A comprehensive approach.* Boston, MA: Allyn & Bacon.

Glover, J. G. (1994). The hero child in the alcoholic home: Recommendations for counselors. *The School Counselor, 41,* 185–190.

Knight, S. M. (1994). Elementary-age children of substance abusers: Issues associated with identification and labeling. *Elementary School Guidance & Counseling, 28*(4), 274–284.

Muro, J. J., & Kottman, T. (1995). *Guidance and counseling in the elementary and middle schools: A practical approach.* Dubuque, IA: Brown & Benchmark.

Naditch, B., & Learner, R. (1987, January–February). The next generation. *Changes: For and about Children of Alcoholics,* 36–38.

O'Rourke, K. (1990). Recapturing hope: Elementary school support groups for children of alcoholics. *Elementary School Guidance & Counseling, 25,* 107–115.

Roberts, C., & Fitzmohan, D. (1987). *Here's looking at you, 2000.* Seattle, WA: CHEF (Comprehensive Health Education Foundation).

Robinson, B. (1989). *Working with children of alcoholics.* Lexington, MA: Lexington Books.

Roosa, M. W., Gensheimer, L. R., Ayers, T. S., & Short, J. L. (1990). Development of a school-based prevention program for children in alcoholic families. *Journal of Primary Prevention, 11,* 119–139.

Schall, J. (1986, April). Alcoholism: When a parent drinks, a child struggles. Here's how to help children cope in healthy ways. *Instructor,* 54–57.

Schoenborn, C. A. (1991). Exposure to alcoholism in the family: United States, 1988. *Advance data from vital and health statistics* (No. 205). Hyattsville, MD: National Center for Health Statistics.

Shell, R. M., Groppenbacher, N., Roosa, M. W., & Gensheimer, L. K. (1992). Interpreting children's reports of concern about parental drinking: Indicators of risk status. *American Journal of Community Psychology, 20,* 463–489.

Sher, K. J. (1991). *Children of alcoholics: A critical appraisal of theory and research.* Chicago, IL: University of Chicago Press.

Thompson, C. L., & Rudolph, L. B. (1992). *Counseling children* (3rd ed.). Pacific Grove, CA: Brooks/Cole.

Vail-Smith, K., Knight, S. M., & White, D. M. (1995). Children of substance abusers in the elementary school: A survey of counselor perceptions. *Elementary School Guidance & Counseling, 29*(3), 163–176.

Webb, W. (1992). Empowering at-risk children. *Elementary School Guidance & Counseling, 27*(2), 96–103.

Webb, W. (1993). Cognitive behavior therapy with children of alcoholics. *The School Counselor, 40,* 170–177.

Wilson, J., & Blocker, L. (1990). The counselor's role in assisting children of alcoholics. *Elementary School Guidance and Counseling, 25,* 98–106.

Woodside, M. (1991). Policy, issues, and action: An agenda for children of substance abusers. In T. Rivinius (Ed.), *Children of chemically dependent parents: Multiperspectives form the cutting edge* (pp. 340–345). New York: Brunner/Mazel.

Woll, P. (1990). Children of chemical dependency: Respecting complexities and building on strengths. *Prevention Forum, 11*(1), 1–15.

Chapter 5

CHILDREN OF DIVORCE

Divorce results when two people in a marital relationship legally dissolve their marital status. When children are a part of that relationship (biological or adopted), they became children of divorce and are equally impacted by the devastating effects of a family in turmoil.

BACKGROUND INFORMATION

According to the 1990 United States Bureau of Census, approximately 48% of all marriages in the United States end in divorce. The divorce rate has tripled since 1960, giving the United States the highest divorce rate in the world (Spencer & Shapiro, 1993). Approximately one third of all children in this country under the age of 18 are thus affected by the divorce of their parents (Strangeland, Pellegreno, & Lundholm, 1989). "In the real world of 1994, only 50.8% of all youths live with both biological parents; 24% live in one-parent families; and 21% live in stepfamilies" (Coontz, 1995, p. 13). These statistics point to one thing—the American family is changing and divorce is a major contributing factor to that change.

Spencer & Shapiro (1993) believed that the sharp increase in divorce rates since the 1960s can, in part, be explained by changing attitudes regarding divorce, the most prevalent being that "Although divorce is traumatic for children, they will survive" (p. 22). Adults, armed with that thought, have felt increasingly more comfortable pursuing their own needs. With thirty five years of history in which to study the impact of divorce on children, research results confirm the devastating short and long term effects that hundreds of thousands of children and adolescents have had to endure.

Effects of Divorce

When children experience the divorce of their parents, their lives are forever changed. In many ways, divorce is comparable to the death of a parent in terms of the stress exacted on the children (Gibson, Mitchell, & Basile, 1993; Parker, 1995). Arnold and Carnahan (1990) reported the following list of stressors, any combination of which children can experience in divorce:

> preceding marital strife (the length and amount of discord in the relationship prior to the divorce);
>
> break-up of the home (house is sold and property is divided);
>
> need to move (a custodial parent relocates);
>
> psychological demands of having two homes (visitation rights and travel between two homes);
>
> lowered standard of living (custodial parent may be without training and experience entering the job market);
>
> loss of noncustodial parent (the contact may be minimal or nonexistent);
>
> loss of father in particular (in most instances, the child resides with the mother);
>
> change in frequency of grandfather contact (either disruption in desired close contact or moving in with a grandparent);
>
> parental stress due to the divorce (parental stress can heighten stress in children);
>
> custodial visitation battles (who gets the children—game playing before a custodial decision and after the decision has been rendered);
>
> pressures to take sides (loyalty, court testimony, abuse allegations, etc.);
>
> decreased parental availability (noncustodial parent has relocated and/ or custodial parent works, dates, has increased responsibilities, has own problems to resolve);
>
> chronic after-shock (continuous reminder that parents are divorced); and
>
> remarriage (children must adjust to different living arrangements, etc.). pp. 375-380

Developmental Considerations

The greater the degree of change (e.g., family, environmental, and personal) to which children of divorce are subjected, the more destructive the results will be that children will experience. However, no child, regardless of how benign the divorce is, escapes the side effects of stress brought on by this family transformation. The following developmental side effects experienced by children of divorce are well documented (Arnold & Carnahan, 1990; Crosbie-Burnett & Newcomer, 1989; Gibson, Mitchell Basile, 1993; Hall, Beougher, & Wasinger, 1991; Morganett, 1994; Muro & Kottman, 1995; Thompson & Rudolph, 1992; Whiteman, 1991).

Children, ages 3 to 5 years

- vague understanding of family situation
- frightened and insecure
- nightmares and fears
- whining and crying
- regression to more infantile behavior
- clinging behavior
- temper tantrums
- change in eating and sleeping habits

Children 6 to 8 years

- unable to separate own needs from those of the parents
- feelings of sadness and loss
- frightened by uncertainty
- generalized anxiety
- disorganized and unsettled
- difficulty with school work
- feel abandoned by missing parent
- angry over the perceived rejection
- may lash out at custodial parent, teachers, and other children in their distraught and confused state
- feel lonely and miss noncustodial parent
- tearful
- denial over what is happening
- engage in self-blame over divorce
- feel alienated from parents
- may attach themselves to other adults for security

Children 9 to 12 years

- feel sense of loss
- rejected
- helpless

- lonely
- feel ashamed and embarrassed about the divorce
- powerless to control parents' behavior
- manifest psychosomatic symptoms (headache, stomachaches, etc.)
- angry
- withdrawn or overactive
- blame one parent for the divorce—direct anger at that parent
- school work is affected (may go down or receive high attention)
- coping with feelings of mixed loyalties, loneliness and depression
- frequent visits to the school nurse
- may seek support from adults outside the home
- in conflict with others—power struggle with authority

Spencer and Shapiro (1993), quoting the research of Wallerstein and Kelly (1980), have stated that there are seven concerns commonly identified in children's responses to divorce. They are fear, sense of sadness and loss, feelings of responsibility, loneliness, feelings of rejection, conflicting loyalties, and anger.

Fear.   Divorce is a fearful experience. Whether children's fears are based on reality or are imaginary, the underlying concerns are ones of abandonment and vulnerability. They question what will happen to them and who will care for them.

Wallerstein found that the children in her research study, when informed about their parents divorcing, were given little information beyond the announcement. They were never provided basic educational information regarding the meaning of divorce, nor were they encouraged to ask questions or express their feelings.

Sadness or Loss.   Children are often tearful and show signs of depression such as sleeping and eating disturbances. Younger children (preschool and early elementary-aged) are distraught over their father's leaving whereas older children are more concerned with the break-up of the family and the loss of structure and continuity it provided. Most children wish to maintain contact with both parents and hope for a reconciliation.

Feelings of Responsibility.   Older children and adolescents often accept an additional burden in divorce. They feel a strong need to take care of their parents who may be experiencing great difficulty coping with their own loss, fears, and uncertainties that accompany divorce (emotional stress, financial concerns, depression, and uncertain living arrangements). As parents rely on their children for support and share their innermost thoughts, feelings and fears, the children feel compelled to offer their care, perhaps taking on the adult role of the missing parent.

Loneliness.   Because the parents are often preoccupied and centered on their own needs, they may distance themselves psychologically and physically from their children. The custodial parent often has to work in order to support the family. This leaves the children either in the care of adult caretakers or home alone to fend for themselves. Children with low self-esteem and who are highly dependent on others are likely to experience a deep sense of loneliness.

Rejection.   Many children experience a sense of rejection because they blame themselves for the divorce. They witness the departure of the noncustodial parent and experience the physical and psychological withdrawal of the custodial parent who is self-absorbed in trying to make things work. Children who feel rejected often question their own loveability and self-worth.

Conflicting Loyalties.   Children of divorce, in most instances, wish to maintain a relationship with both of their parents; however, divorced parents, having needs of their own, may compete for their children's attention and love. One parent seeking to develop an alliance with the children, may attempt to discredit the other. The children become pawns in a relationship that has already gone bad. They often experience further loneliness and rejection because they want to please both parents and fail to satisfy neither's expectations.

Anger.   Most children will show signs of anger at some point during the divorce process. Younger children (preschool and early elementary-aged) often express their anger through temper tantrums and hitting other children. Older children and adolescents tend to express their anger through verbal attacks.

The Divorce Process

Spencer and Shapiro (1993) have stated that divorce represents a process or chain of events that when sequenced consists of the following:

- marital conflict before the divorce,
- disorganization associated with the actual separation and divorce,
- changes in the family following the divorce,
- one or more relocations,
- changes in parental relationships (the divorced parents),
- changes in loss of peer relationships, and
- introduction of next relationship (stepfamily).

The divorce process contributes to the stress that children experience. With each change that occurs, children feel more alienated and disconnected from family members, peers, and even themselves. The stress is likely to escalate unless the children are able to adjust responsibly to the changes taking place in their lives.

Children's Adjustment to Divorce

How children fare in a divorce depends a great deal on the amount and duration of the disharmony they experience before, during, and after the divorce has occurred. Hall et al. (1991) and Hetherington, Stanley-Hagen & Anderson (1989) have stated that the following variables need to be in place if children are to make a reasonable adjustment to the stresses of divorce:

- strong economic support,
- social support,
- minimal environmental change,
- positive parental divorce relationship, and
- effective parenting skills.

In addition, Gibson, Mitchell, and Basile (1993); Morganett (1994); and Thompson and Rudolph (1992) have cited the importance of the child's age, gender, quality of coping skills, self-esteem, and parental preparation provided prior to the divorce as critical child adjustment variables that also impact significantly on the transition process.

Long-term Effects of Divorce

The effects of divorce for many children continue well into their adulthood years. The problem areas most affected are feelings of anger, problems in relationships, feelings of separation, inadequacy, self-esteem, devaluation of the family, and a loss of a sense of belonging (Spencer and Shapiro, 1993). Based on their research, Spencer and Shapiro (1993) have concluded

> . . . we realize that up to one-third of all students experiencing their parents' divorce do relatively well after the initial crisis. They regain their self-esteem, academic performance and growth continue, and they continue to form and keep healthy peer relationships. The other two-thirds or majority, however, have a multitude of problems related to their parents' conflicts and divorce. These problems frequently are with these students years after the divorce process is concluded. Poor academic performance, negative peer relationships,

even delinquency and criminal behavior can result. All children of divorce, however, even those who are in the surviving third, are affected by the experience. (p. 169)

Generally speaking, 25% to 33% of the adult population whose parents divorced when they were children experience long-term effects from the divorce. Kalter (1987) reported that individuals from divorced families were twice as likely to have seen a mental health professional, had significantly higher divorce rates, more work-related problems, and more emotional difficulties than their counterparts from intact families.

Other revealing research by Runyon and Jackson (1988) suggested that the loss of a parent through a conflicted divorce is even more damaging to children than the loss of a parent through death. Knowing what we know about the devastating effects of divorce on children and the staggering numbers of children affected by divorce (40% to 60% of school-age children), the evidence clearly supports the need for children of divorce support groups (Thompson & Rudolph, 1992; Whiteman, 1991).

CHILDREN'S NEEDS

Increased numbers of children are bringing divorce-related problems to school—problems that are effecting them emotionally, socially, academically, and physically (Crosbie-Burnett & Newcomer, 1989). Children's needs seem to touch on seven areas effecting their ability to cope with the divorce of their parents. These areas are health, emotions, learning, peer relationships, images, cognition, and information.

Health. Children in divorce often experience changes in their eating habits and sleeping patterns. They may be overeating or not eating enough and may also be lacking in a healthy diet. Likewise, children may be sleeping more than usual or not able to sleep. These changes are often the result of stress and changes at home regarding parent availability to meet their children's health needs. At school, these children may be experiencing headaches, stomachaches, crying spells, and sleeping in class. They often request to visit the nurse's office more often than other children in class. Children have a need to understand and address these health-related issues that are adversely affecting their lives.

Emotions. Children in the throws of a divorce are experiencing a full range of emotions and feelings that they may not understand fully and find difficult to express. This is particularly true for younger children. Children have a need to talk about and understand their feelings of fear, sadness, sense of loss, feelings of increased responsibility, loneliness, feelings of rejection, abandonment, conflicting loyalties and anger. They also will need ideas as to how they can respond to these feelings when they do occur.

Learning. Many children, especially those with previous academic difficulty may find their grades dropping, experience difficulty staying focused, and lose interest in what they are doing while experiencing the upheavals of divorce. Older elementary school children may skip school, get into conflicts with school authorities, and come to classes unprepared to do their school work (are not doing homework or turning in assignments). Children have a need to maintain as much stability as they can in their lives. They have academic, learning, and school-related needs that must be addressed.

Peer relationships. During a divorce, children's peer relationships often suffer. Younger children may find themselves physically taking their anger and frustration out on their peers, and older children may engage in verbal conflicts with their peers. Children may withdraw gradually from their friends. Other children may have had to endure a family move because of the divorce and are having a difficult time making new friends. Developing sound peer relationships is important to children. They need to feel a sense of self-worth and belonging. At a time when their family is breaking apart, children need some stability in their lives that they may be able to find in their relationships with others.

Images. Children in divorce often conjure up frightening images concerning what will become of them as a result of divorce. They may picture themselves mentally as the cause of the divorce, view themselves as being responsible for getting their parents back together, and picture themselves having low self-worth. Armed with these mental pictures and ones like them, children are likely to become emotionally distraught and behave accordingly. Children need assistance in conjuring up more reality-oriented images, images that will give them some cause for hope that things will get better eventually.

Cognition. Children are predisposed biologically to think irrationally. They tend not to challenge their cognitions to see if those cognitions are reality-based or merely myths that seem plausible but cannot be substantiated. Children harbor many misconceptions about themselves and the world that are intensified during times of stress. Some faulty cognitions that children may harbor are the following:

Once people marry, they should never get divorced.
When parents divorce, their children are often the cause.
Children can get their parents back together again if they change their
    own behaviors (behave better).
When a parent leaves home, that parent is rejecting the child.
The children should keep the divorce a secret.

Faulty cognitions support faulty images that cause children to experience feelings like fear, loneliness, abandonment, and rejection. Children have a need to develop rationally oriented cognitions so that they can enhance their self-worth and self-esteem and view their parents' divorce more realistically.

Information

Often children of divorce lack accurate information about their situation or are provided faulty information that contributes to the formation of their irrational thoughts, fears, faulty images, and physical discomforts. Children have a need to know what divorce is all about, some details about why both parents are divorcing, and that they are not the cause of their parents' divorce. They likewise need information concerning how they can cope more effectively with divorce.

Each of the need areas discussed is interconnected. Collectively they contribute to the manner in which children cope with divorce. Children whose needs are met in each of these areas fare much better than children whose needs have not been met. Wallerstein and Blakeslee (1989) have stated that children have a number of psychological tasks they must resolve if they are to achieve a state of acceptance regarding the divorce of their parents and their own wellness. The psychological tasks are as follows:

Acknowledge the reality of the marital rupture.
Disengage from parental conflict and resume customary pursuits.
Resolve the losses they have experienced.
Work through anger and self-blame.
Accept the permanence of the divorce.
Achieve realistic hope regarding relationships.

If these tasks are to be achieved, children will need to develop the strengths necessary to sustain themselves and to grow from the experience.

STRENGTHS TO BE LEARNED

Children can benefit from developing a number of strengths in responding to the divorce of their parents. In particular, the support group program outlined in this chapter emphasizes

- information acquisition,
- feelings management,
- communication skills development,
- problem solving, and
- stress management.

Information Acquisition

Through activities and group discussion, children will increase their understanding about divorce. They will learn the following concepts:

- the meaning of divorce and family (before and after the divorce);
- all families have problems sometimes;
- many children experience the divorce of their parents—they are not alone;
- family problems are not their fault—they did not cause the break-up of their family;
- children cannot fix serious family problems such as reuniting their parents;
- talking helps children address their fears;
- while parents may have fallen out of love with each other, they still love their children;
- the tough times will not last forever—there is light at the end of the tunnel; and
- children have rights, the most important being that they have the right to balance meeting their needs with those of their family.

With accurate information about divorce, children can learn to separate fact from fiction, dispelling the myths that have captured their attention.

Feelings Management

Children will be encouraged to identify and to share the wide range of feelings they have experienced during their divorce. They also will explore the importance of discussing their feelings versus keeping them a secret from others who can help. Learning to understand, to express, and to accept feelings will help children explore the value of feelings in helping others know what they need. Through activity and discussion, children will learn ways that they can manage their feelings, benefiting themselves and those with whom they interact.

Communication Skills Development

Children will learn ways in which they can express their wants and needs confidently. They will learn their rights and how to respond to others when their rights have been violated. A few of the rights that children have are the following:

You have the right to love both of your parents.
You have the right to express your feelings.
You have the right to share with others.
You have the right to your own privacy and private time.
You have the right to be physically safe and well fed.
You have the right to refuse being a messenger of ill will between your parents.
You have the right to ask others for help.

When children know their rights and how to express them in a responsible manner, they will have learned basic assertive communication skills that will help them through the rough spots.

Problem Solving

Another important strength for children to develop is effective problem solving. Children often feel out of control (powerless) and confused by the many twists and turns their lives seem to take. Problem solving and 3 R's Decision Making provide children with the structure they need to develop and to implement wellness-oriented strategies in meeting their needs.

Children learn through problem solving that they cannot change others but that they do have the power to change themselves. They learn to take ownership of their problems and to resolve them in responsible ways.

Children of divorce face problems related to sibling rivalry, hurt feelings, worries about current home situations, broken parental promises, academic failures, conflicting loyalties, parental spying (one parent requests their child to spy on the other parent), being home alone, and health or stress problems.

Stress Management

Stress is a major factor in the lives of all children, but especially for those in divorce. Children will learn to identify major stressors in their lives and how best to address them. They will learn a variety of self-care strategies and how to apply them in creating their own personal stress management plan. When children master the strengths addressed in the divorce support group, the ultimate effect will be the enhancement of their self-esteem.

Children's self-esteem can be assaulted dramatically in divorce, thus undermining their sense of self-worth. Reduced parental support; feelings of fear, loneliness, rejection and anger; conflicting loyalties; irrational thoughts; and increased vulnerability all take their toll on children in divorce situations. However, self-worth and self-esteem increase when children feel connected to themselves and others, respect their personal assets, and experience a sense of power in response to all of life's challenges. That sense of personal power and increased net worth come from the mastery and utilization of life strengths that help children successfully address life's challenges.

The strengths that children will learn will give them the opportunity to

- acquire accurate information about divorce and how it affects family and family members,
- understand and express their feelings about divorce,
- practice problem solving methods in coping with divorce,
- understand and more effectively manage divorce related stress in their lives, and
- view themselves as having the power to visualize and to create positive futures.

MESSAGE TO FACILITATORS

Divorce, as we have noted, is a difficult life challenge that thousands of children face every year. How they face and are affected by divorce either will serve to strengthen their resolve that they can succeed in spite of it or it will defeat them.

If children are to survive in troubled families, there are some valuable concepts that you can help them understand and apply to their own lives. The following concepts are ones developed by Wells (1993) that can assist all children in troubled families in self-managing more effectively. Be sure to address each point during your support group experience.

All families have some problems sometimes. Help children recognize that all families have problems ranging from minor to major problems. There are no perfect, problem-free families. Having family problems is normal. Although some family problems are embarrassing and challenging, they must nevertheless be faced and resolved. Divorce is one such challenge.

Nobody else but me has problems like these. Children often feel isolated and lonely in the face of adversity. They think that they are all alone and sometimes feel shameful because this awful thing is happening to their family. Help children see that divorce is one family problem shared by many youngsters throughout our society.

Family problems are never your fault. Help child understand that they are not the cause of serious family problems like divorce. Sometimes in the heat of arguments (caused by stress), family members blame each other for the divorce. Divorce occurs because of many forces that gradually mount and come together that causes the family to break up.

Children can never fix serious family problems. Children, in their desire to keep the family together, may assume responsibility for making things better. Help them see that they can not change other people's behaviors. They did not cause the problem nor can they fix it to their liking.

To best help your family, help yourself. Help children understand that while they cannot change others (their parents), they can change themselves in the way they think, feel, and behave. By making certain changes, children can meet their own needs and, by doing so, they can help their family. The divorce support group will teach children how they can manage their own lives more effectively during a divorce.

Enabling seldom helps and often hurts. Sometimes parents ask children to do things for them so that they do not have to face a difficult situation. Parents may have family secrets that the children know about and are not supposed to tell anyone. Sometimes keeping family secrets is helpful in the short run but is harmful in the long run. Some secrets, if kept, could be harmful to children and/or their parents. Children, using 3 R's Decision Making and role-playing, can explore this concept.

There is light at the end of the tunnel. Children often feel hopeless in the midst of a divorce. They are emotionally and physically drained and are in need of some relief. Help children understand that what they are feeling and experiencing is the body's normal response to stress. Let them know that things will improve for them as they learn new and responsible ways of meeting their needs.

Sometimes nobody notices me. Children can and often do experience parental neglect during a divorce. Neglect can occur in many forms, from being left home alone to being ignored. Help children understand that feelings of loneliness, fear, and anger often occur in response to neglect. Also help them understand that few parents are intentionally neglectful. They are hurting too. Let children know that they will be learning ways to let their parents and others know what they want and need.

Balancing your needs with those of the family. Help children understand that both they and their families have needs that must be met. Help them see the importance of taking care of themselves. Impress upon them the importance of eating balanced meals, exercising, and getting enough rest. Only then will they have the energy to help the family with household chores and related responsibilities.

Work it out instead of act it out. When children experience mounting pressure that goes unharnessed, they can explode and say and do things to others that they will come to regret. Help children understand that, while troubled families can produce strong feelings in them, they need to learn acceptable ways to vent their feelings on a regular basis.

How to find help that really helps. Help children recognize that it is okay to seek out help in learning to cope with serious family problems. Help children dispel some of the myths that often prevent people from seeking assistance when needed. Explore some of the resources that they can access in times of need.

Every child has basic human rights. Because we rarely discuss our human rights, many children do not know what they are, much less how to advocate on their own behalf when it comes to protecting their rights. Perhaps a discussion on this topic would be useful in relationship to coping with divorce.

Selecting Group Members

Support groups work best when the group composition is such that children can learn from each other's feelings and experiences. Therefore, consider a group membership whose members vary with regard to length of time since the divorce, level of acquired coping skills, attitudes and values toward divorce, adjustment to the divorce, living arrangements (custody and visitation arrangements), and family composition (adults and children living in the home).

Other variables to consider relate specifically to the children's ability to benefit from a group experience (Morganett, 1994). These could be children who

- currently are dealing with a divorce in the family, but not in immediate crisis;
- are expressing feelings of shame, isolation, loneliness, or poor self-esteem;
- have no major emotional disturbances;
- are expressing the belief that they are in some way responsible for the divorce;
- are exhibiting acting-out behavior to get attention; or
- are expressing anger, hostility, and/or defiant attitudes (p. 84).

We also strongly suggest that you obtain written permission from the custodial parent or caregiver and, where possible, from the noncustodial parent before including a child in the group. The very nature of the group experience is likely to result in the sharing of some sensitive family issues. Parents need to understand the intent of the group sessions and the importance of respecting their child's privacy with respect to group participation. To disregard these considerations is to put your group experience at risk from parents who either do not want their child to participate or who attempt to restrict the participation of their child regarding sensitive topics that they do not want discussed.

Parents are likely to feel more comfortable with a divorce support group when they know that you will be there to answer their questions concerning behavior changes in their children and how they can help them best at home. We advocate a home, school, and community partnership when such partnerships can facilitate the healing process.

Group Process

Your children may be a little apprehensive at first about participating in a divorce support group; however, their fears will begin to dissipate as they connect with each other. Do not try to move too quickly. Give them time to feel comfortable with each other and with you.

Because we have structured our support program around an educational model, the sessions focus on content about divorce as well as process in providing children with an opportunity to talk about their own personal experiences. This format provides you with choices to make regarding the balance that you choose to establish between content and process. If the children feel comfortable focusing on their experiences and feelings during a particular session, that decision is yours to make.

You are now ready to meet your "children of divorce" support group. Your goal is to help children gain a better understanding of divorce and to provide them with some ways in which they can more effectively meet their needs. Being realistic however, an eight session experience is unlikely to resolve all of your children's difficulties, many of which were heightened by the divorce and not the cause of them.

You will need to remain in contact with your group members after the group experience has ended. They undoubtedly will benefit from continued contact with you. While your group will end, their challenges will not. Hopefully, what they will learn from you and the group will continue to benefit them for years to come.

Resources

In Figure 5.1 are provided "Tips for Caregivers" in order to strengthen the healing process at home. In Figure 5.2 are provided lists of resources to be used with and by children in the Children of Divorce Support Group. The resource materials are grouped according to age of child.

CHILDREN OF DIVORCE GUIDE
Tips for Caregivers

Your child soon will be participating in a Children of Divorce Support Group. The goal of this support group is to help children better understand the nature of divorce and to receive assistance in adjusting to the emotional shock associated with the break-up of a family and the loss of a parent. Despite the effectiveness of such support groups, however, children of divorce seem to make better adjustments when parents lend their assistance to this process as well. We have therefore provided a number of tips that will help you help your children adjust more readily to the emotional shock and loss that accompanies the break-up of a marriage and family.

1. Help your child understand that your family relationships have not been terminated but have changed form.
2. Help your child understand that while the marriage will no longer continue, he or she still has two parents who love him or her and that this love will continue.
3. Provide opportunities for your child to be with the missing parent and to see grandparents of both parents.
4. If possible, avoid uprooting your child from familiar surroundings and friends. Stay in the same home, place of worship, school district, etc.
5. If you must move, be sure to provide opportunities for your child to stay

connected with his or her past surroundings while making adjustments to a new location. Having pictures of friends, writing letters, making phone calls, and periodic visits of old friends to the new location can help ease the adjustments. Also encourage your child to move all of his or her favorite belongings to the new location as this will ease the disconnection while establishing new connections.

6. Try to maintain a similar routine with your child. Do as many of the things that you once did as a family. Eat meals at the same time, spend time together, and continue to take an interest in your child's activities.

7. Recognize your child's basic needs for love, security, belonging, and self-esteem. Be there to support your child emotionally. Listen to your child's feelings, hold your child, provide words of reassurance, and be consistent in your relationship.

8. Allow your child time to grieve. Accept these emotions and share your emotions when appropriate. Acknowledge the hurt, pain, anger, confusion, sadness, and all of the other feelings that your child is likely to experience.

9. Provide reassurance and comfort. Let your child know that these are normal feelings and that in time they will pass.

10. Be sure to tell your child that he or she is not the cause of the divorce.

11. Speak kindly of your spouse as a parent in front of your child. Do not use your child as a pawn or a wedge for retaliation to deal with your former mate. Your child needs to love and feel comfortable with both of you.

12. Do not use your child as a substitute for your mate. Refrain from telling your child that his or her role has changed and that he or she must now fulfill the responsibilities of the missing parent.

13. Do give your child some responsibilities at home such as a few chores on which both of you agree.

14. Be sure to plan with your spouse shared parenting responsibilities and agreed upon visitations. Help make these visits fun, meaningful, and something to look forward to in maintaining a positive relationship with the missing parent.

15. Provide ample opportunities to really talk and listen to one another. Children need to be able to count on these times to establish closeness and to discuss joys as well as issues of concern.

16. While both you and your child will be going through some difficult times together, avoid taking out your frustrations on your child.

17. Encourage your child to develop peer relationships and to become involved in a life of his or her own. Your child needs to develop an identity as a normal healthy individual who happens to have parents who are divorced.

18. While you need to encourage your child to strive to be somewhat independent, you also need to be watchful of any changes in behavior or emotional stability that might indicate undue stress.

19. Celebrate special occasions and holidays together when possible.

20. Avoid discussing past negatives and regrets and focus on positives and a future full of potential for you and your child.

Figure 5.1.   Tips for caregivers to be given to parents and/or guardians. Permission to photocopy is granted.

RESOURCES FOR CHILDREN
Children of Divorce

Ages 3 to 7

Abercrombie, B. (1990). *Charlie Anderson.* New York: Margaret K. McElderry Books. (custody issues)

Anderson, P. S. (1979). *A pretty good team.* Elgin, IL: The Child's World. (divorce of parents)

Christiansen, C. B. (1989). *My mother's house, my father's house.* New York: Atheneum Publishers. (different goals, lifestyles)

Dragonwagon, C. (1987). *Diana, maybe.* New York: MacMillan. (fantasy about divorce)

Girard, L. W. (1987). *At Daddy's on Saturday.* Morton Grove, IL: Albert Whitman. (accepting change)

Hazen, B. (1978). *Two homes to live in: A child's eye view of divorce.* New York: Human Sciences Press. (divorce of parents)

Perry, P., & Lynch, M. (1978). *Mommy and Daddy are divorced.* New York: Dial Press. (divorce of parents)

Pursell, M. (1976). *A look at divorce.* Minneapolis, MN: Lerner Publications. (divorce)

Schuchman, J. (1979). *Two places to sleep.* Minneapolis: Carolrhoda Books. (anxiety of accepting change)

Thomas, I. (1976). *Eliza's daddy.* San Diego: Harcourt Brace, Javanovich. (stepbrothers/stepsisters)

Ages 8 to 12

Adler, C. S. (1979). *The silver coach.* New York: Coward, McCann and Geohegan. (parent-child communication)

Betancourt, J. (1990). *Valentine blues.* New York: Bantam, Doubleday, Dell. (remarriage of parents)

DeClements, B. (1990). *Monkey see, monkey do.* New York: Delacorte Press. (parental imprisonment)

Gardner, R. (1978). *The kid's book of divorce.* New York: Science House. (the divorce process, questions and answers)

Greene, C. (1988). *The Jenny summer.* New York: HarperCollins. (divorce, family relationships)

Jukes, M. (1988). *Getting even.* New York: Alfred A. Knopf. (friendship)

LeShan, E. (1978). *What's going to happen to me? When parents separate or divorce.* New York: Four Winds Press. (feelings on divorce)

Newfield, M. (1975). *A book for Jordan.* New York: Atheneum Publishers. (separation of loved ones)

Orgel, D. (1987). *Midnight soup and a witch's hat.* New York: Viking Penguin. (jealousy, accepting change)

Slote, A. (1990). *The trading game.* Philadelphia: J.B. Lippincott. (competition, parental expectations)

Ages 12 and Up

Angell, J. (1981). *What's best for you.* New York: Bradbury Press. (divorce, family relationships)

Bradbury, B. (1975). *Boy on the run.* Boston: Seabury Press. (parental overprotection)

Fine, A. (1988). *Alias Madame Doubtfire.* Boston: Joy Street Books. (divorce, fighting, abuse)

Meyer, C. (1978). *C. C. Poindexter.* New York: Atheneum Publishers. (dependence/independence)

Miller, J. W. (1989). *Newfound.* New York: Orchard Books. (divorce, maturation, extended family)

Pfeffer, S. B. (1979). *Starring Peter and Leigh.* New York: Delacorte Press. (identification with peers)

Platt, K. (1978). *Chloris and the freaks.* New York: Bradbury Press. (parent-child communication)

Rabinowitz, A. (1989). *Bethie.* New York: MacMillan. (boy-girl relationships, depression)

Smith, R. K. (1990). *The squeaky wheel.* New York: Bantam, Doubleday, Dell. (change, new home)

Slate, A. (1979). *Love and Tennis.* New York: MacMillan. (parent-child communication)

Figure 5.2. Resources for use with and by children in Children of Divorce Support Group.

SESSION I—ALL ABOUT ME AND MY FAMILY

BRIEF OVERVIEW OF SESSION

This session will give children an opportunity to become acquainted with each other and also will allow each student to recall times in his or her life within the family unit where he or she had memorable experiences. It also will help group members begin to bond with each other and realize that each person in the group has something in common with other members.

GOALS

1. To help children understand reasons for their presence in the group.
2. To encourage children to become acquainted with the other members of the group.
3. To allow children to begin to focus on and to share feelings about their own family situation.

MATERIALS NEEDED

1. "All about Me and My Family" worksheet (Activity Sheet 5.1) for each child
2. Markers, pencils, and crayons

PROCEDURE

1. Introduce self and have each of the group members introduce self by first name. Talk about the fact that this is a group for those whose parents are divorced. During the course of the sessions, we will talk about the divorce and their feelings and discuss ways each person can deal with these feelings.

2. Begin to set the stage for the group by inviting a brainstorming session on group rules. Examples of possible initial group ground rules may include

a   What is said in the group, stays there (confidentiality).
b   No put-downs are allowed.
c   Only one person talks at a time.
d   It is important to attend all sessions.

Note: If children do not suggest these group rules, you as facilitator should bring them up as part of the brainstorming session.

3. Do the "All About Me and My Family" worksheet (Activity Sheet 5.1). Instruct the children to draw a picture or write words to describe the following:

a   a good time I had with my family

b   a "not good" time I had with my family

c   why I think my parents got a divorce

d   what I'd like to see happen in my family in the next two years

e   something about me that is special (this should go in the center circle)

4. Allow time for children to share one or more sections from their worksheet. If children are reluctant to share, inform them that they have the option to "pass" if they wish.

5. Again, remind the children that everyone in the group has experienced a divorce in his or her family and that in each group we will be talking about family issues. At this point, some children may want to share experiences from their own situation. If time permits, allow this to happen.

CLOSURE

To bring closure to this session, summarize what happened in today's session. Point out that each member of the group is special in some way and that none of us is any less special because there has been a divorce in the family. Conclude by allowing time for each child to share his or her feelings about today's group.

HOMEWORK

Encourage children to think about their current situation and ask them to begin to consider what the word "home" means to them.

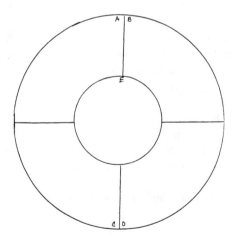

Activity Sheet 5.1.   All about Me and My Family worksheet. Permission is granted to enlarge and photocopy for classroom use.

SESSION II—HOMES MY FAMILY LIVES IN

BRIEF OVERVIEW OF THE SESSION

In this session, children will begin to think about their family and where each family member lives. By sharing this information within the group, each child will begin to see that other group members also have more than one place they call "home."

GOALS

1. To help children realize that, although some of our family members live in different homes, they are still our family.
2. To continue the bonding process within the group.

MATERIALS NEEDED

1. Large sheet of construction paper for each child
2. Crayons or markers

PROCEDURE

1. Briefly review group rules.

2. Talk about family. Ask children to give a definition of family. If someone indicates that family is everyone who lives in the house, point out to the children that sometimes, particularly in situations of divorce, not everyone lives in the same house. Ask for other examples of when a family member may not live in your house, for example, an older sibling in his or her own apartment, in college, or in the military.

3. Provide each child with a sheet of construction paper and some crayons and markers and ask them to draw the number of homes it takes to show their family. The facilitator may want to give an example to the students to show the homes his or her family lives in. (See sample.)

4. Allow time for each child to show his or her family homes to the group and explain the configuration.

5. Briefly discuss the drawings using the following questions as a guide.

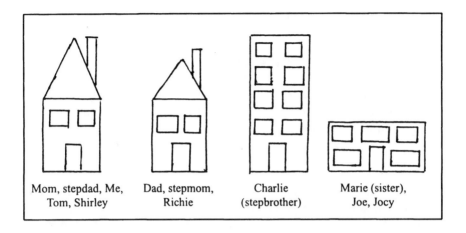

a Can you love someone who lives in a different house as much as you love those who live with you?

b Have you ever wished you could live with your other parent?

CLOSURE

To bring closure to this session, ask children to talk about what they learned in today's session. Again, point out similarities of group members' situations. Allow time for additional questions or discussion.

HOMEWORK

In preparation for next week's group, encourage students to begin to think about all of the feelings they have experienced as a result of their parents' divorce.

SESSION III—MY FEELINGS ABOUT DIVORCE

BRIEF OVERVIEW OF THE SESSION

This session will provide an opportunity for the children to explore the wide range of feelings they experienced as a result of their parents' divorce. The issue of trust also will be reviewed.

GOALS

1. To encourage children to identify the wide range of feelings that they have experienced as a result of the divorce.
2. To discuss trust and how a divorce may effect one's sense of trust in others.
3. To demonstrate to children what can happen when feelings are repressed.

MATERIALS NEEDED

1. Balloon
2. Chart paper and markers

PROCEDURE

Ask the children to think about some of the feelings they remember having when they found out that their parents were getting a divorce. Allow time for a few examples.

1. Divide the group into two or three smaller groups and encourage children to think about all the feelings they experienced as a result of the divorce. Have each group make a list on their chart.

2. Provide time for children to share their lists with the group. Note any similarities in the lists. (Some of the common feelings may include sadness, loneliness, fear, relief, shame, etc.)

3. Encourage children to talk about how their parents' divorce affected their sense of trust in friends and relatives. Children may want to give examples.

4. Talk about how the children deal (or fail to deal) with their feelings. Blow up the balloon to show what happens when we keep all our feelings inside. Keep blowing as a symbol of more and more feelings being held inside.

Ask the children what will happen if you keep blowing. Relate this to what can happen if we keep all our feelings bottled up inside.

5. Encourage children to talk about their feelings—both in the group and with a trusted friend or adult.

CLOSURE

Bring closure to this session by allowing time for questions and comments and reminding children of the balloon experiment. Have children think of a special person in their life who could be a good listener when they need to talk.

HOMEWORK

For the next session, children need to think about sources of stress in their life and begin to think about what can be done about these stressors.

SESSION IV—STRESSORS IN MY LIFE

BRIEF OVERVIEW OF SESSION

In this session, children will have the opportunity to begin to identify some of the stressors that they currently are experiencing in their life. They also will share positive methods for dealing with their stress.

GOALS

1. To assist children in identifying sources of stress in their life.
2. To encourage children to work together to identify positive ways to deal with their stress.

MATERIALS NEEDED

1. Chalk and chalkboard or flipchart and markers

PROCEDURE

1. Begin by reviewing the feelings identified by the group last week. Share with the students that some of these feelings may have caused stress in their lives.

2. Conduct a brief survey of the group to have them indicate feelings they have had. (Children will vote with the following signs: one finger (I've felt like this), two fingers (I've never felt like this), or palm up (undecided).

    a   Fear of failing in school.
    b   Hurt from friends or relatives.
    c   Sadness about not being with absent parent.
    d   Anger at parent, sibling, etc.
    e   Worry about current home situation or absent parent.

3. Allow time for students to brainstorm some sources of stress in divorced families. List the results on the chalkboard or on a chart paper. Some samples of identified areas may include

    a   parents disagree about visitation schedule,
    b   custody battles,
    c   money problems,

d   parent dating or remarriage,
e   broken promises,
f   having a stepparent,
g   different living arrangements, and
h   one parent asking child to "spy" on the other parent.

4. After the list has been completed, provide an opportunity for children to comment on any of the items on the list.

CLOSURE

At the conclusion of this group, remind the children that almost everyone has to deal with the stress of divorce at one time or another. Next session we will begin to identify coping skills that one may use to deal with these stressors.

HOMEWORK

Ask children to think about ways they have used to cope with some of the stressors in their life at the current time. Next week, ask each child to share with the group at least three positive coping skills that they have used.

SESSION V—RECIPE FOR COPING

BRIEF OVERVIEW OF SESSION

All persons need to find positive methods for dealing with stress. In this session, the children will have the opportunity to identify some positive coping methods and also have some fun as they develop their personal coping recipe.

GOALS

1. To encourage children to begin to identify personal preferences for dealing with the stressors in their life.
2. To provide an opportunity for children to develop creatively their personal coping strategy "recipe."
3. To reinforce positively children's efforts to identify personal self-care strategies.

MATERIALS NEEDED

1. 3" × 5" index card for each child
2. Pencils
3. Poster board (11" × 17" for each child)
4. Crayons, markers, and other art media as desired

PROCEDURE

1. Providing each child with a 3" × 5" index card and a pencil and ask them to identify three positive coping strategies that help with life stressors.

2. Allow time for sharing from the group. It may be helpful to list the ideas on the chalkboard as they are shared. Some possible ideas may include the following:

    a watching a favorite TV show,
    b building a jigsaw puzzle,
    c talking on the phone to a friend,
    d playing a game with friends,
    e reading a book,
    f going for a walk,
    g going to a favorite "thinking" spot,
    h exercising, and
    i talking with a favorite adult.

3. Provide a sheet of chart paper and crayons or markers to each child. Encourage each child to develop a personal coping recipe. (Again it may be helpful to do one as a group to get them started or just to have a sample prepared.)

2 C. of exercise
½ C. of quiet thinking time
1 T. of TV time
3 C. of conversation with a friend

Mix thoroughly and wait for a batch of good feelings to appear. This should happen after a short time. Share your recipe with others who need help in coping.

4. Provide time for each child to complete his or her recipe, and be sure to allow an opportunity for creativity on the part of each child. (Most recipe cards are decorative.)

5. Display the finished products for all to see.

CLOSURE

The children's completion of the "recipe" and subsequent display will bring closure to the activity. It may be helpful to end the session by asking: "How did you feel when completing this project? Did you have fun? Do you feel confident that you can cope in many situations?"

HOMEWORK

Remind the children that there are some specific stages one goes through when experiencing a divorce in the family. For next session, ask them to think about what some of those stages may be.

SESSION VI—STAGES OF DIVORCE

BRIEF OVERVIEW OF SESSION

To this point in the group, children have had the opportunity to share feelings and discuss personal concerns about their own situation. This session will help them see that many of the things they have experienced are actually quite "normal" in divorce situations and that these things actually have been documented as "stages of divorce."

GOALS

1. To assist children in gaining an understanding of the stages of divorce.
2. To help children realize that almost everyone will experience these stages at one time or another.

MATERIALS NEEDED

1. Poster that identifies stages of divorce according to Sour (1981) or Bienenfeld (1987).

Stages of Divorce

Sour (1981)	Bienenfeld (1987)
1. Denial	1. Disbelief
2. Anger	2. Anxiety
3. Sadness	3. Anger
4. Reorientation	4. Sadness
5. Acceptance	5. Depression
	6. Acceptance

PROCEDURE

1. Provide a few minutes for any comments, questions, or brief discussion regarding any of the sessions to this point.

2. Introduce the issue of divorce in terms of stages. Remind children that much research has been done to study how persons deal with divorce and that two theories will be shared with them today.

3. Show both posters (or better yet, have them both listed on the same poster so that children may compare and contrast the two lists).

4. Allow time for children to go through each list and identify times that they experienced each of the stages and share these with the group.

5. Remind children that not everyone will experience all of the stages in the same order or in the same way and that this is okay.

6. Suggest that some persons may experience some of the stages more than once. For example, a person may feel that he or she is in the acceptance stage and doing well when an important date (e.g., absent parent's birthday, wedding anniversary date, date absent parent left, etc.) approaches. At this point, the child may feel a great deal of sadness or anger. Reassure the group that this is normal and is to be expected.

7. Ask each child to think about what stage he or she may be in at the present and encourage him or her to share this within the group. (Point out that time may be an important factor in where each person is; that is, the person who has most recently experienced divorce in his or her family may be in the denial or disbelief stage, whereas the person whose parents divorced four years ago may be in the acceptance stage.)

8. Allow time for further discussion and questions.

CLOSURE

Provide time for a brief review of the stages from both lists. Ask children to comment on the session and their feelings regarding the session and the information presented.

HOMEWORK

In preparation for next week's session, ask each child in the group to think of a problem they have dealt with successfully as a result of their parents' divorce. In the next session, the topic for discussion will be problem solving.

SESSION VII—PROBLEM SOLVING

BRIEF OVERVIEW OF SESSION

Since much of what happens in families experiencing divorce is not within the control of the child, many children feel that there are no things in their life that they can control. This session is designed to assist children in identifying areas in their lives that are in their control, and to present a six-step problem solving method for their use.

GOALS

1. To assist children in understanding that some aspects of their life are within their control.
2. To present a six-step, problem-solving method.
3. To provide an opportunity for children to work together to practice the problem-solving method.

MATERIALS NEEDED

1. Chart with the Problem Solving Method on it. (Create chart from Procedure #3 prior to group meeting.)
2. Sample situations to generate thinking for student group work.

PROCEDURE

1. Begin by asking children to identify some problems they have had to deal with during the past few weeks.

2. Discuss the idea that many of the problems we face are solvable; that is, we can do things to resolve the situation.

3. Present the Problem Solving Method

a   State the problem.
b   Identify your feelings about the problem.
c   Talk about the problem with an adult you trust.
d   Decide if the problem can be solved.
e   Remind yourself that the only person you can change is yourself.
f   Decide what you should do.

4. Use some of the problems identified earlier in the session to talk about the process. Can children see how it may have worked in each of the situations discussed?

5. Put the children in groups of two and ask them to develop a scenario in which they could use the problem-solving technique. (Provide 5 to 8 minutes for this discussion.)

6. Provide an opportunity for children to share their scenarios and discuss how the problem-solving method could work with the scenarios.

7. Discuss as many scenarios as time permits.

CLOSURE

Bring the session to a close by reminding children that they do have control of their own reactions and, in many cases, are able to solve many of the problems that they experience.

HOMEWORK

Ask children to attempt to use the Problem Solving Method during the next week. Encourage them to remember specific incidents where it worked (or did not work) for discussion in next week's session.

SESSION VIII—MY CRYSTAL BALL

BRIEF OVERVIEW OF SESSION

To provide closure to this group, children will be given the opportunity to take an imaginary journey into their future. This will be accomplished through the crystal ball activity where they look at their life in 5 years and 20 years and make some predictions based on their own personal hopes and dreams.

GOALS

1. To assist children in looking at their expectations for their future.
2. To encourage children to think about what they will need to do to accomplish their future goals.
3. To bring closure to the group and to evaluate the group in terms of its usefulness to the group members.

MATERIALS NEEDED

1. Copies of "My Crystal Ball" worksheet (Activity Sheet 5.2)
2. Crayons or markers
3. Group evaluation sheet

PROCEDURE

1. Allow time at the beginning to discuss the homework assignment from last session. Encourage each child to talk about a time during the week when he or she successfully used the Problem Solving Method. Reiterate the suggestion that this method be used on a regular basis when problem situations occur.

2. Show a picture of a crystal ball. Ask the children for their interpretation of its use. Spend a few moments talking about what one may see in a crystal ball.

3. Discuss how sometimes we may want to think about our own future and what we would like it to be (or what we think it may be). Ask the children to give examples of what they feel they may be doing in ten years. Allow time for sharing from those who wish to do so.

4. Provide group members with a "My Crystal Ball" worksheet (Activity Sheet 5.2) and crayons or markers and allow sufficient time for them to draw a picture of what they see for themselves in 5 years and 20 years.

5. Encourage all children to share their crystal balls with the group.

6. Provide time for a brief discussion about what the children liked about the group. Have them tell one thing they liked about every other member of the group.

CLOSURE

Ask each child to complete a written evaluation of the group.

HOMEWORK

Since this is the final session, there will be no formal homework, but children will be reminded to practice what they have learned in group and to apply it to everyday situations.

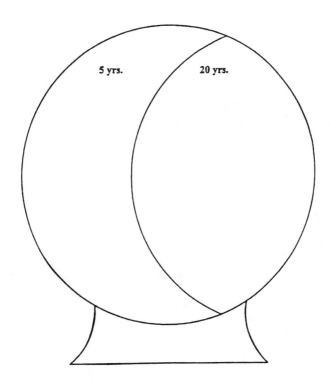

Activity Sheet 5.2. My Crystal Ball worksheet. Permission is granted to enlarge and photocopy for classroom use.

EVALUATION

1. Do you feel that participation in the DIVORCE group was helpful to you? Why or why not?

2. What part of the group did you like best?

3. What part of the group did you like least?

4. If you had a friend who experienced a divorce in his or her life, would you recommend that he or she participate in a similar group? Why or why not?

5. Did you attend all eight group sessions?

_____ Yes   _____ No

If no, how many did you attend?_____

6. Comments, suggestions, etc.:

REFERENCES

Arnold, L. E., & Carnahan, J.A. (1990). Child divorce stress. In L. E. Arnold (Ed.), *Childhood stress* (pp. 373–404). New York: John Wiley & Sons.

Bienenfeld, F. (1987). *Helping your child succeed after a divorce.* Claremont, CA: Hunter House.

Bureau of the Census. (1990). *Statistical abstract of the United States, 1990* (110th ed.). Washington, DC: U.S. Department of Commerce.

Coontz, S. (1995). The American family and the nostalgia trap: Kappan special report. *Phi Delta Kappan, 76,* K1–K20.

Crosbie-Burnett, M., & Newcomer, L. (1989). A multimodal intervention for group counseling with children of divorce. *Elementary School Guidance and Counseling, 23,* 155–156.

Gibson, R. L., Mitchell, M. H., & Basile, S. K. (1993). *Counseling in the elementary school: A comprehensive approach.* Boston: Allyn & Bacon.

Hall, C., Beougher, K., & Wasinger, K. (1991). Divorce: Implications for services. *Psychology in the Schools, 28,* 267–275.

Hetherington, E. M., Stanley-Hagen, M., & Anderson, E. R. (1989). Marital transitions: A child's perspective. *American Psychologist, 44,* 303–312.

Kalter, N. (1987). Long-term effects of divorce on children: A developmental vulnerability model. *American Journal of Orthopsychiatry, 57*(4), 587–599.

Morganett, R. S. (1994). *Skills for living: Group counseling activities for elementary students.* Champaign, IL: Research Press.

Muro, J. J., & Kottman, T. (1995). *Guidance and counseling in the elementary and middle schools: A practical approach.* Dubuque, IA: Brown & Benchmark.

Parker, R. J. (1995). Helping children cope with divorce: A workshop for parents. *Elementary School Guidance and Counseling, 29,* 137–148.

Runyon, N., & Jackson, P. L. (1988). Divorce: Its impact on children. *Perspectives in Psychiatric Care, 23,* 101–105.

Sour, S. (1981). *Children of divorce: How to help.* Sewickley, PA: SRS Associates.

Spencer, A. J., & Shapiro, R. B. (1993). *Helping students cope with divorce: A complete group education and counseling program for grades 7–12.* New York: Center for Applied Research in Education.

Strangeland, C., Pellegreno, D., & Lundholm, C. (1989). Children of divorced parents: A perpetual comparison. *Elementary School Guidance and Counseling, 23,* 167–173.

Thompson, C. L., & Rudolph, L. B. (1992). *Counseling children* (3rd ed.). Pacific Grove, CA: Brooks/Cole.

Wallerstein, J. S., & Blakeslee, S. (1989). *Second chances.* New York: Ticknor & Fields.

Wallerstein, J. S., & Kelly, J. B. (1980). *Surviving the breakup: How children and parents cope with divorce.* London: Grant McIntyre.

Wells, R. H. (1993). *A child's guide to surviving in a troubled family.* Woodburn, OR: Youth Exchange.

Whiteman, T. (1991). *Innocent victims: Helping children through the trauma of divorce.* Wayne, PA: Fresh Start.

Chapter **6**

CHILDREN IN STEPFAMILIES

A stepfamily is a family unit that evolves "as a result of a marriage between two partners, at least one of whom has been married previously, and includes at least one child who was born before the two partners married" (Walsh, 1992, p. 709).

BACKGROUND INFORMATION

Approximately 46% of marriages today involve at least one partner who has been in a previous marriage (US Bureau of Census, 1990). Most of those adults have children (Rice, 1992) resulting in 16% of all American children living in stepfamilies (Coleman & Ganong, 1990). According to Jones and Schiller (1992), 1300 new stepfamilies are formed every day in the United States. By the year 2000, they claim that one out of every four children by the age of sixteen will live in a stepfamily and that more than half of all families in the country will be stepfamilies. With numbers this large and growing, the concept of the traditional American family (biological parents and their children) is quickly becoming a thing of the past, especially when the full range of nontraditional living arrangements is acknowledged (Coontz, 1995; Van Horn, 1995).

Whereas the statistics are pretty self-evident, what is not always clear are the various dynamics that evolve when a stepfamily is born usually out of a loss due to a divorce or the death of a spouse. For many adults entering into a stepfamily relationship, the high expectations for success are quickly substituted with feelings of self-doubt and fear. Most adults, expecting that stepfamily relationships will compare similarly with primary family relationships are often surprised and bewildered to find that there are few similarities (Skeen, Covi, & Robinson, 1985). What follows is a brief, but eye-opening account of some of the many issues that stepparents and their children need to address as they work together in building a healthy, well connected stepfamily.

Why Stepfamilies Are Different

Newman (1994) has stated that stepfamilies come in many different shapes and sizes with varying living arrangements and patterns of interaction. Despite these differences, stepfamilies face similar problems, many of which can be identified when contrasting stepfamilies with other families. Stepfamilies are different (Newman, 1994) for the following reasons:

> At least one partner has experienced marriage and parenthood before or a partner who is a parent has never been married.
> Stepparents who have never married or lived with a partner are unaccustomed to family life (apart from their family of origin).
> Adults and children come into the relationship at the outset.
> The parent and the stepparent often do not have time together alone before having children live with them.
> Stepparents have to live with, care for, and/or relate to stepchildren with whom they have no "history." There is a lack of bonding.
> Single-parent family life often precedes stepfamily life.
> There is at least one "intruder" in the stepfamily.
> Children often lose contact with a parent from the previous family —sometimes this is a loss of daily contact; other times it is forever.
> Children often have two homes with two sets of rules, conditions, discipline, etc.
> Visiting children or stepchildren have to be accommodated into the stepfamily from time to time.
> Family members may experience relocation of home, school, job, activities, etc.
> New responsibilities may emerge.
> Unfinished business from a past marriage (e.g., anger, grief, guilt, anxiety) can come into stepfamily life.
> Suspicion and lack of trust between stepparent and stepchildren may exist.
> Surnames of children can be different and create a sense of not belonging.
> There are more people, all at once, having to get used to each other.
> There is no "legal" relationship between stepparent and stepchild.
> Socioeconomic conditions might change; money can be tight.

Sibling order might change so the oldest, for example, could now
be a middle child.
There might be less space or territory for each person.
At least one person has to adjust to living in a different home—with
different family rules, etc. (pp. 2-4)

Although this is only a partial list of differences that separate stepfamilies
from the traditional family, it does address a number of dynamics any one of
which could create stress in stepfamily relationships.

Stages in Stepfamily Growth

Stepfamilies go through an evolutionary process in their development. All
family members are affected by this growth process beginning with the fantasy
stage and culminating in resolution, the final stage, in which the stepfamily
achieves maturity and its full potential (Newman, 1994).

Whereas other researchers and authors (Barney, 1990; Einstein, 1992; Jones
& Schiller, 1992; Muro & Kottman, 1995; Rice, 1992) have alluded to an evolutionary process of growth, Newman (1994) has identified five specific stages
(fantasy, confusion, conflict, coming-together, and resolution).

Fantasy stage. Reality has not set in at the onset of the marriage. Husband
and wife have high hopes and dreams of a happy married life together
with their children. "There is idealism and, to a certain degree, illusion
and delusion" (Newman, 1994, p. 4). Family members do not really
know each other except superficially. Husband and wife are working
hard at showing their best side. Little thought has gone into anticipat-
ing potential problems and how to solve them with respect to glitches
that are bound to occur with the creation of a new ready made family
unit. This is the stage when family members, especially husband and
wife, are committed to fulfilling their dreams of a good and wonderful
life together.

Confusion stage. Reality begins to emerge and the fantasy starts to crumble
as individual differences make themselves known. There is tension and
confusion in the air signaling signs of emerging trouble between and
among parents, parents and children, and the children themselves. The
family, while experiencing the signs of impending doom, often either
do not recognize the specific issues causing the tension or are in denial
that this is really happening. There is a sense of real fear that the family is in trouble with little understanding as to how to resolve their
dilemma.

Conflict stage. Individual family members recognize that their needs are not being fulfilled. There are hidden and outward expressions of anger and aggression that are often the result of power struggles between and among family members attempting to secure what they believe is rightfully theirs. As tension and stress build and relationships begin to break, either the ensuing conflicts must be negotiated or the marriage is doomed to fail. Conflict is a normal and natural dimension of growth, but such conflicts need to be resolved in a responsible manner "for the maturity of stepfamily life to be achieved" (Newman, 1994, p. 5).

Coming-together stage. Out of conflict and conflict resolution, family members learn to build new connections that are based on respect for self and others. Emotionality gives way to reason as family members learn to work out many of their differences. Out of fantasy emerges the reality that a family unit is evolving. Though far from ideal, more comfortable relationships develop, the family unit operates more smoothly, and hope is renewed.

Resolution stage. While the struggle has not been easy, fraught with frustration, doubt, and despair, the resolution stage signals relief that the bad times have passed. Family members no longer feel the need to be phony or to play games. They can be real and more genuine in their relationships with each other. The family members sense a high degree of optimism, have learned to accept each other for who they are, and have become more skillful in resolving family conflicts.

Newman (1994) was quick to point out that, while all stepfamilies go through this evolutionary process, no two families will experience the process exactly in the same manner. The length of time that families stay in stages, movement back and forth between stages, and the blending of stages will vary from stepfamily to stepfamily. And, of course, there is the sad reality that better than half of second marriages end in divorce.

Myths about Stepfamily Living

Children and adults alike harbor a number of myths related to stepfamily living. Myths, like fairy tales, are not based on truth, but nevertheless seem very believable. When individuals accept assumptions as reality, their expectations often go unfulfilled, leading in many cases to unhappiness and disappointment. The list of myths is endless; the few that follow here demonstrate the impact that faulty beliefs can have on stepfamily solidarity (Cootz, 1995; Einstein, 1982; Einstein, 1992; Einstein & Albert, 1986; Newman, 1994).

There are strong similarities between primary and stepfamily relationships.
Bonding between stepfamily members will occur quickly.
Children will love their stepparents.
The children will be happy together.
Stepfamily marriages stand a better chance of surviving than first marriages because the parents have learned from their mistakes.
Stepparents can replace biological parents.
Stepparent roles are clearly defined.
If stepparents treat children nicely, the children will be happy.
All stepfamily members are committed to making the family work.
Relating to biological or adopted children is the same as relating to stepchildren.
Stepmothers are wicked, jealous, and hostile.
The Brady Bunch constitutes the typical American stepfamily.

Stepfamily Realities

Although many parents and children are familiar with stepfamily myths (that they perceive to be reality), few know about or understand the realities. Denial may play a major role for parents in this regard because they desperately want their next marriage to be successful. Thus, they find themselves focusing on the fantasy rather than on the reality aspects of stepfamily unions. Some of the following realities, if recognized and addressed by family members, would enhance stepfamily relationships, which can take five or more years to develop fully (Koch-Chambers, 1991; Rice, 1992; Walsh, 1992):

Because many second marriages evolve from loss (divorce or death of a spouse), single parents and their children need time to grieve that loss before rushing into a new and more complicated relationship.
Parent-child relationships grow very strong after a loss with the remaining parent (custodian) confiding in their children and involving them in family decisions.
Parent-child relationships, because of shared decision-making traditions and a complex history, often share a much stronger bond than the new couple's relationship.
New stepparents are likely to feel left out, rejected, and ignored when entering a highly connected relationship between the biological and/or custodial parent and his or her children.
Bonding between stepfamily members takes time.
Stepparent roles are ill defined. They are required to assume many of the same responsibilities as the parent but are not perceived as parent or friend to the stepchildren.

Many stepchildren are jealous of the time and attention that their biological and/or custodial parent gives to the stepparent.

All stepchildren are different in terms of their personalities, experiences, and acceptance of stepfamily relationships with stepsiblings, stepparent, and extended families.

Stepparents may disagree with the manner in which their children are being raised.

Stepfamilies often are complicated when spouses from former marriages have not accepted the break-up of their marriages, have joint custody of their children, and are receiving child support for siblings residing with them.

Family cohesion tends to be lower in stepfamilies than in intact families.

Stepfamily members often experience financial stress, reduced privacy, and cramped living conditions.

Once again, this is only a partial list of the realities that stepfamilies must be prepared to address in building stepfamily connections.

Creating the Stepfamily

Because the biological/custodial parent and stepparent are in love and are eager to create a ready-made family, they are motivated to force a sense of togetherness among all family members. The parents tend to discount the realities and accept myths as truths in believing that they can create a second happy marriage by utilizing strategies that will force family members' togetherness, thereby fulfilling their private wishes. What these parents fail to realize is that each person (children and parents) brings into the family a unique package of characteristics. Some of these characteristics are

- a personal set of values and beliefs related to such things as parental roles in child rearing, acceptable child behaviors, family member responsibilities, money management, tidiness, recreation, eating habits, the use of family time, etc.;
- family traditions and rituals;
- religious beliefs;
- individual personality traits and characteristics;
- life experiences;
- birth order of children before and after the stepfamily union;
- exposure to different role models (stepmother, stepfather, step and biological siblings);
- parental and child patterns of behavior established in the biological family;

- unfinished business from the previous marriage(s);
- unfinished business with regard to life issues;
- methods of communication and conflict resolution;
- expression of intimacy;
- parental relationships with biological child;
- hobbies and social interests;
- educational background;
- wellness or illness orientation; and
- previous standard of living.

Failure to recognize and address individual differences in establishing a family is much like attempting to force fit puzzle pieces that do not go together. Some of the strategies that parents use, many of which are unsuccessful, in forcing stepfamily togetherness are (Newman, 1994)

- eating family meals together—no exceptions;
- not recognizing or accepting disagreements;
- requiring children to be nice to each other (siblings and family);
- requiring all family member to participate in family outings-no exceptions;
- insisting that children demonstrate acts of affection toward other family members (kissing or hugging stepparent);
- dressing stepsiblings alike;
- forced involvement of parents into stepchildren's lives;
- changing family name (so that all members share the same surname);
- requiring stepchildren to call stepparent mom or dad;
- requiring stepchildren to establish a sense of closeness with biological parents' family and relatives (e.g., grandparents, aunts, uncles, etc.);
- letting all the children attend the same school;
- requiring children of both parents to love one another and to play together; and
- manipulating environmental conditions so as to promote sameness among family members.

Although some of the strategies may engender positive results in establishing desired stepfamily relationships, others may be viewed as artificial, unrealistic, and manipulative. Instead of bringing family members together, they may have just the opposite affect in that they deny the existence of individual differences, fail to recognize unique personal characteristics, deny the need for personal space and autonomy, and diminish self-esteem.

With all that has been said about the difficulties that stepfamilies face in developing healthy and responsible ties out of diversity, the potential for establishing a sense of family is well within the realm of possibility. "Far from representing the sad fragments of other marriages and family, a stepfamily can grow to be a complex, lively, caring community of people who not only need one another, but respect and love one another" (Barney, 1990, p. 145).

Helping children and parents establish their places in the context of the stepfamily is often painful and confusing. The establishment of the stepfamily unit requires an atmosphere of trust, open communication, honesty, risk taking, respect, and a real genuineness of caring to override the fear of the unknown. To begin that process, stepfamilies must understand the importance of building positive family connections and utilizing strategies that respect individuality and promote togetherness. Newman (1994) has offered some characteristics of positive togetherness:

> Family members know each other and accept differences between themselves.
> There is a feeling of security because family members care for each other by nurturing each other in nonthreatening ways.
> Family members are interested in the lives of each other but do not interfere.
> Family members give comfort and support to each other.
> There is love, devotion, and compassion between family members.
> A sense of belonging, but having freedom at the same time, is experienced by family members.
> Family members are there for each other, for example, at times of crisis or rejoicing.
> Cooperation rather than competition exists.
> Family members communicate honestly with each other.
> There is a working together toward the goal of blending.
> There is enjoyment at being together.
> When family members experience conflict between themselves they are able to resolve it.
> Family members share rituals, traditions, and family celebrations.
> There is respect for each other.
> A strong sense of trust and loyalty exists.
> There is a lack of gossip about each other.
> Family members are united yet retain a strong sense of their own identity. (pp. 29-30)

These positive characteristics result when family members utilize their connectiveness-building assets (e.g., smiling, positive feedback, listening, speaking one at a time, sharing, etc.) in relationships with each other. They create a model of interaction that establishes loving ties while giving family members the power to exercise some of their own individuality. Rules are also established that maintain a spirit of cooperation and sharing. Rules such as the following build family connections:

Listen to one another.
Speak one at a time.
Provide each other with constructive feedback.
Agree to disagree.
Agree to discuss and resolve family conflicts.
Establish some time for family activities.
Encourage everyone to have and to share their ideas even if they differ from other family members.
Establish a bill of rights and responsibilities for all family members.
Respect members' freedom of choice in those areas where choices exist (dress, foods, use of free time, etc.).
Respect personal privacy in those areas agreed upon by the family.

Stepfamilies: A Positive Side

While stepfamilies differ in composition and challenges to be addressed, they can offer potential strengths for children in that they can

- teach them how to be flexible and adjust to new situations,
- provide them with multiple role models,
- teach them self-management skills (communication skills, conflict resolution skills, etc.),
- broaden their sense of family and circle of caring,
- enhance their standard of living (this may not be true for all stepfamilies),
- offer them a second chance at happiness with loving and caring parents, and
- provide them with siblings whose company they can learn to enjoy (Fuller, 1988).

Learning to adjust to stepfamily living is a major challenge for all concerned and especially for the children. Stepfamilies are more likely to achieve a healthy and long lasting relationship if the parents understand the myths and realities associated with stepfamily living, are patient with themselves and their children in making lifestyle adjustments, are persistent in staying with the challenge, and have a workable and responsible plan that will guide them through the stages in stepfamily growth. Ideally, that process should involve all family members and should begin prior to the actual joining together of two family segments. Sometimes that process also benefits from the involvement of a skilled family therapist specializing in stepfamily relationships. The therapist's role is to help family members discuss their feelings, their goals, hopes for the future, and help them develop the skills and understandings necessary to get over the hurdles in each stage of the growth process.

Unfortunately many stepfamilies are neither prepared to address the challenges of stepfamily living nor possess a plan or the skills necessary to support their hopes and dreams for a happy family life. Though there may be little that support group facilitators can do to counsel stepfamilies, they can work with the children in helping them self-manage more effectively during the difficult times. What follows is a discussion of children's needs and the strengths that they can learn that will help them better understand and cope with the life changes they are experiencing.

CHILDREN'S NEEDS

Thompson & Rudolph (1992) have stated in reference to stepfamilies that "adults and children experience changes in role, alliances, parenting arrangements, household responsibilities, rules, expectations, and demands" (p. 370). Furthermore, many children, having experienced the loss of a parent through death or divorce, need time to grieve and express their feelings before they can accept a new stepfamily.

After a divorce or death of a spouse, the biological/custodial parent living in a single parent household often develops a special bond with their children, one based on a shared history of involvement, family traditions, and shared decision making in most family matters. When a biological/custodial parent remarries, the bond that forms in a new partnership is often not nearly as strong as the one that exists between the biological parents and the child (children).

Hostility, anger, confusion, loneliness, guilt, hurt, frustration, shame, and embarrassment are but a few of the emotions that children may experience when thrown into stepfamily relationships. Children experience a sense of powerlessness and abandonment and may feel hostility toward the natural parent but direct the hostility toward the stepparent because it is the safer alternative. They would rather risk losing the stepparent than the remaining parent in their lives.

In addition to mood changes, children in stepfamilies often have to adjust to new communities, households, schools, divided family loyalties, stepsibling relationships, expressions of affection toward stepfamily members, changes in personal status, unrealistic family expectations in developing close relationships, family member role confusion, competition for time and attention, and coping with the stigma often associated with stepfamily living.

Whether the 6.8 million children living in stepfamilies in the United States (Kantrowitz & Wingert, 1990) have more problems than those children living in first marriage families is debatable. What is not open to question is that children living in stepfamilies do have a distinct set of issues and concerns that must be addressed in helping them meet their needs in the following areas:

- accurate information;
- security, belonging, and self-esteem;
- expression of feelings of how they are coping; and
- self-care.

Accurate Information

Children have a need for accurate information regarding unanswered questions that they have. They also have a need to challenge some of the questionable beliefs that they hold about themselves and stepfamily living. Some common questions that children ask about their situation are the following:

Will I get along with my stepbrothers or sisters?
Will my stepmother like me or be mean to me?
Am I the only one going through this experience?
Why do I feel angry, confused, and lonely?
Why am I always being left out of everything?
Why did my mom (dad) have to marry again when things were getting better?
With whom should I show my allegiance, my real mom or my stepmom?
Do I have to love my stepmom? Do I have to call her mom?

These same children also harbor a number of thoughts about themselves and their new living arrangements that may or may not be true. Examples are the following:

I am the cause of my parents' divorce.
Nobody really loves me.
Stepmothers are mean and wicked.
I will never see my real mom (dad) again.

I have been abandoned by my real parent who no longer loves me.
I will make it so difficult for you (stepparent) that you will leave.
You will never take the place of my mom (dad).
I will make you pay for doing what you did to us.
I will act out in school, do poor school work, and fight with other kids,
    and that will make you pay attention to me.
Things should be just like they were before dad (mom) remarried.
If I am mean enough to my stepmother and her kids, they will leave.
My dad is the only one who can tell me what to do.

These questions and thoughts are merely representative of the many concerns and issues with which children are confronted in their search for stability
and predictability in their lives. They have a need for accurate information in
helping themselves sort out their feelings, thoughts, and actions in a world of
confusion. The stepfamily support group can help children obtain answers to
their questions and to reality test their beliefs to see if they are responsible and
working.

Security, Belonging, and Self-esteem

All children have needs for safety, security, and a sense of belonging in
their lives and especially those children whose lives have been doubly disrupted
by the loss of one parent (e.g., death or divorce) and the remarrying of the
custodial parent. These are major life adjustments for anyone, but especially for
children whose lives seem to be out of control. Stepchildren often lack a sense
of security. They do not know what will happen to them next. The family that
they once knew has changed. They are moving into a new family and now
must adjust to new surroundings (e.g., community, school, home) and new ways
of doing things with people, who in many ways, are still strangers. When family stability is rocked and children lose their sense of predictability, they experience a full range of emotions including fear, loss, powerlessness, anger, confusion, and loneliness.

The loss of stability in many ways affects children's sense of belonging.
They desperately want to be a part of something larger than themselves and to
give and receive love. When children do not think or feel like they belong to a
family unit, they may experience rejection, abandonment, and total displace-
ment. This is especially true when stepfamily living requires many of the changes
previously discussed. For many children, they feel totally cut off from past
friendships, a loved community, and separation from one parent. Much energy
is displaced and many emotions are experienced as children are forced to dis-

connect from the safe, secure, and familiar and establish new connections in a world full of uncertainties.

With all of the events surrounding the loss of one family and connecting with a new family, children's self-esteem also is affected. When their world starts to erode, many children will assume some of the blame for the divorce, the death of a parent, and the custodial parent's need to remarry. When children feel powerless to change the course of events in their lives and feel equally powerless to adapt to these changes, they find it easy to devalue themselves. They do not feel loved or worthwhile. They feel totally disconnected from themselves and others. The stepfamily support group is designed to address the issues of security, belonging, and self-esteem in group and provide children with opportunities to learn personal strengths that they can use in their own self-care.

Expression of Feelings

Children have a need to discuss their feelings and to talk about how they are adjusting to stepfamily living. They need to explore what feelings they are experiencing, the cause of those feelings, and how they are expressing them. They need to understand that their feelings are real, serve a purpose, and that feelings are neither good nor bad, but merely their body's physiological reaction to their thoughts regarding personally important life events. They likewise need to identify ways in which they can responsibly and successfully attain emotional wellness.

While children have a need to talk about how they are coping, they also may be reluctant to do so out of fear or failure to recognize the value of discussing their situation with others. Other children may have a need to discuss their lives but may not be consciously aware of what is troubling them. The stepfamily support group provides a warm, stable climate in which children can feel safe and are encouraged to explore their feelings and thoughts about the life transitions they are experiencing.

Self-care

Children have a need to care for themselves. They need to develop the strengths that will help them feel safe, secure, belong, loved, and worthwhile. *They have a need to manage their feelings responsibly, communicate their wants assertively, solve their problems responsibly, and accept gracefully those things that cannot be changed.* Children will learn how to care for themselves by developing the various strengths that follow.

STRENGTHS TO BE LEARNED

Whether remarriage improves children's lives or initially creates more complications for them, there will be a period of transition in which family members learn to make necessary life adjustments. *The purpose of the stepfamily support group is to help children cope with the changes and to offer continued support until things stabilize in their lives.* The coping process can be accomplished best when all family members understand the realities of stepfamily living and what they can do to support the family unit and themselves in coping with the stresses of daily living during the transition period.

The following strengths are designed to help children help themselves in meeting their needs. They will learn that, while they cannot change others, they can make minimal changes in their own self-management strategies that will reduce some stress in their lives. The following strengths are addressed in the stepfamily support group sessions and activities in this chapter:

- information acquisition,
- feelings management,
- assertiveness training,
- problem solving, and
- acceptance.

Information Acquisition

Children are taught that acquiring accurate information about stepfamily living can lead to new understandings that will change their thoughts and feelings about themselves and their stepfamily. Accurate information can help dispel myths and assumptions that needlessly cause stress in children's lives. Children will learn that through discussion, asking questions, and activities, they can learn about some of the truths for which they have been searching. Sharing accurate information can be a powerful strength in the face of distress.

Children are encouraged to talk about life in their new families and how well and in what ways they are coping with stepfamily living. As children discuss their various situations, many will discover that they are not alone. They will share many of the same feelings, thoughts, and questions. Children will need accurate information regarding their fears and beliefs, information that can be provided by the facilitator and children in the group who are at various stages in the stepfamily living transition process.

Feelings Management

As we have indicated, children will bring a broad range of feelings into the support group. They also will offer a multitude of reasons for those feelings and how they are acted out. The support group can help children understand that their feelings come from their thoughts and beliefs about various aspects of family living. Children need an opportunity to explore their thoughts, challenge their accuracy, and decide if these thoughts are helping or hurting themselves. By learning to challenge their initial thoughts, children can learn to manage their feelings. For example, children who believe that they are responsible for the break-up of the first marriage may feel guilty. To compound the guilty feelings, they may also believe that their mom (dad) does not love them anymore and that is why he or she left home. Feelings of abandonment and guilt are heavy feelings for adults and are particularly burdensome for children. Helping children challenge the accuracy of their beliefs and subsequent feelings can help them regain some of their lost self-esteem.

Children need time to explore their feelings, understand their points of origin, challenge their accuracy in portraying reality, and learn acceptable and responsible ways to address those feelings in need of expression. Children need help in sharing their feelings with others, including their parents. They need practice in engaging in self-affirmation activities in which they can experience the benefits from viewing themselves with kind eyes even when things around them do not seem to be very bright.

Assertiveness Training

Children will experience a variety of needs and wants during the transition period. Many children may feel too embarrassed to let others know what they want or need, and others may not recognize that the option exists. Children and facilitators can work together in helping children identify what they want or need and helping children communicate those needs assertively to family or support group members. For example, children who are feeling lonely and in need of a hug could comment to their natural parent, "I'm feeling lonely and I want a hug from you." Children also may have a need for other parental expressions of love or want questions answered regarding the divorce and subsequent remarriage. Teaching children how to assert themselves in responsible ways is a strength that children need to develop.

Children need assistance in understanding their rights and responsibilities and how to secure them in ways that will help them feel more powerful in an environment where they may be experiencing few personal choices. Assertiveness training can help children see that they always have options and that they can make positive things happen in their world. Learning to be assertive requires the acquisition of accurate information, rational thoughts, reality-based beliefs and feelings of success. *When all of these strengths come together, children find themselves developing their own roadmap rather than wondering aimlessly through a maze with no exits.*

Problem Solving

Children in stepfamilies are confronted with many problems or life challenges. The best way in which to develop confidence in self is to practice confronting dilemmas. The stepfamily support group encourages future problem solving using either the 3 R's model or a similar model of choice. Children need practice in defining their problem or challenge, generating alternative solutions, and filtering each through the Right, Reality, and Responsibility filters in search of helpful responses to their dilemma.

Children also can be helped in examining some of their current behaviors in trying to influence what happens to them in their new family. Sometimes children, in their eagerness to exercise personal power, will attempt to control the new family by acting out or by being extremely good. Children need assistance in looking at what they want and whether their behavior is likely to assist them in achieving that end. Looking at their goals and the Right, Reality, and Responsibility factors regarding their chosen path is a great way of helping children make accurate judgments about their behaviors and likely goal attainment.

When children decide that their goal is to behave in ways that will help them, they will need to question their thoughts and feelings about family members and adjust their behaviors accordingly. For example, children who believe in the wicked stepmother myth probably will not be inclined to give their stepmothers much of a chance in developing an amicable relationship with them. However, when they readjust their thinking and recognize that they do not have to love this person immediately just because dad does and that they do not have to call her mom and thereby sever ties with their "real" mom in order to treat this person with respect, new possibilities can unfold as the negative thoughts and feelings give way to ones more neutral.

Acceptance

Perhaps the most difficult of all challenges is helping children recognize that there are things that they cannot change in their stepfamily. Children will need assistance in exploring the things they can do, the choices they can make, and the actions they can take in making their lives and stepfamily living more tolerable if not enjoyable. They also will need assistance in exploring those things unlikely to change.

Learning acceptance is a courageous act of adjustment and evolves when children recognize that some things cannot be changed or fixed. Acceptance requires its own set of skills but is a necessary step toward tranquility. Facilitators can discuss with children the meaning of acceptance and examples of acceptance. When people experience loss through the death of a loved one, lost mobility through illness or injury, or structural losses through natural disasters, these people can never go back to what was. They learn to readjust their thinking and to let go of the past, to set new goals, and to move forward. While this process takes time and often occurs in stages, acceptance can be facilitated through sharing, talking to others who have made the transition, and utilizing a variety of symbolic techniques to bury the past. Many children who will participate in the stepfamily support group undoubtedly will be able to share things that they have learned to accept and how they did it.

MESSAGE TO FACILITATORS

Children need time and personal support from you and their peers as they adjust to new family living arrangements. For some children, the adjustments will be quite traumatic, for others less so. Regardless of individual needs, all of the children in your group will be confronted with change and coping as best as they can with it.

The goal of your family support group is not to solve their many problems but to develop and to sustain a sense of family in your group. These children need to feel safe and secure, to belong, and to experience a sense of personal worth in their lives. You can do more for them by building a solid connectiveness between and among members of your group than you ever will know. These children are looking for some degree of stability and predictability in their lives that comes from a tightly knit group that genuinely cares for each other.

Whatever you can do to help children obtain accurate information about themselves and stepfamily living, manage their feelings, communicate their wants and needs, solve personal problems, and accept those things that cannot be changed, you will have gone a long way in assisting children in achieving the proper balance between meeting their needs and contributing to family unity.

Selecting Group Members

No special directions are needed for selecting group members. Follow the directions provided in Chapter 3 for establishing your group. Share with parents and/or guardians Figure 6.1 so that they will have suggestions on how they can help their children.

Group Process

As we have indicated, your greatest challenge will be developing a sense of family in your group. Help children understand that, while each of them is different, they still can work together in benefitting themselves individually and their support group collectively. Help the children draw some parallels between their support group and their family groups in developing a sense of family.

The support group sessions and activities are designed to help children

- understand that they share a number of things in common, one of which is stepfamily living,
- realize that their family includes those people with whom they live and those living in different homes,
- develop a sense of family in their group even though they share different homes,
- explore their questions and feelings about stepfamily living,
- explore ways in which they cope with their many feelings,
- identify and explore stressful situations in their lives and develop strategies for dealing with stress,
- explore their personal daily habits and how they many help or hurt them and their families,
- explore positive self-care activities in which they engage,
- explore ways in which they can enhance family harmony and cooperation,
- practice cooperation and communication skills that they can use at home, and
- explore the many things that they can give each member of their family in helping build family unity (e.g., a smile, hard work, free time, etc.).

One of the messages that you are trying to communicate to children is that they can only pass on to others what they have to give. By the same token, you need to help children identify some of the negative and hurtful things that they also have been passing on to family members, such as bad attitudes, negative beliefs, and hurtful behaviors.

Developing a positive stepfamily life is about passing on to others the very best of ourselves that we have to give. The achievement of this goal begins with the children in your group and what they learn that can be passed on to their own families.

You are now ready to begin the process of passing on the very best of yourself and your ideas about family living to your group. Good luck and have fun making a positive difference in the lives of those children whom you are about to touch.

Resources

In Figure 6.1 are provided "Tips for Caregivers" in order to strengthen the healing process at home. In Figure 6.2 are provided lists of resources to be used with and by children in the Stepfamilies Support Group. The resource materials are grouped according to age of child.

STEPFAMILY LIVING GUIDE
Tips for Caregivers

Your child soon will be participating in a Stepfamily Support Group. The goal of this support group is to help children adjust more readily to stepfamily living. We are offering a few tips concerning things that you can work on at home while your child participates in the Stepfamily Support Group. We have found that children adjust more readily to new family living arrangements when some of the following suggestions are addressed by the biological and stepparent.

Do's

1. Do encourage your stepchildren to have and to express their own ideas even if they do differ from your own.
2. Do let your stepchildren know that you care about them (e.g., smiles, touches, a kind word, a listening ear, etc.).
3. Do allow your stepchildren some freedoms commensurate with their ages and stages of development (e.g., arrangement of their room, choice of dress, time when they do their school work, etc.).
4. Do allow your stepchildren time to be with and converse with their biological parent if this contact time is important to them. Letter writing, exchanging gifts, and telephone calls can provide opportunities for contact.
5. Do temper your own values, attitudes, and beliefs concerning child raising, family life, and related matters as they impact on your stepchildren and spouse. Take time to share your values with other family members and, where they differ, discuss amicable solutions in lieu of conflict.
6. Do realize that there are many ways to resolve family differences—not just your way.
7. Do provide your stepchildren with as much privacy as possible.
8. Do look for and encourage unique qualities in your stepchildren.
9. Do treat your stepchildren as you would want to be treated.
10. Do give your stepchildren permission to discuss whatever is on their minds and to express their anger in socially acceptable ways.
11. Do let your stepchildren know that you understand that adjusting to stepfamily living takes time and, at times, may be difficult.
12. Do have stepfamily meetings on a regular basis so that you can share in the joys and concerns and make necessary adjustments when possible. Do not wait until little problems escalate into crises.
13. Do treat your stepchildren as individuals.
14. Do acknowledge your spouse and his or her children.
15. Do avoid being judgmental regarding issues of family management.
16. Do be open to change and ready to try new ways of doing things.

17. Do believe in yourself and your capabilities as a person.
18. Do allow time for family relationships to develop.
19. Do accept the fact that stepfamily life will not always be happy.
20. Do accept the courage to be imperfect.
21. Do try to help your own children and stepchildren accept the realities of change—what they can and cannot do to make things better.
22. Do allow your stepchildren the freedom to be members of two families.

Don'ts

1. *Don't try to take the place of your stepchildren's parents.* Your stepchildren have biological parents and feel a sense of loyalty to them. They may see you as an intruder; however, with time and loving support, gradual acceptance as a family member will grow.
2. *Don't expect instant love.* Any affection that develops will take time. On average, it takes up to four or five years for stepfamily members to bond. The older the stepchildren at the time of marriage, the longer it takes for a relationship to develop.
3. *Don't try to buy the love and affection of your own children or stepchildren.* This can lead to manipulation on the part of your children as they may view your love for them as conditional based on their performance.
4. *Don't take sides, blame, or show favoritism when responding to family matters involving the children.*

These suggestions represent only a partial list of the many things that you can do to help your stepchildren adjust to their new family. To succeed as a stepparent, you need to redefine your role from that of a traditional biological parent to viewing yourself in some of the following ways:

- as a friend,
- as a confidant,
- as a parent figure,
- as a mentor, and
- as a role model.

These roles allow you the freedom to be yourself and not a biological replacement for the missing parent. These are important roles that can provide you with a significant and meaningful relationship with your stepchildren without having to compete with the missing parent. Try some of these ideas. I am sure they will work for you. If you need further assistance, there are many good books on stepparenting and willing professionals (e.g., counselors, psychologists, and mental health workers) who can provide you with needed assistance.

Figure 6.1. Tips for Caregivers to be given to parents and/or guardians. Permission to photocopy is granted.

RESOURCES FOR CHILDREN
Stepfamilies

Ages 3 to 7

Berman, C. (1982). *What am I doing in a stepfamily?* Secaucus, NJ: Lyle Stuart. (stepsiblings, accepting change)

Boyd, L. (1978). *The not so wicked stepmother.* New York: Viking Penguin. (having a stepmother)

Boyd, L. (1990). *Sam is my half-brother.* New York: Vicking Penguin. (stepsiblings, accepting change)

Bunting, A. E. (1979). *The big red barn.* San Diego: Harcourt Brace Jovano-vich. (stepmother, accepting change)

Drescher, J. (1986). *My mother's getting married.* New York: Dial Press. (getting ready for a stepparent)

Jukes, M. (1984). *Like Jake and me.* New York: Alfred A. Knopf. (stepfather)

Leach, N., & Browne, J. (1992). *My wicked stepmother.* New York: Macmillan. (having a stepmother)

O'Connell, P., & Flynn, B. (1994). *Land of many shapes* (coloring book). Minneapolis: Johnson Institute. (feelings about divorce/stepfamilies)

Tax, M. (1981). *Families.* New York: The Atlantic Monthly Press. (stepparent/stepsiblings)

Vigna, J. (1980). *She's not my real mother.* Morton Grove, IL: Albert Whitman. (remarriage of parents)

Ages 8 to 12

Evans, M. (1986). *This is me and my two families.* New York: Magination Press. (journal keeping for stepfamily issues)

Gardner, R. (1982). *The boys and girls book about stepfamilies.* Creative Therapeutics. (stepfamily issues)

Henkes, K. (1987). *Two under par.* New York: Greenwillow Books. (parent remarriage/stepfather)

Hest, A. (1989). *Where in the world is the perfect family?* Boston: Clarion Books. (accepting change, parental custody)

Mark, J. (1986). *Trouble halfway.* New York: Atheneum Publishers. (resisting change, stepfamilies)

Miller, M. J. (1990). *Me and my name.* New York: Viking Penguin. (adoption, meaning of love)

Park, B. (1989). *My mother got married (and other disasters).* New York: Alfred A. Knopf. (resisting change, stepsiblings)

Petersen, P. J. (1993). *I want answers and a parachute.* New York: Simon and Schuster. (remarriage of father)

Rosenberg, M. (1990). *Talking about stepfamilies.* New York: Bradbury Press. (stepbrothers, stepsisters, and communication)

Schanback, M. (1990). *Does third grade last forever?* Mahwah, NJ: Troll Books. (remarriage of mother)

Ages 12 and Up

Berger, F. (1983). *Nuisance.* New York: William Morrow. (parent remarriage)

Cooney, C. B. (1987). *Family reunion.* New York: Bantam, Doubleday, Dell. (parental expectations, peer jealousy)

Derman, M. (1983). *And Philippa makes four.* New York: Four Winds Press. (stepsibling issues)

Gilmour, H. B. (1985). *Ask me if I care.* New York: Ballantine Books. (remarriage of parent, drug abuse)

Killien, C. (1989). *Sister of quints.* Boston: Clarion Books. (search for identity, boy-girl relationships)

Reading, J. P. (1989). *The summer of Sassy Jo.* Boston: Houghton Mifflin. (abandonment, belonging, change)

Shannon, J. (1986). *Too much T.J.* New York: Delacorte Press. (stepsibling issues)

Townsend, J. R. (1988). *Rob's Place.* New York: Lothrop, Lee and Shepard Books. (feelings of loss, escaping reality)

Wright, B. R. (1986). *The summer of Mrs. MacGregor.* New York: Holiday House. (stepfather, search for identity)

Figure 6.2. Resources for use with and by children in Stepfamilies Support Group.

SESSION I—GETTING IN "STEP"

BRIEF OVERVIEW OF SESSION

This session will introduce the children to the purpose of the group, help them realize that many others are also living in stepfamily situations and provide an opportunity to become acquainted with others who are in similar situations.

GOALS

1. To provide the structure and purpose for the group.
2. To help the children realize that living in a stepfamily is common to all group members.
3. To encourage "getting acquainted" through a fun activity.

MATERIALS NEEDED

1. Copies of "Getting in Step" worksheet (Activity Sheet 6.1)
2. Chart paper or chalkboard
3. Chalk or markers

PROCEDURE

1. Introduce self and have each of the group members introduce self by first name. Tell the children that everyone in the group lives in a stepfamily. During the course of this group, we will begin to talk about the changes that occur when one lives with step siblings and, hopefully, learn some ways to adjust to those changes.

2. Begin to set the stage for the group by discussing ground rules. List the ground rules on a chart or on the chalkboard for future reference. Possible group rules may include

a   What is said in the group, stays there (confidentiality).
b   No put-downs are allowed.
c   Only one person talks at a time.
d   It is important to attend all sessions.

Note: If children do not suggest these rules, you as facilitator should bring them up as part of the brainstorming process.

Activity Sheet 6.1. Getting in Step worksheet. Permission is granted to enlarge and photocopy for classroom use.

3. Give each child a copy of the "Getting in Step" worksheet (Activity Sheet 6.1) and tell children this is how we will be getting acquainted.

   a   On Step 1, write down something about you that is really neat—something that makes you special.
   b   On Step 2, write down something about you that has changed in the past year.
   c   On Step 3, write down something about you that you would like to change.
   d   On Step 4, write down one thing that has changed for you as a result of living in a stepfamily.
   e   On Step 5, write down something that is good about your stepfamily.
   f   On Step 6, write down something you would like to change about your stepfamily.
   g   On Step 7, write something about the best time you ever had with your stepfamily.

4. Provide time for the children to share their answers as a way of getting acquainted.

5. Point out to the children that the first three questions centered on personal questions about them while the last four centered around their stepfamily. Just as they change and grow, so do their stepfamily situations. It is these changes that we will be discussing in these groups.

CLOSURE

To bring closure to this initial session, allow time for the children to talk of their feelings about this first group session. If there is a sense of uncertainty, share with the group that you, too, frequently feel nervous and uncertain at the beginning of a group session.

HOMEWORK

Encourage the children to think about some of the things that have helped make their stepfamily situation work smoothly.

SESSION II—HOMES MY FAMILY LIVES IN

BRIEF OVERVIEW OF THE SESSION

In this session, children will begin to think about their original family as well as their stepfamily. They will identify through a pictorial representation where each "family" member lives. By sharing this information within the group, each child will begin to see that other group members also have more than one place they call "home."

GOALS

1. To help children realize that, although some of our family members live in different homes, they are still our family.
2. To continue the bonding process within the group.

MATERIALS NEEDED

1. Large sheet of construction paper for each child
2. Crayons or markers

PROCEDURE

1. Briefly review group ground rules.

2. Talk about family. Ask children to give a definition of family. If someone indicates that family is everyone who lives in the house, point out to the children that sometimes, particularly in situations of divorce, remarriage, and stepfamilies, not everyone lives in the same house. Ask for other examples of when a family member may not live in your house, for example, an older sibling in his or her own apartment, in college, or in the military.

3. Provide each child with a sheet of construction paper and some crayons and markers and ask them to draw the number of homes it takes to show their family. The facilitator may want to give an example to the children to show the homes his or her family lives in. (See sample.)

4. Allow time for each child to show his or her family homes to the group and explain the configuration.

5. Briefly discuss the drawings using the following questions as a guide.

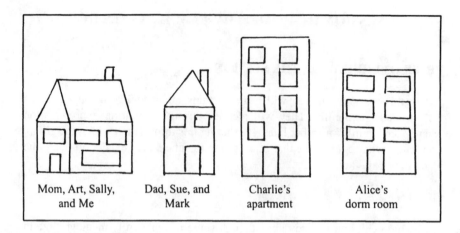

| Mom, Art, Sally, and Me | Dad, Sue, and Mark | Charlie's apartment | Alice's dorm room |

a   Can you love someone who lives in a different house as much as you love those who live with you?

b   Have you ever wished you could live with your other parent?

CLOSURE

To bring closure to this session, ask children to talk about what they learned in today's session. Again point out similarities of group members situations. Allow time for additional questions or discussion.

HOMEWORK

In preparation for next week's group, encourage children to begin to think about all of the feelings they have experienced as a result of their stepfamily situation.

SESSION III—STEP FEELINGS

BRIEF OVERVIEW OF SESSION

In this session, children will have an opportunity to identify all of the feelings that they have experienced as a result of living in a stepfamily. Both positive and negative feelings will be discussed and children will have the opportunity to identify coping skills.

GOALS

1. To assist children in identifying feelings that have surfaced as a result of living in a stepfamily.
2. To encourage children to talk about positive coping skills for dealing with feelings.
3. To provide an opportunity for children to identify feelings they have experienced during a specific period of time.

MATERIALS NEEDED

1. "STEP Feelings Journal" worksheet (Activity Sheet 6.2)
2. Chart paper or chalkboard
3. Markers or chalk
4. 5" × 8" index card and pencil for each child

PROCEDURE

1. Begin by asking the children to recall the homework assignment of identifying feelings they have had as a result of their stepfamily situation.

2. List the feelings on a chart or on the chalkboard and ask children to copy down any of the feelings they have experienced personally.

3. When a somewhat exhaustive list has been developed, go back over the list and allow time for each of the feelings to be discussed in some depth. As each feeling is mentioned, ask all of the children who listed that feeling on their card to share a personal experience of that feeling. Two examples are as follows:

"Step" Feelings Journal

_____

_____

_____

_____

_____

_____

_____

_____

Activity Sheet 6.2.   Step Feelings Journal worksheet. Permission is granted to enlarge and photocopy for classroom use.

Jealous	Excited
when my stepsister gets better grades	when I have more kids to play with
when mom gives more attention to my stepbrother	when my stepmother likes basketball as much as I do
when I have to share my bedroom and my older sister doesn't	when there are more kids to do the family chores

4. Discuss with the children that, although we all may have different reasons for feelings, we have experienced many of the same feelings.

5. Begin to identify some of the coping skills that the children use to deal with the negative feelings. Spend a few minutes allowing the children to share coping skills and ideas.

6. Point out that, in almost every case, there are both positives and negatives to living in a stepfamily, just as there are positives and negatives to going to school, being on vacation, playing with friends, etc. Much of how we get along with our stepfamily members will, in the long run, depend on how we perceive the situation.

CLOSURE

Review the things that were covered in today's group with the children. Remind them that how they get along in their stepfamily can, to some extent, be within their control.

HOMEWORK

Give each child a copy of the "STEP Feelings Journal" page (Activity Sheet 6.2) and ask the group members to keep a week-long journal of the feelings they have that are related directly to living in a stepfamily. When they write down the feeling, they also should indicate the cause of that feeling. Ask the children to bring the journals back to group next week for discussion at the beginning of the session.

SESSION IV—STEPFAMILY STRESSORS

BRIEF OVERVIEW OF SESSION

During this session, the children will have an opportunity to identify sources of stress within their situation, and to discuss just how much stress these particular situations have caused. They will also have an opportunity to learn some stress reducing techniques that they can use when they feel a large amount of stress.

GOALS

1. To assist children in identifying stressful situations in their life.
2. To provide an opportunity for children to think about just how stressful the situations are for them.
3. To teach children how to utilize a relaxation strategy for dealing with stress.

MATERIALS NEEDED

1. A "Stressometer" (Activity Sheet 6.3) for each child

   a   2" × 8" sheet of card stock paper for each child
   b   For each child, a ½" × 8" colored ribbon and a ½" × 8" white ribbon sewn/glued end to end to identify amount of stress on the "stressometer"

2. Chalkboard or chart paper
3. Chalk or markers

PROCEDURE

1. Spend a few minutes discussing the feelings journal from their homework assignment. Allow for as much sharing as the children wish to do. Talk briefly about the value of the assignment in helping us to get in touch with our feelings. Remind children that writing about feelings sometimes can be a great tension reducer.

2. Encourage the children to brainstorm some of the things that are stressful in their stepfamily life. List these on a chart or on the chalkboard. Some possible stressors may include

   a   More people in the house—no place for privacy.
   b   Having to share a room, toys, clothes, etc.

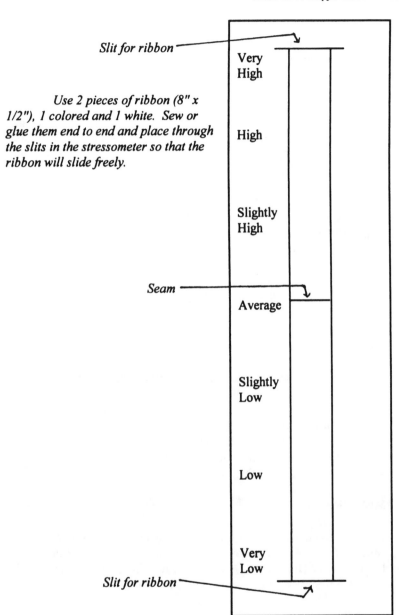

Activity Sheet 6.3.   Stressometer example and instructions.

b   Having to share a room, toys, clothes, etc.
c   Not having mom's or dad's full attention.
d   Feeling "left out."
e   The possibility of a new baby in the home.
f   The possibility of having a new last name.

3. Provide each child with a "stressometer" and reintroduce the stressors from the list. Ask each child to indicate on the "stressometer" how stressful that particular item is for him or her. Compare and contrast the items in terms of how much stress they cause for each person.

4. Allow time for children to talk about why some of the items on the list are not stressful for them and what they have done to deal with this potentially stressful situation. (This sharing may give some of the others ideas to deal with their particular stressors.)

5. Introduce the idea of relaxation techniques or imagery as a way to deal sometimes with stress. Choose your favorite relaxation or imagery script, and spend the final 5 to 10 minutes having the children participate in the activity.

CLOSURE

Talk about how the relaxation-imagery script affected each child by asking the following questions:

1. Do you feel relaxed?
2. Can you feel less stress in your body?
3. What was it that helped you become less stressed?
4. How can you apply this technique in everyday life?

HOMEWORK

Allow the children to take their "stressometer" home with them. Remind the children to use the relaxation or imagery technique when their stress level reaches the "Very High" level. Ask them to be willing to share stress reducing successes (and failures) at the beginning of next week's session.

SESSION V—THE "STEPFAMILY GAZETTE"

BRIEF OVERVIEW OF SESSION

In this session, the children will have an opportunity to produce a group newsletter based upon the experiences they have had in their stepfamily. They will utilize their creativity to share experiences and issues in a fun manner.

GOALS

1. To assist children in developing a newsletter about life in a stepfamily.
2. To provide an opportunity for the children to express their creativity throughout the activity.
3. To continue to discuss and explore issues related to stepfamily life.

MATERIALS NEEDED

1. Computer equipped with a newsletter program
2. Scrap paper
3. Pencils
4. Newspaper

PROCEDURE

1. Talk briefly about the experiment with the "stressometers." On a continuum of 1 (lowest) to 10 (highest), ask the children to describe their stressors for the previous week. Allow for a brief discussion of any strategies used to assist them in relaxing and dealing with the stressors.

2. Pass out the newspapers and allow a few minutes for the children to review briefly the specific types of articles that can be found in a newspaper. Tell them that today we are going to do a newsletter about stepfamilies (the "Stepfamily Gazette"). Ask them what types of columns they would like to have in their newsletter. Some possibilities could be News, Sports, Food, Comics or Cartoons, Opinions, Births/Deaths, etc.

3. Pass out scratch paper and pencils and provide time for each child to write his or her article or contribution to the newsletter. Assist as needed with wording, grammar, spelling, etc. (*Note*: This activity actually may involve two group periods, plus some special time for the children to type their articles into the computer.)

4. When the newsletter has been completed, make sufficient copies for the children and allow them time to share their newsletters based on their feelings regarding who should receive copies. (They may want to just have the copies remain in the group.)

5. Talk about the experience.

a Was it fun to produce your own newsletter?

b What did you learn about yourself as a result of participating in this exercise?

c What did you learn about others in the group that you didn't know prior to this time?

d How do you think your family will react to your article (if you choose to share it with them)?

e What did you like best about this activity? What did you like least about this activity?

f Do you think that at sometime in the future you may like to work on the school newspaper?

CLOSURE

In bringing closure to this session or group of sessions (depending on how long it takes to complete this activity), allow time for the children to talk about the fact that there is a lot of "good news" in stepfamilies.

HOMEWORK

Alert the children to the fact that in next week's session we will discuss "self-care." Ask them to begin thinking about what they can do to really take care of themselves each and every day.

SESSION VI—TAKING CARE OF ME

BRIEF OVERVIEW OF SESSION

This session will assist children in identifying and thinking about their daily rituals and how these affect their personal state of well-being. They also will think of at least one thing they can do in each of the periods of time that will provide a "spark" to that time of the day.

GOALS

1. To help children become aware of their personal daily habits.
2. To assist children in identifying some things they can do to energize them at each of the time periods in their day.

MATERIALS NEEDED

1. A copy of the "My Day" worksheet (Activity Sheet 6.4) for each child
2. Pencils or markers

PROCEDURE

1.   Spend a few moments talking about the reactions to the "Stepfamily Gazette." Allow time for the children to talk about their feelings about completion of this project.

2.   Remind the children about their homework assignment to think about ways in which they take care of themselves. Give them a few minutes to share things they do just for themselves.

3.   Talk briefly about daily rituals or things we do every day to take care of ourselves. Some of these things are fun, whereas others just need to be done. Do a brief overview of "Wake Up Routine" to give them an example of how the activity will work.

Wake Up Routine
Turn off the alarm
Wake up little sister
Brush my teeth
Eat breakfast
Finish any homework assignments
Wait for the bus with my friend, Bob

My Day

Wake Up Routine:

Lunchtime Routine:

After School Routine:

Evening Routine:

Activity Sheet 6.4.   My Day worksheet. Permission is granted to enlarge and photocopy for classroom use.

4. Provide a copy of the "My Day" worksheet (Activity Sheet 6.4) for each child and ask the group members to complete it based on their daily routines. Allow enough time for all children to complete the worksheet.

5. Ask the children to rate their routines in terms of whether or not they have an uplifting effect on their day. They can use the following scale to rate the items.

Great +2
Good +1
Neutral 0
Not So Good –1
Yuk! –2

6. After the children have evaluated their routines, ask them to go back and try to think of one thing they can do to provide a neat uplifter for each of the times in their day. Provide time for the children to give suggestions.

7. Ask each child to share his or her very best energizer and list these on the board. Encourage the children to "borrow" good ideas from others to energize their own day.

8. Challenge the group to use these new ideas every day to take care of themselves.

CLOSURE

To conclude this session, talk with the children about the importance of self-care in dealing most effectively with any situation. If they look and feel well, they will find they can deal more effectively with life's stressors.

HOMEWORK

For homework, encourage the children to think about as many things as they can that will help them achieve maximum happiness and success in their stepfamily.

SESSION VII—STEPS TO SUCCESS

BRIEF OVERVIEW OF SESSION

In this session, the children will have an opportunity to think about things they have done or can do that will promote stepfamily cooperation and harmony. Children will brainstorm ideas to promote positive family communication and will be encouraged to implement these ideas within their family situation.

GOALS

1. To provide an opportunity for the children to identify ideas to promote family cooperation and harmony.
2. To assist children in learning cooperation and communication skills within the group that they then can utilize in everyday life situations.

MATERIALS NEEDED

1. Large "STEPS to Success" poster prepared prior to meeting (see sample in Activity Sheet 6.5)
2. Copies of "STEPS to Success" student worksheet (Activity Sheet 6.5)
3. Markers and pencils

PROCEDURE

1. Briefly review the self-care energizers that the children identified last session. Provide a few moments for them to talk about successes in utilizing the strategies and encourage them to allow these energizers to become a part of their daily routines.

2. Show the "STEPS to Success" poster to the children and ask them to brainstorm some positive steps they can take to provide for more positive communication and cooperation within their home. Write these ideas on the "steps" of the poster. (You probably will have enough suggestions so that you can write several ideas on each step.)

3. Spend enough time for a wide variety of suggestions to come forward.

4. Give each child a copy of the "STEPS to Success" worksheet (Activity Sheet 6.5) and ask him or her to choose 5 steps that he or she wishes to try as a means of improving communication and cooperation within the stepfamily.

Steps to Success:

1.

2.

3.

4.

5.

6.

Activity Sheet 6.5.   Steps to Success worksheet. Permission is granted to enlarge and photocopy for classroom use.

5. Provide about 5 minutes at the conclusion of the session for the children to share their charts and describe to the group which one of the steps they have chosen to implement for next week.

CLOSURE

As a means of closure, remind the children that they have chosen at least five steps that they are willing to try to increase communication and cooperation within their stepfamily. Suggest that they implement at least one "step" each week so that at the end of the five weeks they will be using all five of the STEPS.

HOMEWORK

As a homework assignment, each student will choose one of the steps to implement during the upcoming week.

SESSION VIII—THE MAGIC BOX

BRIEF OVERVIEW OF SESSION

In this final session of the stepfamily group, the children will have the opportunity to fantasize a bit about what they have (or should have) to make their life more "perfect." They also will begin to focus on what the group has done for them in terms of helping them in their stepfamily situation.

GOALS

1. To encourage the children to think about what would need to happen to make things more positive for each person in their stepfamily.
2. To review with the children the material and topics that we have covered in this group.
3. To bring closure to the group.
4. To provide time for the children to do a group evaluation.

MATERIALS NEEDED

1. Copies of "The Magic Box" worksheet (Activity Sheet 6.6)
2. Evaluation surveys
3. A sample "Magic Box" (shoebox wrapped in gift wrapping with a ribbon) filled with pretzels or some other type of nutritious snack

PROCEDURE

1. Spend just a few minutes having each child describe his or her experiment with the "Steps for Success." What worked? What didn't work? Which of the steps will you choose to implement next week?

2. Show the children "The Magic Box." Ask the following questions: What do you think could be in this box? What would you like to have in the box? If you could choose anything at all that could be in the box, what would it be? (Remind the children that they can fantasize all they want on this—the item doesn't necessarily need to fit in the box.)

3. Talk about what kinds of things each child would choose for the rest of the persons in his or her stepfamily. (The items do not need to be material things; they also may be qualities, skills, etc.)

The Magic Box

The things that the "Magic Box" holds for my family members would be:

Family Member's Name   Item in the Box

_____   _____

_____   _____

_____   _____

_____   _____

_____   _____

Activity Sheet 6.6. The Magic Box worksheet. Permission is granted to enlarge and photocopy for classroom use.

4. Give a copy of the "The Magic Box" worksheet (Activity Sheet 6.6) to each of the children and provide time for completion. Encourage them to share their insights with the group if they so desire.

5. Begin to bring closure to the group by asking the following question, "If you could give something from the 'The Magic Box' to each person in the group, what would it be?" Allow time for each child to tell every other person what he or she would like to give that person. (The facilitator may want to model this activity for the group by going first and suggesting, "John I'd like to give you space to put your model airplanes, because it seems as if that is something that has really concerned you." "Mary, I would like to give you a new outfit because I know you sometimes get tired of wearing your older sister's hand-me-downs," etc.). Help the children understand that they have much to give each family member (e.g., love, respect, understanding, a smile, etc.)

CLOSURE

Provide opportunities for each of the children to talk about their feelings in regard to the "stepfamily" group. When each child has shared his or her feelings, open "The Magic Box" and pass out the treats for them to eat while they complete the group evaluation sheet.

HOMEWORK

Because this is the final group meeting, there is no "homework" assignment other than for each group member to continue practicing the "STEPS for Success." Wish the group luck and success with their stepfamily and encourage them to keep in touch.

EVALUATION

1. Do you feel that participation in the STEPFAMILY group was helpful to you? Why or why not?

2. What part of the group did you like best?

3. What part of the group did you like least?

4. If you had a friend who lived in a stepfamily, would you recommend that he or she participate in a similar group? Why or why not?

5. Did you attend all eight group sessions?

_____ Yes   _____ No

If no, how many did you attend? _____

6. Comments, suggestions, etc.:

REFERENCES

Barney, J. (1990). Stepfamilies: Second chance or second rate? *Phi Delta Kappan, 72,* 144–147.

Coleman, M., & Ganong, L. H. (1990). Remarriage and stepfamily research in the 1980's: Increased interest in an old family form. *Journal of Marriage and the Family, 52,* 925–940.

Coontz, S. (1995). The American family and the nostalgia trap: Kappan special report. *Phi Delta Kappan, 76,* K1–K20.

Einstein, E., & Albert, L. (1986). *Strengthening your stepfamily.* Circle Pines, MN: American Guidance Service.

Einstein, E. (1992). *Strengthening stepfamilies: Understanding bonds, boundaries, and stumbling blocks.* Indiana, PA: MATTI Summer School Workshops.

Einstein, E. (1982). *The Stepfamily: Living, loving, and learning.* New York: Macmillan.

Fuller, M. (1988). Facts and fiction about stepfamilies. *Education Digest, 54*(2), 52–54.

Jones, M. B., & Schiller, J. A. (1992). *Stepmothers: Keeping it together with your husband and his kids.* New York: Carol Publishing Group.

Kantrowitz, B., & Wingert, P. (1990, Winter-Spring). Step by step. *Newsweek Special Issue, 114,* 24–28.

Koch-Chambers, C. (1991, November). You can choose the steps to healthy, happy stepfamilies. *PTA Today, 13.*

Muro, J. J., & Kottman, T. (1995). *Guidance and counseling in the elementary and middle schools: A practical approach.* Dubuque, IA: Brown & Benchmark.

Newman, M. (1994). *Stepfamily realities: How to overcome difficulties and have a happy life.* Oakland, CA: New Harbinger Publishers.

Rice, F. P. (1992). *Human development: A life-span approach.* New York: Macmillan.

Skeen, P., Covi, R., & Robinson, B. (1985). Stepfamilies: A review of the literature with suggestions for practitioners. *Journal of Counseling and Development, 64,* 121–125.

Thompson, C. L., & Rudolph, L. B. (1992). *Counseling children* (3rd ed.). Pacific Grove, CA: Brooks/Cole.

U. S. Bureau of the Census. (1990). *Statistical abstract of the United States, 1990.* Washington, DC: Government Printing Office.

Van Horn, J. (1995, Tuesday, March 7). Stepparent families rapidly increasing. *The Indiana Gazette, 91,* 1–10.

Walsh, W. (1992). Twenty major issues in remarriage families. *Journal of Counseling and Development, 70,* 709–725.

Chapter 7

LATCHKEY CHILDREN

The term latchkey originated during the eighteenth century and referred to lifting the door latch in order to gain access into the home. The term reemerged during the 1940s to describe children who took care of themselves while their fathers were away at war and their mothers entered the labor market. Latchkey children exist today and are responsible for their own self-care during those hours of the day when they are not at school and adult supervision is unavailable.

BACKGROUND INFORMATION

Today more working parents than ever before are faced with serious and difficult choices in child care. One choice that is becoming more popular is letting children care for themselves alone at home during those hours of the day (before and after school) when their parents are working.

The latchkey phenomenon continues to be an ever present condition in our society due to changes in the American family. Between 1940 and 1976, the number of working mothers escalated five fold (Long & Long, 1982). By 1985, the United States Bureau of Labor Statistics (1985) cited 69.9% of women with children ages 6 to 13 participating in the labor force. In addition, there has been a dramatic increase in single parent households that also has contributed to the "home alone" phenomenon (Coontz, 1995). Other factors cited for the ever increasing numbers of latchkey children are fewer adult caretakers in the child's environment, cost of formal child care, school schedules that overlap with parental work responsibilities, the paucity of after school programs, lack of adequate transportation, the lack of extended family members in the home, lack of parental awareness of child care alternatives, and unexpected environmental changes (e.g., loss of baby-sitter, change in parental status, and state regulations that preempt services) (Grollman & Sweder, 1992; Padilla & Landreth, 1989). In addition, many parents believe that their children are mature enough to take care of themselves after completing the third grade (Hedin, Hanes, Saito, Goldman, & Knich, 1986). Hedin et al. (1986) found that 50% of the children in kindergarten through grade three, 65% in grades four through six, and 80% of seventh and eighth graders were at home without adult supervision at least one day a week.

According to *PTA Today* (1990, April), about one-third of all school-aged children (an estimated 5 million) between the ages of 5 and 13 are latchkey children. These children are spending two to three hours on most days in self-care arrangements. They get themselves ready and off to school in the morning, secure the home before they leave, and enter empty homes at the end of the school day. Some researchers believe the PTA estimates to be conservative and place the numbers at about 8 to 10 million American children staying home alone (Grollman & Sweder, 1992). We may never know the specific figure, but we do know that the number of children staying home alone is on the increase. Finding adequate adult supervision is a major problem for many parents.

While we advocate the use of adult supervision, we recognize locating good child care options at an affordable cost is not always possible. Therefore, many parents, because of a variety of circumstances beyond their control, will have to opt for having their children stay home alone for short periods of time each day. In order to insure for their child's safety, security, and their peace of mind, parents will need to rely on a self-care plan for their home-alone children.

Many organizations such the PTA, YMCA, YWCA, BSA, and 4-H have developed comprehensive latchkey safety programs for children. Many school districts, in cooperation with parent and community service organizations, also provide latchkey safety programs. *Support Groups for Children* advocates that all children, even those in adequate before and after school adult supervision programs, participate in latchkey self-care groups. Parents find that even the best of plans can break down. Children get sick, baby-sitters move away or accept new jobs, children mature and are embarrassed to continue their involvement in day care programs, and child care programs are cancelled due to bad weather and illness. Despite all that parents can do in providing for adult supervision in their absence, children occasionally may find themselves home alone. Therefore, proper planning and child training are necessary if children are to be prepared to stay home alone whether occasionally or on a regular basis (Kraizer, Witte, Fryer, & Miyoski, 1990; Powers & Anderson, 1991).

Home Alone: Negative and Positive Consequences

Being a latchkey child is not without complications. In a literature review, Padilla and Landreth (1989) found that one third or more of children who stay home alone experience a loss of peer socialization, fears (e.g., recurring nightmares, noise, the dark, personal safety), and intense feelings of isolation and loneliness. Children in grades four to six were concerned about getting hurt, being kidnapped, getting involved with the wrong kind of friends, getting into fights, and being abused. Older children (7th- and 8th-graders) were concerned with being bored, wasting time, and not getting homework and chores finished. Parents in various studies seemed most concerned about the possibility of injury to their children, neighborhood safety, emotional needs of their children not being met, and drop in school performance.

Negative complications aside, many researchers (Glass, 1990; Hedin et al., 1986; Peterson & Magrab, 1989; Stoudnour & Klimas, 1991; Vandell & Corasaniti, 1988) have reported that the latchkey experience can produce valued outcomes if handled properly. Some children enjoy their new found freedom, independence, feelings of competence, and opportunity to experience responsibility with respect to their own self-care.

Research findings (Glass, 1990; Gray & Coolsen, 1987; Long & Long, 1982) also have concluded that children left alone without siblings were given better home safety instructions, taught better survival skills, and were provided with established and consistent routines when compared with children who had adult supervision or were left alone with a sibling. Children who were taught self-care responsibilities also were found to be more effective in handling potential emergency situations than adult-care children.

Myths Versus Reality

Despite the paucity of research and the sometimes conflicting results pertaining to latchkey children, we must be careful not to perpetuate the long line of myths cited when there is little existing evidence to support them. Some of these myths include the following (Robinson, Rowland, & Coleman, 1986):

They are hurried children.
They face serious social and emotional damage.

They are more sexually active than adult-supervised children.
They get low marks in school and score low on achievement tests.
They have poor self-concepts and social relationships.
They develop more poorly than children in school-age child care programs.
They are more self-reliant than children cared for by adults.
They are more fearful, apprehensive, and insecure than adult-supervised children.
They have very little inner control, compared to their age mates under adult supervision.

These myths have created an unfounded negative perception of latchkey children that conjures up images of child neglect and parental irresponsibility. When, to the contrary, the home alone phenomenon represents a sociological fact of life for which many children have been well prepared. Our intention is to de-emphasize the social stigma attached to "latchkey" and to refrain from criticizing parents who, for a variety of reasons, must depend on their children to care for themselves. Rather, our goal is to assist facilitators in creating the most conducive support groups possible in helping children and their parents obtain self-care information, develop strengths, and execute action plans that will meet child needs and satisfy parental expectations in home alone situations.

CHILDREN'S NEEDS

From what we know about children who have been thrust into latchkey situations, they often express needs that fall into the following categories:

- physiological,
- safety and security,
- love and belonging, and
- self-guidance

Physiological Needs

Children have a need for food, water, shelter, and warmth. While we might assume that those needs have been met, all we need to do is remind ourselves of the number of children in this country who are undernourished, live in inadequate housing, and suffer from the cold. Children, because they do not enjoy the same degree of autonomy as their parents, often are not capable of insuring a nourishing food supply, preparing adequate meals, looking after their own health needs, and assessing and maintaining a safe living environment. Children's physiological needs are more likely to go unmet in home alone situations where parents have not provided child self-care training that address these issues.

Safety and Security Needs

One of the major concerns of children who stay home alone is that they do not feel safe in their own homes. Many express fears and worries associated with imaginary and real dangers such as fires, break-ins by intruders, violent storms, strangers at the door, the lights going out, and strange sounds in the house. For many home alone children, their homes can become places where they do not feel safe and secure.

Even those children who feel safe and secure at home could be living in unsafe environments and practicing unsafe behaviors in their own homes. For this reason, children must be taught how to answer the phone when alone, handle emergency situations, and respond to strangers at the door. Appropriate self-care training can help children reduce their fears and worries and learn safe ways to help insure their own safety while home alone.

Love and Belonging Needs

All children have a need to feel loved and to belong. Some children may experience loneliness and feel isolated at home because there is no one there with whom they can relate. The long and repeated separation from peers and family can produce stress and anxiety (Long & Long, 1983). Some children may experience psychological distance between themselves and their parents. They may not understand why their parents are not at home with them. Many of these children do not share their concerns, fears, and worries with their parents and suffer in silence.

Children have a need to receive affection, love, and understanding. They likewise have a need for relationships with family and friends. Self-care programs are designed to help children meet their emotional needs for love and belonging.

Self-guidance Needs

Children have a need for an internal guidance system that will help them do the right things when home alone. Discerning right from wrong, knowing how to respond to emergency situations, and being able to solve special problems are representative of the kind of understandings and decisions that children must make while home alone. If children are to meet their physiological, safety and security, and love and belonging needs, they must learn appropriate models of self-care on which they can rely. Self-care programs are designed to help children address the daily realities of being home alone.

From the early 1970s through the late 1980s, research findings have been contradictory regarding the effects of being a latchkey child. Whereas some studies report no significant differences between "home alone" children and adult supervised children (Hedin et al, 1986; Rodman, Pratto, & Nelson, 1985; Vandell & Corasaniti, 1988) regarding emotions, social skills, self-esteem, and control, others such as Coleman and Apts (1991), Gray and Coolsen (1987), and Steinberg (1986) suggest otherwise. They support the belief that latchkey children do not feel safe and secure and experience periods of loneliness, fear, and worry. Most likely the truth lies somewhere in between. The position that we take is that every child faced with being home alone, whether on a daily basis or intermittently, can benefit from a support group experience aimed at self-care.

STRENGTHS TO BE LEARNED

Our latchkey support group provides children with the information, personal strengths, self-confidence, and opportunities to meet their needs (e.g., physical, safety and security, love and belonging, and guidance) in home-alone settings. We do not promote or encourage self-care but recognize the importance of working with children and assisting parents who have opted for self-care based on their own unique situations.

The self-care support group sessions that follow are designed to help children develop personal strengths in a variety of areas. Children will be taught home safety rules, how to conduct a home safety review, and learn a variety of personal safety skills.

Simple Home Safety Rules

Children are asked to brainstorm a number of simple home rules that will help them make their home alone stays safer. Rules like the following can be addressed during group discussions and family homework assignments (Grollman & Sweder, 1992):

Go straight home after school. If you are going to be late, call your parents and let them know.

When you get home, lock the doors and then call a parent to let Mom or Dad know that you are safe at home.

Have the name and phone number of a close neighbor that you can contact in emergency situations if you cannot reach your parents.

Be sure to make a list of phone numbers that you can call in case of a fire, illness, injury, break ins, etc.

If a window is broken or a door is unlocked or things just do not look right to you, do not enter the house; go to a neighbor's instead.

Never let anyone know that you are home alone.

Carry your house key on a strong string around your neck and under your clothing.

Be sure that you know how to use your key to unlock the door. Practice using it a few times when you parents are around to help you.

Do not talk on the telephone for long periods of time so that your parents can reach you.

Do not use the stove when you are home alone.

Home Safety Check and Repairs

Children can discuss ways in which they can make their homes and property safe. A checklist can be prepared that children can take home. Together parents and children can expand on their checklist and then conduct a home safety review and make corrections where appropriate. Some safeguards to be addressed are

- appropriate repairs to doors, windows, locks, and the placement of usable peepholes for children;
- installation of appropriate lighting (indoors and outdoors);
- trimmed bushes near doors and windows;
- corrected potential home hazards such as electrical wiring, defective or malfunctioning water heater, smoke alarms, furnace and appliances;
- checking for the presence of usable first aid kits, fire extinguisher, carbon monoxide detectors, and fire alarms;
- be sure phones are in working order and the emergency numbers are properly affixed to the wall or the phone; and
- making sure that all poisonous chemicals, flammable materials, and dangerous equipment and weapons are secured appropriately.

Personal Safety Skills

If young people are to take good care of themselves while home alone, there are a number of skills they need to learn and practice in their support group and at home. Some very pertinent skills include learning how to (Koblinsky & Todd, 1991)

- answer the phone when home alone;
- answer the door when home alone;
- make emergency 911 phone calls;
- practice basic first aid;
- discriminate between emergency and nonemergency situations and how to respond to each;
- make decisions based on Right, Reality, and Responsibility;
- make an activity schedule to follow while home alone;
- organize space for recreation, homework, and hobbies;
- care for younger brothers and sisters; and
- openly discuss feelings of fear, loneliness, anxiety, and boredom and ways to respond to them.

Our latchkey support group not only provides children with useful information and skills but also teaches them how to apply what they know through responsible decision making. Children's self-confidence is enhanced by using 3 R's Decision Making and playing the "What If" game. Children can be presented with a number of incidents that could happen to them when home alone. They then are asked to decide how they would handle each.

"What if . . . the lights go out?"
"What if . . . a stranger came to your door and wants to use your phone?"
"What if . . . the telephone rings and the caller asks to speak to your mother?"
"What if . . . there is a fire in your house?"
"What if . . . your sister or brother gets a minor cut or bruise?"

Children are given the opportunity to discuss "What if" situations and then decide on the best course of action to take. Their goal is to select safe choices based on what they have learned in their support group. With time and practice at home and in support group activities, children will experience confidence in themselves in making home-alone decisions.

MESSAGE TO FACILITATORS

Your latchkey support group should focus on the following topics (Coleman & Apts, 1991):

- home alone rules,
- responsibilities at home,
- home safety check and repair,
- personal safety skills,
- emergency and non-emergency situations,
- dealing with emotions, and
- handling the unexpected (problems that arise at home).

Whenever possible, involve parents in the homework phase of your support group activities. By keeping parents informed regarding session activities and providing them with tips on how they can support their children, parents will be able to make the home-alone experience safer and less traumatic for their children. Above all, encourage parents to talk with their children. They should let them know that they love them and that they think about them when they are away. Encourage parents to call their children and to spend as much time with them as possible when they are at home. Encourage them to show interest in their children's school work and special projects and to compliment them on a job well done regarding chores, handling home responsibilities, and managing themselves in a responsible manner. (See Figure 7.1.)

Although it is difficult to place an age minimum on staying home alone, we believe that children under eight years of age may not be fully mature enough to assume home alone responsibilities. That is not to say, however, that younger children cannot benefit from various aspects of the content to be covered in a latchkey support group. Depending on the needs of the children, a modified group experience can be developed.

During group sessions, make a point to attend to the children's emotional needs. Many children will harbor worries, fears, and anxieties they have not shared with their parents. This is your opportunity to help children talk about their feelings and discuss ways in which they can manage them more effectively. You also may want to talk with parents and make child referrals if home-alone stresses and worries require attention beyond what you can provide in the group.

Studies conducted by Bundy and Boser (1987), Gray and Coolsen (1987), the National PTA (1990), and Stoudnour and Klimas (1991) suggest that it is possible to communicate self-care practices. While we all agree that self-care is no substitute for adult supervised child care, few would argue that all children should be prepared to care for themselves in emergency situations. Consequently, we believe that all children can benefit from learning some self-care practices regardless of the amount of time they spend home alone.

Resources

In Figure 7.1 are provided "Tips for Caregivers" in order to strengthen parent/ guardian involvement in the Latchkey Children Support Group. In Figure 7.2 are provided lists of resources to be used with and by children in the Latchkey Support Group. The resource materials are grouped according to age of child.

LATCHKEY CHILDREN GUIDE
Tips for Caregivers

Your child soon will be participating in a Latchkey Support Group. The goal of this support group is to provide children with information, skills, and confidence in themselves to take on adult responsibilities while home alone. We are offering you a few tips that you can use in better preparing your children to stay alone when adult supervision is not possible. We have found that children generally do better in home-alone situations when they are prepared for this experience.

1. *Assess the safety of your neighborhood.*
   a   Crime rate.
   b   Types of crimes.
   c   Availability of community services in case of an emergency.
   d   Safety (e.g., pollution, dangerous objects and equipment, etc.)
   e   Police and/or security guard availability.
   f   Availability of families in the neighborhood who can provide emergency care.
   g   Parents' distance from home.
   h   Include any additional items that will help you do a neighborhood safety assessment.

2. *Assess the safety of your home. Your children can help you put a checklist together that can be used in doing a safety check.*
   a   Electrical and mechanical equipment are locked up.
   b   Locks on all doors and windows are in working order and in use.
   c   Smoke alarms are distributed in key places throughout your home and are in working order.
   d   Medicines are accurately labeled, current, and stored properly.
   e   All of your appliances are in good working order.
   f   Directions are posted and easily understood for using appliances.
   g   Electrical outlets are covered.
   h   Old wiring and broken electrical cords have been replaced.
   i   Fire extinguishers are in good working order and are accessible.
   j   Your children have access to a posted map of the community noting emergency services.
   k   Emergency phone numbers (e.g., 911, doctor, fire department, poison control, ambulance, etc.) are posted.
   l   A schedule of after school activities is posted.
   m   Areas where children could become injured or trapped have been secured.
   n   Broken furniture has been repaired.

o   Overgrown bushes around the house have been trimmed.
p   Proper outside lighting has been installed.
q   Procedures for answering the telephone have been taught.
r   Include other items on your checklist that seem appropriate.

3. *Be sure to teach your children the following in-home safety strategies.*
a   Memorize your name, address, and emergency phone numbers.
b   Learn how to make phone calls (long distance and local) using your home phone (role-play and practice using the phone).
c   Check in with a neighbor and at least one parent immediately upon arrival at home (by phone).
d   Check outside the home for anything unusual before entering (e.g., window open or broken, door ajar, lights on that should not be, strange car in the driveway). If anything is out of the ordinary, do not enter. Go to a designated neighbor's house and report the incident.
e   Do not make any side trips from school to home. Go straight home.
f   Never go anywhere with another adult even if that person tells you that your parent(s) asked for you to be picked up. Develop a secret family code name that children can ask third parties.
g   When possible, never walk or play alone.
h   If you feel like you are being followed, either by foot or car, run to the nearest public place, neighbor, or safe house.
i   Have your children report to you any unusual situations or happenings out of the ordinary (e.g., strangers on your property, unfamiliar vehicles, solicitors coming to the door).
j   Be sure to tell your children not to open the door to anyone. Tell the party that your parents are busy at the moment and that you will take a message through the door.
k   Teach your children basic first aid.
l   Teach your children how to discriminate between emergencies and situations that they can handle on their own.
m   Provide your children with a pad and pencil so they can record information, questions, and concerns about staying home alone.
n   Create a daily activity, schoolwork, and chores list so that children can plan how to use their time.

4. *Add any additional items that come to mind that will make your children's home alone experiences safe, less fearful, and fun.*

Although we have provided only a partial list of "home alone tips," these ideas represent a good beginning. In addition to these ideas, we cannot emphasize enough, the importance of developing a positive family climate when everyone can be together. You and your children need opportunities to connect with each another. Plan quiet times to talk, share in your children's interests, and let them know you love them.

Your children need to feel safe, belong, and feel good about themselves and their accomplishments. They have a need to experience childhood to its fullest even though they have the added responsibilities of self-care.

Figure 7.1.   Tips for Caregivers to be given to parents and/or guardians. Permission to photocopy is granted.

RESOURCES FOR CHILDREN
Latchkey Children

Ages 3 to 7

Bauer, C. F. (1981). *My mom travels a lot.* New York: Frederick Warne. (family unity, working mother)

Kessler, E., & Kessler, L. P. (1985). *The Sweeney's from 9D.* New York: Macmillan. (new house, mother working)

Power, B. (1979). *I wish Laura's mommy was my mommy.* Philadelphia: J. B. Lippincott. (working mother, meaning of love)

Schick, E. G. (1980). *Home alone.* New York: The Dial Press. (independence, accepting change)

Skurzyniski, G. J. (1979). *Martin by himself.* Boston: Houghton Mifflin. (loneliness, change in lifestyle)

Smith, L. B. (1979). *My mom got a job.* New York: Holt, Rinehart & Winston. (change in lifestyle)

Stanek, M. N. (1985). *All alone after school.* Morton Grove, IL: Albert Whitman. (independence, dependence)

Stecher, M. P., & Kendell, A.S. (1981). *Daddy and Ben together.* West Caldwell, NJ: Lothrop, Lee & Shepard. (communication, mother working)

Ages 8 to 12

Bunting, E. (1988). *Is anybody there.* Philadelphia: J. B. Lippincott. (latchkey, maturation)

Duder, T. (1985). *Jellybean.* New York: Oxford University Press. (autonomy, feelings of ambivalence)

Hayes, S. (1986). *You've been away all summer.* New York: E. P. Dutton. (fighting between parents, resisting change)

Howard, E. (1986). *Gillyflower.* New York: Atheneum Publishers. (mother working, unemployment, incest)

Jarrow, G. (1987). *If Phyllis were here.* Boston: Houghton Mifflin. (loneliness, love for grandparent)

Lowry, L. (1985). *Anastasia on her own.* Boston: Houghton Mifflin. (family unity, working mother)

Seabrooke, B. (1990). *Jerry on the line.* New York: Bradbury Press. (fear, loneliness, latchkey)

Tapp, K. K. (1986). *Smoke from the chimney.* New York: Atheneum Publishers. (parental unreliability)

Ages 12 and Up

Smith, R. K. (1990). *The squeaky wheel.* New York: Bantam Doubleday Dell. (change, new home, divorce)

Terris, S. D. (1986). *The latchkey kids.* New York: Farrar, Straus, & Giroux. (accepting responsibility, involuntary baby-sitting)

Tolan, S. S. (1983). *The great Skinner strike.* New York: Macmillan. (family unity, working mother)

Figure 7.2.   Resources for use with and by children in Latchkey Children Support Group.

SESSION I—WE ARE ALL "HOME ALONE"

BRIEF OVERVIEW OF SESSION

This session will introduce children to the purpose of the group, help them realize that others are also dealing with self-care, and provide an opportunity for the children to become acquainted while sharing an idea of something they enjoy doing when they are "home alone."

GOALS

1. To provide the structure and purpose for the group.
2. To encourage the children to realize that being "home alone" is a situation common to all group members.
3. To provide an opportunity for children to share an idea for something fun to do when they are "home alone."

MATERIALS NEEDED

1. 5" × 8" cards for name tags
2. Crayons or markers
3. Masking tape

PROCEDURE

1. Introduce self and have each of the group members introduce self by first name. Tell the children that everyone in the group is "home alone" and taking care of himself or herself either before or after school (or both). During the course of this group we will be learning many skills that will help them be happier, more confident, and safer in their self-care situation.

2. Begin to set the stage for the group by discussing ground rules. Examples of possible group rules may include

a   What is said in the group, stays there (confidentiality).
b   No put-downs are allowed.
c   Only one person talks at a time.
d   It is important to attend all sessions.

Note: If children do not suggest these rules, you as facilitator should bring them up as part of the brainstorming process.

3. Give each child a 5" × 8" card and a crayon or marker and ask each to write his or her name in the middle of the card. The remainder of the card will be completed as follows:

a   Upper right corner—a small picture or word to describe your favorite thing to do when you are "home alone"
b   Lower right corner—a small picture or word to describe a snack you make for yourself (without using the stove or microwave).
c   Upper left corner—a small picture or word to show what chores you do when you are alone.
d   Lower left corner—a small picture or word to show how you feel about getting your homework done when you are by yourself.

4. Provide time for children to share each of the corners from their tag (or just tape them on their shirt and walk around and read each other's tag). Encourage them to "store away" any good ideas they heard that they may be able to use in the future.

5. Compliment the children on their cooperation and involvement in the initial group session.

CLOSURE

Bring this session to a close by encouraging the children to try some of the ideas they have heard and think about how they can use them in their own self-care situation.

HOMEWORK

Alert the children to the fact that next week's group will focus on rules and responsibilities at home. Ask each child to make a list of at least five rules he or she has while "home alone."

SESSION II—I HAVE RULES AND RESPONSIBILITIES

BRIEF OVERVIEW OF SESSION

During this session, children will begin to identify rules in their self-care situations that will help keep them safe. Again they will have the opportunity to see how these rules and responsibilities are similar to others.

GOALS

1. To assist children in identifying the rules and responsibilities they have while in self-care.
2. To provide an opportunity for children to compare and contrast their rules and responsibilities with those of others in the group.
3. To encourage practice of specific rules and skills through role-play.
4. To help children realize that having rules can prevent problems.

MATERIALS NEEDED

1. One piece of chart paper for each child
2. Markers

PROCEDURE

1. Give each child a piece of chart paper and marker and ask them to list five of their home rules and also five of their responsibilities (from their homework assignment).

2. Provide time for children to share their chart with other group members, and encourage discussion of similarities in the lists. (During this time, you as facilitator should make one complete list of all the rules and responsibilities mentioned by group members. If possible, these completed lists should be displayed somewhere in the room for future reference.)

3. Allow time to role-play and practice one specific rule that is no doubt on each child's list—answering the phone when you are "home alone."

   a Provide the following example of a fictional phone call. "Hello, this is Margie. No one is home but me. My mom won't be home until late tonight. I'll tell her you called."

   b Discuss these questions: What was wrong with Margie's answer? What could she have said instead? ("My mom can't come to the phone right now. May I have your number so she can call you back?")

c Have the children work in dyads to practice answering the phone, being careful not to allow the caller to know they are home alone.

4. As a group, review the technique of answering the phone. Remind children that they should always use this technique when the phone rings or when someone comes to the door.

5. Allow time for discussion and questions.

CLOSURE

To bring closure to this session, spend some time discussing why rules and responsibilities must play an important part in self-care at home.

HOMEWORK

For homework, the children should be encouraged to practice and to use consistently the rules that they have discussed. Also for next week, they should begin to think about ways they keep themselves personally safe when "home alone." Ask them to be prepared to talk about three things they do to keep themselves safe.

SESSION III—KEEPING ME SAFE

BRIEF OVERVIEW OF SESSION

In this session, children will identify some things they can do to assure that their home is safe and that they are safe. Each child will develop a checklist of safety measures that he or she can control to assure his or her safety.

GOALS

1. To assist children in identifying some personal safety skills that they must develop.
2. To encourage children to work with their parent(s) to assure household safety.

MATERIALS

1. Copies of "My Safety Checklist" (Activity Sheet 7.1)
2. Chart paper and markers

PROCEDURE

1. Briefly review the information presented in the previous session.

2. Encourage each child to share with the group the three homework items for keeping safe. Compare the items from the list for similarities and differences. Make a composite list and post it in the room for reference as the group continues.

3. Spend some time discussing each of the items listed on the chart. Encourage the children to give personal examples of things they have done or learned that have helped them feel or be safer at home.

4. Give a copy of "My Safety Checklist (Activity Sheet 7.1) to each child. Encourage him or her to discuss it with his or her parent(s).

CLOSURE

To end this session, remind the children that much of their safety is well within their control because they can do and know many things that will keep them safe at home.

HOMEWORK

For homework, each child should talk with his or her parent(s) and complete the safety checklist. If there is more than one item from each list that is not completed, parent and child should work together to correct the situation.

MY SAFETY CHECKLIST

Parent Checklist

_____1. Are doors, windows, locks in good repair?

_____2. Are bushes and shrubs near doors and windows trimmed?

_____3. Are the following available and in good working order?

    _____fire alarms and/or smoke detector
    _____carbon monoxide detector
    _____first aid kits

_____4. Are flammable materials, poisonous chemicals and dangerous equipment appropriately secured?

_____5. Are indoor and outdoor lighting appropriate?

_____6. Are the following maintained in good working order?

    _____furnace
    _____water heater
    _____wiring
    _____electrical appliances

My Checklist

Do I know how to

_____1. answer the phone when I'm "home alone"?

_____2. answer the door when I'm "home alone"?

_____3. make an emergency call? (911)

_____4. do basic first aid?

_____5. discriminate between emergency and nonemergency situations?

Activity Sheet 7.1. My Safety Checklist worksheet. Permission is granted to enlarge and photocopy for classroom use.

SESSION IV—"THE EMERGENCY SORT GAME"

BRIEF OVERVIEW OF SESSION

In this session, children will begin to realize that many situations will arise while they are in self-care. They need to prepare to react responsibly to a given situation.

GOALS

1. To assist children in identifying situations as "major," "minor," and "no" emergency.
2. To provide information on action steps needed to handle major and minor emergencies.
3. To encourage children to develop a list of phone numbers that may be needed in emergency situations.

MATERIALS NEEDED

1. 3" × 5" index cards for each child (prepared as per sample under procedure #5)
2. Fine line markers
3. Cards labeled "major," "minor," and "no"

PROCEDURE

1. Introduce the session by discussing the fact that situations may arise that will require assistance from adults. These emergency situations basically fall into three categories:

> **Major**—fire, smoke in the house, a gas leak, an accident where you or one of your siblings is bleeding badly or has a broken bone. THIS SITUATION REQUIRES A CALL TO THE EMERGENCY NUMBER OR TO YOUR PARENT.
>
> **Minor**—some type of damage to the home such as backed-up drain pipe, toilet overflow, or no heat or electricity. YOU COULD CALL YOUR NEIGHBOR OR OTHER CONTACT PERSON.
>
> **No**—fighting with brothers or sisters, juice spilled on the rug, losing your homework. YOU CAN HANDLE THIS UNTIL MOM OR DAD GETS HOME.

2. Explain to the children that the group will play the emergency sort game to help them determine the type of emergency each is. Ask for three volunteers (each one will hold one of the emergency type cards—Major, Minor, and No).

3. As an emergency situation is read, the children will be asked to vote to identify the type and to tell what they would do in that situation. Some card samples could include

a   Little brother fell and cut his head and is bleeding badly.
b   The TV is not working.
c   There is no water in the faucet.
d   You smell a strong smoke smell when you open the door.
e   You spilled spaghetti sauce on your clothes.
f   You had a fight with your little brother.
g   The basement is flooded.

4. Spend some time discussing each of the situations and how they could be handled.

5. Provide each child with a preprinted emergency card and have them put in the appropriate numbers. Encourage the children to post the card at home near the phone.

POLICE   _____
FIRE   _____
POISON CONTROL   _____
AMBULANCE   _____
MOM AT WORK   _____
DAD AT WORK   _____
NEIGHBOR   _____
RELATIVES   _____

CLOSURE

Provide closure to this session by reminding children that, although they can handle many situations on their own, others need adult intervention. It is critical to know which situations are which.

HOMEWORK

Prepare for next session by thinking about some of the feelings that being "home alone" generate.

SESSION V—DEALING WITH FEELINGS

BRIEF OVERVIEW OF SESSION

This session will provide an opportunity for the children to talk about a variety of feelings they have experienced as a result of being in self-care. The group will discuss that these feelings include both comfortable and uncomfortable and that everyone experiences many of these feelings when they are "home alone."

GOALS

1. To assist children in identifying the wide variety of feelings and emotions that one faces when in self-care.
2. To help children realize that the feelings that they experience are normal and to be expected.
3. To encourage the children to share these feelings with other group members.
4. To discuss ways to cope with difficult feelings.

MATERIALS NEEDED

1. Colored construction paper (precut into 8" circles)
2. Glue or tape
3. Crayons and markers

PROCEDURE

1. Spend a few moments discussing the previous session and giving the children an opportunity to discuss any emergencies they have handled while in self-care.

2. Bring up the subject of feelings one has as a result of self-care situations. Provide a few minutes for the children to identify some of the feelings they have experienced (and the reason for each of the feelings). Some examples of some feelings they may have experienced include the following:

- **proud,** because parents trusted them enough to leave them alone;
- **lonely,** because they had nothing to do;
- **scared,** because the house seemed spooky when no one else was there; and
- **responsible,** because they completed their chores without being reminded.

3. Give each child six precut 8" paper circles, crayons, and glue or tape and ask them to make a personal "Feelings Bug" to identify at least five feelings they have had as a result of being in self-care. (On the front of each circle, they will write the feeling; on the back, the reason for the feeling). See example below:

4. When children have completed their bugs, allow time for sharing and discussing ways they have been able to cope with the uncomfortable feelings.

5. Remind children that all of the feelings are normal, that even adults have experienced some of the feelings when they are "home alone."

CLOSURE

Display the Feelings Bugs in an area where the children will see them and be reminded that all of these feelings are normal.

HOMEWORK

Encourage the children to keep a diary of feelings for the next week by writing down all of the feelings they have experienced while they are in self-care.

SESSION VI—BEING BORED

BRIEF OVERVIEW OF SESSION

This session will give children an opportunity to think about causes for boredom when they are home alone. It also will provide an opportunity for each child to make his or her very own "bored bag" to which he or she can go when feeling bored.

GOALS

1. To help children identify positive ways to avoid becoming bored.
2. To allow time for each child to make a "bored bag" full of ideas for things to do to avoid boredom.
3. To encourage sharing of ideas for avoiding boredom.

MATERIALS NEEDED

1. Brown bag for each child
2. Crayons, markers
3. Scissors
4. Slips of paper (for writing ideas)
5. Chart paper or chalkboard
6. 3" × 5" card for each child for homework assignment

PROCEDURE

1. Begin with a brief discussion of the feelings bug. Allow a small amount of time for children to share some of the feelings from their feelings diary. (The word "bored" will probably come up in at least one instance.)

2. Ask the children to name some things they can do when they are feeling bored. List these on the chalkboard or on a piece of chart paper for future reference.

3. Give each child a paper bag, markers or crayons, scissors, and slips of paper. Ask them to decorate their "bored bag" on the outside and to write ideas of things to do to keep from being bored on the slips of paper. Put these slips of paper in the "bored bag" for use when they are feeling bored.

4.   Remind the children to use the "bored bag" for ideas when they do not have anything to do. When they are feeling bored, they are to pull one idea out of the "bored bag." If they do not like it, they can pull out another one. They have to do the second one. They can put the ideas back into the bag for use on another day.

5.   Provide time for the children to share some of the ideas from their "bored bag." If some new ideas come up, have a few extra slips of paper for children to add additional ideas to their bag.

6.   Encourage the children to take their bags home and keep them in a place that it is easily accessible to be used when they are feeling bored.

CLOSURE

Conclude this session by reminding the children that being bored is a choice they make. If they want to be bored they can just sit around and do nothing, but if they really want to do something to keep from being bored, they can use some or all of the ideas in the "bored bag" they have just completed.

HOMEWORK

For homework the children should try to think of a wide variety of situations that may come up when they are in self-care. Ask each child to think of at least two "What if . . ." situations for use in next week's group. We will use these ideas as we play the "What if . . ." game. (Provide 3" × 5" cards for each child to write his or her "What if . . ." situations).

SESSION VII—THE "WHAT IF . . ." GAME

BRIEF OVERVIEW OF SESSION

In this session, the children will be introduced, through a game format, to handling unexpected situations. They will be aware of things they need to consider when making decisions in cases of unexpected situations.

GOALS

1. To assist children in identifying some situations that may arise while they are in self-care.
2. To help children analyze situations in which they need to become a decision maker.
3. To provide practice in a role-playing atmosphere.

MATERIALS NEEDED

1. 3" × 5" cards for "What if . . ." situations

PROCEDURE

1. Ask the children if they remembered to complete their "What if . . ." situation cards. (If any of them forgot, provide a few minutes for them to jot them down on the 3" × 5" cards.)

2. Identity some possible "What if..." situations that may arise while they are in self-care. Some examples include

a What if the lights go out?
b What if a stranger comes to your door and wants to use your phone?
c What if the telephone rings and the caller asks to speak with your mother?
d What if there is a fire in your house?
e What if your sister or brother gets a minor cut or bruise?
f What if a friend wants to bring cigarettes into the house?

3. Talk about each of the situations and what things need to be done to deal with each situation. Remind them of the 3 R's filters for good decision making (chapter 2).

4. Use some of the situations identified in their homework assignment as role-play problems. Have volunteers play the part of the child who is home alone as he or she deals with the "What if . . ." situations.

5. Spend as much time as is necessary to discuss the unexpected situations and potential solutions for dealing with them effectively.

6. Review the decision making steps briefly with the children. Remind them that making a good decision in an unexpected situation will help them feel more confident and able to handle the unexpected in the future.

CLOSURE

To bring closure to this session, again remind the children that they have many choices to make when they are in self-care situations. Using the 3 R's filters of Right, Reality, and Responsibility will assist them in feeling more confident and in control when they are faced with unexpected situations.

HOMEWORK

Ask the children to think about how having a younger sibling at home with them changes the self-care situation (particularly if they are responsible for the care of the younger child). Encourage them to consider these three questions for next session:

1. What are some things I can do to make the situation more fun for the younger sibling?
2. What are some responsibilities we can share?
3. What should I do to be ready to handle problems that may arise with the younger sibling?

SESSION VIII—BEING IN CHARGE OF YOUNGER SIBLINGS

BRIEF OVERVIEW OF SESSION

This session will provide an opportunity for the children to begin to assess the added responsibility of caring for a younger sibling. Although not all of the children will need to deal with this situation, they all can benefit from this discussion.

GOALS

1. To assist children in discovering how to entertain younger siblings in the home.
2. To help children develop skills for being a peacemaker when necessary.
3. To assist children in identifying methods of dealing with difficult situations with younger brothers and sisters.

MATERIALS NEEDED

1. Copies of "Compli-Notes" worksheet (Activity Sheet 7.2) for each child
2. Chart paper and markers
3. Copies of evaluation form

PROCEDURE

1. Briefly review last week's session. Did anyone have to deal with any unexpected situations during the past week? How did you handle it?

2. Ask the children how many of them are responsible for the care of a younger sibling when they are in self-care situations. Discuss some of the added problems that may arise as a result of this responsibility. List them on a large piece of chart paper. They may include

    a safety concerns,
    b keeping younger sibling entertained,
    c handling arguments, and
    d making sure chores get done

3. Talk about some techniques for handling each of the situations listed. Other suggestions for involving younger siblings may include

a read a story to them—select a story that has lots of pictures;
b talk and play with them;
c try not to be bossy;
d do not punish for spills and accidents—ask them to help you clean it up;
e praise for a job well done; and
f be alert for dangers—remove them if possible rather than telling the child to get away.

4. Allow time for the children to discuss other situations that encourage the children to continue to do the best job they can in assuming the responsibility of caring for a younger sibling.

5. Talk about how compliments can be helpful in working with younger siblings. Sometimes compliments can be much more helpful in getting youngsters to cooperate. Remind them of the old sayings such as "A spoonful of sugar helps the medicine go down" and "You can catch more flies with honey than with vinegar." We all like to be complimented.

CLOSURE

Give each child a "Compli-Note" worksheet (Activity Sheet 7.2) and ask him or her to put his or her name on it. He or she then will pass it to the person on his or her right who will write a compliment to tell the person one thing the writer has liked about being in group with the person. When the "Compli-Note" has been passed the whole way around the group, each person will have received a compliment from every other person in the group. Talk about the good feelings that develop as a result of giving and receiving compliments. Encourage the children to use this technique as they work with younger siblings in the home. Ask the children to fill out the evaluation forms.

HOMEWORK

Since this is the final session, there will be no homework except to encourage the children to use all of the skills they have developed in the group.

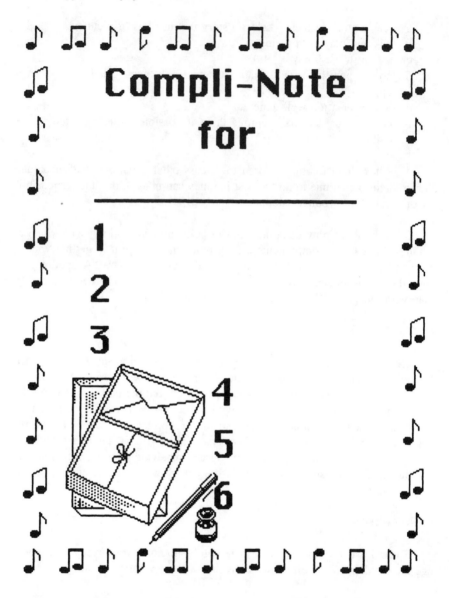

Activity Sheet 7.2. Compli-Note worksheet. Permission is granted to enlarge and photocopy for classroom use.

EVALUATION

1. Do you feel that participation in the "Home Alone" group was helpful to you? Why or why not?

2. What part of the group did you like best?

3. What part of the group did you like least?

4. If you had a friend who was home alone each day after school, would you recommend that he or she participate in a similar group? Why or why not?

5. Did you attend all eight group sessions?

_____ Yes_____ No

If no, how many did you attend? _____

6. Comments, suggestions, etc.:

REFERENCES

Bundy, M. L., & Boser, J. (1987). Helping latchkey children: A group guidance approach. *The School Counselor, 35*(1), 58–65.

Coleman, M., & Apts, S. (1991, Spring). Home-alone risk factors. *Teaching exceptional children,* 36–39.

Coontz, S. (1995). The American family and the nostalgia trap: Kappan special report. *Phi Delta Kappan, 76,* K1–K20.

Glass, T. L. (1990, September-October). Is your child ready to be in self-care? *Children Today,* 4–5.

Gray, E., & Coolsen, P. (1987, July-August). How do kids really feel about being home alone? *Children Today,* 30–32.

Grollman, E. A., & Sweder, G. L. (1992). *Teaching your child to be home alone.* New York: Macmillan.

Hedin, D., Hanes, K., Saito, R., Goldman, A., & Knich, D. (1986). *Summary of the family's view of after school time.* St. Paul University, MN: Center for Youth Development and Research.

Koblinsky, S. A., & Todd, C. M. (1991, Spring). Teaching self-care skills. *Teaching Exceptional Children,* 40–44.

Kraizer, S., Witte, S., Fryer, G. E., & Miyoski, T. (1990). Children in self-care: A new perspective—special report. *Child Welfare, 69*(6), 571–581.

Long, T. J., & Long, L. (1982). *Latchkey children: The child's view of self care.* Urbana, IL: ERIC Clearinghouse on Elementary and Early Childhood Education. (ERIC Document Reproduction Service No. ED 211229).

National Parent-Teacher Association. (1990, April). Kids with keys, parents with jobs: Keeping latchkey kids safe. *PTA Today,* 15–16.

Padilla, M. L., & Landreth, G. L. (1989). Latchkey children: A review of the literature—special report. *Child Welfare, 68*(4), 445–453.

Peterson, L., & Magrab, P. (1989). Introduction to the special section: Children on their own. *Journal of Clinical Child Psychology, 18,* 2–7.

Powers, D. A., & Anderson, P. J. (1991, Spring). Advocacy for latchkey children: A new challenge for special educators. *Teaching Exceptional Children*, 49–51.

Robinson, B. E., Rowland, B. H., & Coleman, M. (1986). *Latchkey Kids: Unlocking doors for children and their families*. Lexington, MA: Lexington Books.

Rodman, H., Pratto, D. J., & Nelson, R. S. (1985). Child care arrangements and children's functioning: A comparison of self-care and adult care children. *Developmental psychology, 21*, 413–418.

Steinberg, L. (1986). Latchkey children and susceptibility to peer pressure: An ecological analysis. *Developmental Psychology, 22*(4), 433–439.

Stoudnour, J., & Klimas, A. W. (1991). *Kids in control: When you're home alone*. University Park, PA: Penn State Cooperative Extension.

United States Bureau of Labor Statistics. (1985). Labor force activity of mothers of young children continues at a record pace. *News, USDL* No. 85-381. Washington, DC: Department of Labor.

Vandell, D. L., & Corasaniti, M. A. (1988). After-school care and social, academic, and emotional functioning. *Child Development, 59*(4), 868–875.

Chapter **8**

ANGER MANAGEMENT

Anger Management is the act of handling one's feelings of displeasure in a socially acceptable and constructive manner.

BACKGROUND INFORMATION

Anger is a basic human emotion often arising out of children's frustrations in response to an injury, perceived mistreatment by others, or opposition to a situation or event particularly displeasing to them (Olthof, Ferguson, & Luiten, 1989). While everyone experiences angry feelings at one time or another, it is a much maligned emotion in that most people identify anger with negativity. They tend to pair anger with hurting others, conflict, and violence. And while anger can lead to aggression, it also can be a positive and motivating force for constructive social, political, and personal change. Anger can move people to action, help them hurdle personal barriers, and champion unpopular causes in support of basic goodness.

Anger is an emotion that is neither good nor bad. How anger is expressed and channeled is the real issue. Because anger is an inescapable emotion as is the distress that produces it, a critical developmental task for children to learn is "how to modulate, tolerate, and endure negative experiences" (Beland, 1992, p. 45). Children must be taught how to control the manner in which they express their anger and how to direct it in helpful and positive ways (Rice, 1992).

Aggressive Children

Although all children experience angry feelings, they all do not handle anger in socially acceptable ways. Children are exposed to a multitude of role models, both in and outside of the home, who may demonstrate impulsive and aggressive behaviors in response to conflict. They display their anger in harmful and hurtful ways, thus sending a message that acts of violence are socially acceptable responses to venting anger.

Teachers, in particular, are faced with ever increasing displays of disruptive and angry outbursts by children in their classrooms. They are spending less time teaching and more time managing interpersonal conflicts. Some children begin to display socially unacceptable behavior patterns during early childhood with regard to the following (Spivack & Cianci, 1987):

- a tendency to engage in such annoying social behaviors as hitting, pushing, poking, etc.;
- a tendency toward impulsiveness;
- negative and defiant behavior; and
- self-centered verbal responses in social situations (interrupting others, blurting out responses, and irrelevant talk regarding the current conversation).

Aggressive children, while doing damage to themselves (e.g., rejection by peers, poor academic success, and school dropout risk), also exact a negative toll on classroom instruction and peer relationships. Teachers are unable to cover the academic material they need to teach nor are they able to provide as much individual academic attention to those in need of additional help. Also, many children, and especially the socially neglected, are victimized by their more socially aggressive peers (Coie, Dodge, & Supersmidt, 1990). These socially neglected children often suffer such ill effects as low self-confidence, poor academic success, and eventually may drop out of school. Some of these children may commit suicide later or engage in violent acts of retaliation against their aggressors.

Causes of Aggressive Behavior

Children, whether exhibiting minor behavior problems or being excessively aggressive, often fail to manage their emotions and behaviors because they are experiencing difficulty in one or more of the following areas (Beland, 1992; Dodge, 1993; Lochman & Lenhart, 1993; Stern & Fodor, 1989):

Encoding social cues. "Aggressive children have been found to attend to fewer relevant cues before interpreting an event, to attend selectively to hostile rather than benign areas, and to have recent biases in their recall of cues" (Lochman & Lenhart, 1993, pp. 6 & 7).

Making accurate interpretations and attributions about the social event. Aggressive children tend to have a hostile attributional bias in which they believe that others have acted toward them with purposeful and hostile intentions. This bias is more prevalent in children with reactive aggressive tendencies than in those children who are more proactively aggressive.

Generating a variety of appropriate solutions to the perceived problem. Aggressive children have been found to display deficiencies in the quality and quantity of their solutions. With regard to interpersonal conflicts, these children tend to generate more physically aggressive solutions to their problems than their more socially inclined counterparts.

Deciding on which solution(s) to enact based on probable outcome. Aggressive children, when evaluating their strategies and the notable consequences of each, believe that the best results will come from their more aggressive strategies. They believe that a more aggressive stance will reduce the aversive behavior in others, help them avoid a personal negative image, and would not cause others to suffer. These children also believe that they will be more successful in enacting aggressive behaviors versus enacting more prosocial behaviors. Their beliefs are that aggressive behaviors are not all that bad, will lead to positive outcomes, and that they will be more successful implementing the aggressive strategy.

Skillfully enacting the chosen strategy. Many aggressive children have been found to be less successful in implementing proactive, socially acceptable behaviors when compared with less aggressive children. Their lack of success is due to a variety of variables that include some of the following:

- lack of responsible role models,
- lack of acceptable alternatives and skills,
- lack of knowledge,
- emotional response that inhibits the performance of desired behaviors (e.g., fear, anger, anxiety),
- faulty beliefs regarding aggression, and
- developmental delays and psychological deficits.

Categorized Expressions of Anger

As we have indicated, all children do not turn their angry feelings into destructive and violent acts of aggression. Children express their anger in a variety of ways. Although all children may not be aggressive, they may choose to express their anger in ways that are just as damaging. Schmidt (1993) has categorized the expression of anger into six anger styles that she has identified as the stuffer, the withdrawer, the blamer, the triangler, the exploder, and the problem solver. A brief description of each follows.

Stuffers.   Children who hold in their anger or deny its existence are said to be stuffers. Some children may attempt to avoid conflict by repressing their anger. Children who habitually stuff their anger are particularly vulnerable to depression, somatic complaints, and related emotional problems.

Withdrawers.   Passive aggressive behavior is often characteristic of the withdrawers. Children fitting this label often withdraw from participation with others as a way of expressing their anger. Withdrawers deal with their anger by cutting themselves off physically, emotionally, and geographically from the anger-producing stimuli. They distance themselves from the stressors (difficult personal relationships) in their lives and find it difficult to show their needy, vulnerable and dependent dimensions. Children who refuse to participate in school activities and family chores may be disconnecting themselves from family and friends as a means of making a statement regarding their angry feelings.

Blamers.   Children who project their anger onto others through name calling, put-downs, and teasing are blamers. These children tend to hold others responsible for their feelings, thoughts, and actions. They see others (friend and peers) as the cause of their anger and the barriers to their success. Blamers avoid responsibility and abdicate their personal power by putting it in the hands of someone else. Blamers view others as having the power in determining their own destiny.

Trianglers.   These children reduce their anger in a relationship by involving a neutral third party. Rather than resolve their anger directly with the involved child, trianglers share their anger with a third party, thereby getting rid of their anger and creating an ally who now supports their position. In this case, a third party has been triangled into a dispute in which he or she was never directly involved. Trianglers find it difficult to confront their anger directly. Rather, they find it easier and safer to share their anger with someone who will support them and not have to risk a confrontation with the involved person.

Exploders. These children express their anger through direct confrontation and violence. Exploders tend to be aggressive children with short fuses. They manage their anger through fighting, hitting, verbal abuse, and related acts of aggression. They are not effective nonviolent problem solvers. Rather, they respond to their own angry feelings by acting out.

Problem Solvers. These children have patience, persistence and a nonviolent plan for responding to anger. They are open and accepting of other children's feelings, do not try to change others but look to themselves in managing their anger, and possess the skills necessary to operate within socially acceptable boundaries of right and wrong in their dealings with others.

CHILDREN'S NEEDS

Based on years of research, as has been indicated, there are a number of early indicators of violence and aggression in children. These indicators translate into specific skill deficits representing five areas of need that must be addressed if anger coping interventions (strengths training) are to succeed. The skill deficit areas to which we allude are the following (Beland, 1992):

- a lack of empathy,
- a lack of impulse control,
- a lack of problem-solving skills,
- a lack of behavioral skills, and
- a lack of anger management strategies.

Empathy

Children have a need to be empathic in their relationships with others. Empathy can be defined as "understanding, being aware of, being sensitive to, and vicariously experiencing the feelings and thoughts of another person" (Webster's Dictionary, 1990). Children who are empathic are sensitive to others' needs, can relate to varying points of view, and are more likely to understand and tolerate the behaviors of others. They are less likely to exhibit impulsive behaviors and are therefore not as quick to act out under stress when compared with their more aggressive counterparts.

Empathy is an important child need to be addressed if children are to be successful in their relationships with others, especially during times of anger. How children handle their anger is very much related to their capacity to empathize with others.

Impulse Control

Children who are quick to express their anger often do so in socially unacceptable manners. They act before they think about their options and the potential consequence of each. Much of their behavior is predicated on habit and represents a knee jerk response to environmental conditioning. Children have a need to be in control of their impulses if they are to self-manage more responsibly in times of anger. Impulse control methods teach children to slow down their reaction time between STOP and GO so that they can THINK about their choices and the consequences of each before acting (chapter 2).

Problem Solving

If children are to learn the virtues of patience, persistence, and a plan, they have a need to recognize the value of planning. Children who possess a problem-solving plan are more likely to use it than those who do not. Rather than always reacting to environmental stimuli, children need a "game plan" that they can implement, thereby assuming some control over their own destiny.

Learning to apply a problem-solving model requires patience in that it takes time to feel comfortable with a new way of doing things. Persistence is also required. Moving from acting totally on impulse to problem solving is going to result in some frustration and a lack of success. Change requires patience and persistence (i.e., staying with the task until success is attained).

Behavioral Skills

Children have a need to learn a variety of overt behavioral skills (strengths) in processing their chosen course of action in response to their problem. For example, Susan wants to play with a group of girls, but they seem to be ignoring her. Through problem solving, she generates a number of choices to consider in solving her problem. Susan decides to assert herself and ask these girls if she can play with them. While Susan has selected a socially acceptable solution to her problem, she does not know how to actually approach these girls. Susan needs help in being assertive. Through strengths training, Susan can learn the behaviors she will need to use in processing her solution (e.g., asking the girls if she can play with them).

Anger Management

Children have a need to understand anger, anger cues, and those personal and environmental conditions that trigger anger responses in them. They likewise have a need to develop strategies that will help them calm down in times of anger, prevent the onset of angry feelings when possible, and to utilize their anger, when it does occur, in positive and responsible ways. Children also need to reflect on these anger-provoking incidents in their lives so that they can better understand their causes and effects and make wiser future decisions in times of stress.

STRENGTHS TO BE LEARNED

If children are to understand how to handle their angry feelings in a productive manner, they must have a variety of personal strengths that will help them do so. A number of curricula exist that tend to approach the study and management of anger rather simplistically, failing to recognize its complex nature. We believe that there are at least five integrated strengths that anger management support groups must address. They are (Beland, 1992) as follows:

- empathy training,
- impulse control,
- problem solving,
- behavior skills training, and
- anger management strategies.

Empathy Training

Empathy training focuses on helping children identify and experience the feelings of others. Children possessing empathy skills respond often and appropriately to the needs and feelings of others. They possess the ability to

identify the emotional state of others. Children who are able to empathize with others are capable of identifying the various cues associated with different emotional states. They are capable of discriminating one emotional state from another based on the cues of each.

see through the eyes of another. In order to empathize with others, children must be able to view the world from another person's perspective.

respond to the emotional state of another. Children who are empathetic are able to identify with the emotional state of another person and respond accordingly.

Empathy is a necessary condition in developing positive social relationships with others. Children who are able to perceive, predict, and identify with others' feelings are capable of making decisions and solving problems that are sensitive to the needs of those who will be affected by their actions. Empathic children tend to be thoughtful and caring individuals who enlist the cooperation and support of their peers in all that they do.

Empathy is a learned behavior that can be taught to children via the application of proven strategies as noted by the likes of Beland (1988, 1989, 1991), Feshbach (1984), Hoffman (1982), Saltz & Johnson (1974), and Selman (1980). Empathy training was originally developed to benefit aggressive children but now is thought to be of most benefit when applied to children before they begin to display habitual antisocial behavior. Beland (1992) has identified a number of objectives that, when met, will help children learn to

identify feelings from a variety of physical (face, body) and situational cues. Children can be taught to recognize a variety of emotions in others once they learn the basic components of each.

recognize that people may have different feelings about the same thing. How children feel about various situations is a matter of perspective and accounts for individual differences in emotional responses to the same stimuli.

recognize that feelings change and why this is so. Children learn that their feelings can change regarding the same event. Changing circumstances and maturation can account for a shift in feelings.

predict feelings. With practice, children can learn to predict other's feelings, remarks, and actions. They can learn to anticipate these predicted outcomes by placing themselves in the same situation and imagining their own reactions.

understand that people may have different likes and dislikes (preferences). Children can learn to recognize that people have differing perspectives and therefore do not always share the same likes and dislikes. They also can learn that even though people are different they still can like each other.

differentiate intentional from unintentional acts. Children can learn to assess other people's motives in response to their actions.

apply fairness rules in simple situations. Children can learn about the meaning of double standards and the 3 R's in equating fairness and equality.

communicate feelings using "I" messages and actively listen to another person. Children can learn to take responsibility for their actions and the importance of two-way communication.

express care and concern for others. Children can learn and practice a variety of ways that they can connect with others in caring ways.

As children learn to be empathetic, they are encouraged to identify opportunities open to them for doing so. The last step of the Keystone Learning Model (utilization) requires children to set goals in which they can demonstrate their empathy for others. Later the children are asked to share their goals and action-oriented outcomes with their peers.

Children can learn about empathy through the curriculum. They can study people (past and present) who demonstrated their empathy for others. They can write papers on the topic, read stories, and watch video presentations that portray the virtues of being empathetic. Children can likewise practice what they have learned about empathy at home, in school, and in their places of worship. Empathy is a central condition to building a sense of community and harmony among people.

Impulse Control

Children will learn a variety of techniques that will help them manage their impulsive actions in response to stressful situations. Many of the methods discussed here can also be used in the stress management support group discussed in Chapter 13. In particular, we advocate the use of

- thought stopping strategies,
- relaxation training,
- positive imagery,
- self-talk techniques,
- deep breathing, and
- momentarily walking away from the stressors.

These techniques, and others like them, are designed to help children momentarily distance themselves from stressful situations. They provide children with the time needed to replace habitual impulsive responses with more responsible and well thought out options. When confronted with name calling, teasing, and bullying, children discover that they can distance themselves from these situations long enough to develop and execute plans based on reason versus pure emotion and impulsive actions.

Problem Solving

Whereas impulse control methods will help children break the impulsive cycle to anger, problem solving can provide the plan for helping children create more rational solutions to their problems.

Problem solving can be viewed as an extended impulse control method in which children learn to use the 3 R's Model described in Chapter 2. The 3 R's Model requires children to

Step 1:   STOP (Identify and describe their problem or challenge.)
Step 2:   THINK (Brainstorm and filter solutions to the problem using the Right, Reality, and Responsibility filters.)
Step 3:   GO (Select a solution or solutions that are based on Right vs. wrong, Reality vs. myth, and Responsibility vs. desire. Implement and evaluate your solution[s].)

Behavioral Skills Training

What some people call behavioral skills training, we have labeled strengths training. Helping children identify 3 R's solutions to their problems does not go far enough. Children must possess the necessary strengths (behaviors) to carry out their solutions. Knowing *what* to do does not insure that children will know *how* to do it.

Strengths training is designed to provide children with the necessary information, skill step, confidence, and opportunity to help ensure a successful resolution of their problems. Strengths training is described in detail in Chapter 2. When a child understands the four-step process of building strengths, he or she will be able to utilize strengths training whenever the process can serve personal needs.

In sessions and activities that follow, children will engage in role-plays, practice sessions, and discussions in learning new strengths. Performance feedback, positive reinforcement, and self-assessment will guide children through the strengths training process.

As an example of its use, some children might find themselves having difficulty understanding a class assignment. Rather than get angry with themselves and the teacher, they could use the 3 R's problem-solving process to generate solutions to their problem, one of which might be to ask for help in a positive way. With this choice in mind, strengths training would be used to teach these children appropriate skills that they could use in "asking for help in a positive way." Children might be taught how to get the teacher's attention in a positive way and how to ask the kinds of questions that will assist them in understanding their assignment. Perhaps other skills will be needed in helping children achieve success. If so, they can be developed in the same manner as described.

Children, using empathetic skills coupled with 3 R's problem solving and strengths training, no longer have to act on impulse to be in control. They can manage their emotions and act with confidence in achieving their wants and needs in socially acceptable ways.

As with empathy training, children will need practice using problem solving and behavioral skills (strengths) in responding to difficult life situations. These techniques must be repeatedly modeled in the support group. Children need to be coached and taught to think out loud as they practice problem-solving and strengths training procedures.

In order to ensure for success in problem solving and strengths training, charts should be developed that outline the steps for both. Every opportunity to use these models in addressing daily life occurrences should be utilized. Also, children should be helped to imagine their day and identify opportunities to use what they have learned. At the end of the day, children should be encouraged to examine how they processed the day's events. Children can examine their emotions, empathetic responses, and their success with impulse control. With patience, persistence, and a plan (impulse control), children can learn to manage their lives in positive self-caring ways.

Anger Management: Putting It All Together

As indicated earlier, "anger management is a compilation of stress reduction techniques for channeling one's angry feelings into socially acceptable directions" (Beland, 1992, p.45). Before children can engage in developing empathy for others or solve problems, they first must be able to manage their internal state especially in response to stressful situations.

Children as young as six years of age can be taught how to deal with stressful emotions (Feindler, Marriott, & Iwata, 1984). Anger management utilizes *thinking out loud,* commonly referred to as *self-talk,* in teaching children how to guide themselves through their anger. This method is used because children who experience intense anger in stressful situations use self-talk (self-statements) in ways that provide insight into, maintain, and influence their angry emotions. Angry feelings often are accompanied by a combination of physical arousal and cognitive labeling of that arousal, which further intensify the reactions being experienced. For example, Susan might confront a problem involving a classmate cutting in front of her in the lunch line. Susan becomes physically aroused (tense, accelerated heart rate, hot) and then labels those feelings by stating, "you make me so mad when you push ahead of me."

Using self-talk to teach anger management makes good sense in that we are helping children recognize and refocus their use of a familiar technique for their own benefit. "Self-talk can help children break or reverse the cycle of anger escalation by substituting positive coping statements and psychological techniques to reduce the physical arousal pattern" (Beland, 1992, p. 47).

Anger management is a multidimensional process consisting of empathy training, impulse control, problem solving, and strengths training. These components are taught in the following sequence in helping children channel their angry feelings in socially acceptable ways (Schmidt, 1993; Beland, 1992).

Help children recognize that they are angry. Children need assistance in identifying the bodily signs (internal and external) of anger that they experience when fully aroused. Some examples of bodily signs are fast heart rate, muscle tension, hostile thoughts, sweaty palms, raised voice, etc.

Help children accept their anger. Children need to recognize that they are angry and that though angry feelings are uncomfortable, angry feelings do not make them bad people. Help them accept that their feelings of anger are normal and are experienced by all human beings.

Teach children how to calm down when first overcome by anger. Relaxation training can benefit children in times of anger. They can learn to take deep breaths; imagine pleasant thoughts; and engage in calming, positive self-talk. "Stay calm, I'm going to be OK. These feelings will pass."

Have children decide if their problem is something they can or cannot change. Some problems cannot be changed because they require other people to change their behaviors. For example, Billy's parents have recently divorced. Billy is angry with his parents and wants them back together. Because Billy cannot change his parents, he must look at ways that he can change himself in dealing with his anger in a positive way. If a child is angry about a problem that can not be changed, that child can (a) learn to accept what can't be changed and (b) express his or her anger in positive and safe ways (exercise, punch a pillow, draw, write a letter, or talk to someone). If the problem can be changed, encourage children to use 3 R's problem solving. Help them channel their anger into positive energy in generating 3 R's solutions.

Have children think out loud to solve their problems. After the children have decided that they can resolve their problem, teach them to use the 3 R's problem solving process. The process works best when children are asked to verbalize their thoughts as they go through each step. This helps them stay focused in using a tool (3 R's) with which they are unfamiliar. Other children in the group can benefit from hearing the process verbalized and can offer assistance to each other as needed. Out loud problem solving also provides the kind of useful reinforcement and helpful feedback that results in responsible learning.

Have children study their options based on "Right, Reality, and Responsibility." As children filter their choices (options), they increase the odds in their favor of selecting solutions that will be helpful to themselves and others. Using the 3 R's requires children to pause long enough between Stop and Go to break old habits based more on impulse than reason. The filtering process is designed to help children think about helpful versus harmful ways to express their anger.

Have children create and implement their plan. Children will need assistance in developing the chosen solution to their problem. They will need a behavioral plan detailing each step leading to goal attainment. Strengths training and role-playing should be used to help ensure success.

Help children evaluate how they handled their anger. This can be done by asking a few reflective questions such as

What were you angry about?
How did you feel?
What did you want to do?
What did you do?
Did it work?
What did not work?
What changes would you make?
How would you evaluate your success in using Anger Management?

Anger management requires the application and practice of appropriate anger-control strategies and anger-reducing self-talk. The more that children understand about anger and how it affects their own behavior, the better prepared they will be to accept and apply anger management practices to their own lives.

MESSAGE TO FACILITATORS

All children can benefit from participating in an anger management program because all children experience feelings of anger and must decide how those feelings will be expressed. Anger can be used as a positive motivator for the purpose of doing good or it can be channeled into acts of aggression or turned inwardly and experienced as depression.

Your role must be one of providing children with an opportunity to interact with each other in a safe environment for the purpose of helping them explore their feelings, thoughts, values, attitudes, and hopes concerning anger and anger control. Many of the children in your group may not know how to regulate their emotions safely and responsibly. They may come from homes where parents as well have not learned to manage their emotions responsibly.

Many children are afraid to feel; they pretend that they are without feelings. They live in fear of becoming overcome with their emotions or losing control of their emotions. No matter how hard they try to control their emotions, they find their emotions in control of them. One of the emotions that children and adults fear most and understand least is anger. They believe that anger is a bad emotion and that they are bad because they sometimes feel angry. When "bad children" experience anger, they respond in "bad ways" or try to "stuff their anger," because they do not want others to see them that way.

Many children harbor the following inaccurate beliefs about anger and these inaccuracies are effecting how they respond to feelings of anger in their lives.

Anger is a bad feeling.
Children who experience anger are bad people.
Anger is not a normal emotion and should not be displayed.
Only certain people get angry; it doesn't happen to everyone.
Anger is synonymous with aggression and violence.
The only way to get rid of anger is to act it out.
Feelings of anger will not go away on their own.
Other people/children are responsible for "my anger."
When children feel angry, there is nothing positive they can do for themselves to feel better.
Angry feelings cannot be tolerated by anyone.
Angry feelings just happen; they cannot be prevented.

Much of your work in group will be spent helping children understand the realities of anger and how to manage their anger in socially acceptable ways.

Basic Facts

More specifically, you will be helping children challenge their myths about anger by addressing the following facts on the subject (Schmidt, 1993).

The use of violence to express anger is unacceptable.
Children are responsible for choosing responsible and nonviolent ways to express anger.

Feelings are neither good nor bad, right nor wrong. They just are.

Learning to THINK between STOP and GO (3 R's decision making) will enable children to choose 3 R's ways of expressing their feelings.

There are six ways to express anger: stuffing, withdrawing, blaming, triangling, exploding, and problem solving (Schmidt, 1993).

Children and parents usually love each other despite the fact that some parents choose to use violent ways to express their anger and their children are angry with them for doing so.

When children are angry about a problem that they can not change, they can learn to accept the unchangeable, find positive ways to let their anger go, and do nice things for themselves.

When children are angry about a problem they can change, they should channel their anger into 3 R's problem solving in search of nonviolent solutions.

Anger management (process) helps children control their impulses by converting habitual, thoughtless responses to ones based on thought and reason.

The steps of anger management help children

- recognize their anger;
- accept their anger;
- calm down when overcome by anger;
- decide if their problem is one they can or cannot change;
- think out loud to solve their problem;
- explore their options based on Right, Reality, and Responsibility;
- create and implement their plan (a 3 R's solution); and
- evaluate how they handled their anger.

Anger can be a positive motivating force for bringing about positive and helpful change.

Children can learn to manage their anger in nonviolent, peaceful ways.

Group Selection

You are encouraged to follow the general guidelines for group selection found in Chapter 3. Give particular attention to your group's composition. Be sure not to overload your group with children who are violent or particularly aggressive in their handling of anger. As we have indicated, all children can benefit from learning about anger and how to manage it productively. Therefore, try to balance your group's composition with children who can serve as positive role models and who possess some anger coping skills. To do otherwise could very well result in a group that will be out of control and very difficult to manage. Remember that your group sessions are few in number so you will not want to spend a lot of time focusing on inappropriate and non-supportive behaviors.

Group Process

Help children explore the various social situations that trigger angry feelings in them. They may mention such things as the following:

- being cut ahead of in line,
- other children taking things of theirs without asking,
- seeing other children cheat on tests,
- enduring name calling and teasing,
- being bullied by others,
- not being invited to participate in a particular activity,
- children wanting to copy their school work,
- being told by others they can't do something that they want to do,
- being ridiculed by a parent or teacher, and
- trying to succeed at something and failing.

Help children see that everyday events can engender anger depending on how their personal beliefs, attitudes, thoughts, and values are impacted by the event or situation. How children perceive others' actions also can be a significant factor in understanding violence and aggression. Some children, because of misconceived notions about others, may interpret the smallest slight as an act of hostility toward them. Children may believe that everyone is out to get them and act accordingly.

Your role must be one of helping children understand that it is not events or people that cause anger but their interpretations of both. They will need assistance in learning to interpret their beliefs and to evaluate their responses when confronting events, people, or situations that are upsetting to them. Children need to understand that they are responsible for their own behaviors and that they do have choices with regard to their actions. Your support group members will want to learn more about anger, how they cope with their angry feeling, and develop new coping skills that will help them become more effective anger managers. More specifically you will want to help children

- understand that anger is a normal emotion;
- understand that anger is not a bad emotion, instead, how they manage their anger can have helpful or hurtful consequences;

- discriminate helpful versus hurtful responses;
- recognize internal and external signs of anger within themselves;
- learn impulse control techniques (strengths) that will slow down their anger responses giving them time to think before they act;
- explore a variety of ways in which they can manage life's frustrations and disappointments in nonviolent ways;
- learn and practice their own anger management plan;
- understand that anger either can be a positive motivating force leading to responsible action or it can be a prelude to aggression and violence—the choice is theirs;
- apply what they have learned about themselves and anger management to life situations outside the group experience; and
- review what they have learned about themselves and anger through their support group experience.

Remember that children learn to act prosocially through modeling, practice, and positive reinforcement. Much of what they will learn about anger management will come from the group experience. Use the support group experience to model empathy, impulse control, problem solving, strengths training, and anger management. Provide children with the opportunity to affect their environment (in and out of group) in positive ways and to experience a variety of emotions (e.g., pride, happiness, security, belonging, and feeling loved) in your anger management support group.

The time has come for you to meet your group and to begin a journey of self-exploration, self-understanding, and practicing new ways of coping with anger. Good luck and much success with your anger management support group.

Resources

Share with parents and/or guardians Figure 8.1 so that they will have suggestions on how they can help their children. In Figure 8.2 are provided lists of resources to be used with and by children in the Anger Management Support Group. The resource materials are grouped according to age of child.

ANGER MANAGEMENT GUIDE
Tips for Caregivers

Your child soon will be participating in an Anger Management Support Group. The goal of this support group is to help children better understand the emotion of anger and how they can redirect their feelings in positive ways. We are offering you a few tips that you can use at home with your children. Children who learn to manage their anger in positive and socially acceptable ways are more likely to develop lasting peer and adult relationships and generally do better in school. Help your child understand the following ideas:

1. The use of violent or aggressive behavior as an expression of anger is unacceptable. Fighting, hitting, and hurtful words are not okay even when you are angry.

2. All feelings are okay. How you express your feelings is what matters.

3. Children can become angry when they are teased, called names, not allowed to play with others, when things do not go the right way for them, and when their feelings are hurt by others. Have your children talk about things, situations, events, and people that cause them to become angry.

4. When children become angry, they experience different signs of anger on the inside and the outside. Children may tense their muscles, get red in the face, have a knot in their stomach, get sweaty palms, talk loudly, feel like crying, and have angry and hurtful thoughts toward others. Ask your children to describe the signs of anger that they experience.

5. When children become angry, they handle their anger in different ways. Children may pretend not to be angry, blame others for their anger, withdraw from the anger-producing situation, explode, and solve their problems by brainstorming helpful and responsible ideas that they can try. Have your children discuss how they handle their angry feelings.

6. Solutions to angry situations can be helpful or hurtful. Discuss with your children the differences between helpful and hurtful responses to anger.

7. Children who have the most success in handling their anger in positive and responsible ways are those that have a plan for doing so. What follows is an anger management plan that you can use with your children. This plan will help your children learn what they can do about angry feelings. The steps are as follows:

Step 1: **How am I feeling right now?** What bodily signs are you experiencing that help you know that you are angry?

Step 2: **Calm down.** Before the feelings become too strong and over-powering, help your children reduce their anger by taking deep breaths; thinking pleasant thoughts; and telling them-selves to calm down—"I'm OK, things will get better, etc."

Step 3: **Problem Solve.**

> **STOP**—What is my problem? Have your children describe their problem—what has happened.
>
> **THINK**—What are my choices? (Help your children make a list of all the things that they could do. After making the list, consider each solution separately by asking "Will this solution help or hurt me, others, or property?" "What evidence do I have that tells me this is the right thing to do?" "What are the consequences?" "What are the good things and bad things that could happen to me or others if I pick this solution?"
>
> **GO**—Go with a solution that is helpful, safe, supported by facts, and is likely to have positive consequences.

Step 4: **Evaluate.** After you have acted on your choice, think about what happened. What did you do? How did you feel? Did it work? Was it the right thing to do (helpful vs. hurtful)? What might you have done differently? Are you satisfied with how you handled your anger?

You can be a positive role model for your children by demonstrating positive and acceptable methods in expressing your own anger. You like-wise can catch your children modeling appropriate methods of anger management and positively reinforce them for their actions.

Let your children know that hitting, biting, screaming, and temper tan-trums are unacceptable expressions of anger. Let your children know that you understand their anger. Tell them that there are positive things that they can do to help them get rid of their uncomfortable feelings such as punching a pillow, going outside and playing, and using the anger management 4-step plan that we have provided for your use.

If anger becomes excessive and persistent in your child despite all your efforts to understand and correct it, consult a professional counselor for help. Your local school district or community mental health services may also be able to provide assistance.

Figure 8.1. Tips for Caregivers to be given to parents and/or guardians. Permission to photocopy is granted.

RESOURCES FOR CHILDREN
Anger Management

Ages 3 to 7

Alexander, M. (1972). *And my mean old mother will be sorry, Blackboard Bear.* New York: Dial Press. (getting angry, imaginary activity)

Berridge, C. (1992). *Hannah's temper.* New York: Scholastic. (anger when everything goes wrong)

Erickson, K., & Roffey, M. (1987). *I was so mad.* New York: Viking Penguin. (anger, self-discipline)

Everitt, B. (1992). *Mean soup.* San Diego: Harcourt Brace. (anger, getting help from adults)

Joosse, B. M. (1989). *Dinah's mad bad wishes.* New York: Harper Collins. (anger, meaning of love)

Lasky, K. (1993). *The tantrum.* New York: Macmillan. (anger, temper tantrums)

Rogers, F. (1987). *Making friends.* New York: Putnam & Grossett Group. (accepting emotions)

Shapiro, L. (1994). *The very angry day that Amy didn't have.* King of Prussia, PA: Childswork/Childsplay. (anger, problem solving)

Viorst, J. (1988). *The good-bye book.* New York: Atheneum Publishers. (anger, separation anxiety)

Waber, B. (1988). *Ira says goodbye.* Boston: Houghton Mifflin. (anger, accepting change)

Ages 8 to 12

Betancourt, J. (1983). *The rainbow kid.* New York: Avon Books. (anger at divorce of parents)

Carris, J. (1990). *Aunt Morbelia and the screaming skulls.* Boston: Little, Brown. (anger, fear, dealing with learning disabilities)

Faber, A., & Mazlish, E. (1994). *Bobby and the Brockles.* New York: Avon Books. (compromising to handle anger)

Geller, M. (1987). *What I heard.* New York: Harper Collins. (anger-trust issues)

Merriam, E. (1992). *Fighting words.* West Caldwell, NJ: Morrow and Company. (name calling)

Moser, A. (1994). *Don't rant and rave on Wednesdays: A children's anger control book.* Kansas City, MO: Landmark Editions. (anger reduction techniques)

Osborne, M. P. (1986). *Last one home.* New York: Dial Press. (anger, resisting change)

Snyder, C. (1987). *Leave me alone, Ma.* New York: Bantam Doubleday Dell. (anger, parental absence)

Townsend, J. R. (1988). *Rob's Place.* New York: Lothrop, Lee and Shepard Books. (anger, feelings of loss)

Woolverton, L. (1987). *Running before the wind.* Boston: Houghton Mifflin. (anger, physical abuse)

Ages 12 and Up

Adler, C. S. (1987). *Carly's back.* Boston: Clarion Books. (anger, feelings of guilt)

Calvert, P. (1986). *Yesterday's daughter.* New York: Charles Scribner's Sons. (anger, abandonment)

Fox, P. (1986). *The moonlight man.* New York: Bradbury Press. (anger, parental unreliability)

Hoffman, A. (1988). *At risk.* New York: Putnam and Grossett Group. (anger, fear, rejection, AIDS)

Klass, S. S. (1986). *Page four.* New York: Charles Scribner's Sons. (anger, maturation)

Meyer, C. (1989). *Wild Rover.* New York: Margaret K. McElderry Books. (anger, parent-child communication)

Pfeffer, S. B. (1987). *The year without Michael.* New York: Bantam Doubleday Dell. (anger, fear, emotional abuse)

Talbert, M. (1985). *Dead birds singing.* New York: Little, Brown, and Company. (anger, grief issues)

White, E. E. (1987). *Live without friends.* New York: Scholastic. (anger, guilt, ostracism)

Willey, M. (1986). *Finding David Dolores.* New York: Harper & Row Publishers. (anger, friendship)

Figure 8.2. Resources for use with and by children in Anger Management Support Group.

SESSION I—WHAT BUGS YOU?

BRIEF OVERVIEW OF SESSION

This session will serve as an introduction for the children to group process. It also will provide an opportunity for the children to become acquainted, to share at least one thing that makes them angry, and to realize that everyone in the group is interested in learning how to deal more effectively with anger.

GOALS

1. To provide the structure and purpose for the group.
2. To help children realize that the need to learn to manage anger more appropriately is common to all group members.
3. To encourage each child to identify at least one anger-producing situation.

MATERIALS NEEDED

1. Various colors of construction paper
2. Pipe cleaners
3. Scissors
4. Paste or glue
5. Chart paper
6. Markers

PROCEDURE

1. Introduce yourself and have each of the group members introduce himself or herself by first name. Tell the children that everyone in the group is interested in learning to manage anger more effectively. During the course of this group, we will begin to talk about the causes of anger, reactions to anger, and coping with anger.

2. Begin to set the stage for the group by discussing ground rules. List the ground rules on a chart or on the chalkboard for future reference. Examples of possible group rules are as follows:

a   What is said in the group, stays there.
b   No put-downs are allowed.
c   Only one person talks at a time.
d   It is important to attend all sessions.

Note: If children do not suggest these rules, you as facilitator should bring them up as part of the brainstorming process.

3. Introduce the topic of anger with the question, "What are some things that really bug you?" Provide plenty of time for the children to identify these anger causing situations.

4. Provide construction paper, glue, scissors, and other work materials, and tell the children that they are going to make "bugs" for the bulletin board to describe some things that really "bug" them. Tell them that these bugs can be as strange, way out, and weird as they want them to be.

5. Allow enough time for the artistic bug creations to be developed. (While the children are working, continue to talk about the anger producing situations and allow for general group chatter.)

6. When each bug is completed, allow each child to place his or her bug on the bulletin board. Beneath the bug, place a piece of paper or notecard that describes the situation that "bugs" that child.

7. When all bugs have been placed on the bulletin board, allow time for each child to tell about his or her bug and anger-producing situation.

CLOSURE

To bring closure to this session, tell the children that everyone has things that bug them and that anger is a perfectly legitimate feeling. What gets us all in difficulty is our response to that anger. Remind the children that in the upcoming weeks, we will begin to identify ways to deal more productively with that anger.

HOMEWORK

For homework, ask the children to begin to think about the things they do when they get angry and what have been some of the consequences of that anger. This will be the topic for next week's session.

SESSION II—DON'T EXPLODE

BRIEF OVERVIEW OF SESSION

In this session, children will begin to look at the consequences of "exploding" anger, how it causes problems both for them and for the people around them. They also will begin to look seriously at ways to help them deal more effectively with their anger.

GOALS

1. To assist children in looking critically at their reactions to anger-provoking situations.
2. To begin to present some techniques for more effectively handling anger.
3. To provide time for practicing the techniques through role-play.

MATERIALS

1. Balloon.
2. Role-play situations on 3" × 5" cards

PROCEDURE

1. Briefly review the anger-provoking situations that were identified in the previous session. Ask the children to describe their reactions to those situations.

2. Show the deflated balloon to the children and compare it to how we are prior to the anger-provoking situation. Then begin to blow it up a little at a time and compare it to what happens when anger builds up in us. Continue to blow the balloon almost to the breaking point and compare this to the explosion of our anger when we get out of control.

3. Ask the children how we can keep the balloon from popping. Show them what happens when we let the air out a little at a time. Compare this to finding ways to talk out our anger and letting out angry feelings out a "little bit at a time." Provide a few moments to allow the children to describe times that they were able to diffuse their anger by talking things out with someone who cares about them. Remind them to think about the balloon experiment as a way of handling anger-provoking situations.

4. Present the following anger-provoking situation for the children: "You have worked very hard to earn enough money to go to the movies with your friend and his parents. Now your mother is refusing to allow you to go because you failed your spelling test yesterday (even though you had studied very hard for it)."

5. Discuss the situation in terms of (a) What could you do? and (b) What would happen if you did that?

6. After you have discussed several options, encourage group members to role-play the child and his or her mother in a discussion of the situation. Talk about the effects of "blowing one's cool" as a possible reaction.

7. Encourage role-play of the other role-play situations as listed below (each may be printed on a 3" × 5" card).

a A friend wants to borrow your homework and tells you that if you do not share it he will tell the teacher you copied from Davy Smith.
b Someone in your class took 25 cents from the teacher's desk. Because you sit closest to the teacher, you are being blamed.
c The principal gives you two nights' detention for running in the hall. The girl who was running with you didn't get any detention.

CLOSURE

Following the role-plays, bring closure to the session by telling the children that not all anger-provoking situations are "fair"; that is what makes it so frustrating. However, we need to find some appropriate ways to deal with the situations rather than exploding. Again, blow up the balloon and let the air out slowly as a reminder to "let off steam" a little bit at a time.

HOMEWORK

For a homework assignment, ask the children to make a list of five clues to anger for them. These may be physical reactions, emotional reactions, or cognitive (thinking) reactions. Provide a 3" × 5" card for each child to make his or her list.

SESSION III—CLUES TO MY ANGER

BRIEF OVERVIEW OF SESSION

In this session, children will begin to personalize anger producing situations in terms of the clues that may precede an anger response from them. These clues will be categorized in terms of whether they are physical, emotional or "thinking" clues.

GOALS

1. To assist children in gaining an awareness of physical, emotional, or cognitive clues to anger.
2. To help students identify their personal response to anger.

MATERIALS NEEDED

1. Copies of "Anger Anecdotes" worksheet (Activity Sheet 8.1)
2. Chart
3. Markers

PROCEDURE

1. Begin by discussing the reality that anger does not just happen, that there are situations or "triggers" that provoke anger. These situations are followed by some type of reaction from us that is either physical (in the body), emotional (in the feelings), or cognitive (in the mind).

2. Ask the children to share items from their homework assignment in terms of how anger-provoking situations most often affect them. Categorize them on a chart in the following manner:

Physical	Emotional	Cognitive
Face gets flushed	Yelling	Thinking about getting in
Fists clench	Crying	trouble—someone talking
Stomach gets tight	Name calling	about you, etc.
Heart pounds		

3. Discuss the anger clues that seem most common among group members. Ask the following questions:

a   What do you most often do when you get angry?
b   What can you do with this awareness?
c   Will you be alert to these clues in the future?

4. Work with the children on suggestions for avoiding these angry responses. List the brainstormed ideas on the chart. Some of these ideas may include

a   Find a way to relax (deep breathing, counting).
b   Try ignoring the situation.
c   Talk yourself out of anger by using calming self-talk (e.g., "I can deal with this.").
d   Think about what will happen if you follow through on your angry response.
e   Walk away.

CLOSURE

Ask the children to talk about how any of the suggestions have worked for them and what were the positive effects of the actions.

HOMEWORK

As a homework assignment, ask the children to keep track of anger-producing situations and their reactions for the week. This record should be kept on the Anger Anecdote worksheet (Activity Sheet 8.1).

Anger Anecdotes

WHAT HAPPENED?	WHO WAS INVOLVED?	HOW DID YOU REACT?
_____	_____	_____
_____	_____	_____
_____	_____	_____
_____	_____	_____
_____	_____	_____
_____	_____	_____
_____	_____	_____
_____	_____	_____
_____	_____	_____
_____	_____	_____
_____	_____	_____
_____	_____	_____
_____	_____	_____
_____	_____	_____

Activity Sheet 8.1.   Anger Anecdotes worksheet. Permission is granted to enlarge and photocopy for classroom use.

SESSION IV—STAYING IN CONTROL

BRIEF OVERVIEW OF SESSION

In this session, the children will have an opportunity to look at how their feelings, thoughts and what they tell themselves about a situation influence how they act. They will have an opportunity to learn and practice ways to cope with anger in more productive ways.

GOALS

1. To assist children in understanding that our reactions to anger are often precipitated by what we tell ourselves about the situation.
2. To provide opportunities for children to utilize coping statements to help them control anger.
3. To encourage children to utilize the coping statements they practiced in real life situations.

MATERIALS NEEDED

1. Copies of "Coping Statements" worksheet (Activity Sheet 8.2)
2. Situations for role-plays (taken from children's "Anger Anecdotes" worksheets from Session III)

PROCEDURE

1.   Provide a few minutes at the beginning of the session for the children to share information from their "Anger Anecdotes" worksheets (Activity Sheet 8.1). (Save some of these situations for role-plays after they have discussed the coping statements.)

2.   Ask the children the following questions about their anger-producing situations:

    a   What was your reaction?
    b   Did you get what you wanted as a result of your anger?
    c   What were the consequences of your anger?
    d   Did you try to think of a better way to handle the situation?

3.   Explain to the children that today we are going to look at one way to deal more appropriately with our anger by using "self-talk." (Provide a brief

description of self-talk and give an example, such as, If someone tells me I have on a weird looking outfit, I could get mad or I could say to myself, "Well, she doesn't like my outfit, but then I don't like everything she wears either. We just have different tastes in clothes.")

4. Give the children a copy of the "Coping Statements" worksheets (Activity Sheet 8.2) and allow a few moments for them to read and react to them. Ask if they feel that using "self-talk" to tell themselves these positive things might help diffuse their anger.

5. Use one of the anger-producing situations from the "Anger Anecdotes" and have two of the children role-play the situation, first using the anger reaction, then using "self-talk" from the "Coping Statements" worksheet as a possible option.

6. Discuss the differences with the children. Suggest that once they become comfortable with using this technique, they often will be able to diffuse their own anger and not have it escalate into a blowup.

CLOSURE

Ask the children to use the information they learned in today's session when they become involved in anger-producing situations. Remind them that we will again discuss this technique briefly next session.

HOMEWORK

Provide another "Anger Anecdotes" worksheet for each child and encourage the children to use the statements from the "Coping Statements" worksheet to deal with anger-producing situations this week.

Coping Statements

Things I can say to myself:

This will pass, my life will get better.

It's okay to be temporarily upset.

I am able to remain calm.

I am not a helpless person.

I will do what I have to do to deal with this.

I am a unique and capable person.

I will not overreact to this situation.

I will deal with it. I will not hide from it.

I will do the best I can.

I have come a long way. I can do it.

It's okay to make mistakes.

I won't sweat the small stuff.

In the future, will this seem like such a major issue?

Activity Sheet 8.2. Coping Statements worksheet. Permission is granted to enlarge and photocopy for classroom use.

SESSION V—OUR ACTIONS

BRIEF OVERVIEW OF SESSION

In this session, the children will begin to differentiate between appropriate and inappropriate responses to anger-producing situations. Since they have been practicing coping skills, they now need to begin to identify appropriate ways to handle anger on an ongoing basis in everyday life situations.

GOALS

1. To assist children in identifying and differentiating appropriate and inappropriate responses to anger.
2. To help children role-play appropriate responses to anger.
3. To provide an opportunity for children to begin to realize that, if they can handle anger-producing situations appropriately, they will be more effective communicators in everyday life situations.

MATERIALS NEEDED

1. 3" × 10" sheets of poster paper with words "Appropriate" and "Inappropriate" written on them
2. Situations from "Anger Anecdotes" worksheets for role-plays

PROCEDURE

1. Encourage the children to share items from their "Anger Anecdotes" in which they used the "Coping Statements" that they learned last session. Spend a few minutes talking about times when the statements were successful and when they were not successful. (Save some of the unsuccessful situations for role-playing later on in this session.)

2. Place the cards with "Appropriate" and "Inappropriate" written on them on the wall where the children can see them. Remind them that today we are going to discuss these two terms in relation to reactions that they feel would fall into each category. Then provide the following scenarios and have the children discuss whether the reaction was "Appropriate" or "Inappropriate." The 3 R's Decision Making Model can be used to evaluate "appropriate" and "inappropriate."

a When it was snowing out and Mary could not go to the movies with her friends, she slammed her bedroom door and spent the afternoon in her room.

b When Chad hit his hand with the hammer, he cursed loudly and threw the hammer in the closet.

c When Stacy heard that the other girls were gossiping about her, she just ignored them and played with her other friends.

d When Tom was teased for missing the basket in the basketball game, he gave the other guys the "silent treatment" for the next week.

3. After discussion of each of the situations, have the children role-play the situation and use an "appropriate" action to play out the scenario. Following the role-plays, talk with the children about their feelings about using more appropriate reactions:

a What are the benefits?

b What are the frustrations?

c How will it help in the long run?

4. Select one or more of the items from the "Anger Anecdotes" and discuss how an "appropriate" response could have helped in that situation.

CLOSURE

Encourage the children to practice using more appropriate reactions to anger-producing situations. With frequent use, these reactions will become a part of their daily actions.

HOMEWORK

For a homework assignment, ask each child to be prepared to talk about one anger situation that he or she felt was handled in a way that made him/her feel proud of himself or herself.

SESSION VI—WAYS PEOPLE EXPRESS ANGER

BRIEF OVERVIEW OF SESSION

In this session, the children learn that everyone has different styles of handling and expressing anger. They will look at six different ways that people deal with anger. They will identify which of the methods best describes their reaction to anger.

GOALS

1. To assist children in understanding that people handle anger in different ways.
2. To present six different ways people handle anger.
3. To help children identify which of the six ways most appropriately describes their reaction to anger.

MATERIALS NEEDED

1. Chart on the "Six Ways of Handling Anger" (adapted from Schmidt [1993], *Anger Management and Violence Prevention,* Minneapolis, Johnson Institute) as shown in Procedure #2
2. 3" × 5" card for each child

PROCEDURE

1. Allow a few minutes for the children to describe their successes from the previous week. Congratulate them on their hard work in trying to deal more appropriately with their anger-producing situations.

2. Show the chart on the "Six Ways of Handling Anger" (Schmidt, 1993) and describe each of the six types. The six types are as follows:

Stuffers—People who are stuffers tend to avoid anger at any cost. They always want things to be peaceful. They often have a lot of tension inside like the balloon that is just about to pop.
Withdrawers—These people hide their anger by ignoring situations, avoiding communication with others, or just by doing something else. They never get a chance to solve the underlying problem.
Blamers—People who are blamers tend to blame their anger on others: parents, teachers, other kids. They are not willing to accept responsibility for their own actions.

Trianglers—These people handle their anger by trying to pull other persons into the situation. For example, a girl who is angry at a friend may try to get another friend on her side. The problem with this technique is that the person never gets to the root of the problem.

Exploders—People who are exploders use violence to express their anger. This may show itself through hitting, pushing, and yelling. A major problem with this way of dealing with anger is that one never knows what to expect.

Problem Solvers—These people handle their anger by thinking about the situation and their feelings about it. They decide if it is a situation they can do something about and how they can handle it.

3. Present a situation to the group and ask if they can describe how each of the six styles would handle the situation. Use an actual problem from the group or pose one of the following situations:

a Mary was friends with Sally for many years but then Erin came to the school. Now Erin and Sally are friends and Mary feels left out.

b Charlie worked very hard on his science worksheet and was sure he would get an A. When he went to the office on an errand for the teacher, Mark copied all of the answers from his paper. Now the teacher is going to give both of the boys an F for cheating.

4. Role-play the situations based on the six anger styles.

CLOSURE

Ask the children to think about how they most often handle their anger situations and which of the six types best describes them.

HOMEWORK

As a homework assignment, ask the children to keep a list of at least three anger situations they deal with during the week and describe which of the anger styles they used to react to each. Provide a 3" × 5" card for them to list the situations and their reactions.

SESSION VII—CHANGING ANGRY THINKING

BRIEF OVERVIEW OF SESSION

In this session, children will begin to look systematically at their anger-producing situations and work on ways to "rethink" the situation for more productive problem resolution.

GOALS

1. To help children realize that "rethinking" a situation may help them see the scenario in a more positive light.
2. To provide an opportunity for the children to practice this technique so that they will feel more comfortable using it in everyday life situations.

MATERIALS NEEDED

1. Situations from "Anger Anecdotes" (from Sessions III, IV, and V)
2. Chart with the following headings:

What was the situation?
What did you think about it?
How did you feel about it?
What else could you have thought that would be more positive?

3. Copies of "Positive Thinking Worksheet" (Activity Sheet 8.3) for homework

PROCEDURE

1. Provide a bit of time for the children to share their three situations from the homework assignment. Ask if their knowledge of the six styles of handling anger made them more aware of how they react to anger-producing situations.

2. Tell the children that today we are going to further consider situations and learn a new way to think about those situations in a more positive light.

3. Present the following situation to the children.

Sharon has been having a lot of problems making friends at her new school. She has tried being nice to the kids and sharing things with them, but she often sees them whispering and looking in her direction.

4. Use the questions from the chart to assist the children in discussing Sharon's situation. An example of how this might work out would be

a   What was the situation? (see description above)
b   What did Sharon think? (e.g., that the kids were making fun of her, that they didn't want to be her friends)
c   How did Sharon feel? (e.g., sad, left out, disappointed, lonely)
d   What else could she have thought that would be a bit more positive? (e.g., *Since I am new here, it may take a bit more time for the kids to get to know me—I guess I just have to give them a little time.*)

5. Select one or two situations from the "Anger Anecdotes" for discussion and evaluation using the questions above.

CLOSURE

Bring closure to this session by encouraging the children to begin to use the technique learned this session in their everyday life situations.

HOMEWORK

Provide copies of the "Positive Thinking Worksheet" (Activity Sheet 8.3) for the children and ask that they complete it for one of their anger-producing situations during the upcoming week.

Note: An expanded anger management process is described on pages 226 and 227 that can be used with older children.

Positive Thinking Worksheet

1. Describe the situation._____

_____

2. What did you think?_____

_____

3. How did you feel?_____

_____

4. What could you have thought that would have been more positive?_____

_____

_____

Activity Sheet 8.3.   Positive Thinking Worksheet. Permission is granted to enlarge and photocopy for classroom use.

SESSION VIII—PRODUCTIVE PROBLEM SOLVING

BRIEF OVERVIEW OF SESSION

In this session, children will have an opportunity to look at problem-solving techniques as a way to deal more appropriately with life situations. They also will become acquainted with passive, aggressive, and assertive reactions to situations.

GOALS

1. To assist children in realizing that there are some situations in their lives that they cannot change.
2. To help children become familiar with passive, aggressive, and assertive reactions to life situations.
3. To present problem-solving suggestions.
4. To bring closure to the group by having children validate each other.

MATERIALS NEEDED

1. Chart with "Passive," "Assertive," and "Aggressive" and their definitions

   Passive—handle conflict by doing nothing
   Aggressive—handle conflict by harming others (verbally or physically)
   Assertive—handle conflict by using problem solving

2. Student "Name Sheets" (a sheet of paper for each child with the child's name on it) for validation activity

PROCEDURE

1. Spend a few moments encouraging the children to share items from their homework assignment. Congratulate them for the efforts they have made to change their thinking as a way to handle anger.

2. Show children the chart with the words "Passive," "Aggressive," and "Assertive" on it. Explain each of the terms and give an example of how each conflict style may be played out using the following situation:

> *Joe and Charlie have been having a conflict over a library book that Joe borrowed from Charlie. When Charlie put the*

book in his locker to return it to Joe, it was stolen. Joe wants his book back.

Passive—Joe pays for the book and does not mention it again.
Aggressive—Joe beats Charlie up after school.
Assertive—Joe asks Charlie if they can meet to talk about what they will do about the lost book. They decide together on a situation that is agreeable to both.

3. Encourage children to talk about how the "Assertive" method of behavior will help them solve problems.

4. Provide "Name Sheets" for the validation activity. Ask each child to write something positive about every other person in the group on that person's name sheet.

5. Allow a few minutes for sharing.

CLOSURE

To bring closure to the group, encourage the children to share their feelings about group participation and complete the written evaluations.

HOMEWORK

Because this is the final session for the anger group, there will be no homework except to practice the skills they learned through participation in the Anger Management group.

EVALUATION

1. Do you feel that participation in the ANGER MANAGEMENT group was helpful to you? Why or why Not?

2. What part of the group did you like best?

3. What part of the group did you like least?

4. If you had a friend who needed help in dealing with anger, would you recommend that he or she participate in a similar group? Why or why not?

5. Did you attend all eight group sessions?

_____ Yes ____ No

If no, how many did you attend? _____

6. Comments, suggestions, etc.:

REFERENCES

Beland, K. (1992). *Second step: A violence-prevention curriculum, grades 1–3* (2nd ed.). Seattle, WA: Committee for Children.

Beland, K. (1988). *Second step, grades 1–3.* Seattle, WA: Committee for Children.

Beland, K. (1991). *Second step, preschool-kindergarten.* Seattle, WA: Committee for Children.

Beland, K. (1989). *Second step, grade 4–5.* Seattle, WA: Committee for Children.

Coie, J. D., Dodge, K. A., & Supersmidt, J. B. (1990). Peer group behavior and social status. In S. R. Asher & J. D. Coie (Eds.), *Peer rejection in childhood* (pp. 17–59). New York: Cambridge University Press.

Dodge, K. A. (1993). Social cognitive mechanisms in the development of conduct disorder and depression. *Annual Review of Psychology, 44,* 559–584.

Feindler, E. L., Marriott, S. A., & Iwata, M. (1984). Group anger control training for junior high school delinquents. *Cognitive Therapy & Research, 8,* 299–311.

Feshbach, N. D. (1984). Empathy, empathy training, and the regulation of aggression in elementary school children. In R. W. Kaplan, U. J. Koneani, & R. W. Novaco (Eds.), *Aggression in youth and children* (pp. 192–208). Boston, MA: Martinus Nijhoff Publications.

Hoffman, M. L. (1982). Development of prosocial motivation: Empathy and guilt. In N. Eisenberg (Ed.), *The Development of Prosocial Behavior* (pp. 281–311). San Diego, CA: Academic Press.

Lochman, J. E., & Lenhart, L. A. (1993). Anger coping intervention for aggressive children: Conceptual models and outcome effects. *Clinical Psychology Review, 13,* 785–805.

Olthof, T., Ferguson, T. J., & Luiten, A. (1989). Personal responsibility antecedents of anger and blame reactions on children. *Child Development, 60,* 1328–1336.

Rice, F. P. (1992). *Human development: A life-span approach.* New York: Macmillan.

Saltz, E., & Johnson, J. (1974). Training for thematic fantasy play in culturally disadvantaged children: Preliminary results. *Journal of Educational Psychology, 66,* 623–630.

Schmidt, T. M. (1993). *Anger management and violence prevention: A group activities manual for middle & high school students.* Minneapolis, MN: Johnson Institute.

Selman, R. L. (1980). *The growth of interpersonal understanding.* New York: Academic Press.

Spivack, G., & Cianci, N. (1987). High-risk early behavior pattern and later delinquency. In J. D. Burchard & S. N. Burchard (Eds.), *Prevention of delinquent behavior* (pp. 44–74). Newbury Park, CA: Sage Publication.

Stern, J. B., & Fodor, I. E. (1989). Anger control in children: A review of social skills and cognitive behavioral approaches to dealing with aggressive children. *Child & Family Behavior Therapy, 11*(3/4), 1–20.

Webster's ninth new collegiate dictionary. (1990). Springfield, MA: Merriam-Webster.

Chapter 9

CONFLICT MANAGEMENT

Conflict represents a state of opposition that occurs between two parties (individuals or groups) who are at odds with each other in their attempt to secure their respective wants or needs. Conflict management is a process that brings conflicting parties together in search of a peaceful settlement in attaining their respective goals.

BACKGROUND INFORMATION

Because children are not exactly alike coming from varying backgrounds, sharing different experiences, and living according to different values and beliefs, conflicts are bound to happen. They are a natural part of life and living. Without them, life would be uninteresting and not very challenging. With too many conflicts, life can become very stressful and anxiety ridden.

Children need to learn about conflicts and what causes them. They need to understand their benefits and pitfalls and how to develop the skills to prevent those that can be avoided, reduce the unnecessary, and peacefully resolve the seemingly unresolvable. Only then perhaps will we see a drop in childhood violence as a means of settling differences being replaced by more rational and responsible peacemaking alternatives.

Understanding Conflict

Understanding how conflict can emerge from a level of obscurity to heightened tension and "all out" confrontation is described by Hart (1981) in seven phases, which she referred to as the conflict cycle. Confrontation begins with *Anticipation* in which children (unconsciously or consciously) prepare for an anticipated attack on themselves by known or imagined challengers. Children brace themselves physically and mentally in response to cues from others (e.g., an angry face, mean spirited words) that conflict is a possibility.

Phase two takes on a *Wait and See* posture in which children gather information and assess the situation and those in it trying to decide what to do next. Unless the causes of the conflict are reduced or eliminated, however, the conflict will manage to keep *Growing* (phase three), moving from the possible to the very probable with respect to its occurrence.

In phase four, the conflict is *In the Open.* The parameters of the conflict come into sharper focus and both parties become more entrenched in their positions. Tensions rise and defenses are up. At this phase, one or both parties may choose to retreat from the conflict by denying its existence, giving in to the other party, or just suppressing the whole thing; however in the absence of a retreat, the two parties may choose to press on to phase five, *Application.* A single method or combination of methods are applied to resolve the conflict resulting in some form of *Settlement* (phase six). A truce is called and tensions are reduced as the two parties gradually shift gears getting back to other life activities. If the settlement was an amicable one, the two parties gradually may resume a more favorable relationship.

The last phase, and the one most overlooked, is *Reflection.* The parties involved are encouraged to review the conflict, their involvement in it, whether the conflict was settled to their liking, and what personal changes (attitudes, thoughts, actions) they would make in retrospect in achieving a more desired and peaceful settlement. *Reflection* gives both parties a chance to learn from conflict.

Causes of Conflicts

Thompson and Rudolph (1992) indicated that most of the problems that children experience can be divided into the five categories listed here.

1. *Interpersonal conflict.* Children have relationship problems with their peers, siblings, teachers, and parents.
2. *Intrapersonal conflict.* Children experience internal conflict in resolving personal problems in relationship to achieving their wants and needs.
3. *Lack of information about self.* Children have a need to understand and apply their abilities, strengths, interests, and values in attaining their goals.

4. *Lack of information about the environment.* Children need current and useful information about school, home, and community regarding legal, ethical, and moral principles that will help them discern right from wrong in all that they do.
5. *Lack of skill.* Children need to develop specific life skills that will help them make responsible life choices.

While Thompson and Rudolph focused on two categories of conflict experienced by children, the remaining three categories, in a limited sense, are related to conflict as well. Conflict occurs because children often lack information about themselves, the other party, the environmental conditions related to the conflict, and the skills required to reach win-win settlements.

With respect to specific examples contributing to interpersonal conflict between children and their peers, siblings, parents, and teachers, we offer the following: fighting, teasing, verbal and physical abuse, destructive behaviors, tantrums, tattling, swearing, lying, stealing, and competing with others. *Children are likely to engage in interpersonal conflicts when their values are at odds with their overpowering need for love and worth.*

Children, for example, may find themselves in a personal tug of war deciding whether or not to cheat on an exam, face their shyness or withdraw from others, face their tensions and anxieties responsibly or become truant, day dream or stay focused, become dependent on others or strive for autonomy, trying to be perfect or settle for self-improvement. These represent only a few of the wars that go on in some children's heads as they struggle to self-manage in the absence of self-knowledge, environmental understandings, and needed personal success skills.

Benefits and Pitfalls

Conflict is neither good nor bad nor is it right or wrong. Like power, conflict is a force with destructive and constructive potential. Therefore, conflict needs to be "harnessed" in ways so that children can benefit from the possibilities it has to offer. Conflict is beneficial when it

- clarifies both sides of an important issue;
- results in both parties being heard in a spirit of cooperation;
- focuses on problem identification and a win-win resolution;
- serves as a safe release of pent-up anxiety, stress, and emotion;
- helps children resolve their conflicts and invest in their relationship with each other; and

- becomes a learning experience providing opportunity for responsible conflict management.

Conflict is destructive (a pitfall) when it

- promotes name calling, labeling of others, and fighting;
- diverts attention away from the problem and a cooperative win-win solution;
- destroys children's sense of self-worth;
- polarizes individuals and groups and widens the gap between the parties in conflict; and
- promotes a win-lose competition fueled by deception and manipulation.

Fostering Constructive Relations

If children are to live in harmony with each other, they must be taught how to do so (Lantieri, 1995). While this chapter focuses primarily on conflict resolution, three other key components are necessary in providing children with the knowledge, attitudes, and skills that can foster constructive relations. These components are cooperative learning, the constructive use of controversy in teaching subject matter, and the creation of dispute resolution centers in schools. A brief description of each component follows.

Cooperative Learning.   There are five key components to cooperative learning. They are positive interdependence, face-to-face interaction, individual accountability, interpersonal and small group skills, and processing (Deutsch, 1993). Children are taught the value of *positive interdependence* in which they learn the importance of total group cooperation. Group members come to understand that it is to their advantage for all members of the group to succeed if the group as a whole is to attain success. Group projects that promote goal interdependence, task interdependence, the sharing of resources, and joint rewards are also promoting cooperative learning. Because children must work together *face-to-face* in order to succeed, they must learn to express themselves in ways that build strong, positive connections. Children in cooperative learning settings each must assume responsibility for completing their portion of the task and in supporting other group members in ways that will help insure the group's success. *Individual accountability* in achieving group goals is an essential ingredient in cooperative learning.

Learning to work together as a team is enhanced further when children are taught *interpersonal and small group skills*. This, coupled with children being taught group and task *processing* skills, allows for self-analysis and group analysis and ultimately self-improvement and group improvement in future cooperative learning ventures.

Constructive Use of Controversy. Johnson and Johnson (1987, 1992) have advocated the use of constructive controversy in teaching subject matter in the classroom as a means of promoting academic learning and the teaching of conflict resolution skills to children. Deutsch (1993) explained that the process of constructive controversy begins with the formation of equal size heterogeneous groups that are then assigned a topic to be discussed. Each small group is subdivided and assigned a position to take on the topic. For example, the topic could be one being discussed in science class regarding the cutting of the rain forest. Two students in a group of four would be assigned the task of supporting the cutting of the rain forest, and the remaining two would support the rain forest's preservation.

After each pair researches its position, the children are required to discuss their positions and reach a consensus on the issue. There are five phases to the process.

1. Pairs learn their respective positions and then present their positions to each other.
2. An open discussion follows in which each pair argues its position with conviction using the evidence collected.
3. The pairs engage in a perspective reversal in which they trade positions and present the opposite points of view as strongly and convincingly as they are able.
4. Following the perspective reversal, both pairs drop their advocacy positions and strive for a consensus position that is supported by the evidence.
5. In this the final phase, the group (four members) writes and presents its joint statement that includes a position rationale supported by the evidence.

Constructive controversy works because children are instructed to follow a prescribed set of operational rules. Those rules are (Deutsch, 1993) as follows:

> be critical of ideas not people;
> focus on making the best possible decision, not on winning;
> encourage everyone to participate;
> listen to everyone's ideas even if you do not agree;
> restate what someone has said even if it is not clear;

bring out the ideas and facts supporting both sides and then try to
put them together in a way that makes sense;
try to understand both sides of the issues; and
change your mind if the evidence clearly indicates that you should
do so. (p. 516)

Following the structured controversy, children are encouraged to identify
the skills used, the process applied, and the outcome achieved. Constructive
controversies is an engaging and stimulating process fostering the use of ana-
lytical decision making and communication skills. Although the existence of
systematic research on the process is limited, its potential is overwhelming.

Conflict Resolution.   Most child conflict resolution training programs seek
to instill attitudes, knowledge, and skills that are conducive to effective and
cooperative problem solving between and among the affected parties. Children
can be taught how to resolve conflicts in a cooperative and peacemaking environment (Lantieri, 1995).

Support Groups for Children teaches children how to accept disagreements;
agree to work toward win-win solutions; and to do so in ways that will strive
to improve relationships, increase self-esteem, and reduce tension among the
parties involved. While a number of child conflict resolution training programs
exist (Arrington, 1987, Deutsch, 1993; Drew 1987; Dysinger, 1993; Gentry &
Beneson, 1993; Lane & McWhirter, 1992; Maruyama, 1992; McClure, Miller,
& Russo, 1992; Morganett, 1994; Prutzman, Stern, Burger, & Bodenhamer, 1988)
there are common threads that seem to run throughout each in terms of the
process taught.

Basic objectives taught in conflict resolution training programs focus on
helping children

- establish a win-win philosophy;
- focus on problems and behaviors, not each other;
- express their feelings, needs, and wants in peaceful ways;
- listen to others' views rather than attack or react;
- define their problem(s);
- identify common ground on which they can agree;
- generate multiple options from which to choose;
- agree in principle and action to resolve their conflict by applying their
  plan; and
- learn and practice the skills of conflict resolution for future use when
  the need arises.

Conflict resolution training not only involves teaching children the process of resolving conflicts but also demands the guidance of an experienced facilitator to guide children through the process once it has been learned. Teachers, guidance counselors, parents, and students can become effective conflict mediators with training and supervised practice sessions. We will address peer mediation training later in this chapter.

Conflict resolution training can be described as a multi-step process in which children are taught how to identify and resolve conflicts in a manner that best meets the needs of those involved in a dispute. Children can be taught this process in small groups as illustrated in this book or in classroom size groups.

While there are many conflict resolution models used with children, the similarities far outweigh the differences. Essentially every model does the following in preparing children to resolve conflicts.

1. The purpose of conflict resolution training is explained.
2. Disputants agree that they want to solve their problem.
3. Rules to facilitate mediation are discussed with the disputants.

   Agree to solve the problem.
   No put-downs or name calling are allowed.
   Do not interrupt while others talk.
   Listen to what others are saying.
   Maintain confidentiality.
   Be truthful when presenting your side.

4. The disputants must agree to follow the rules before mediation can begin.
5. The mediator (group facilitator) agrees to confidentiality except in those cases where the welfare of the disputants or related parties is endangered.
6. The disputants are given individual talk time to describe what happened and how they feel about the situation.
7. The disputants repeat what they heard each other say and feel.
8. The disputants then are asked to define the problem and to state separately what they want.
9. Common ground (i.e., areas of agreement) is identified by the disputants. This becomes the basis on which to build a resolution.
10. Ideas for resolving the conflict are developed using brainstorming.
11. Disputants are asked to explain what they are willing to do to resolve the conflict.

12. Both disputants review the plans and agree to a solution.
13. A contract is developed describing the terms of the resolution that both parties sign.
14. The mediator congratulates the disputants for their hard work.
15. Disputants are encouraged to put the dispute behind them and to practice positive interactions with each other.

This process, as described, can and should be modified for children under 10 years of age. A simple four-step process works well with primary age children. Provide the children with a short story that presents a conflict and then ask the children to

1. Describe the conflict—What does each child want? How does each child feel?
2. Brainstorm some solutions to the problem.
3. Select solutions that will help both children win.
4. Role-play or discuss each solution. Ask children to select the solutions that they think are best for both children.

Peer Mediation.   Children can be taught to be peer mediators. Unlike the process described in conflict resolution where children learn how to resolve conflicts by being guided through the process by a group facilitator (mediator), the children are taught how to function as mediators. They not only must learn the steps involved in conflict resolution but also must learn how to guide their peers through that process. Peer mediation training first must begin with skilled mediators who have the ability to train others in the process. Most peer mediation programs for children require 16 or more hours of training and role-playing before child mediation teams (two children per team) are prepared to assist their peers in resolving conflicts (Deutsch, 1993; Lane and McWhirter, 1992).

Children as young as 10 years old have been trained as peer mediators. Although little systematic research has been done on the effects of peer mediation, there is considerable anecdotal evidence to suggest that children make effective peer mediators (Adler, 1987; Araki, Takesita, & Kadamoto, 1989; Cahoon, 1988; Jason & Rhodes, 1989; Kelly, Munzo, & Snowden, 1979; Klepp, Halper, & Perry, 1986; Lane & McWhirter, 1992; Maxwell, 1989; McCormick, 1988; Roderick, 1988). These same researchers report that elementary and middle schools with peer mediation programs seem to be making a difference in the following ways:

• drop in school discipline problems;
• decrease in self-reported aggressive conflicts;

- more prosocial attitude toward conflict;
- increased use of the peer mediation process to settle disputes;
- positive improvement in the school climate;
- school to home transfer of conflict management skills used in resolving sibling disputes;
- improved leadership, language, and problem solving skills of mediators;
- improved peer status, self-esteem, self-discipline, and responsibility of mediators; and
- improved self-esteem and respect for peer mediators by disputants.

Peer mediation programs involving child mediators represent a natural extension to conflict resolution training for children. Children first must understand and apply the principles of resolving conflicts peacefully before they should move to a more advanced level of functioning, that of mediator. As more children become acquainted with how to resolve conflicts constructively, perhaps some will wish to become peer mediators.

Conflict management, as we have presented it, can abound if presented and supported in the context of a comprehensive program that fosters constructive relationship building (Sautter, 1995); however, children first must be taught the values and skills of cooperative learning, the benefits of which foster greater commitment, helpfulness, and caring for each other regardless of differences (Deutsch, 1993). When this type of climate has been fostered, children will see the value of investing themselves in conflict resolution, peer mediation, and constructive controversy programs as means of preserving constructive, peace keeping relationships in times of conflict.

CHILDREN'S NEEDS

All children will face conflict in their lives. According to Erickson (1963), conflicts and how children adjust to them play a significant role in personality formation. How children manage conflict in their lives has a cumulative effect over time in that a conflict management style begins to evolve that affects the manner in which future conflicts will be handled (Sautter, 1995).

Erickson addressed the importance of conflict and how personality evolves in his eight stages of psychosocial development. Thompson and Rudolph (1992) have drawn a comparison between Havighurst's developmental tasks and Erickson's eight stages of development. In doing so, they have captured the interplay of expectations, human needs, and developmental tasks for the childhood years. They stated

> The two basic tasks for people are to learn how to cope with the demands and expectations of others when these demands and expectations conflict with their own needs and how to meet these demands with the limited abilities they have in each developmental stage. (p. 30)

For the middle childhood years (ages 6 to 11), children have a number of needs and tasks to complete that are critical to their development and ultimate success. The ones that we are about to mention can be unduly threatening if children do not learn how to manage life's conflicts in responsible ways. Children have a need to get along with agemates, learn the skills of tolerance and patience, develop a sense of morality and a scale of values, achieve personal independence, and develop attitudes toward social groups and institutions through experience and imitation (Havighurst, 1972; Noddings, 1995). During these middle childhood years, children require encouragement and praise from adults as they strive to be competent, well liked, young people with healthy self-esteem.

Stated more specifically, the Conflict Management Support Group addresses the following needs that relate specifically to helping children manage conflict in their lives successfully:

Cooperation—Children have a need to invest in each other and to value the importance of community in working together and accomplishing common goals. Through cooperation, children learn the value of building win-win connections, to trust, and to share.

Communication—If children are to learn how to cooperate with each other and value team building, then they must be astute observers, sensitive listeners, and accurate message senders. They have a need to know how to enhance accurate communications and to "bust" communication barriers.

Tolerance—Children have a need to understand, respect, and appreciate diversity. They must likewise learn to understand the roles that perception and prejudice play in the creation of conflict situations. Differences among people have the potential for human enrichment or can fuel conflicts depending on how those differences are perceived and acted upon. Children first must experience the value of diversity if they are ever to practice tolerance in their lives.

Emotional expression—Children have a need to understand, express, and manage their emotions in a constructive manner. Children who do not know how to handle anger, frustration, and aggression in positive and responsible ways still have the need to express their feelings and often do so in ways that lead to conflict.

Conflict resolution—Conflict is a natural aspect of life and living. Children have a need to prevent conflicts when they can be prevented, reduce the frequency of conflicts where possible, and learn how to manage unavoidable conflicts more constructively. Children have a need to learn how to settle disputes peacefully in ways that promote win-win solutions.

When children learn to cooperate, communicate, tolerate, manage their emotions, and resolve conflicts in nonviolent ways, they will satisfy their needs for safety, belonging, self-esteem, and self-actualization. They will become peacemakers in a world that needs more peace and less violence. These are the needs that are addressed in this conflict support group.

STRENGTHS TO BE LEARNED

If children are to develop positive relationships with siblings, peers, parents, teachers, and adults and enhance their physical and mental wellness, they must learn to become skillful peacemakers. The conflict management support group activities that follow are designed to help children meet their needs, as described, by learning the following strengths associated with conflict management. In this unit, children will

- understand the nature of conflict,
- identify types of conflicts that effect their lives,
- practice effective communication skills in resolving conflict,
- practice using a conflict resolution model, and
- participate in problem solving and role-playing conflict resolution activities (role-playing and problem solving).

Nature of Conflict

Children will define the meaning of conflict and will come to understand some of the causes of conflict such as competition, intolerance, poor communication, inappropriate expression of emotion, and lack of conflict management skills (Kreidler, 1984).

Types of Conflict

Conflict can be described in terms of three categories (Kreidler, 1984).

1. **Conflict over resources**—When two or more people want the same things and supply is limited.
2. **Conflict of needs**—Children have many needs such as the need for friends, to belong, power, self-esteem, etc. Conflict can arise between children or groups of children as they try to satisfy their needs in ways that may threaten the need satisfaction of their peers.
3. **Conflict of values**—Children learn their values and beliefs from those closest to them. Because children do not share the same values and beliefs with regard to diversity and lifestyle, conflicts are likely to arise.

When children experience heightened emotions, feel threatened, take sides on an issue, are not connected in positive ways with the disputants, and possess few peacemaking skills, conflict will escalate. By the same token, conflicts will dissipate more quickly when children learn to focus on the dispute and not each other, have their emotions in check, have a friendship investment with the disputants, and utilize their peacemaking skills effectively.

Effective Communication Skills

Learning to communicate effectively is necessary if conflicts are to be managed successfully. Disputants must learn how to connect with each other in positive ways so that they can resolve their conflicts. Therefore, children must learn how to

affirm others—As children learn that all people have some positive qualities, they can recognize those qualities in others and begin the process of relationship building.

send I messages—"I" messages help children focus on their behaviors and to take ownership for the positive things they do as well as holding themselves responsible for their part in contributing to conflicts.

use reflective listening—Many conflicts occur because the disputants have not heard each other. They tend to focus on their own discomfort and expect the other person to change so that they can feel better. Reflective listening teaches children how to send and receive clear messages. They learn how to give feedback and reflect feelings and content.

brainstorming—Conflicts may not get resolved because people are habitual in nature. They tend to behave the same way whether their actions are productive or not. Some children have learned a conflict management style that consists of one solution—fighting, name calling, etc. Brainstorming is a technique that requires children to generate and examine many solutions before settling on the right one(s) for their situation.

Conflict Resolution Model

Children will learn a basic problem-solving approach to managing their conflicts. The model that we present teaches children to find alternate ways to resolve conflict without become combative. The essential components of conflict resolution are as follows:

Give each disputant a chance to present his or her feelings and the problem as he or she sees it using "I messages."

Children are to refrain from attacking each other physically or verbally. They are to stay focused and give each other a chance to be heard.

Each disputant restates the problem from the other's perspective and does so to the other's satisfaction.

When the problem has been clearly stated, the disputants look for common ground on which to build a solution.

The disputants brainstorm together, a list of possible solutions.

The disputants look for ways in which they can change their own behaviors to achieve a win-win solution to their conflict.

The disputants affirm each other for their efforts in resolving their conflict.

Techniques and Activities

The Conflict Management Support Group makes use of role-playing, case situations, and 3 R's Decision Making in providing children with simulated conflict experiences. In this way, children receive the practice they need in learning to self-manage in times of conflict. Once children understand and are skillful at managing conflicts, we encourage using teachable moments so that children can apply what they have learned to real conflict situations.

MESSAGE TO FACILITATORS

While you may think that community building is somewhat of a paradox in a support group on conflict management, keep in mind that the most successful conflict managers are those who practice cooperation, effective communication, tolerance, and positive emotional expression. When children learn to connect and invest in each other, they can see the value in managing conflicts in constructive ways. Teaching children how to manage conflict is a skill building process. The children in your group will not all possess the same skills as one another nor will they have developed the same quality in those skills that they do share. Consequently, there will be some setbacks and hurdles to overcome along the way; however, do not despair. Aim for improvement not perfection.

We provide you with a sequenced and structured format for teaching conflict resolution. That format will address the children's general needs and the strengths to be taught in resolving conflict peacefully. Follow the process as presented, making whatever adjustments seem appropriate, given the children's needs in your group.

Conflict management can be taught to children from five years of age upward; however, the process needs to be simplified for younger children. We provided a less involved conflict management process earlier on in this chapter. For children ages 9 to 11, the model and activities, as presented in the following sessions, are appropriate. Although we encourage diversity in your group, we suggest that children be grouped as closely as possible to the same age so that you can take a more developmentally appropriate position in facilitating group process.

We encourage you to provide many examples, activities, role-plays, and case discussions as possible since children learn best through involvement. We also encourage using conflict management skills to address "real disagreements" when they occur. If you are working in a school environment, teachers can integrate conflict resolution training into their curriculum. For example in social studies, they can have children study about the lives of people who are peacemakers. In language arts, they can create and role-play conflict stories. In science, children can study values related conflicts pertaining to such topics as the use of animals in medicine, organ transplants, and crime and punishment. With respect to math class, children can study conflicts as they relate to issues of supply and demand (use of our natural resources). Conflicts related to moral decision making also can be addressed.

As you practice the conflict resolution process, help children see that, while many conflicts can be resolved between the disputants themselves, this may not be the case always. Sometimes a conflict mediator is necessary to guide and monitor the process. Help the children see that you are functioning as a mediator as you teach and guide them through the conflict resolution process.

Tell the children (ages 10 to 12) that they too can learn to be conflict mediators. If time permits and the interest is there, and the children feel comfortable with the conflict resolution process, you can teach them to be conflict mediators. As we have indicated, children in the 10- to 12-year age bracket have made wonderful peer mediators serving on peer mediation teams in their elementary schools.

Review the group sessions that follow, and have fun teaching children how to resolve conflicts constructively in their homes (see Figure 9.1), schools, and communities.

Resources

Share with parents and/or guardians Figure 9.1 so that they will have suggestions on how they can help their children at home. In Figure 9.2 are provided lists of resources to be used with and by children in the Conflict Management Support Group. The resource materials are grouped according to age of child.

CONFLICT MANAGEMENT GUIDE
Tips for Caregivers

Your child soon will be participating in a Conflict Management Support Group. The goal of this support group is to help children understand and peacefully resolve conflicts in their lives. Though conflict is inevitable, how children learn to manage conflict is a matter of choice. Children who learn to use conflict management skills successfully develop positive peer relationships, are at ease with themselves emotionally, and are less likely to resort to fighting, teasing, name calling and competition in settling their differences with others. Rather, they are more inclined to seek out cooperative and caring solutions in resolving their differences with others. We are happy to share a few tips with you that you can try at home in teaching the children in your care how to resolve conflicts peacefully.

1. Conflict is less likely to occur when you and your children communicate clearly. Be sure to say what you mean and mean what you say.

2. Establish clear rules of responsibility and right and wrong behavior in teaching kindness, cooperation, sharing, taking turns, speaking one at a time, listening to one another, putting things back where they belong, manners, etc.

3. Anticipate conflicts between your children before they occur and discuss a plan with your children that will reduce the possibility of conflicts before they have a chance to start.

4. When a conflict does arise, teach your children how to fight fairly. Establish some ground rules.

   a You and your brother (sister) have been fighting.
   b This behavior is unacceptable.
   c Fighting and arguing are not working. We need to find a better way.
   d Encourage your children to see a peaceful solution.
   e I will help you solve your problem, but you must agree to the following:

- no put-downs or name calling,
- no interruptions while your brother/sister is talking,
- listen to each other's side, and
- be truthful with what you say.

f Ask each child to take turns describing the conflict. What does each child want? How does each child feel? Write down what each child says.

g Brainstorm some solutions to the problem. Make a list of ideas to solve the problem.

h Help your child select solutions that will help both children win.

i Discuss each solution.

j Ask your children to select solutions that they think are best for each other.

k Get your children to agree to a solution and try it. If some modifications are required, have both children discuss the modifications and implement those that are acceptable to each other.

5. Congratulate your children for being successful conflict resolvers.

6. Always encourage your children to put their conflicts behind them.

7. Encourage your children to examine what they have learned about themselves and their conflict so that they can use what they have learned to avoid similar conflicts in the future.

This conflict management plan can be modified to suit your needs. The type of plan discussed here works well with children nine years old and above. With younger children (five to eight years old), you can follow the same plan, but simplify it to meet their needs. The idea is to look for a peaceful, win-win solution that both children can accept. You may wish to receive additional suggestions or ideas from the person leading your child's support group.

Figure 9.1. Tips for Caregivers to be given to parents and/or guardians. Permission to photocopy is granted.

RESOURCES FOR CHILDREN
Conflict Management

Ages 3 to 7

Bourgeois, P. (1993). *Franklin is bossy.* New York: Scholastic. (being bossy doesn't help one get one's way)

Boyd, L. (1989). *Bailey the big bully.* New York: Viking Penguin. (dealing with bullies)

Brown, M. T. (1989). *Arthur's birthday.* Boston: Joy Street Books. (problem solving and sharing)

Caple, K. (1990). *The coolest place in town.* Boston: Houghton Mifflin. (dealing with being teased)

Gould, D. (1989). *Aaron's shirt.* New York: Bradbury Press. (dealing with personal conflict)

Henwood, S. (1991). *The troubled village.* New York: Farrar, Straus, Giroux. (working together to solve problems)

Petty, K., & Firmin, C. (1991). *Playing the game.* Hauppauge, NY: Barron's. (fairness helps resolve conflict)

Scholes, K. (1990). *Peace begins with you.* Boston: Little, Brown. (cooperation and problem solving)

Titherington, J. (1987). *A place for Ben.* New York: Greenwillow Books. (finding one's own private place)

Wilhelm, H. (1988). *Tyrone the horrible.* New York: Scholastic. (dealing with bullies)

Ages 8 to 12

Auch, M. J. (1987). *Cry uncle.* New York: Holiday House. (conflict with live-in relatives)

Clifford, E. (1987). *Harvey's marvelous monkey mystery.* Boston: Houghton Mifflin. (conflict over dishonesty)

Conrad, P. (1987). *Seven silly circles.* New York: Harper Collins. (conflict with friends)

Duffey, B. (1990). *The math wiz.* New York: Viking Penguin. (pupil-teacher relationships)

Duncan, L. (1988). *The wonder kid meets the evil lunch snatcher.* Boston: Little, Brown. (conflict with bully)

Hiller, B. B. (1988). *Rent a third grader.* New York: Scholastic. (classmate relationships and problem solving)

Rosenbaum, E. (1993). *Friends afloat.* Milwaukee: Raintree Publishers. (cooperation as a means of solving conflict)

Taha, K. T. (1988). *Marshmallow muscles, banana brainstorms.* San Diego: Harcourt Brace Jovanovich. (problem solving in sports, sportsmanship)

Terrell, R. (1992). *A kid's guide to how to stop the violence.* New York: Avon Books. (realistic conflict resolution)

Wright, B. R. (1989). *Rosie and the dance of the dinosaurs.* New York: Holiday House. (problem solving regarding separation from loved ones)

Ages 12 and Up

Blakeslee, A. R. (1989). *After the fortune cookies.* New York: Putnam & Grossett Group. (dealing with teasing)

Childre, D. L. (1991). *Heart smarts: Teenage guide for the puzzle of life.* Boulder Creek, CA: Planetary Publications. (dealing with life's conflicts)

Cohen , B. (1990). *The long way home.* New York: Lothrop, Lee & Shepard Books. (problem solving in family issues)

Holl, K. D. (1987). *Hidden in the fog.* New York: Atheneum Publishers. (dealing with family conflict and responsibilities)

Kunjufu, J., & Hubbard, L. J. (1991). *Up against the wall.* Chicago: African-American Images. (conflicts of real people)

Mango, K. (1987). *Somewhere green.* New York: Four Winds Press. (teen sexuality conflicts)

Ruby, L. (1987). *Pig out inn.* Boston: Houghton Mifflin. (conflicts within an eccentric lifestyle)

Scott, S. (1986). *How to say no and keep your friends.* Amherst, MA: Human Resource Development Press. (teen issue conflicts)

Scott, S. (1988). *When to say no and make more friends.* Amherst, MA: Human Resource Development Press. (making a difference through helping others)

Stone, J. D., & Keefauver, L. (1990). *Friend to friend.* Minneapolis: Educational Media Corporation. (peer helping to solve conflicts)

Figure 9.2.   Resources for use with and by children in Conflict Management Support Group.

SESSION I—CONFLICT IN MY LIFE

BRIEF OVERVIEW OF SESSION

In this session, children will become acquainted with each other, learn group ground rules, define conflict and share with others their view of conflict in their life.

GOALS

1. To provide the structure and purpose for the group.
2. To enable children to determine what the term "conflict" means in their life.
3. To establish a working definition of "conflict."

MATERIALS NEEDED

1. 12" × 18" construction paper for each child
2. Markers or crayons
3. Chart paper for listing group ground rules

PROCEDURE

1. Introduce yourself and have each of the group members introduce himself or herself by first name. Tell the children that everyone in the group is participating so that we all can learn more effective ways of coping with conflict. During the course of the group, we will be learning many skills that will help us resolve conflict more effectively.

2. Begin to set the stage for the group by discussing ground rules. Examples of possible group rules may include the following:

a   What is said in the group, stays there (confidentiality).
b   No put-downs are allowed.
c   Only one person talks at a time.
d   It is important to attend all sessions.

Note: If children do not suggest these rules, you as facilitator should bring them up as part of the brainstorming process.

3. Pose the following questions to the group:

a   What is conflict?
b   What things do most conflicts have in common?
c   What makes conflict worse?
d   What things seem to decrease conflict?

4. Following the discussion of the questions, give each child a sheet of paper and some markers or crayons and ask them to draw a picture of a conflict. (Do not give additional directions; just allow the children to put down on paper a graphic representation of what conflict is to them.)

5. Encourage each of the children to share his or her picture of conflict with the group. Talk about the fact that "conflict" means many different things to each of us but that there are some commonalities in all of our pictures in that conflict always is represented by differences of opinion or feelings.

6. Display the conflict pictures in the room for future reference during the course of the group.

7. Compliment the children on their involvement and participation (if appropriate) in this first session.

CLOSURE

Bring closure to this first session by again reminding the children of the fact that conflict is a normal part of life, that all of us will experience conflict at some time or another, and that there are some skills we will be learning in this group that will help us deal more effectively with the conflict in our lives.

HOMEWORK

As a homework assignment, ask the children to think about causes of conflict in their life. Encourage them to think of at least three things that cause conflict for them. We will discuss causes and sources of conflict during the next session.

SESSION II—CAUSES AND SOURCES OF CONFLICT

BRIEF OVERVIEW OF SESSION

In this session, children will begin to look at the causes and sources of conflict in their lives. They also will identify what areas seem to cause the most conflict for them personally and look at what are some possible ways for dealing with these conflicts.

GOALS

1. To provide an opportunity for children to identify the causes and sources of conflict in their life.
2. To encourage the children to think about what are the "roots" of their conflict.
3. To begin to identify ways to deal with personal conflict in one's life.

MATERIALS NEEDED

1. 3" × 5" cards for sorting conflict categories
2. 3" × 12" label cards for sorting activity (at least 3 sets with the labels "NEEDS," "RESOURCES," and "VALUES" on them)

PROCEDURE

1. Ask for examples of conflicts. Give a few if necessary. These can include conflicts between friends, conflicts in families, conflicts within oneself, conflicts between countries, and conflicts between students and teachers.

2. Show the group the cards with the words NEEDS, RESOURCES, and VALUES on them. Discuss their meanings with the group (p. 270).

3. Have one of the group members give an example of a conflict that he or she thought about for the homework activity. Does that conflict revolve around one of the three categories of NEEDS, RESOURCES, or VALUES? (Since almost all conflicts fall under one of these three categories, no doubt it will be easy to identify the appropriate category.)

4. Ask the children to work in groups of two or three and to discuss their "homework" conflicts. As they discuss them, they should categorize them as NEEDS, RESOURCES, or VALUES conflicts. (Remind them that any vague

or hard to classify conflicts should be set aside to be discussed with the whole group at a later time.)

5. Bring the group back together for a discussion of the activity. These questions may be helpful in that discussion.

a   What were some (resource, need, value) conflicts?
b   How did your group decide where to put them for sorting purposes?
c   What were some factors you looked at?
d   What were some of the conflicts you couldn't classify easily?

6. Point out to the group that most conflicts are caused by a threat to NEEDS, RESOURCES, or VALUES; however, there may also be other ways to classify conflicts. This could include the following:

a   friendly—angry,
b   silly—important,
c   violent—nonviolent, and
d   resolvable—unresolvable.

CLOSURE

To conclude this session, it is important to remind the children that everyone has conflicts in their life, that conflicts can be classified and that they almost always involve a threat to needs, resources, or values.

HOMEWORK

Encourage the children to keep track of the conflicts they have in their life during the next week. We will spend a few minutes next session discussing the types and causes of conflict.

SESSION III—WIN-WIN: THE WAY TO GO

BRIEF OVERVIEW OF SESSION

This session will provide an opportunity for the children to become aware of the best method for solving conflicts—the Win-Win resolution.

GOALS

1. To introduce the concept of win-win conflict resolution.
2. To provide an opportunity for children to participate in a situation that can involve a Win-Win situation.
3. To help children realize that there are three types of conflict resolution.

MATERIALS NEEDED

1. Conflict resolution chart (see sample in procedure #6)
2. Pieces of candy or other type of snack (10 pieces per team of two)

PROCEDURE

1. Take a few minutes at the beginning of the session to talk about conflicts the children have had during the past week. Briefly discuss whether they were NEED, RESOURCE, or VALUE conflicts and how the parties solved their conflict. Remind the children that today we are going to talk about a way to solve conflicts.

2. Pair the children in groups of two with a table or other flat surface between them. Ask them to grasp right hands with their partner and keep their elbows on the table. Place 10 snack items between them and tell them that the one who keeps the back of his or her hand from touching the table will receive a snack. They are to continue until all snacks have been distributed. (Make no mention of a contest—just see how the groups go about dealing with the directions. Most will probably arm wrestle each other to gain the snack. Hopefully, some will realize that the best way to solve the problem is to share the snacks with each person receiving five.)

3. After a few minutes, ask the children to stop and call their attention to the following chart:

Win-Lose (one person wins, the other loses)
Lose-Lose (both parties lose)
Win-Win (both parties win)

4. Ask the children what type of resolution they had with the snack activity. Most will have a Win-Lose situation. Talk about how the winner feels and how the loser feels. How could this situation have been handled so that both parties come out a winner?

5. Describe to the group the following scenario. Jim and Chad are working with a set of building blocks. Jim wants to build a fort, but Chad wants to make a space station he has been designing for his science project. What does Jim want? What does Chad want? Does there have to be a winner and a loser? Would there be another way of solving this issue?

6. Place the following chart on the board:

	Chad gets what he wants	Chad does not get what he wants
Jim gets what he wants	Win-Win	Win-Lose
Jim does not get what he wants	Win-Lose	Lose-Lose

7. Talk about how this problem could be resolved into a win-win situation.

CLOSURE

Encourage the children to briefly review the conflicts that were discussed at the beginning of today's session. Could any of these have been resolved by Win-Win?

HOMEWORK

Each child should be encouraged to try to solve one conflict so that a win-win solution is achieved. This will be the topic for initial discussion at next week's session.

SESSION IV—VOCABULARY OF CONFLICT

BRIEF OVERVIEW OF SESSION

This session will provide an opportunity for the children to begin to develop a common frame of reference in terms of conflict through a brainstorming activity designed to elicit words that describe conflict. It can be as simple or as complex as the children in the group make it.

GOALS

1. To assist children in developing a common frame of reference in terms of the vocabulary of conflict.
2. To help children understand how knowledge of specific conflict resolution terms will be helpful to them both now and in the future.
3. To make the acquisition of conflict resolution terminology a fun activity.

MATERIALS NEEDED

1. Chart paper
2. Markers
3. ½" blocked graph paper or graph of some kind (for word find puzzle)

PROCEDURE

1. Provide time for a brief review of the win-win resolutions the children have made during the past week. Congratulate them for their efforts in attempting to come to win-win resolutions. Spend a little time talking about failed efforts and possible changes that could have made them more successful.

2. Ask the children to brainstorm a list of conflict vocabulary. Some words that may come up include the following

apologize	escalate	violence
negotiate	deescalate	mediate
aggressive	assertive	anger
peace	war	reconcile
prejudice	trust	intolerance
cooperation	tolerance	frustration
anxiety	compromise	argument

3. At the addition of each word to the list, allow time for a discussion of how the word may be used in relation to a conflict, particularly to a conflict in their own lives.

4. Point out that some of the words are negative but many are positive, that conflict resolution can be a very positive process.

5. Give a piece of graph paper to each child and ask him or her to develop a word find puzzle using at least 10 of the conflict terms from the vocabulary list. When each child has completed the puzzle, allow him or her to exchange with a partner who will try to find the 10 words in the puzzle. (If time is growing short for the session, it may be helpful to allow the puzzle to be a homework assignment to be completed for the next session.)

CLOSURE

To bring closure to this session, redirect the children's attention to the chart for the list of words they have identified. Remind them that knowledge and understanding of the vocabulary of conflict will assist them in becoming more effective and confident mediators.

HOMEWORK

If the puzzle is not completed in the session, it can be given to the children as a homework assignment. An additional assignment will be to think of a conflict situation that affects many children their age and to begin to think of possible solutions. Next session will be spent on developing the technique of brainstorming as a part of the mediation process.

SESSION V—BRAINSTORMING

BRIEF OVERVIEW OF SESSION

This session will provide an opportunity for the children to learn the technique of brainstorming in a fun manner. They will then utilize this brainstorming technique in the mediation process to identify possible problem solutions.

GOALS

1. To introduce the topic of brainstorming in a fun and entertaining manner.
2. To assist children in understanding how this skill may be used in resolving conflicts.
3. To enable children to practice brainstorming.

MATERIALS NEEDED

1. A variety of interesting materials that will be used to make an object (These could include various sizes and shapes of boxes, a variety of cloth, pieces of jewelry, paints, etc.)
2. Chart paper for brainstorming
3. Crayons or markers

PROCEDURE

1. Take a few minutes to review the last session. Ask if any of the children were able to complete their puzzle. Remind them that this exercise has enabled them to be more familiar with the vocabulary related to conflict.

2. Introduce the concept of brainstorming. Explain to the children that the goal of brainstorming is to introduce as many ideas as possible and to do it in the least amount of time possible. There are three rules:

    a   Do not judge. Record ideas as quickly as possible.
    b   Use ideas already mentioned to build upon and modify. Do not always feel that new ideas have to be presented.
    c   Write down everything, even if the idea sounds silly. We are looking for quantity at this point.

3. Place the materials you have brought in front of the children. Inform

them that you want them to build something, but you are not sure what they can make. Suggest that they begin to brainstorm possible ideas.

4. Write down on the chart all of the ideas presented by the children. Add a few of your own if the pace drags. Remind the children not to criticize any ideas.

5. When all ideas have been presented, go back over the list and erase those that cannot receive consensus. Try to narrow the list to three or four possible ideas.

6. Follow through on ideas by completing the project.

7. Discuss the following questions at the conclusion of the project:

a   When might brainstorming be useful in a conflict situation?
b   How can you brainstorm by yourself?
c   Why is it important not to judge ideas during the initial brainstorming?

CLOSURE

A very smooth closure can be achieved by asking one of the children to pose a conflict situation that he or she is involved in and asking the group to brainstorm possible solutions to that situation. Remind them that they will use this technique more in the next session.

HOMEWORK

Encourage the children to use the technique of brainstorming to think of potential conflict situations during the next week.

SESSION VI—MEDIATING CONFLICTS

BRIEF OVERVIEW OF SESSION

This session will provide children with the opportunity to work together to learn the process of mediation. They will gain an awareness of the process as well as have an opportunity to practice the skills they have learned.

GOALS

1. To introduce a conflict resolution or mediation process to the children.
2. To provide opportunities for the children to practice the skills necessary for conflict resolution.
3. To encourage the children to utilize their own newly acquired skills as they deal with conflicts in their life.

MATERIALS NEEDED

1. Chart paper (enough for two sheets per group of two children)
2. Markers
3. Copies of "Agreement Form" (Activity Sheet 9.1)

PROCEDURE

1. Take a few moments at the beginning of the session to give the children an opportunity to talk about whether they tried brainstorming as a way to identify conflict resolutions. Talk about successes, failures, and problems that may have surfaced.

2. Tell the children that today they are going to begin to learn and practice a process for solving conflicts. It is a process that involves the following steps:

    a   Identify the problem.
    b   Agree to listen to each other's sides with no interrupting or name calling.
    c   Each person tells his or her story being certain to describe how the situation makes him or her feel.
    d   The two disputants brainstorm possible solutions.
    e   The list is discussed and one or two potential solutions are agreed upon.
    f   Each person tells what he or she will do to assure that the conflict is resolved.

g If possible, the two disputants agree to sign an agreement that details what they will do to solve the problem (Activity Sheet 9.1).

h The disputants talk about what they will do next if the solution does not work.

3. Spend the necessary amount of time to allow the children to understand the process.

4. Role-play a situation with one of the children while the others watch the process.

5. Allow the children to work in pairs to role-play and seek 3 R's solutions to the following problem.

> John loaned Larry a copy of a book his grandmother had given him for his birthday so that Larry could do a report. Larry's little brother wrote on one of the pages with crayon and tore out another page. Now John is insisting that Larry return the book immediately and pay him for it. Larry still wants to keep the book so that he can finish the report.

CLOSURE

Spend some time discussing the process the children have just used. Do they think it can work? How will they use it?

HOMEWORK

Provide children with a copy of the steps in the process and encourage them to use it in conflicts that arise during the next week. Also, ask them to think about some "Inner Conflicts" that they have experienced.

AGREEMENT FORM

We agree to _____

_____

_____

_____

_____

_____

_____

_____

_____

_____

_____

Signature

_____

Signature

_____

Date

Activity Sheet 9.1.   Agreement Form worksheet. Permission is granted to enlarge and photocopy for classroom use.

SESSION VII—INNER CONFLICTS

BRIEF OVERVIEW OF SESSION

During the session, children will have an opportunity to identify some of the inner conflicts they have experienced. They also will begin to think about some of the skills they have learned and how these skills can assist them in dealing with the inner conflicts as well.

GOALS

1. To provide an opportunity for each child to identify some of the inner conflicts he or she deals with each day.
2. To encourage the children to think about how they can deal with the inner conflicts in their life.
3. To provide continued opportunities to practice the skills of conflict resolution.

MATERIALS NEEDED

1. A large (life-size) piece of paper (newsprint) for each child
2. Crayons
3. Scissors

PROCEDURE

1. Talk briefly with the children about conflict resolution attempts they have made during the past week.

   a   Did you use the skills we practiced?
   b   How did it work?
   c   What problems surfaced as a result of using that conflict resolution model?

2. Ask the children to work in pairs to make life-size models of each other. (One child lies down on the newsprint while the other traces his or her body outline onto the paper; then reverse roles.)

3. When the models have been cut out, ask for volunteers to talk about choices they have made this week. They need not be difficult choices—choosing gelatin or pudding for dessert, deciding to read a new mystery rather than watching TV, etc.

4. Then ask each child to draw a line from top to bottom in the center of his or her body outline. On the opposite sides, ask each child to list some of the choices he or she made this week. Suggest that each child list at least five choices he or she had to make. An example is shown as Activity Sheet 9.2.

5. When the children have completed the activity, explain that inner conflicts arise when one has uncertain feelings about needs, resources, or values.

6. Encourage the children to describe some of their inner conflicts over needs and values rather than resources, if possible. (This is when you may get into a discussion of peer pressure and conflicts over smoking, alcohol, etc.)

7. Ask the children to list at least two of these difficult inner conflicts on their models.

8. Allow time for discussion among the children. Some questions that may be helpful in directing the discussion include the following:

a   How can you resolve inner conflicts?
b   How do your inner conflicts affect others?
c   What role does your conscience play in inner conflicts?

CLOSURE

As a method of closure for this session, remind the children that they learned ways for dealing with conflicts with others that will also help in dealing with inner conflicts. The steps will work just as well alone as with others.

HOMEWORK

Again, encourage the children to continue to use the skills of conflict resolution they have learned in all conflicts they face during the next week. Remind them that they will get better and better at conflict resolution skills with practice; thus, this is a very important homework assignment.

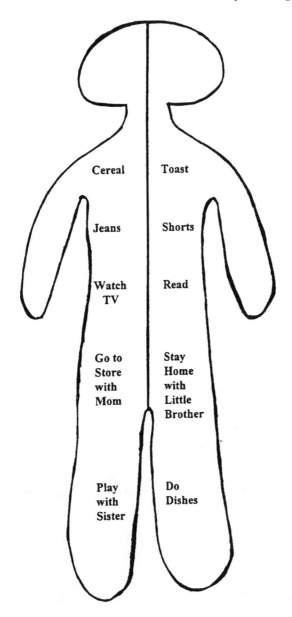

Activity Sheet 9.2.   Example of life-size choices exercise.

SESSION VIII—ANOTHER TYPE OF CONFLICT: HANDLING BULLIES

BRIEF OVERVIEW OF SESSION

In this session, children will begin to talk about how conflict occurs as a result of bullying. They will identify characteristics of bullies and of persons who are the targets of bullies. They also will begin to identify what they do to deal with bullies.

GOALS

1. To assist children in identifying characteristics of bullies and those who are targets of bullies.
2. To discuss ways to handle bullies most effectively.
3. To bring closure to the group.

MATERIALS NEEDED

1. Chart paper
2. Markers
3. Copies of "Give Me a Hand" worksheet (Activity Sheet 9.3)

PROCEDURE

1. Provide a very brief review of how the children are doing at using the conflict resolution model. Are they experiencing problems? If so, discuss.

2. Ask the children to think of a bully they have known and what that person did that made him or her a bully.

3. Have the children work in pairs to tell each other about a bully they have known, without using names. (This should only take about three minutes).

4. Bring the group back together and begin to make a list of characteristics of bullies. List these on a chart. Some of the characteristics that may be identified can include

- try to beat people up,
- lie to others,
- hit people,
- pick on you,

- talk about you,
- look for fights,
- do mean things,
- threaten people, and
- brag about how tough they are.

5. Talk about characteristics of people who are bullied. What makes them targets? List these also on a chart.

- sometimes cry when they're picked on,
- are afraid to say something back,
- do things that make bullies pick on them,
- act scared, and
- act nerdy or wimpy.

6. Talk about what people should do when they get bullied. Suggest that it usually will be helpful to get an adult involved, particularly if the bully continues to threaten. (This may be a type of conflict that they can not handle alone.)

7. Conclude the session by giving each child a copy of the "Give Me a Hand" worksheet (Activity Sheet 9.3). Ask that they write something positive on each of the fingers about themselves in terms of conflict resolution. Some examples of things they may write could include the following:

a   I'm willing to listen to the other person's side of the story,
b   I'll tell how I feel, and
c   I'm confident that I can deal with some of my conflicts.

8. Allow a few minutes for sharing of items from the worksheet, for saying goodbye to the group, for talking about feelings, and for reviewing what they have learned in the group.

CLOSURE

Have children complete the group evaluation form.

HOMEWORK

Although there is no formal homework for the group, each child should be encouraged to keep in touch with the facilitator and let him or her know how things are going. They also should continue to practice the conflict resolution skills they have learned.

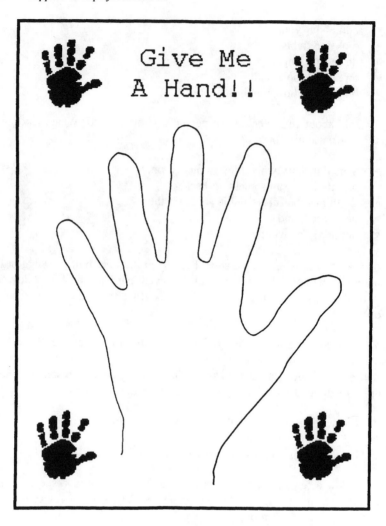

Activity Sheet 9.3. Give Me a Hand worksheet. Permission is granted to enlarge and photocopy for classroom use.

EVALUATION

1. Do you feel that participation in the Conflict Resolution group was helpful to you? Why or why not?

2. What part of the group did you like best?

3. What part of the group did you like least?

4. If you had a friend who was experiencing a good deal of conflict in his or her life, would you recommend that he or she participate in a similar group? Why or why not?

5. Did you attend all eight group sessions?

_____ Yes _____ No

If no, how many did you attend? _____

6. Comments, suggestions, etc.:

REFERENCES

Adler, P. (1987). Is ADR a social movement? *Negotiations Journal, 3*(1), 59–71.

Araki, D., Takesita, C., & Kadamoto, L. (1989). *Research results and final report for the Dispute Management in the Schools Project.* Honolulu: Program on Conflict Resolution, University of Hawaii at Manoa.

Arrington, E. W. (1987). Managing children's conflict: A challenge for the school counselor. *The School Counselor, 3,* 188–194.

Cahoon, P. (1988). Mediator magic. *Educational Leadership, 45*(4), 92–95.

Deutsch, M. (1993). Educating for a peaceful world. *American Psychologist, 48*(5), 510–517.

Drew, N. (1987). *Learning the skills of peacemaking: An active guide for elementary-age children on communicating, cooperating, resolving conflict.* Rolling Hills Estates, CA: Jalmar Press.

Dysinger, B. J. (1993). Conflict resolution for intermediate children. *The School Counselor, 40,* 301–308.

Erickson, E. H. (1963). *Childhood & society.* New York: Norton.

Gentry, D. B., & Beneson, W. A. (1993). School-to-home transfer of conflict management skills among school-age children. *Families in Society: The Journal of Contemporary Human Services, 74,* 67–73.

Hart, L. B. (1981). *Learning from conflict: A handbook for trainers & group leaders.* Reading, MA: Addison-Wesley.

Havighurst, R. J. (1972). *Developmental tasks and education* (3rd ed.). New York: David McKay.

Jason, L., & Rhodes, J. (1989). Children helping children: Implications for prevention. *Journal of Primary Prevention, 9,* 203–211.

Johnson, D. W., & Johnson, R. T. (1987). *Creative conflict.* Edina, MN: Interaction Book.

Johnson, D. W., & Johnson, R. T. (1992). *Creative controversy: Intellectual challenge in the classroom.* Edina, MN: Interaction Book.

Kelly, J., Munzo, R., & Snowden, L. (1979). Characteristics of community research projects and the implementation process. In R. Munzo, L. Snowden, & J. Kelly (Eds.), *Social and psychological research in community settings* (pp. 343-363). San Francisco, CA: Jossey-Bass.

Klepp, K., Halper, A., & Perry, C. (1986). The efficacy of peer leaders in drug abuse prevention. *Journal of School Health, 56,* 407–421.

Kreidler, W. J. (1984). *Creative conflict resolution: More than 200 activities for keeping peace in the classroom.* Glenview, IL: Scott, Foresman.

Lane, P. S., & McWhirter, J. J. (1992). A peer mediation model: Conflict resolution for elementary and middle school children. *Elementary School Guidance & Counseling, 27,* 15–23.

Lantieri, L. (1995). Waging peace in our schools: Beginning with the curriculum. *Phi Delta Kappan, 76*(5), 386–388.

Maruyama, G. (1992). Lewin's impact on education: Instilling cooperation and conflict management skills in school children. *Journal of Social Issues, 48*(2), 155–166.

Maxwell, J. (1989). Mediation in the schools. *Mediation Quarterly, 7,* 149–154.

McClure, B. A., Miller, G. A., & Russo, T. J. (1992). Conflict within a children's group: Suggestions for facilitating its expression and resolution strategies. *The School Counselor, 39,* 268–272.

McCormick, M. (1988). *Mediation in the schools: An evolution of the Wakefield Pilot Peer Mediation Program in Tucson, Arizona.* Washington, DC: American Bar Association.

Morganett, R. S. (1994). *Skills for living: Group counseling activities for elementary students.* Champaign, IL: Research Press.

Noddings, N. (1995). A morally defensible mission for schools in the 21st century. *Phi Delta Kappan, 76*(5), 365–368.

Prutzman, P., Stern, L., Burger, M. L., & Bodenhamer, G. (1988). *The friendly classroom for a small planet: A handbook on creative approaches to living and problem solving for children.* Santa Cruz, CA: New Society Publishers.

Roderick, T. (1988). Johnny can learn to negotiate. *Educational leadership, 45*(4), 86–90.

Sautter, C. R. (1995). Standing up to violence: Kappan special report. *Phi Delta Kappan, 76*(5), K1–K2.

Thompson, C. L., & Rudolph, L. B. (1992). *Counseling children* (3rd ed.). Pacific Grove, CA: Brooks/Cole.

Chapter 10

COPING WITH DEATH, GRIEF, AND LOSS

Personal loss represents a voluntary or involuntary separation (permanent or temporary) from people, places, and things in children's lives that have been personally significant and/or familiar.

BACKGROUND INFORMATION

Loss, death, and grief are as much a part of life as life itself. They affect all children's lives regardless of age. Children are not immune to loss and experience its effects in a multitude of ways. They suffer physically, emotionally, and spiritually in response to losses such as the following:

- loss of childhood dreams,
- loss of health,
- family moves,
- changing schools,
- loss of personal belongings,
- failure (grades, sports, respect),
- loss of security,
- loss of safety,
- loss of self-esteem,
- loss of a pet, and/or
- parental separation and divorce.

- loss of relationships (friendships)
- death of a significant other

How children are affected by loss and cope with it will shape how they respond to future losses in their lives (Rice, 1992). The focus of this chapter and support group experience is to help children learn more about life by learning about death, loss, and grief. While children will experience a variety of life losses, we will highlight death education because death of a peer, family member, or caregiver is the ultimate loss and the most difficult for adults to address in helping children self-manage responsibly (Grollman, 1991; Lewis, 1992; Wass, 1991). The need for support groups on death, loss, and grief was supported by Garanzini (1987) when he stated the following:

> Attempts to shield children from the reality of death reinforces in them the perception that death is either not real, too frightening to examine, or, worst of all, that the ending of life is not worth noting with respect and reverence. These unintended lessons are unhealthy. . . . For the sake of a healthy . . . sound appreciation of the meaning of death, parents and teachers must face the topic realistically and naturally—for themselves and for the children they teach. (p. 30)

The fear, isolation, loneliness, and confusion that children experience when their needs are not met after experiencing any loss, and particularly the death of a significant other, creates unhealthy stress that can interrupt their growth and development. When children's needs are supported and provided for in times of loss, however, children will gain the information, skills, and self-confidence needed for handling future life situations involving loss.

Death, Loss, and Grief: Our Approach

There are two approaches in addressing death, loss, and grief. One approach utilizes the "teachable moment," which occurs when children raise questions about the topic or when a loss is experienced by children that must be addressed. In such cases, the facilitator(s) must decide how best to respond to children's needs and develop a planned course of action based on immediate need.

A second approach in learning about death, loss, and grief involves participating in a planned course of study consisting of objectives and activities that evolve over several sessions. While both approaches are necessary, we advocate a support group experience that relies on planned objectives and activities that will provide children with a well-rounded and healthy learning experience.

Children's Perceptions of Loss

How children view loss and death is a matter of development, personal experiences, adult guidance, and innate abilities. Although the following categories are arranged by age levels, educators should treat them as reference points only, paying more attention to sequence of understandings rather than to specific ages (Seibert, Drolet, & Fetro, 1993).

Under Age Three.   Furman (1978) and Wenestam and Wass (1987) have studied children under the age of three and have noted understandings and reactions related to death; however, the data pertaining to children's reactions to death under the age of three are limited at best. Because some children in this age range have exhibited reactions in response to death does not mean that we can generalize these findings to all children under the age of three years.

Age Three through Five.   Death is viewed as a temporary state in that children may speak of a loved one being dead today but expect to see this person next week. Unless the death of someone touches them directly, they may appear to show little or no reaction to the loss. The terms "death" and "dead" hold little meaning for young children. They are unable to distinguish the physical differences between life and death. Because young children engage in magical thinking, they are able to see death as being avoidable and reversible when it does occur. Also, because children are unable to distinguish between reality and fantasy, some may even blame themselves for the death of a loved one regarding something they may have said or done. Helping children understand that they are not responsible for a loved one's death is a necessary challenge in helping children eliminate guilt and harmful thoughts.

Ages Six through Eight.   Children are beginning to understand that death is final and yet many do not attribute the finality of death to themselves; however, as they mature in their ability to reason, some children will take on a more personal perspective of death.

Children are particularly interested in the biological facts and physical details about death. They ask many questions about the causes of death, what happens after death, the purpose of viewings, why and how the body is prepared after death, and questions regarding funeral homes, burial, cremation, coffins, tombstones, and various rituals at the time of death. Some children will experience fears and anxiety as they respond to internal conflicts regarding the inevitability of death for all and their own magical thinking of "not me," which is beginning to erode.

Ages Nine and Over.   Children are beginning to accept an adult perspective of death. By age ten, most children understand that death is final, inevitable, and personal. They can define death, understand the biological implications, and are capable of thinking in the abstract regarding death. These same children, however, while understanding and accepting death from an adult perspective, may be limited in their actual experiences with death and coping with their emotions in response to such a loss.

Grieving Process

The grieving process, while unique for each child, does seem to occur in stages for all children. Bowlby (1980), Fox Valley Hospice (1987), Jewett (1982), Wolfelt (1983), and Costa and Holliday (1994) substantiated the stage theory of grief originally pioneered by Kubler-Ross in 1969.

The stage theory of grief helps explain the grieving process but should not be used as a diagnostic or predictive instrument force fitting children into a static description of a fluid process. Children will proceed through the stages of grief at varying rates, skipping some and experiencing others out of sequence.

Whereas much of the early research on the grieving process was done with adults, Wolfelt (1983) studied how children experience grief and developed the following framework describing the process.

Shock, Denial, Disbelief, and Numbness.   Immediately following the death of a loved one, many children experience disbelief and emotional shock. They are unable to comprehend the magnitude of their loss. Often they will deny their loss in an attempt to protect themselves. They may perceive everything that is happening to them as a dream from which they will awaken and that everything will be okay.

Lack of Feelings.   To parents, children may appear to lack emotions during a time when family members are overwrought with grief in response to the death of a loved one. Yet what often appears to be a lack of emotions is more often than not their attempt to protect themselves in an environment that is no longer predictable and safe. Their apparent inability to feel emotion is an expression of denial and disbelief. Children are attempting to "hang on" to their world, thus giving themselves time to ease into the pain that for now is too much for them to bear.

Physiological Changes.   As children begin to process mentally what they have been told and are now experiencing, their bodies respond accordingly and experience common somatic changes in response to their bereavement. Some of those changes are (Wolfelt, 1983)

- tiredness and lack of energy;
- difficulty in sleeping or prolonged sleeping;
- lack of appetite or excessive appetite;
- tightness in the throat;
- shortness of breath;
- general nervousness, trembling;
- headaches;
- stomach pain;
- loss of muscular strength; and
- skin rashes. (p. 34)

These conditions are temporary, normal bodily reactions to acute stress. Children need support and the opportunity to express their thoughts and feelings when they are ready to do so. With time, these symptoms will gradually dissipate.

Regression.   Under the physical and psychological stress of grief, children's sense of connectiveness can be interrupted. They no longer feel safe and secure. In their yearning for comfort and protection, many children will regress to an earlier developmental level when they experienced the physical and psychological warmth that is now missing in their life. Wolfelt (1983) has indicated that the most common regressive behaviors of childhood bereavement are the following:

- overdependence on parent to point of declining to go outside to play as they have in the past;
- a desire to be nursed or rocked as they were at an earlier stage of development;
- a desire to sleep with parent;
- an inability to separate from parent for any length of time;
- request others to perform tasks for them that they were previously able to do for themselves (e.g., ask to be carried, etc.);
- refuse to work independently in school setting and/or demand constant individual attention and demonstrate dependent seeking behaviors to teacher and peers;
- taking on a "sick role" in an effort to avoid attending school;
- regression to talking "baby talk" and in general presenting themselves in an infant-like manner; and
- breakdown in ability to function adequately in peer relationships. (p. 36)

Regressive behaviors, like the ones mentioned, are temporary expressions of grief and gradually disappear as children, with caregiver support, adjust to their loss.

"Big Man" or "Big Woman" Syndrome.   Wolfelt characterized this dimension as being the opposite of regressive behavior in which children attempt to become the man or woman of the house in an effort to replace the deceased parent. Children who play the "big man" or "big woman" may do so in an attempt to maintain things as they once were or to help others with their grief by fulfilling the responsibilities of the deceased parent. When children are seen taking on adult roles, they need to be encouraged and supported to follow as normal a routine as possible commensurate with their stage of development.

Disorganization and Panic.   Children may experience periods of overwhelming thoughts, feelings, panic, and disorganization that may occur suddenly and unpredictably. Such reactions are not uncommon as children begin to come to grips with the reality of the death. For the first time, they may question who will take care of them and what will happen to them if their other parent dies. They likewise may be frightened by scary dreams and memories of the deceased and, at other times, try to connect with the departed by remembering their voice, bodily features, and pleasant events.

During this dimension, children may appear to be restless, irritable, find it difficult to concentrate, and may experience changes in eating and sleeping patterns. They also may experience confusing changes in emotions, laughing one moment, and for no apparent reason, crying the next moment.

Wolfelt (1983) stated that disorganization and panic tend to occur from one to six months following the death of a significant loved one. Children need to be reassured that what they are experiencing is a normal reaction to grief. They likewise need to be comforted and held as a counter response to their feelings of being disconnected (e.g., aloneness, loss of security, and fear).

Explosive Emotions.   Children in their response to feelings of pain, hopelessness, frustration, and hurt may lash out at those around them. They may exhibit expressions of anger, hatred, and terror in response to their perceived sense of abandonment. Their explosive emotions often are aimed directly at the deceased for leaving them. They may feel vulnerable having invested themselves totally in this relationship only to lose the one they loved so much. Some children may fear getting too close to others because they might lose them as well.

Children need support during those times when their behavior is unpredictable and difficult to accept because of its abusive nature. Caregivers must lend an open ear even while they are being abused. They must not criticize or punish, rather be accepting, supportive, and understanding until these uncomfortable, yet natural feelings subside. Anger and hostility turned inward can result in depression, anxiety, and withdrawal or escalate into violence and unmanageable behavior. Children who exhibit such symptoms, may need professional assistance.

Acting Out Behavior.   Some children may experience the pain of grief by physically acting out. Temper tantrums, fighting, unusually noisy and loud behavior, and defiance against authority are typical physical responses to grief. Other children may experience a drop in grades, associate with children outside of their peer group, and in some cases run away from home. Such outward expressions of anger provide a release for pent-up frustrations, feelings of deprivation, and abandonment. These children may feel unloved or utilize their aggressive behaviors to distance themselves from others so they can not be hurt again.

Fear.   Children often experience fear during the grieving process. They fear being left alone to care for themselves, death of the surviving parent, and, in some cases, their own death. They may be frightened by their inability to help others with their grief and fear the slightest hint of illness in themselves that mimics that of the deceased.

Children also may fear loving again, because to love again means to risk loss and endure the same pain. Children need help understanding and accepting their fears as a part of life, living, and loving.

Guilt and Self-blame.   Many children will blame themselves for the death of their loved one and experience the guilt associated with self-blame. Young children especially are prone to making connections between their thoughts and the death of their loved one. Thus, when a loved one dies, children are quick to blame themselves for expressed wishes and angry thoughts that were aimed at the now deceased parent.

The guilt that children feel often surfaces in statements such as "If only I would have . . ." or "I wish I could have . . ." or "Why didn't I. . . ." As the guilt mounts, children may think that they deserve to be punished or engage in self-punishment as a means of responding to their sense of guilt, helplessness, and worthlessness. Because children feel responsible for their loved one's death, they also may bargain with God or the deceased that they will be good if the deceased person returns.

Children need to experience unconditional love and support. They need to be encouraged to discuss their feelings and thoughts regarding the deceased. They likewise need to understand that death is not a form of punishment and that their being angry or upset with a person does not cause that person to die.

Relief.   When children have experienced prolonged stress associated with the long illness of a loved one, they are likely to feel a sense of relief. Relief is a natural and normal bodily response to extended periods of tension. Relief is the body's way of achieving peace after a heightened period of alertness. Children who are not prepared to experience relief may feel guilty at a time when they believe they should be grieving for the deceased. Children need help understanding that relief is an emotion to be accepted when it is felt. Relief does not mean a lack of love for oneself or the dead person.

Loss, Emptiness, and Sadness.   The full sense of loss takes place over time. Loss does not occur all at once. Children may not totally experience the full impact of the loss until months after the death. That is when sadness, emptiness, and, for some, depression sets in. These feelings are truly felt when children realize the finality of the loss and that the dearly missed will not be coming back.

Children may wonder why it is that 6 to 10 months after the death they are feeling alone, sad, and tearful. During this time, children may demonstrate the following (Wolfelt, 1983):

- a lack of interest in self and others,
- change of appetite and sleeping patterns,
- prolonged withdrawal,
- nervousness,
- inability to experience pleasure, and
- low self-esteem. (p. 46)

Reconciliation.   The last dimension of grief is a process of adjustment in which children come to terms with their loss. Life never will be the same again, because death is a life changing experience. Though children will never "get over" the loss, they can reconcile themselves to it. They can gain a new sense of meaning and purpose to life.

Children should be supported in their struggle in addressing one of life's adversities, the loss of a loved one. As children grow from their loss, they will experience the following (Wolfelt, 1983):

- a return to stable eating and sleeping patterns,
- a renewed sense of energy and well-being,
- a subjective sense of release from the person who has died,
- increased thinking and judgment making capabilities,
- the capacity to enjoy life experiences,
- a recognition of the reality and finality of the death, and
- the establishment of a new and healthy relationship. (p. 49)

D'Andrea and Daniels (1992), in their review of how children react to personal loss, have presented a four-stage process described as numbness, yearning, disorganization and depression, and reorganization.

Numbness Phase. Immediately following a significant loss in their lives, children seem to react as if in a daze of disbelief. They will experience a sense of unreality, empty feelings, and psychological numbness (Siegelman & Shaffer, 1991). This numbness serves as a form of protection that insulates children from the full brunt of the devastation allowing them to experience the loss gradually.

Yearning Phase. As the numbness wanes, children will become more acutely aware of their loss. They will experience emotional feelings of sadness and loneliness, and the anxiety and agony that accompanies the reality of separation in response to the loss. Whiting (1990) also notes that underlying the pain is a preoccupation with that which has been lost.

Also during the yearning phase, children may experience behavioral changes like those noted by Wolfelt (1983). Among the more common behaviors exhibited are restlessness, agitation, insomnia, nightmares, sudden bouts of uncontrollable crying, physical aches and pains, and feelings of panic (Siegelman & Shaffer, 1991). Because children are unaccustomed to these feelings and behaviors, they may be on edge, irritable, and quick to lash out at those around them. They yearn to have things as they once were and may blame themselves and others for their loss.

Disorganization and Depression Phase. In this stage, children begin to adjust to the reality that there is nothing they can do to "fix" their loss—to make things as they once were. Children may become depressed in response to their hopeless situation. They may show a total lack of interest in themselves, school work, peer relationships, and family activities. They seem to lack energy and direction. In many ways, they truly are experiencing the loss in their confusion, sadness, anger, and powerlessness. They need time and assistance from adult caregivers and peers to work through and reorganize their thoughts, feelings, and behaviors in response to their loss.

Reorganization Phase.   During the last phase of grief, children come to terms with their loss. The grieving process requires patience, persistence, and a plan. Children and family members must be patient and not try to rush the grieving process. They likewise must persist in working through their feelings, thoughts and questions as they relate to their loss. And, finally, they need a plan for moving on—not to put the loss behind them, but to accept the loss and draw strength from it. Daniels (1990), in her examination of the growth potential inherent in personal loss, found that her adult subjects reported increased inner strength, more self-confidence, a greater appreciation for friends and family, new interests, and a clearer focus with regard to life and living. Children also can grow and become stronger as a result of their loss by learning more about themselves and how they have grown in the face of adversity (Edgar & Howard-Hamilton, 1995).

Factors Influencing a Child's Response to Death

Children will vary in their response to the death of a loved one. Wolfelt (1983) identified the following six elements that caregivers must consider in helping children face significant losses in their lives:

- the child's relationship with the person who has died—the "meaning" of the death;
- the nature of the death—when, how, and where the person died;
- the child's own personality and previous experiences with death;
- the child's chronological and developmental age;
- the availability of family/social/community support; and
- most importantly the behavior, attitudes, and responsiveness of parents and other significant adults in the child's environment.

Types of Loss

Although the major focus of this chapter has been on death and grief, children will experience many different types of losses in their lives. Understanding loss and grief have application in helping children respond to a broad range of loss experiences. What follows is a brief discussion of some of the more typical examples of loss that many children will experience.

Lost Toy.   Children of all ages develop attachment to toys and personal belongings. When a toy is lost or broken, children are faced with having to cope with the loss. Blankets and stuffed animals are often symbols of comfort, protection, and safety. Children become attached to their belongings and count on their presence day in and day out. One only can imagine the impact felt by a child whose favorite teddy bear has been left at Grandma's house many miles away. For the first time in the child's life, he or she must face bedtime without that favorite companion.

Moving Away.   When parents change jobs and the family has to move, a major separation is inevitable. Children must disconnect from all that is familiar and safe. They will be facing a new life absent of old friends, familiar routines, a loving home, and a comfortable community. There is little in life that is more scary and difficult for children to accept than to have to disconnect from their homes, schools, communities, and friends because of a move.

Divorce.   Many children today will be facing a divorce in their future. Their parents will separate and the children's lives will be changed forever. The loss of a parent through divorce can be devastating. Physically, the family changes in structure and psychologically, children experience all of the emotions and thoughts that loss triggers. Divorce is discussed in further detail in Chapter 5.

Stepfamilies.   When two families join together in marriage, a new relationship is formed. Children who are unrelated now share common parents, a common household, and a common bond as they strive to make the necessary adjustments in building one new family where previously there had been two. Stepfamilies, at least in theory, would seem to be a workable possibility benefiting all concerned; however, in reality children are forced to cope with many losses and the grief that accompanies each. Children must cope with having to share their parent with other family members. They must adjust to new living arrangements and share bedrooms, the dinner table, love, and family resources. Before sharing can take place, children need support and assistance in grieving the loss of their autonomy and all previous life connections affected by the new living arrangements. See Chapter 6, Stepfamilies, for further information on this topic.

Death of a Pet.   A common experience that many children have shared is the death of a pet. Dogs, cats, birds, hamsters, and fish are important family pets often in the care of children who love them very much. When a pet dies, children are left with a gap in their lives. Because of the close physical and psychological attachment to their pet, the loss can be every bit as difficult to accept as the loss of a loved one. Missing or deceased pets will generate questions, feelings, and thoughts in children that must be addressed in helping them grieve their loss.

Remember that loss can represent a voluntary or involuntary separation (permanent or temporary) from people, places, and things in children's envi-

ronments that are personally significant or familiar to them. This definition covers a breadth of loss possibilities from the breaking of a toy to the death of a loved one. Children need caring adults on whom they can rely in learning how to express and share their grief. With such support, children will come to understand that loss is a natural part of life.

CHILDREN'S NEEDS

Children learn about death, loss, and grief in small steps throughout their formative years of development (Baker, Sedney, & Gross, 1992). The messages they receive about loss are wide and varied ranging from exposure to the mass media, customs, language related to the culture, religious training, and personal family experiences. The messages received during the early years of life, while having an impact, take on more clarity and meaning with advanced stages of development. Having knowledge and understanding of the grieving process will help facilitators better meet children's needs in response to loss (Glass, 1991; McHutchion, 1991; Silverman & Worden, 1992). While specific needs will vary depending on developmental levels of understanding and personal experiences with death, loss, and grief, all children need to

- receive accurate information,
- share their feelings,
- share their beliefs,
- grieve, and
- take action.

Share Feelings

Children have a need to share and understand their feelings (emotions) in response to loss and grief. Children are often confused and frightened by the vast array of emotions they will experience. Feelings of loneliness, abandonment, anger, sadness, emptiness, and low self-esteem are likely to trigger a multitude of thoughts and behaviors that are equally confusing and frightening as children search for ways to get back to the way things once were.

Share Beliefs

Children are likely to harbor a number of beliefs about death. Some of these beliefs are cultural and religious in nature whereas others will evolve from children's vivid imaginations and fascination with death. Children, as with feelings, have a need to share their beliefs with others. Understanding children's beliefs provides insight into their feelings and behaviors in response to loss. Sometimes beliefs are based more on myth than fact and need to be addressed in responsible ways.

Grieve

Grief is a normal and natural aspect of loss. Because children experience feelings of grief, they have a need to understand their sense of hopelessness and loss of control in relationship to the adversity they have experienced. In many ways, helping children relate to the grief process is aided through accurate information and the sharing of feelings and beliefs about death and loss.

Take Action

Children need not be mere bystanders in the ebb and flow of the grieving process. They have a need to take constructive action in relationship to loss. Although children, in most instances, can do little to prevent a loss or keep a loved one from dying, they can become involved in self-care activities the will help them facilitate a healthy adjustment to loss, death, and grief.

STRENGTHS TO BE LEARNED

Children must learn how to acknowledge, grieve, and resolve loss in their lives. Some losses will be addressed easily, whereas other losses will require time and the application of personal strengths to resolve. The support group sessions that follow will provide children with the information, skills, self-confidence, and opportunity to play an active role in their own self-care.

Information

Accurate and useful information can help children meet their physiological, safety and security, love and belonging, and self-esteem needs that often are assaulted during loss. Children can benefit from information that will help them better understand themselves and their needs (Bertoia & Allan, 1988; Morganett, 1994; Muro & Kottman, 1995; Rando, 1988). More specifically, children have a need to know that

- there are many types of loss;
- when they experience a significant loss, they will grieve;

- grief is a normal process that takes time;
- there is no timetable for resolving a loss;
- there is no one right way to grieve and grieving is personal;
- working through grief can be difficult, but they can do it;
- they can express their grief through pictures, talking to others, writing a poem, being by themselves, taking a walk in the park, and so forth;
- anger, sadness, loneliness, guilt, frustration, and numbness are normal feelings;
- they may experience highs and lows, feeling fine one minute and sadness the next;
- they are not going crazy even though they feel totally disorganized and confused;
- they can and should take breaks from their grieving by spending time with friends, listening to music, and doing healthy things that give them personal pleasure;
- while it may be difficult to eat properly, exercise, and get plenty of rest, this is what they must strive to do; and
- with time and work, things will get better and they will be able to remember the good times and cherish comforting memories that never can be taken away.

Sharing Feelings

Learning to understand and share feelings with others is a personal strength that children can develop. During the following activities, children will be given the opportunity to share their feelings in discussion and in pictures. They will experience the power that comes from sharing. Children will explore a variety of feelings that they have experienced when their loved one died and will learn a variety of ways in which they can manage difficult feelings responsibly. With practice in understanding, expressing, and managing their feelings, children will recognize that they can survive and grow in the face of adversity. They will be able to ask for the help they need, share their grief, and relieve themselves of some of the stress and tension they have been experiencing. They will learn that painful feelings do not last forever and that there are helpful things they can do to benefit themselves in coping with loss.

Sharing Beliefs

Sharing beliefs about loss and death will help children recognize the power that their thoughts play in affecting their feelings and actions. Many fears about death that children harbor often occur because developmentally they are unable to understand or comprehend the differences between myth and reality. As children develop and mature, they can explore religious and cultural beliefs about death and learn to question and challenge some of their own irrational thoughts. For example, children in various developmental stages may believe that people who die today will be seen tomorrow; that because Uncle Joe died in his sleep, they themselves will die in their sleep; and that because they have had ill thoughts about a loved one, they are responsible for that loved one's death.

Teaching children to appreciate differing cultural and religious beliefs about life and death and the various ceremonies and rituals that support both will help children understand that death is very much apart of life. Likewise, children can be taught to examine their own beliefs about life and death and the extent to which reality and myth influence their perceptions. With practice, children can learn to challenge their irrational beliefs and replace them with rational thought and more responsible action.

Taking Action

Action oriented activities can help children respond to loss in their lives. Children can be taught the value of taking action in reducing stress, eliminating fear, and restoring confidence in themselves. Learning to take action can help children make the necessary life adjustments in disconnecting from their loss experiences while setting new goals that will lead to future growth. For example, children may have little choice but to relocate with their family following a parental job promotion; however, they do have choices they can make that will help them adjust to the move. They can remain in contact with their old friends by phone, letter writing, and occasional visits. Likewise they can learn about their new community and what it has to offer by obtaining information from the Chamber of Commerce, visiting the new school, and joining familiar groups at school and in the community.

Similarly, when children lose a friend or relative through death, adults can include them in such activities as cooking a meal, delivering food, planning part of the service, selecting flowers, sending cards, and attending the funeral. Children have a special need to be connected to self and others during times of loss. One way of helping them achieve a sense of closeness is to include them in as many family related activities as is practical. Support group activities emphasize the importance of connecting with the deceased through pictures, mementos, and memories. Even though their loved ones are no longer present in life, their memories and teachings will live on in them and will be passed onto future generations through them.

MESSAGE TO FACILITATORS

Helping children understand and manage death, loss, and grief in their lives is a major challenge. Your primary goal must be one of presenting a positive view of loss. Seibert et al. (1993) have stated that these topics (i.e., death, loss, and grief) must be treated in a factually accurate manner, appropriate to children's levels of understanding, and be presented in ways that will help children view death, loss, and grief as a natural part of life.

As you review the support group activities, you also need to examine your own feelings, attitudes, and beliefs about death, loss, and grief. The groups that you facilitate will be successful to the extent that you can create an open atmosphere where children can feel safe to explore, what for many, are taboo topics. Children are quick to pick up verbal and nonverbal signals noting any discomfort that you may be experiencing as you listen to them share their innermost thoughts and feelings.

Because children's beliefs come from home and are often culturally and religiously based, your role is to teach and accept a variety of beliefs. Children can be encouraged to explore death, loss, and grief with their families and members of their religious communities (see Figure 10.1). These beliefs then can be shared with the support group. As you listen to children share their feelings and beliefs, keep in mind that some children have had negative experiences with loss and death. Such experiences may trigger tears, anger, fear, or cynicism that can become misdirected and have a negative influence on the group. All the more reason for you to explore your own death, loss, and grief experiences before you begin facilitating a support group on these topics.

Selecting Group Members

Because your support group is designed to meet general and specific needs of children who have experienced recent losses, it is helpful to interview perspective group members and their parents. Your goal is to select children that can best benefit from a support group and to identify others who may need more intense therapeutic interventions. These children and their families should be referred to appropriate counseling services.

While we have provided general selection guidelines in Chapter 3, the following specific indicators offered by Morganett (1994) may suggest that a child is a good candidate for a support group intervention on this topic:

- is currently dealing with the loss of a parent, relative, friend, or pet;
- is able to function academically and socially at school without major disturbances—that is, neither severely acting out nor acting extremely withdrawn;
- is having difficulty grieving, as indicated by an inability to stop talking about the death or acting as though the loss never occurred (e.g., by talking about the person as if he or she were still alive or constantly referring to the dead person); and
- is experiencing depression as evidenced by withdrawal, moodiness, irritability, problems sleeping and/or eating or difficulty concentrating or remembering.

Some children may not benefit from a group experience. Morganett (1994) indicated that a child who exhibits any of the following characteristics should be referred for more individualized assistance:

- engages in bizarre behavior such as self-destruction, hurting animals, giving away possessions, playing with knives, and the like;
- has frequent panic attacks or otherwise appears still to be in a state of shock over the loss;
- engages in serious socially inappropriate or delinquent behaviors, such as stealing or vandalism;
- withdraws or refuses to socialize with other children;
- refuses to do school work or go to school; and
- is assessed as being suicidal.

Group Goals

The goals of our support group are designed to help children

- learn about death, loss, and grief as dimensions of life;
- participate in a supportive, open climate where they can explore their thoughts, feelings, and attitudes;
- receive accurate information that will help them challenge unrealistic fears and myths about death, loss, and grief;
- express their grief in responsible ways using coping skills learned in group; and
- talk with their parents and loved ones about their grief.

Guidelines for Discussing Death, Loss, and Grief

Whether responding to children's questions or discussing activities, remember to

- provide specific, clear, and short responses;
- be honest, truthful, and loving;
- take time and listen to the children discuss their concerns;
- describe activities to the children before they participate;
- let them know that there are no wrong answers;
- give them permission to feel a full range of emotions;
- thank children for participating;
- help children understand the value of sharing; and
- review what children have learned from each activity and in group.

Because children experience death, loss, and grief differently, you should monitor their progress both in and out of the group experience. We have found it helpful to meet with children individually each week, even for just a few minutes. These brief contacts will give you an opportunity to answer "private" questions and to identify specific needs that can be addressed individually or in group.

Helping children understand death, loss, and grief and teaching them new ways to self-manage is an important gift that we can pass on to them through a support group experience. Be open and sensitive to their needs and your group will give every bit as much back to you as you give to them. With each new support group experience, your expertise, sensitivity, and facilitative skills will grow. You are now ready to begin what will be a valuable experience for you and all the children whose lives you will touch in positive ways.

Resources

Share with parents and/or guardians Figure 10.1 so that they will have suggestions on how they can help their children at home. In Figure 10.2 are provided lists of resources to be used with and by children in the Death, Grief, and Loss Support Group. The resource materials are grouped according to age of child.

DEATH, GRIEF, AND LOSS GUIDE
Tips for Caregivers

Your child soon will be participating in a Death, Grief, and Loss Support Group. The goal of this support group is to help children better understand death and to provide support to those children who are coping with loss and grief. We are happy to share with you some general tips that you can use in helping your child cope with loss, grief, or life-threatening illness; however, we also suggest that you consult with counselors, clinicians, funeral directors, and religious professionals for additional guidance in helping you provide a supportive role to your child (children).

1. Should children be shielded from death?

Children experience grief and need an opportunity to share what they are feeling. Although you may not have all the answers to your child's questions, you can provide the needed emotional support that your child desires. Answer your child's questions openly and honestly, and do not be afraid to acknowledge that you do not have all the answers.

2. How do I explain death to a child?

You can approach the topic quietly and gently by helping your child connect with the life cycle of plants, trees and leaves, insects, small animals, and pets. The story of *The Fall of Freddie the Leaf* by Leo Buscaglia (1982) explains life and death through the eyes of a leaf.

3. Can children understand death?

As children grow and mature, their ideas about death change. For preschoolers, death is reversible. When a loved one dies, a young child may believe that the person has taken a long trip but will one day return. Children 5 to 9 years of age understand the meaning of physical death and yet do not attribute this physical state to themselves. By ages 9 or 10, children are beginning to accept an adult perspective of death. Age ranges, however, tell only part of the story. They do not reflect what individual children may understand, believe, or feel. Treat your child as an individual. Listen and learn from your child, and answer his or her questions truthfully, compassionately, and with brevity.

4. How do I tell my child about the death?

Figure 10.1. Tips for Caregivers to be given to parents and/or guardians. Permission to photocopy is granted.

Tell your child right away. Do not delay. Inform them about the death in familiar surroundings. Do so gently and lovingly. Be open but only provide as much detail as necessary to communicate understanding. Hold your child and provide comfort as needed and desired. Do not be surprised if your child does not respond like an adult would to the death. Be there to answer your child's questions, hear concerns, and express emotions. Also be ready to accept your child's need for distance from the stress and shock in response to hearing about the death. Some children will want to change the subject while others will temporarily escape by going outside to play.

5. What are some responses my child may exhibit?

Children can respond to the death of a loved one in a variety of ways. They may experience

Denial: "I can't believe it. This could not have happened."
Body stress: Stomachaches, headaches, tightness in the chest, sleep disturbances, anxiety, and fears are a few of the many bodily reactions that
children can experience.
Hostility: Some children will become angry with the deceased or lash out at
other family members and friends in response to the loss.
Idealization: Seeing the deceased as perfect and transformed in death can
occur and helps children connect with this person following the loss.
Fear: Some children may fear what will become of them after the death of a
parent. They also may fear the loss of the remaining parent as well.
Guilt: Children can experience guilt if they believe that they in some way
caused the death because of something they may have said or done when
the deceased was alive.

Maintaining a watchful and caring perspective may alert you to some of these reactions that then can be addressed in an understanding and supportive manner.

6. Should I use words like die, death, and dead?

When explaining the death of a loved one or friend, be truthful and use words that convey what has happened. Children should be told that Uncle Bill has died, not gone on a long trip or passed away. Your child has a need for trust and the truth.

7. Should I explain an afterlife to my child?

If you have a strong belief in an afterlife, you and your child should discuss this matter with a clergy person. While an afterlife explanation can be comforting to a child, it also can be confusing. Children may have a difficult time under-standing how Mommy can be in heaven when her body is in the ground. If you do decide to share your belief about an afterlife with your child, be prepared to answer questions of confusion that may arise.

8. Should I discourage my child from crying?

Crying is a natural emotion often expressed in times of pain and despair and is nature's way of experiencing emotional release. Allow yourself and your child the freedom of expressing a full range of emotions. Children neither should be expected to cry nor told not to do so. Allow honest expressions of emotion to be displayed without prejudice.

9. Should my child attend the funeral?

Children should be given the option as to their attendance at the funeral. For those children wishing to attend, the funeral can give them a chance to say their good-byes and to experience the finality of death. If your child chooses to attend, be sure to prepare him or her for what to expect in terms of the service. Your explanation will help reduce your child's fears and help him or her connect with the funeral service. If your child chooses not to attend the funeral, accept your child's wishes and do not use force to the contrary.

10. What about going to the cemetery?

The internment service is an extension of the funeral. If your child wishes to attend, you should explain what to expect in terms of the service and the burial. Witnessing the burial can help your child connect with the finality of death and what has happened to the body; however, your child should be given the choice as to whether or not to attend.

11. What about after the funeral?

The mourning process and grief can extend for months beyond the actual death. Be sure to inform your child's day care or school about the death. In this way, other adults and children can support your child in addition to keeping you alert as to adjustment needs to be addressed. Child support groups and death education classes are always options for children who could benefit from a little extra support.

If after several months beyond the death you have doubt about your child's adjustment, do not be afraid to consult with your family doctor, school counselor, religious affiliation, funeral director, or other professionally trained caring adults for assistance.

Figure 10.1. (*Continued*) Tips for Caregivers to be given to parents and/or guardians. Permission to photocopy is granted.

RESOURCES FOR CHILDREN
Death, Grief, and Loss

Ages 3 to 7

Carlstrom, N. W. (1990). *Blow me a kiss, Miss Lilly.* New York: HarperCollins. (death of friend).

Cazet, D. (1987). *A fish in his pocket.* New York: Orchard Books. (attitude toward death).

Cohn, J. (1987). *I had a friend named Peter.* New York: Morrow & Co. (loss of friend)

Douglas, E. (1990). *Rachel and the upside down heart.* Los Angeles: Price Stein Sloan. (death of father)

Gould, D. (1987). *Grandpa's slide show.* New York: Lothrop, Lee & Shepard Books. (death of grandparent)

LeTord, B. (1987). *My Grandma Leonie.* New York: Bradbury Press. (death of grandparent)

Palmer, P. (1994). *I wish I could hold your hand: A child's guide to grief and loss.* New York: Impact Publishers. (death of a loved one)

Powell, E. S. (1990). *Geranium morning.* Minneapolis: Carolrhoda Books. (death of mother)

Prestine, J. (1993). *Someone special died.* New York: Fearon Publishers. (loss of a special person)

Rogers, F. (1988). *When a pet dies.* New York: Putnam & Grosset Group. (death of pet)

Ages 8 to 12

Auch, M. J. (1988). *Pick of the litter.* New York: Holiday House. (death of sibling)

Berry, J. (1990). *Good answers to tough questions about death.* Chicago: Childrens Press. (questions and answers about death)

Boyd, C. D. (1985). *Breadsticks and blessing places.* New York: Macmillan. (funeral issues)

Clardy, A. F. (1984). *Dusty was my friend: Coming to terms with loss.* New York: Human Sciences Press. (death of a friend)

Clifford E. (1987). *The man who sang in the dark.* Boston: Houghton Mifflin. (death of father)

DeClements, B. (1988). *The fourth grade wizards.* New York: Viking Penguin. (death of mother)

Dyzak, E. (1990). *I should have listened to Moon.* Boston: Houghton Mifflin. (death of pet)

Foley, P. (1990). *John and the fiddler.* New York: HarperCollins. (death of friend)

Goble, P. (1989). *Beyond the ridge.* New York: Bradbury Press. (funeral issues)

Hartling, P. (1990). *Old John.* New York: Lothrop, Lee & Shepard Books. (death of grandparent)

Temes, R. (1992). *The empty place: A child's guide through grief.* Far Hills, NJ: New Horizon NJ. (death of sibling)

Ages 12 and Up

Asher, S. F. (1984). *Missing pieces.* New York: Delacorte Press. (death of father)

Cross, G. (1987). *Chartbreaker.* New York: Holiday House. (death of mother)

Davis, J. (1987). *Good-bye and keep cold.* New York: Orchard Books. (death of father, maturation)

Ferris, J. (1987). *Invincible summer.* New York: Farrar, Straus & Giroux. (death of friend to leukemia, attitude toward death)

Gulley, J. (1988). *Wasted space.* Nashville: Abingdon Press. (death of friend, lack of communication)

Mazer, H. (1985). *When the phone rang.* New York: Scholastic. (death of mother)

Miklowitz, G. D. (1983). *Close to the edge.* New York: Dell Publishing. (suicide of friend)

Maggio, R. (1990). *The music box Christmas.* New York: William Morrow. (death of grandparent, accepting change)

White, E. E. (1987). *Life without friends.* New York: Scholastic. (murder)

Wood, P. A. (1986). *Then I'll be home free.* New York: Dodd, Mead & Co. (death of grandparent, attempted suicide)

Figure 10.2. Resources for use with and by children in Death, Grief, and Loss Support Group.

SESSION I—GETTING ACQUAINTED/
SETTING THE STAGE

BRIEF OVERVIEW OF SESSION

This initial group will set the stage for an eight week support group on dealing with death or loss. Members should have been chosen because they have had a loss in their life and should have been interviewed and invited to be a part of the group. At this session, ground rules will be set, children will have the opportunity to become acquainted with other group members, and they will have their first opportunity to talk about the loss they have experienced.

GOALS

1. To assist children in understanding the reason for their presence in the group.
2. To allow children to become acquainted with other group members.
3. To assist children in beginning to talk about losses in their life.

MATERIALS NEEDED

1. Copies of "Coat of Arms" worksheet (Activity Sheet 10.1)
2. Markers, pencils, crayons
3. Chalkboard and chalk (or chart paper)

PROCEDURE

1. Introduce yourself and have each of the students in the group introduce himself or herself by first name. Talk about the fact that this is a group for those who have lost a loved one. During the course of the sessions, we will talk about these losses and also will discuss ways we can deal with loss.

2. Begin to set the stage for the group by inviting a brainstorming session on group rules. Examples of possible initial group ground rules may include

a What is said in the group, stays there (confidentiality).
b No put-downs are allowed.
c Only one person talks at a time.
d It is important to attend all sessions.

Note: If children do not suggest these group rules, you as facilitator should bring them up as part of the brainstorming session.

3. Do the "Coat of Arms" worksheet (Activity Sheet 10.1). Instruct the children to draw a picture or write words to describe the following:

a three words that describe you,
b something you really like to do,
c a safe place for you,
d things you like to do with a friend,
e something you do well, and
f something you would like to improve.

4. Allow time for children to share one or more sections from their "Coat of Arms" when they are completed. Remind children that they have the opportunity to "pass" if they wish.

5. Reintroduce the topic of loss and remind the children that each person in the group is there because he or she has lost a loved one. If students feel comfortable talking about their loss, time should be provided. (The facilitator may want to model by sharing a loss in his or her life.)

CLOSURE

At the conclusion of the sharing session on loss, summarize for the children and begin to set the stage for next session by stating that we will begin to look at types of losses. Conclude by asking each person to describe his or her feelings about today's group.

HOMEWORK

For their homework assignment, group members are to think about some possible kinds of loss. (It may be prudent to give examples such as loss of a material object, loss of a friend, when someone moves away, etc.)

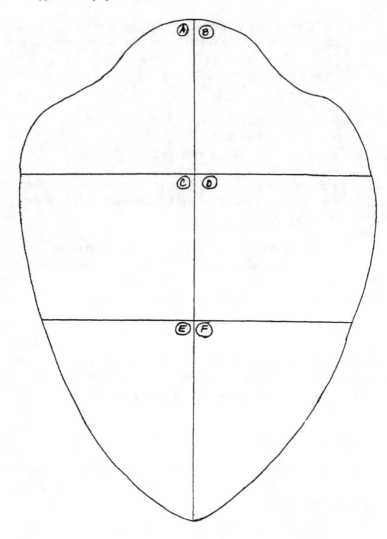

Activity Sheet 10.1.   Coat of Arms worksheet. Permission is granted to enlarge and photocopy for classroom use.

SESSION II—TYPES OF LOSSES

BRIEF OVERVIEW OF SESSION

This session will provide children with the opportunity to look at loss in a broader focus as they begin to identify the wide variety of losses that occur in one's life. They also will begin to realize that some losses have a much greater impact on our life than others and that all losses are not negative—in fact, some loss is a choice.

GOALS

1. To provide children with an opportunity to begin to identify the many types of loss they have experienced.
2. To assist each child in the group in identifying at least four personal losses he or she has had.
3. To encourage children to realize that not all loss has to be negative.

MATERIALS NEEDED

1. Chart papers and markers
2. Chalkboard and chalk
3. Copies of "Four Losses" worksheet (Activity Sheet 10.2)

PROCEDURE

1. Begin with a brief review of last session. Remind children that at the conclusion of the session, we began to look at losses we have had in our lives. (If anyone wants to comment further, or if someone who did not share last session would like to share, allow a few minutes for sharing.)

2. Talk about things we have lost. Ask each student to pair up with a partner and talk about losses they thought about for their homework assignment.

3. Provide each pair with a sheet of chart paper and a marker and ask him or her to list the losses discussed. Allow about 5 to 8 minutes for dyad activity.

4. Display charts from the various pairs and discuss similarities and differences in types of losses that were described.

5. Point out that not all losses are negative. Some things such as a loss of weight actually may be a choice that a person makes. Or the loss of a friend who moves away actually may give one the opportunity to make a new friend while still communicating by mail with the one who moved away.

6. Allow children the opportunity to talk about some losses that were listed on the charts. Can they identify positives and negatives about any of the losses they listed?

7. Provide each child with a copy of the "Four Losses" worksheet (Activity Sheet 10.2) and ask each to write or draw a picture of four personal losses he or she has experienced in life.

8. Permit children who wish to do so an opportunity to share one of the four losses from their worksheet.

CLOSURE

Summarize the session by sharing the types of losses identified by the students. Conclude the session by asking each person to describe their feelings about today's group.

HOMEWORK

Remind students that, for the next session, we plan to begin to identify feelings identified with the loss of their loved one. Stress that, at different times in the grieving process, each person may have a variety of feelings.

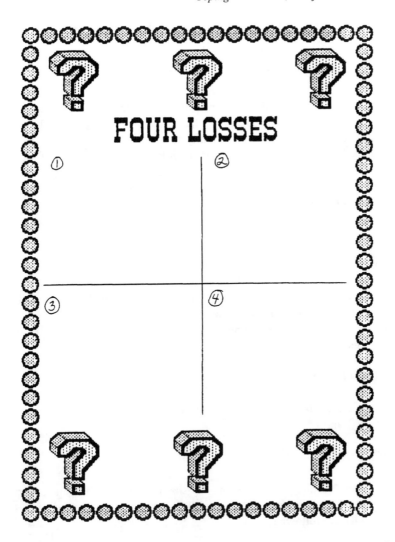

Activity Sheet 10.2.　Four Losses worksheet. Permission is granted to enlarge and photocopy for classroom use.

SESSION III—FEELINGS ABOUT LOSS

BRIEF OVERVIEW OF SESSION

During the course of this session, children will have the opportunity to recall feelings they experienced during the time of the loss of their loved one. Each child will be given the opportunity to recall and describe for the group the four feelings he or she experienced upon learning of the death of the loved one. Follow-up discussion will focus on the fact that not everyone experiences the same feelings, that all feelings are okay, and that no one should tell you how you *should* feel.

GOALS

1. To assist children in realizing that one may experience a wide range of feelings when a loved one dies.
2. To encourage children to identify and recall the feelings they experienced upon the death of their loved one.
3. To provide a secure atmosphere in which the children may talk about their feelings.

MATERIALS NEEDED

1. Chalk and chalkboard or chart paper and markers
2. Crayons and paper

PROCEDURE

1. Introduce the topic of feelings by sharing with the children some possible feelings one may have upon learning of the death of a loved one. These may include the following:

fear—that they may die or that they will be left alone,
guilt—that they may be responsible for causing the death,
sorrow—at the loss of a loved one,
anger—that the person has left them,
jealousy—that this hasn't happened to other kids, and
relief—that suffering has ended.

2. Invite children to share other possible feelings that one may experience. List all of these on a chalkboard or chart for further reference.

3. Allow each child the necessary time to think about the feelings they experienced

a   upon learning of the death,
b   the first night after the death,
c   at the funeral home or funeral, and
d   after the funeral.

4. Reassure children that all feelings are okay, that not everyone feels the same way because each person is having a personal experience.

5. Encourage each child to share with the group at least one feeling he or she experienced. Recognize that it may be difficult for some children.

6. Ask each child to draw a picture of one of the feelings he or she experienced and share it with the group.

CLOSURE

Conclude by reviewing what has been said about feelings and by reiterating that people have different feelings in reacting to the death of a loved one. Again, complete the activity by asking each child to describe how he or she felt about today's group.

HOMEWORK

Remind students that, as a homework assignment for next week's group, they are to think about how their life has changed as a result of the loss.

SESSION IV—COPING WITH CHANGE

BRIEF OVERVIEW OF SESSION

Throughout this session, children will be afforded the opportunity to begin to look at the changes that have taken place in their lives as a result of their loss. They also will begin to identify coping strategies they have utilized in order to assist them in dealing with their loss.

GOALS

1. To encourage children to identify ways their life has changed as a result of their loss.
2. To assist children in looking carefully at how they have changed as a result of their loss.
3. To provide an opportunity for children to develop coping strategies for dealing with their loss.

MATERIALS NEEDED

1. Chalkboard (or chart paper)
2. Chalk (or markers)
3. 9" × 12" sheet of paper and pencil for each child

PROCEDURE

1. Provide a few minutes to review the material from last session and remind students that a variety of feelings were identified to describe how people feel as a result of a loss of a loved one. Allow a few minutes for discussion of any additional feelings anyone may want to share.

2. Pose the question, "What things have changed in your life as a result of your loss?" As students begin to share items, list them on the chart paper or chalkboard for all to see. (Children will probably say such things as, "I have to go to a baby-sitter after school," "I have lots more jobs to do at home," or "We don't have as much fun."

3. Encourage children to communicate with others' comments through comments or questions such as "Has anyone else had a similar experience?" or "I'll bet others in this group may have experienced the same kinds of things."

4. Follow up this discussion with the question, "How have you changed as a result of your loss?" Again list the children's responses on the chart paper or chalkboard. These may include such things as, "I seem more grown up than other kids in my class" or "I can do a lot of things that others my age can't do." Point out to the children that not all of these things are negative.

5. Draw a continuum on the chart paper or chalkboard and label it as the sample shown here:

Positive   Negative

6. Ask children to identify ways they have coped with their loss. You may want to ask them, "What are some things kids can do to help deal with their feelings?" As they identify different strategies, encourage them to decide whether the strategies are more positive or negative and label them on the continuum. (Some possible items that may be identified can include playing with a friend, reading a book, watching TV, talking with someone, fighting with siblings, taking drugs, etc.)

7. Provide each child with a sheet of paper and have them develop their own coping strategies continuum. If possible, allow time for sharing and discussion at the end of the session.

CLOSURE

By this point in the group, children should be feeling fairly comfortable with each other. Take a few moments to encourage discussion as to how they feel the group is going, to review ground rules, and to praise the group for adhering to the ground rules.

HOMEWORK

Remind children that next session we will be looking at the stages of loss. Ask them to do some thinking about what those stages might be.

SESSION V—STAGES OF GRIEVING

BRIEF OVERVIEW OF SESSION

In this session, children will begin to learn that different stages occur in the grieving process and each will affect everyone at some time in their life. They will be helped in understanding that not everyone experiences the stages in the same order or for the same length of time and that one may experience the stages more than once.

GOALS

1. To assist children in gaining an understanding of stages of loss.
2. To help children realize that everyone will experience some of these stages.

MATERIALS NEEDED

1. Poster that identifies stages of loss according to Kubler-Ross (1969) and Hannaford and Popkin (1992)

Stages of Loss or Grief

Kubler-Ross (1969)	Hannaford and Popkin (1992)
	1. Shock
1. Denial	2. Panic
2. Anger	3. Denial
3. Bargaining	4. Release
4. Depression	5. Guilt
5. Acceptance	6. Anger
	7. Depression
	8. Returning
	9. Hope
	10. Acceptance

PROCEDURE

1. Provide a few minutes for any comments, questions, or brief discussion regarding any of the sessions to this point.

2. Introduce the issue of loss in terms of stages. Remind children that much research has been done to study how persons deal with grief and that two theories will be shared with them today.

3. Show both posters (or better yet, have them both listed on the same poster so that children may compare and contrast the two lists).

4. Allow time for children to go through each list and identify times that they experienced each of the stages and share these with the group.

5. Remind children that not everyone will experience all of the stages in the same order or in the same way and that this is okay.

6. Suggest that some persons may experience some of the stages more than once. For example: A person may feel that he or she is in the acceptance stage and doing well when the anniversary of the loved one's death approaches. At this time the person may find the he or she feels a great deal of sadness and depression. Reassure the children that this is very normal and is to be expected.

7. Ask each child to think about what stage he or she may be in at this time and encourage him or her to share this information with the group. (This may be a good time to point out that each person in the group experienced his or her loss at a different time, thus many stages may be represented within the group.)

8. Allow time for further discussion and questions.

CLOSURE

Provide time for a brief review of the stages from both lists. Ask children to comment on the session and their feelings regarding the session and the information presented.

HOMEWORK

For a homework assignment, ask each child to locate and bring to next week's group a shoebox with a lid. The box will be used for the next two group sessions.

SESSION VI—MAKE A MEMORY BOX

BRIEF OVERVIEW OF SESSION

To this point in the group, all of the sessions have dealt with the loss in a direct manner. This group will provide the opportunity for the children to relax a bit and get involved in an activity. It also will enable them to make something that will, in the future, be a pleasant reminder of the group and the learnings and understandings gained from participation.

GOALS

1. To provide time, materials and opportunity for the children to make a "Memory Box."
2. To encourage the children to think about all of the special memories they have of their loved one.

MATERIALS NEEDED

1. Shoebox for each child (Children should supply these, but it might be a good idea to bring a few extras.)
2. Contact paper
3. Construction paper, scissors, glue, etc.
4. Other materials (depending on how creative you wish to be)

PROCEDURE

1. Begin by providing time for any questions, comments, or discussion from previous sessions.

2. Talk briefly about "memories." What are some things that may help us remember a person? Children's comments probably will include things such as special events, food, pictures, and souvenirs.

3. Tell children that today everyone is going to make a "Memory Box." They may decorate their box in any way they wish and will have the whole session to work on it.

4. Allow children to relax and have some fun as they make their "Memory Boxes."

5. Encourage children to think about how they could use their boxes for special memories of their loved one. Provide time for brief discussion and suggestions.

CLOSURE

Conclude today's session by reviewing the session and allowing the children to comment on the activity. Remind them that the most significant portion of this activity actually will take place during next session.

HOMEWORK

Instruct children to, for a homework activity, collect at least four or five items that remind them of their loved one in a special way and put the items in the box to bring to group next week. Each person will have an opportunity to help us get to know the things that made the loved one special.

SESSION VII—SHARING OF MEMORY BOXES

BRIEF OVERVIEW OF SESSION

The children will have the opportunity to "share" their loved one with the group as the "Memory Box" activity is completed. This will provide an arena for them to begin to remember all of the special things about their loved one. This probably will be a very emotional experience for many of the children and will tend to develop an even stronger bond with group members.

GOALS

1. To provide children an opportunity to remember their loved one in a special manner.
2. To assist children in realizing that, even though their loved one is gone, they have many special memories and remembrances that will remain with them throughout their lifetime.

MATERIALS NEEDED

1. The "Memory Box" that was completed last session
2. Items for the box (supplied by each child)

PROCEDURE

1. Begin by sharing something from your "Memory Box" that is very special to you. Remind the children that we all have many things in our homes that help us remember our lost loved one in a very personal and special way. (I usually share a plaque, "Friends are Forever," which was given to me by a friend who died of cancer at a young age.)

2. Encourage each child to share with the group the items from his or her Memory Box and to describe what it is about the particular item that makes it special.

3. Provide time for children to make comments and ask questions after each "box" has been shared.

4. Remind children that, even though the loved one has died, the items in the box will serve as constant reminders of how special that person was in our lives and that we may keep these items as long as we live.

5. Encourage children to comment on the activity and how it made them feel. (It is not uncommon for a child to say that, even though it was difficult to talk about the items, it was very helpful to be able to let others know how special the person was to him or her.)

CLOSURE

Because this may have been an emotional experience for some of the children, provide time for processing of feelings about the activity. Allow for comments and questions. Also begin to prepare the children for the fact that next week will be the final session of group. Encourage them to share their feelings about what group has done for them.

HOMEWORK

As a homework assignment, ask students to think about what they have done during the sessions and be willing to share some comments at the final session. Also they need to think about something positive about each of the other members of the group.

SESSION VIII—TERMINATION

BRIEF OVERVIEW OF SESSION

At this final session of the group, children will have an opportunity to review their coping skills and to begin to look toward the future. They also will be given time to put their future plans and dreams into a letter to be shared with the group. Finally, children will be asked to provide a brief evaluation of the sessions.

GOALS

1. To encourage children to begin to think about what their plans are for the future.
2. To enable children to again identify coping strategies that help them deal with their loss.
3. To provide an opportunity for children to evaluate the group.

MATERIALS NEEDED

1. Paper and pencil for each child
2. Group evaluation sheet for each child

PROCEDURE

1. Allow initial time for children to review the coping skills they identified in session four. Ask if they have been remembering to use these strategies at appropriate times.

2. Provide time for the children to begin to think about dreams for the future. What do they see themselves doing in ten years?

3. Give each child a paper and pencil and ask children to write a letter to their lost loved ones describing their dreams or plans for the future. Encourage the children to share feelings as well as dreams.

4. Encourage each child to read his or her letter to the group. (Or have children exchange letters and read each other's aloud.)

5. Provide time for children to begin to bring closure to the sessions by asking them to share with the group their feelings about their participation by

using a stem sentence such as, "When this group started, I felt_____,
and now I feel_____."

6. Complete this session by inviting children to say one positive thing about
having each of the other members in the group. This helps to end the sessions
on a very positive note.

CLOSURE

At the conclusion of this session, each child will be asked to complete a
written evaluation of the group.

HOMEWORK

Because this is the final session, there will be no formal homework assignment. Children should be reminded to remember what they have learned in group
to assist them in the future.

Note: Help the children understand that as their group comes to an end, they
must prepare themselves for and adjust to another loss—the loss of their group
and all that it has come to represent.

EVALUATION

1. Do you feel that participation in the "Loss" group was helpful to you? Why or why not?

2. What part of the group did you like best?

3. What part of the group did you like least?

4. If you had a friend who experienced a loss in his or her life, would you recommend that he or she participate in a similar group? Why or why not?

5. Did you attend all eight group sessions?

_____ Yes   _____ No

If no, how many did you attend?_____

6. Comments, suggestions, etc.:

REFERENCES

Baker, J. E., Sedney, M. A., & Gross, E. (1992). Psychological tasks for bereaved children. *American Journal of Orthopsychiatry, 62*(1), 105–116.

Bertoia, J., & Allan, J. (1988). School management & the bereaved child. *Elementary School Guidance & Counseling, 23,* 30–38.

Bowlby, J. (1980). *Attachment and loss* (Vol. 3, Loss). New York: Basic Books.

Costa, L., & Holliday, D. (1994). Helping children cope with the death of a parent. *Elementary School Guidance & Counseling, 28*(3), 206–213.

D'Andrea, M., & Daniels, J. (1992). When children's parents go to war: Implication for counseling development. *Elementary School Guidance & Counseling, 26*(4), 269–278.

Daniels, J. (1990). *Loss: A developmental approach to transition and its impact on the work environment.* Unpublished doctoral dissertation Vanderbilt University, Nashville, TN.

Edgar, L. V., & Howard-Hamilton, M. (1995). Noncrisis death education in the elementary school. *Elementary School Guidance & Counseling, 29*(1), 38–46.

Fox Valley Hospice. (1987). *Child grief: A teacher handbook.* Bataira, IL: Fox Valley Hospice.

Furman, E. (1978). Helping children cope with death. *Young Children, 33*(4) 25–32.

Garanzini, M. J. (1987). Explaining death to children: The healing process. *Momentum, 18*(4), 30–32.

Glass, J. C. (1991). Death, loss, and grief among middle school children: Implications for the school counselor. *Elementary School Guidance & Counseling, 26*(2), 139–148.

Grollman, E. A. (1991, November). Explaining death to children and ourselves. In D. Papadatou & C. Papadatou (Eds.), *Children and death.* New York: Hemisphere.

Hannaford, M. J., & Popkin, M. (1992). *Windows: Helping and healing through loss.* Atlanta, GA: Active Parenting.

Jewett, C. (1982). *Helping children cope with separation and loss.* Harvard, MA: The Harvard Common Press.

Kubler-Ross, E. (1969). *On death and dying.* New York: Macmillan.

Lewis, J. K. (1992). Death and divorce: Helping students cope in single-parent families. *National Association of Secondary School Principals Bulletin, 75*(543), 55–60.

McHutchion, M. E. (1991). Student bereavement: A guide for school personnel. *Journal of School Health, 61*(8), 363–366.

Morganett, R. S. (1994). *Skills for living: Group counseling activities for elementary students.* Champaign, IL: Research Press.

Muro, J. J., & Kottman, T. (1995). *Guidance & counseling the elementary & middle schools: A practical approach.* Madison, WI: Brown & Benchmark.

Rando, T. A. (1984). *Grief, dying, and death: Clinical intervention for caregivers.* Champaign, IL: Research Press.

Rice, F. P. (1992). *Human development: A life-span approach.* New York: Macmillan.

Seibert, D., Drolet, J. C., & Fetro, J. V. (1993). *Are you sad too? Helping children deal with loss & death.* Santa Cruz, CA: ETR Associates.

Siegelman, C. K., & Shaffer, D. R. (1991). *Life-span human development.* Pacific Grove, CA: Brooks/Cole.

Silverman, P. R., & Worden, J. W. (1992). Children's reactions in the early months after the death of a parent. *American Journal of Orthopsychiatry, 62*(1), 93–104.

Wass, H. (1991). Helping children cope with death. In D. Papadatou & C. Papadatou (Eds.), *Children and Death.* New York: Hemisphere.

Wenestam, C. G., & Wass, H. (1987). Swedish & U. S. children's thinking about death: A qualitative study and cross-cultural comparison. *Death Studies, 11,* 99–121.

Whiting, P. (1991). *The experience of personal loss: A comprehensive vision.* Unpublished manuscript, Vanderbilt University, Nashville, TN.

Wolfelt, A. (1983). *Helping children cope with grief.* Muncie, IN: Accelerated Development.

Chapter 11

CHILDREN AND SELF-ESTEEM

Self-esteem is the emotional result of an ever-changing collection of accurate and/or inaccurate assessments one continually makes of oneself. The assessments are based on the way one *views* oneself (self-image) and *thinks about* oneself (self-concept) relative to numerous personal characteristics such as physical appearance, personality traits, status in various groups, and the like. (Akin, Cowan, Dunne, Palomares, Schilling, & Shuster, 1990, p. 2)

BACKGROUND INFORMATION

Self-esteem represents a self-evaluation process in which children repeatedly ask themselves the question, "How am I doing?" The response that they give themselves may be followed by feelings of satisfaction or perhaps fear, anger, loneliness, or despair. Many children are imprisoned by their own nagging feelings of helplessness associated with low self-esteem. They dislike the down feelings that they experience and only find momentary relief from adults and other children who try to cheer them up with smiles, kind words, pats on the back, and related moral boosters. These techniques work for a time and then these children gradually slip back into experiencing those uncomfortable feelings so familiar to them.

Why is it that some children have high self-esteem whereas others do not? Why is it that despite everything that well meaning parents and teachers do to raise their children's self-esteem, the results appear to be only temporary? The answer to both questions is that self-esteem is an inner state of well being that can be controlled only by the children themselves. Our children can learn how to self-manage in ways that not only will increase their chances for achieving personal success but also will place them in control of their own inner state (Briggs, 1977; Kohn, 1994; Maples, 1992).

Just as we control the comfort zone in our homes with a thermostat, children can learn how to manage their own thoughts, feelings, and actions, in achieving personal satisfaction in their lives (Shapiro, 1993). Children who experience high self-esteem do so, not because of what we do to them, but rather from what they do for themselves. Children with high self-esteem appreciate living in a self-esteem enhancing environment but are not totally dependent on their surroundings to experience feelings of satisfaction and well-being (Kohn, 1994).

Importance of Self-esteem

Branden (1988) has stated that self-esteem is the key to success or failure and the key to understanding ourselves and others.

> Apart from problems that are biological in origin, I cannot think of a single psychological difficulty—from anxiety and depression, to fear of intimacy or of success, to alcohol or drug abuse, to under-achievement at school or at work, to spouse battering or child molestation, to sexual dysfunctions or emotional immaturity, to suicide or crimes of violence—that is not traceable to poor self-esteem. Of all the judgements we pass, none is as important as the ones we pass on ourselves. Positive self-esteem is a cardinal requirement of a fulfilling life. (Branden, 1988, p. 5)

McKay and Fanning (1987) stated that self-esteem is essential for psychological survival and that, without some measure of self-worth, life can be enormously painful, with many needs going unmet.

> One of the main factors differentiating humans from other animals is the awareness of self: the ability to form an identity and then attach value to it. In other words, you have the capacity to define who you are and then to decide if you like that identity or not. The problem with self-esteem is this human capacity for judgement. It's one thing to dislike certain colors, noises, shapes, or sensations. But when you reject parts of yourself, you greatly damage the psychological structure that literally keeps you alive. (McKay & Fanning, 1987, p. 1)

Pope, McHale, and Craighead (1988) have stated that self-esteem is an important aspect of a child's overall functioning.

It [self-esteem] appears to be related to other areas, including psychological health and academic performance, in an interactional manner; that is, self-esteem may be both a cause and an effect of the type of functioning which occurs in other areas. (Pope, McHale, & Craighead, 1988, p. 5)

Generally speaking, self-esteem has been linked to five basic areas of children's lives (Wiggins, Schatz, & West, 1994). Those areas are social, academic, family, body image, and global self-esteem. Socially, children are concerned about their peer relationships. They want to have friends and have others view them as a friend. Children are constantly evaluating themselves as to whether or not their social needs are being met.

Academically, children are concerned with whether they are good enough. Do they measure up to their own academic standards? Are they satisfied with their academic performance? Standards of academic performance are influenced by family, friends, and teachers and, thus, contribute to a child's academic self-esteem.

Family self-esteem is based on children's perceived status in the family unit. Do children see themselves as respected and valued family members who are loved and accepted for who they are?

Body image is based on children's perceptions of how they look physically and their ability to perform in satisfying ways. Boys and girls want to see themselves and be seen by others as being physically attractive and capable performers.

Global self-esteem, unlike the other mentioned areas of self-esteem, is a more general approval of self. Children with high global self-esteem are satisfied with themselves, feel successful, and like most things about themselves.

Self-esteem and Self-concept

In order to understand more fully the meaning of self-esteem, it helps to differentiate it from self-concept. Although these two components are very much related, they are also quite different. Self-concept describes how children think about themselves. Children may think of themselves as baseball players, students, and as friends to others. Self-esteem, as described earlier, is the evaluation of the information contained in the self-concept. Children will evaluate their various concepts of self by asking the question, "How am I doing?" If children place a high value on being a "good student" but see themselves as a "poor student" (self-concept), then their self-esteem (feelings about self) will suffer.

Pope et al. (1988) stated that self-esteem is thus based upon perceived objective information about oneself and the subjective evaluation of that information.

Essentially, all children have two pictures of self, a perceived self and an ideal self. The perceived self is a child's concept of self formed from feedback received from others and the child's perception of that information. The ideal self is what children hope to be. When both perceptions of self are realistic and rational and represent a close match, these children will experience positive self-esteem. For example, a boy who sees himself as having athletic ability in football (perceived self) and who also strives to do better (ideal self) will focus on self-improvement rather than perfection in his quest to do better as a football player. When he asks the question, "How am I doing?" he will experience satisfaction and a good feeling knowing that he is making progress toward his goal.

Positive self-esteem is therefore contingent upon children possessing a realistic, fact-supported perceived self and an ideal self that is challenging but not totally out of reach (perfection). Likewise, children must be taught how to be reality oriented in their self-assessments in order to insure a positive self-esteem (Cutright, 1992).

How children judge themselves will influence the kinds of friends they choose, how they get along with their peers, and how productive they will be. Self-esteem according to Briggs (1975), will effect a child's creativity, integrity, stability, and whether that child will be a leader or follower. "Self-esteem is the mainspring that slates every child for success or failure as a human being" (Briggs, 1975, p. 3).

CHILDREN'S NEEDS

Self-esteem represents a quiet sense of self-respect and feelings of self-worth. Children must experience feelings of love and worth and internalize them in ways that will stimulate a sense of wholeness within.

Because children are complex human beings, they have many needs that they must learn to satisfy if they are to experience a positive self-esteem. Bean (1992), in his writings about self-esteem, characterized self-esteem as a multi-dimensional phenomenon that coincides with children's basic needs for love and worth. Self-esteem, said Bean (1992), is a state that results from four conditions being met both within the child and the environment in which the child lives. What follows is a brief overview of Bean's four dimensions of self-esteem. These four dimensions not only identify children's needs in terms of self-esteem but also provide a very strong and defensible plan for building children's self-esteem through a support group experience.

In order for children to experience positive self-esteem, they must learn how to satisfy the four conditions associated with love and worth. Those conditions are connectiveness, uniqueness, power, and models.

Connectiveness

Children have a need to be connected to people, places, and things in their environment that are important to them and are respected and approved by others. Being connected to oneself and others is important to maintaining a sense of security, safety, and predictability in children's lives. Children learn to trust and invest in their connections.

A lack of connectiveness or a threat to connectiveness will result in children experiencing some degree of fear, isolation, loneliness, and a general loss of security. Sometimes children in their need to be connected may engage in thoughts, feelings, and actions that can be detrimental to themselves and others. Children's overall self-esteem is enhanced when their sense of connectiveness is enhanced. They will experience the positive feelings that come from satisfying and responsible connections.

Uniqueness

Children have a need to acknowledge and respect the personal characteristics and assets that make them special and different from others. They likewise have a need to receive the approval and respect from others regarding what makes them unique. Children strive to be unique in positive ways and seek opportunities to use and be recognized for their special assets, talents, attributes, and personality characteristics.

The lack of uniqueness will cause children to experience feelings of low personal worth and a loss of love for themselves and others. Such children may feel bored, unimaginative, depressed, or frustrated with daily routines. Their lives are depleted of excitement and challenge. Some children, in their drive to be unique, may engage in inappropriate and harmful behaviors to themselves and others. Children's self-esteem will increase when they recognize that they have value and worth and that their unique attributes can be used to help them build and maintain satisfying connections.

Power

Children have a need to use their assets, skills, personality attributes, and related resources to influence the circumstances of their lives. Power gives children independence and the freedom to shape themselves and their respective environments in meaningful and responsible ways. Children's true power is internal and is fueled by the utilization of their strengths that help them manage their lives effectively.

A lack of power causes children to feel helpless because they fail to act. Children feel powerless because they lack information, skill, self-confidence, or the opportunity to make a difference in their lives. Sometimes they feel powerless because of internal (e.g., fear, anxiety, irrational thinking, etc.) or environmental barriers that appear insurmountable. When children feel powerless, they may engage in actions that are irresponsible, unethical, or illegal. Children's self-esteem increases when their need for power is satisfied in ways that will benefit themselves and others.

Models

Children have a need for an internal guidance system. That system is designed to help children with the "how-to's" of life. Children have a need to understand right from wrong and to have a set of values that will guide them in making responsible decisions. The personal standards and ideals that children develop at home, school, and in their religion will provide the models that will assist them in their own self-management.

A lack of models makes children feel uncertain about what choices to make or how to do the right things that will benefit themselves and others. They may not know how to set goals in achieving their wants. Some children learn models that are detrimental to themselves and others. Children hitting other children because of a disagreement represents an inappropriate model for addressing conflicts. Children's self-esteem increases when they have people models, moral principles, and age appropriate skills that will guide them in making responsible life decisions.

STRENGTHS TO BE LEARNED

The support group experiences that follow are designed to teach children the strengths that they will need to boost their self-esteem in response to the four mentioned conditions.

Connectiveness Strengths

Children with a low sense of connectiveness are often not in touch with themselves, feel separated from their environment, and lack satisfying peer relationships. Children with a low sense of connectiveness can learn to enhance their self-esteem in this area through group activities that help them

- identify their strengths and weaknesses;
- practice strengths that will enhance their peer relationships;
- practice strengths that will enable them to connect with themselves in positive ways;
- explore new ways in which they can build connections with group members;
- identify thoughts, feelings, and actions that may be causing disconnections in their lives and how to stop doing them;
- identify thoughts, feelings, and actions that work for them in building connections and make plans for their continuation; and
- suggest ways in which group members can build connections with each other.

When children recognize that they can achieve personal satisfaction in their relationships with self and others by making responsible connectiveness choices, their self-esteem will rise.

Uniqueness Strengths

Children with a low sense of uniqueness may be unaware of their special talents, assets, and personality attributes. They may lack respect for themselves and others, experience a lack of personal accomplishment, express themselves in counterproductive ways to get attention, and lack in creativity and imagination. Children with a low sense of uniqueness can learn to enhance their self-esteem in this arena through group activities that will help them

- view themselves as people of value;
- appreciate what makes them unique and special; and
- recognize, value, and utilize their personal assets in the service of self and others.

When children recognize that they are loved and valued for who they are and are given the opportunity to exercise their unique qualities, they will learn to appreciate themselves and others. Their self-esteem will rise to new heights.

Power Strength

Children with a low sense of power lack confidence in themselves in accomplishing their wants. They often become dependent on others, view the environment and others as the cause of their predicaments, engage in manipulative behaviors to meet their needs, and withdraw from or avoid situations in which they feel helpless.

Children with a low sense of power can learn to enhance their self-esteem in this area by participating in a self-esteem support group that will help them

- understand that power comes from the utilization of their personal strengths in achieving their goals;
- identify examples of personal power in their own lives;
- learn power strengths like decision making, goal setting, problem solving, rational thinking, communication strategies, and interpersonal skills; and
- make choices based on Right, Reality, and Responsibility.

When children recognize that they can manage their lives successfully by utilizing their assets, talents, and personality attributes, their self-esteem will increase. They will feel more in charge of their lives.

Model Strengths

Children with a low sense of models do not have adequate human models to emulate. Often, they have not been exposed to moral, ethical, and legal standards of right and wrong. These children often lack a rich array of experiences that otherwise would have contributed to their development of socialized behaviors such as good manners, proper etiquette, and common decency.

Inadequate or inappropriate models, when applied to life situations, often result in failure, disapproval, pain, embarrassment, and punishment. Children with a low sense of models can learn to enhance their self-esteem in this area through group activities that will help them

- recognize the importance of rules and the consequences for breaking them;
- develop clear standards of right and wrong;
- practice values of common decency such as honesty, respect, and kindness;

- connect with adults who are worthy role models; and
- achieve their goals by practicing the 3 R's of Right, Reality, and Responsibility.

When children have positive models, they can tell right from wrong, have clearly stated values and beliefs, are goal oriented, and are able to make sense of what is going on in their lives. As children's sense of models begin to take on meaning in their lives, their self-esteem will rise.

MESSAGE TO FACILITATORS

Your role is to help children understand that they can learn to manage their own self-esteem. How children feel about themselves is based on their ability to make desired life connections in ways that are based on Right, Reality, and Responsibility (Braucht & Weime, 1992).

Life connections are developed through the utilization of children's unique attributes. When children are able to equate their value and worth in terms of their assets, talents, and personality attributes, they will begin to see how they can use their unique assets to build life connections.

Help children understand that they must utilize their assets if they are to derive power from them. Once they understand that power comes from the utilization of their assets (strengths) they will be well on their way to managing their lives successfully.

Models provide children with understandings of how to make life connections based on what is Right not wrong, what is Reality not myth, and what is Responsible not irresponsible. Models provide children with an internal guidance system that will allow them to make life connections that will meet their needs and leave them feeling satisfied.

Selecting Group Members

All children can benefit from a positive self-esteem. We therefore encourage you to identify children who fall along the continuum from high self-esteem to low self-esteem when forming your support group. Children can learn much from each other and need the opportunity to interact with peers who can share a range of self-perceptions and personal strengths.

To help you and others identify children with specific self-esteem needs, we advocate using the four conditions of self-esteem discussed earlier in this chapter. Children who are struggling to build meaningful and satisfying connections (i.e., self, others, and the environment); who perceive themselves as being unique but for all the wrong reasons (i.e., diminished self-worth); who feel powerless in satisfying their needs; and who lack a responsible internal guidance system in making 3 R's decisions are all likely candidates for your support group. As we emphasized earlier, however, nearly every child can grow in an understanding and utilization of self.

Group Goals

Self-esteem, as we have indicated, evolves from a self-evaluative process in which children accurately or inaccurately assess their worth as human beings. Their assessment is based on how they believe others perceive them coupled with their own perceptions of self. Consequently self-esteem is not likely to be improved by what we *do to* or *for* children but rather by what we can teach children to do for themselves. Therefore, the goals of a successful self-esteem support group must focus on helping children develop a perception of self (real and ideal) that is reality-oriented that helps them achieve their life purpose in four areas:

- to relate to others and be part of the world (connectiveness);
- to appreciate and utilize their unique attributes in ways that will benefit themselves and others (uniqueness);
- to be self-determining and competent in influencing the circumstances of their lives (power); and
- to develop an internal guidance system that will help them choose 3 R's paths in achieving their goals (models).

As is evident from these four goals, self-esteem is an action-oriented process that permeates all dimensions of children's lives. Self-esteem goes far beyond merely helping children feel good about themselves (Beane, 1991). Nor can self-esteem be nurtured in isolation via 30-minute exercises once a week set aside for that purpose. Helping children develop positive self-esteems ultimately is the combined responsibility of children and adults working together to accomplish that end.

Therefore, you must help children understand that their feeling about self (self-esteem) is related to how they perceive themselves and their capabilities. They will need to be taught how to examine their perceptions and how to challenge their accuracy in light of the evidence. They likewise need to understand that their self-esteem is based on their assessment of their ability to fulfill their needs as they relate to the four conditions of self-esteem. By learning to take appropriate actions in these four areas, children can successfully manage their self-esteem.

Four Key Questions

The four conditions of self-esteem relate specifically to four key questions that effect children's self-esteem. Those questions are

What do you want to be?
What do you want to do?
What do you want to have?
What do you want to give?

What do you want to be?   Children, consciously or unconsciously, are struggling to be a variety of different things. They want to be friends to others, physically fit, helpful to others, trusted, and academically successful. While the lists of what children want to be will vary, their ability to achieve their wants will impact their self-esteem. When they ask themselves "How am I doing?" their mental response to that question will evoke an emotional response. Their assessment of their ability to make important life *connections* in terms of their wants will effect their self-esteem in positive or negative ways. Your responsibility as a facilitator will be to help children identify and assess their wants to see if they are reality-oriented and achievable. For example, children who either are striving for perfection in their lives or are trying to change others have wants that are unrealistic and unattainable. These are wants that can lower self-esteem.

What do you want to do?   In order for children to achieve their wants, there are actions they must take. Sometimes children fail to act on their wants by doing the right things and, in other instances, they just simply fail to act. Children's wants can be achieved only by their applying (power) their personal assets and attributes (uniqueness) in ways that are based on Right, Reality, and Responsibility (models). For example, if children *want* to be liked by others, they must *do* the things that will help them connect with their peers. They must use their connectiveness-building assets and personality characteristics to build relationships. If they apply ineffective models of relationship building (e.g., hitting, name calling, or withdrawing from social contact), they will be unsuccessful in attaining their wants and their self-esteem will drop. Your role must be one of helping children understand the importance of acting on their wants and how doing so relates to their self-esteem.

What do you want to have?   Children are motivated to attain their wants because there is a personal payoff in it for them. They want to have something. For example, children who *want* to have friends and *do* the right things will *have* satisfying peer relationships. Children who fail to get what they want will not have anything to show for their efforts and their self-esteem will drop. Help children understand that they must be clear about their wants and what they must do to achieve them so that they will *have* those things that give meaning to their lives. In other words, if children wish to *have* respect, friends, good grades, and so forth, they must be clear about their *wants* and do the right things to obtain them.

What do you want to give?   Help children understand that they can give to others only what they themselves have to give. Life is about "passing it on." The question is, what do they want to pass on to others? Children's self-esteem is very much related to being an effective giver. For example, if children know how to smile, give positive feedback, and listen to others, they can pass on their smiles, positive feedback, and listening attention to others. The end result is that what children pass on to others will either serve to enhance their self-esteem or deplete it.

The four questions come full circle because what children have to give to others comes from their having attained their wants. Now by giving away what they have to give, they will continue to personally reap the benefits by enhancing their connections to self and others. The result is an increase in self-esteem.

Think of your support group not just as a place where you will transform children's lives but as an environment in which you can help children understand the meaning of self-esteem and what they can do to influence their emotions in a positive direction. Good luck in helping your group members unlock the mystery of self-esteem enhancement.

Resources

Share with parents and/or guardians Figure 11.1 so that they will have suggestions on how they can help their children at home. Figure 11.2 provides lists of resources to be used with and by children in the Self-esteem Support Group. The resource materials are grouped according to age of child.

SELF-ESTEEM MANAGEMENT GUIDE
Tips for Caregivers

Your child soon will be participating in a Self-esteem Management Support Group. The goal of this support group is to help children develop positive perceptions of their worth and abilities. How children feel about themselves is crucial to their mental health, their relationships with others, and their successes in life. Children need to feel loved, liked, accepted, valued, capable, and competent if they are to like and respect themselves. This support group experience will help your child develop a positive self-esteem; however, your child's self-esteem is influenced by you as well. We have provided some tips that you can use with your child that have proven self-esteem enhancing possibilities.

1. Hold your child.

2. Praise your child often for responsible behaviors.

3. Share your feelings with your child. Teach your child how to share personal feelings with you.

4. Listen to your child without judging, advising, or commenting.

5. Help your child to find goodness within himself or herself.

6. Brainstorm a list of positive ways to connect with your child and then implement some of these ideas every day.

7. Practice positive ways to cooperate, resolve conflicts, and respect one another.

8. Your child is different from you. Learn to accept your child's unique qualities.

9. Give your child space and the opportunity to do things his or her way as much and as often as possible. Be sure to set responsible limits when giving your child freedom to choose.

10. Provide your child with opportunities to do new things, to be creative, and to use his or her imagination.

Figure 11.1. Tips for Caregivers to be given to parents and/or guardians. Permission is granted to photocopy.

11. Your child does need to be taught right from wrong.

    a   Criticize your child's behavior privately.
    b   Offer positive comments while being very specific about the inappropriate behavior.
    c   State why the behavior is inappropriate and then decide together better alternatives.
    d   Have your child practice one of the selected behaviors and offer praise.

12. Treat each of your children as individuals. You do not need to treat them alike, but you do need to treat them fairly and respectfully.

13. Establish rules for privacy, give your child responsibilities at home, and allow your child to make choices (e.g., clothing, chores, study time, etc.).

14. Your child needs to understand what makes him or her unique and needs to be respected for that uniqueness. Your child needs to see himself or herself as special, capable, and loved.

15. Teach your child how to influence people in positive ways, how to do things, to make decisions, ask questions, make choices, and solve problems. Your child needs to possess skills that will help him or her respond successfully to life's challenges.

16. Teach your child to be a responsible person.

17. Share your beliefs and values with your child (e.g., honesty, trust, courage, kindness, acceptance, etc.).

18. Help your child understand the consequences of his or her actions.

19. Set clear standards of acceptable behaviors and performance.

20. Be a responsible role model for your child. Practice what you preach.

Although this is only a partial list of things that you can do to influence your child's self-esteem in a positive direction, it does represent a good place to begin. As you think about building your child's self-esteem, try to remember what it was like when you were a child. What were some things that your parents did or you wish that they had done for you when you were growing up? Write these ideas down and add them to this list of ideas.

Figure 11.1.   (*Continued*) Tips for Caregivers to be given to parents and/or guardians. Permission is granted to photocopy.

RESOURCES FOR CHILDREN
Self-esteem Management

Ages 3 to 7

Adorjan, C. (1990). *I can, can you?* Morton Grove, IL: Albert Whitman & Co. (attitude toward self)

Carlson, N. (1988). *I like me.* New York: Viking Penguin. (self-confidence, accepting self)

Engel, D. (1989). *Josephine hates her name.* New York: William Morrow. (attitude toward name)

Fleming, B. (1992). *Scott the dot.* Manassas Park, VA: Impact Publishers. (being happy with self)

Hallinan, P. K. (1991). *I know who I am.* Center City, MN: Hazelden. (being yourself, liking yourself)

Hoffman, M. (1987). *Nancy no size.* New York: Oxford University Press. (body concepts)

McDonnell, J., & Ziegler, S. (1988). *What's so special about me? I'm one of a kind.* Emeryville, CA: Children's Book Press. (accepting self)

Mendez, P. (1989). *The black snowman.* New York: Scholastic. (accepting self)

Sharmat, M. (1992). *The 329th friend.* New York: Four Winds Press. (seeing self in a positive light)

Weiner, M. (1994). *I want your moo.* New York: Magination Press. (self-acceptance)

Ages 8 to 12

Adler, C. S. (1990). *Ghost brother.* Boston: Clarion Books. (accepting self)

Grove, V. (1990). *The fastest friend in the west.* New York: Putnam & Grossett Group. (belonging, making friends)

Haynes, M. (1990). *The great pretenders.* New York: Bradbury Press. (self-confidence, lack of friendship)

Figure 11.2.   Resources for use with and by children in Self-esteem Management Support Group.

Holl, K. D. (1984). *Footprints up my back.* New York: Atheneum Publishers. (expectations of self, responsibility)

Moser, A. (1991). *Don't feed the monster on Tuesdays.* Kansas City, MO: Landmark Editions. (building positive attitudes)

Olofodotter, M. (1993). *Sofia the heartmender.* Minneapolis, MN: Free Spirit Publishers. (self-esteem and feelings)

Parkinson, J. (1994). *Pequena the burro.* Shawnee Mission, KS: Marshmedia. (self-discovery)

Slote, A. (1989). *Make believe ball player.* Philadelphia, PA: J.B. Lippincott. (self-esteem, lack of friendship)

Yarbrough, C. (1989). *The shimmershine queens.* New York: Putnam Berkley Group. (accepting self, feelings of inferiority)

Ages 12 and Up

Adler, C. S. (1989). *The lump in the middle.* Boston: Clarion Books. (feelings of inferiority)

Ames, M. (1989). *Who will speak for the lamb?* New York: HarperCollins. (search for identity, self-confidence)

Carter, A. R. (1990). *Robodad.* New York: Putnam and Grossett Group. (weight control, concern about appearance)

Chambers, J. W. (1985). *The colonel and me.* New York: Atheneum Publishers. (self-esteem, boy-girl relationships)

DeClements, B. (1983). *How do you lose those ninth grade blues?* New York: Viking Penguin. (parental rejection, attitude toward self)

Gilmore, H. B. (1985). *Ask me if I care?* New York: Ballantine Books. (family relationships, boy-girl relationships)

Greene, C. C. (1988). *Monday I love you.* New York: HarperCollins. (body concept, feeling different)

Irwin, H. (1987). *Kim/Kimi.* New York: Margaret K. McElderry Books. (feeling different)

Rabinowich, E. (1983). *Underneath I'm different.* New York: Dell Publishing. (body concept, adolescent mental illness)

Walker, M. A. (1988). *Brad's box.* New York: Atheneum Publishers. (self-esteem, boy-girl relationships)

Figure 11.2. (*Continued*) Resources for use with and by children in Self-esteem Management Support Group.

SESSION I—GETTING READY TO GROW

BRIEF OVERVIEW OF SESSION

This session will provide an opportunity for children to begin to focus on the purpose for the group, to become aware of group ground rules, and to begin to see the structure for the eight sessions on self-esteem.

GOALS

1. To help children understand their reasons for involvement in the group.
2. To encourage children to become acquainted with the other members of the group.
3. To present information on the four conditions of self-esteem.

MATERIALS NEEDED

1. Name tags (see samples on Activity Sheet 11.1)
2. A green plant
3. Chart with the four conditions of self-esteem (connectiveness, uniqueness, power, and models) written on it
4. Crayons or markers

PROCEDURE

1. Introduce yourself and have each of the group members introduce himself or herself by first name. Talk about the fact that this is a group where we will begin to look for the good things about us. During the course of our eight sessions, we will try to identify many things that make us special—things that we can do well—and people who are an important part of our lives either because they are special to us or because they help us be the kind of people we want to be.

2. Begin to set the stage for the group by inviting a brainstorming session on group rules. Examples of possible initial group ground rules may include the following:

a   What is said in the group, stays there (confidentiality).
b   No put-downs are allowed.
c   Only one person talks at a time.
d   It is important to attend all sessions.

Note: If children do not suggest these group rules, you as facilitator should bring them up as part of the brainstorming session.

3. Give each child the name tag that has been prepared beforehand and a marker or crayon. Ask each child to write his or her name down the left hand side of the tag, one letter per line. Example:

K
A
T
E

4. When all children are ready to go on, ask them to describe some of their positive qualities by using the letters of their name. Again, it may be helpful to provide an example:

K—kind to others
A—artistic
T—takes turns with classmates
E—energetic

5. When the children have completed their name tags, allow time for sharing of the qualities. (If possible, display them in the group room during subsequent sessions.)

6. Show the children the green plant and ask them if they were to be given a plant such as this, what they would need to do to keep it growing. (Chances are all children will identify that the plant would need adequate amounts of sunlight, nutrients, water, and air.)

7. Then ask children if they know what four conditions would be necessary to help them grow and feel good about themselves. Share with them the four conditions of self-esteem and provide a brief explanation of each condition. Remind them that the remaining sessions will be focusing on identifying positive qualities of each of them based on these four conditions.

8. Provide time for questions or discussion if necessary.

CLOSURE

Conclude this first session with a brief review of the four conditions of self-esteem and allow children to share their feelings about today's group.

HOMEWORK

Remind the children that the next two week's sessions will deal with UNIQUE-NESS. For homework, they are to think of at least three things that make them unique.

Activity Sheet 11.1. Sample name tags. Use geometric or seasonal shapes as appropriate.

SESSION II—THIS IS ME—I AM SPECIAL

BRIEF OVERVIEW OF SESSION

In this session, children will have an opportunity to share with the group some things about themselves that they feel are special. Each child will do this by describing three special qualities about himself or herself.

GOALS

1. To assist children in realizing that they are each unique and special.
2. To encourage each child to identify at least three things that make him or her special.

MATERIALS

1. Polaroid camera and film (enough for two pictures of each child)
2. Poster board on which to mount one of the pictures
3. Glue or paste
4. Crayons or markers

PROCEDURE

1. Begin with a brief review of the ground rules and a refresher of the four conditions of self-esteem.

2. Briefly discuss the homework assignment. Ask the children if they were able to think about three things that are special about themselves.

3. Tell the children that each of them will have the opportunity to have two pictures taken of them. One of them will be used to create a poster entitled "This Is Me—I Am Special"; the other one will be taken just for fun—they can take it home to put up in their bedroom to remind them how special they are.

4. Take pictures and allow time for the children to make their poster and write three statements beginning "I am special because. . . ."

5. Encourage children to share the information from their posters. Encourage discussion, comparison of similarities, and so forth. If space permits, display the posters in the group room as a reminder of the special qualities of group members.

6. Provide a few moments for the facilitator and group members to identify one additional thing that is special about each member of the group by using the stem sentence, "My favorite thing about (John, Mary, etc.) is. . . ."

CLOSURE

The children will, no doubt, feel pretty positive about themselves after this activity. Remind them that each of them was able to identify at least three things that were special about himself or herself, and that they probably have many more special things that they had not even thought of. Also remind them that sometimes people do or say things that make them feel they are not special but that we always need to remind ourselves that each of us is a very special human being.

HOMEWORK

The children actually will have two homework assignments for this week. The first will be to keep a running count of the times when others tell them they were special or valued in some way and when others put them down and make them feel that they are not special. At the beginning of next session, we will compare the numbers of positive and negative comments for each person.

The second homework assignment will be to begin to collect pictures and words from magazines that they could use to describe themselves in terms of their interests.

SESSION III—"ME" COLLAGE

BRIEF OVERVIEW OF SESSION

In this session, the children will continue to work on the condition of uniqueness and will participate in an art activity designed to assist them in further exploring the things that make them special and unique.

GOALS

1. To provide an opportunity for each child to explore further his or her uniqueness by identifying interests, hobbies, and characteristics.
2. To enable children to express themselves through an art activity.
3. To begin to discuss coping skills that may be used when others make them feel "less special."

MATERIALS NEEDED

1. Old magazines and catalogs
2. Scissors
3. Glue or paste
4. Crayons or markers
5. Chart paper for each child

PROCEDURE

1. Begin by reviewing the special characteristics that were identified for each child last week. If the posters are displayed, take a moment to look at them again.

2. Encourage children to share their homework count of positive and negative comments from others during the past week. Discuss the feelings that accompanied the comments.

3. Briefly discuss the types of things one can do when someone says something positive (e.g., say thank you, smile, etc.) and when someone says something negative (e.g., ignore, refute the comment in some way, use positive self-talk, etc.).

4. Provide chart paper and other needed materials for the children to complete their "Me" Collage. Remind them that all of the items on their collage

should, in some way, tell something about them. (If some of the children are having difficulty, suggest that they could show an interest in reading by putting a picture of a book on their collage, an interest in TV by using a page from TV Guide or the local TV listings in the newspaper.). Also remind them that they may use crayons or markers to draw other special items on their collage.

5. When the collages are completed, allow time for the children to share themselves again with the other members of the group by showing and explaining their collage.

CLOSURE

Complete this session by reminding the children that they have proven again that they are very special and unique in their own way. Encourage them to take their collages home and display them in their room to remind them of this fact. Children use their unique attributes to connect with themselves, others, and their environments.

HOMEWORK

As a homework assignment for this session, ask children to think of as many interests as they can so that they can be prepared to write down at least 10 things that they really enjoy doing.

SESSION IV—WEB OF CONNECTIONS

BRIEF OVERVIEW OF SESSION

This session will provide a visual reminder to the children as to how they are connected to others in the group and how these connections help them feel that they belong.

GOALS

1. To assist children in understanding that everyone feels more secure when they feel they belong, whether it be to a family, a school, a church, or any other group.
2. To show children how, by virtue of their interests, they can form connections with others in the group.
3. To provide an additional opportunity for children to identify at least 10 interests.

MATERIALS NEEDED

1. A 5" × 8" card for each group member
2. Pens or pencils
3. A ball of yarn

PROCEDURE

1. Begin this session by informing the children that we are now moving on to the second condition of self-esteem, connectiveness. Tell them that, when they leave group today, they will be aware of several "connections" that they have within the group.

2. Provide a card and pencil for each child and ask them to write down the 10 interests they identified in their homework assignment.

3. When the children have completed their cards, remind them to keep them on their lap during the activity so that they can refer to them as we begin to spin the web of connections.

4. This exercise begins with the ball of yarn in the facilitator's hand. The facilitator then names one of the interests from his or her card and asks if any other children in the group have that particular item written on their card. (There

probably will be at least one other person; if not, the facilitator should identify the second interest on the card and continue on until another group member also has the same interest.)

5. At the point where a common interest is found, the facilitator should hold an end of the yarn and throw the ball to the person with the common interest. If there is more than one, the second person should hold a piece of the yarn and again throw the ball to the new connection.

6. When all of the persons with the initial interest area have been connected, the last person with the ball of yarn names another interest from his or her card and again connections are noted. The ball of yarn continues to be thrown (with everyone still holding their piece of yarn to complete the web).

7. At the conclusion of the activity, allow time for the children to view the web of connections they have made with other members of the group. Remind them to keep in mind that they share many "interest connections" with fellow group members.

8. If time permits, untangle the web by throwing the ball of yarn in reverse order to form the ball again. This will give the children one more opportunity to maintain visual contact with their "interest connections."

CLOSURE

Allow time for children to share feelings and comments about the activity. Again, reinforce the idea that one of the ways we make connections with others is through sharing of common interests.

HOMEWORK

Encourage the children to think of other interest connections they have with children outside the group. Ask them to think of at least two ways they can use these interests to form friendships with other children.

SESSION V—CONNECTIONS ARE "COOL"

BRIEF OVERVIEW OF SESSION

This session will help children identify the numbers of people connections they have through their involvement in school, sports, activities, church, and family. Through a brief experiment, they will see that many connections are indeed "cool."

GOALS

1. To assist children in identifying the many "people connections" they have through their involvement in groups and activities.
2. To discuss ways persons can make more "people connections."
3. To help children develop some basic socializing skills.

MATERIALS NEEDED

1. Card stock paper or other similar weight paper cut into 1" × 4" strips
2. Stapler
3. Pencil
4. Chart paper and markers or chalkboard and chalk

PROCEDURE

1. Briefly review the interest connections the children made last session. Remind them that today we are going to continue identifying connections, but this time we are going to talk about "people connections."

2. Provide each child with at least eight paper strips and a pencil or marker. Ask each child to write down the name of a family member on one of the strips.

3. Then instruct the children to "fan" themselves with the paper strip fan. (Point out that very little air can be felt from just one strip.)

4. Continue with this activity by allowing the children to put the names of other "people connections" on the strips of paper and add them to their fan by stapling them at the bottom and placing them in the shape of a "fan." Again instruct them to "fan" themselves. (After a few additions, someone will, no doubt, point out that the fan now produces much more cool air with each addition.)

5. Allow time for the children to name persons who make up their "people connections" and add the strips to make the complete fan. Point out that numerous connections are really "cool."

6. Provide opportunity for sharing from those group members who wish to do so.

7. When children have completed the sharing, pose the following question, "What are some do's and don'ts for making more connections?" As children share ideas, list them on a chart and talk about how each of the ideas could contribute to the development of more positive connections. Some of the types of suggestions that the children may share could include the following:

Do's	Don'ts
Share	Hit others
Smile	Take things without asking
Be willing to help	Call names
Take turns	Talk about people behind their backs
Show good sportsmanship	Tell lies about others

8. If time permits, role-play some of the do's of making positive connections. (Be sure to ask for volunteers to do the role-plays.)

CLOSURE

Conclude this session with a brief review of the people connections they have identified and point out that one feels good when he or she belongs to a group and is accepted by the others in that group. Remind the children that next session we will be moving on to the Power condition of self-esteem.

HOMEWORK

Encourage the children to try at least two of the identified "do's" before next session and be willing to discuss the results of their efforts with the group.

SESSION VI—A PRIZE FOR POWERFUL ME

BRIEF OVERVIEW OF SESSION

This session will enable the children to identify their power characteristics and to identify ways they can use this power and confidence to set and achieve goals.

GOALS

1. To assist children in identifying at least three strengths that they have.
2. To help children realize that everyone has strengths, yet no one is good at everything.
3. To encourage children to see themselves in a positive light in regard to their strengths.

MATERIALS NEEDED

1. Construction paper
2. Scissors
3. Paste
4. Markers

PROCEDURE

1. Begin the session with a brief discussion of their homework assignment. How did the *do's* work for them in building additional connections? Allow time for brief sharing of experiences.

2. Ask the children to define what power means to them. Brainstorm a list of powerful people or animals. What makes them powerful? Spend some time talking about power as being likened to strength but not just physical strength. Point out that, when we feel powerful, we most often have a strong sense of self-confidence that we can do what we need to do to be successful.

3. Provide time for the children to each share three "powers" or strengths they have. If they are having trouble thinking of any, point out that such things as keeping ones room neat, being a good helper at home, being dependable, being a good friend, and doing well in math are all strengths. Explain to children that power comes from using their unique attributes (strengths) to build connections.

4. When the children have all shared their three strengths, give each child a piece of construction paper, scissors, and markers with which to design a prize ribbon for himself or herself for one of the strengths. Provide enough time for each child to complete the ribbon and share it with the class.

5. Display the prize ribbons on a bulletin board entitled "And the Winner is. . . ."

6. After the children have shared their ribbons, ask them to identify ways they can use the information from their particular strengths in everyday life and how they can develop additional strengths. Spend some time encouraging them to set goals and work toward developing additional strengths.

CLOSURE

To bring closure to this session, ask each child to write down one goal that he or she would like to begin to work on in the next two weeks. (Find some time between now and the next group to discuss the personal goal with each child in the group.)

HOMEWORK

For homework, encourage the children to begin to develop a plan for reaching their goal. Let them know that you will be talking individually to each of them sometime during the next week and prior to the next group session.

SESSION VII—A SPECIAL MODEL FOR ME

BRIEF OVERVIEW OF SESSION

In this session, the children will begin to identify people and things that are models in their life. Hopefully they will make the connection that these models have provided structure and a sense of purpose for them.

GOALS

1. To assist children in identifying persons who have been models in their life.
2. To provide an opportunity for children to consider what types of beliefs and ideas have formed a structure for their behaviors and actions.
3. To encourage children to identify some additional models they would like to emulate.

MATERIALS NEEDED

1. Copy of letter paper (Activity Sheet 11.2) for each child
2. Pencils or pens
3. Envelopes and stamps

PROCEDURE

1. Allow a few moments for each child to share a goal and initial action plan for reaching that goal. If there is some sharing of suggestions or ideas, give a few extra minutes for this to take place. Compliment children on their efforts and encourage them to continue to goal attainment.

2. Ask the children to define "models." Help them understand that models may be in the form of either people whom we wish to emulate or other types of structures such as rules for good behavior and teacher's directions for doing an assignment. Encourage the children to talk briefly about some people or structures that have provided models for their life.

3. Provide time for each child to think about a specific person who has been a model in his or her life and think about what he or she would say to that person if the opportunity to express their appreciation arose. Allow time for the children to share some of the statements that they would use.

4. Give each child a piece of letter paper (Activity Sheet 11.2) and a pen or pencil with which to write a letter to express appreciation to that person for being a model.

5. If children wish to share their letters, provide time for this to take place. Stress that it would be a very positive step if they would want to send the letter to the person. Provide envelopes and stamps for those who wish to do so.

CLOSURE

Compliment the children for their efforts in showing their appreciation to the models in their lives. Encourage them to think about how they can begin to be models for others.

HOMEWORK

In preparation for the final session, ask the children to think of one item for each of the four conditions so we can begin to put all things together and look at the whole person that each of them is. Our final activity will deal with integrating all of the conditions into a very special person.

Dear _____

Love,

Activity Sheet 11.2.   Letter paper. Permission is granted to enlarge and photo-copy for classroom use.

SESSION VIII—PUTTING IT ALL TOGETHER

BRIEF OVERVIEW OF SESSION

This concluding session will enable the children to pull together all of the information they have gained during the previous sessions and will encourage them to utilize the qualities, connections, models, and strengths they have identified to live a more successful and productive life.

GOALS

1. To assist children in looking at their power, uniqueness, connections, and models and to discuss how they can utilize this information most effectively.
2. To encourage children to develop strategies to adapt this information to everyday life situations.
3. To bring closure to the group sessions.

MATERIALS NEEDED

1. Chart that was used in Session I with the four conditions for self-esteem listed
2. Copies of "Four Conditions" worksheet (Activity Sheet 11.3)
3. Pens or pencils
4. Evaluation sheet for each child

PROCEDURE

1. Allow a few minutes for children to talk about their feelings regarding the conclusion of the group sessions and to review the four conditions of self-esteem.

2. Remind the children about all the positive aspects of themselves that they have identified during the past seven weeks. Did they learn some things about themselves that they were not previously aware of?

3. Give a copy of the "Four Conditions" worksheet (Activity Sheet 11.3) to each group member and instruct the children to write at least one sentence under each of the four conditions to remind them of the qualities and strengths that they have identified.

4. Encourage the children to utilize this information to assist them in adapting strategies for being more successful in everyday life. Brainstorm ways this can happen. Some examples of the types of things they may identify include

- use an ability in art to help design sets for play,
- use a good communication ability to volunteer to be a peer helper,
- use a strength in getting along with small children to take a baby-sitting course, and
- use dependability to get an after school job.

5. Stress to the children how important it is for them to keep and use the information they have learned from this group to lead a happier and more productive life.

CLOSURE

Since this is the final session, time should be allotted to permit the children to complete the evaluations and to have a few minutes to express their appreciation to every other group member. This can be done by having each child, in turn, sit in the center of the group and listen while every other group member tells him or her what he or she liked about having that child in the group.

HOMEWORK

There is no actual homework for this session but it would be very advisable for the facilitator to encourage the children to use what they learned in this group continually in the years to come.

Activity Sheet 11.3. Four Conditions worksheet. Permission is granted to enlarge and photocopy for classroom use.

EVALUATION

1. Do you feel that participation in the self-esteem group was helpful to you? Why or why not?

2. What part of the group did you like best?

3. What part of the group did you like least?

4. If you had a friend who needed to identify some positive characteristics about himself or herself, would you recommend that he or she participate in a similar group? Why or why not?

5. Did you attend all eight group sessions?

_____ Yes _____ No

6. Comments, suggestions, etc.:

REFERENCES

Akin, T., Cowan, D., Dunne, G., Palomares, S., Schilling, D., & Shuster, S. (1990). *The best self-esteem activities: For the elementary grades.* Spring Valley, CA: Innerchoice Publishing.

Bean, R. (1992). *The four conditions of self-esteem: A new approach for elementary and middle school.* Santa Cruz, CA: ETR Associates.

Beane, J. A. (1991). Enhancing children's self-esteem: Illusion and possibility. *Early Education and Development, 2*(2) 153–160.

Branden, N. (1988). *How to raise your self-esteem.* New York: Bantam Books.

Braucht, S., & Weime, B. (1992). The school counselor as consultant on self-esteem: An example. *Elementary School Guidance & Counseling, 26*(3), 237–250.

Briggs, D. C. (1975). *Your child's self-esteem.* New York: Dolphin Books.

Briggs, D. C. (1977). *Celebrate your self-esteem: Enhancing your own self-esteem.* New York: Doubleday.

Cutright, M. C. (1992, February). Self-esteem: The key to a child's success and happiness. *PTA Today,* 5–6.

Kohn, A. (1994). The truth about self-esteem. *Phi Delta Kappan, 76*(4), 272–283.

Maples, M. F. (1992). Teachers need self-esteem too: A counseling workshop for elementary teachers. *Elementary School Guidance & Counseling, 27*(1) 33–38.

McKay, M., & Fanning, P. (1987). *Self-esteem: A proven program of cognitive techniques for assessing, improving, and maintaining self-esteem.* Oakland, CA: New Harbinger.

Pope, A. W., McHale, S. M., & Craighead, W. E. (1988). *Self-esteem enhancement with children and adolescents.* New York: Pergamon Press.

Shapiro, L. E. (1993). *The building blocks of self-esteem.* King of Prussia, PA: The Center for Applied Psychology.

Wiggins, J. D., Schatz, E. L., & West, R. W. (1994). The relationship of self-esteem to grades, achievement scores, and other factors critical to school success. *The School Counselor, 41*(4), 239–244.

Chapter 12

SOCIAL SKILLS TRAINING

The phrase *social skills* is defined herein as a repertoire of verbal and nonverbal behaviors by which children affect the responses of other individuals (e.g., peers, parents, siblings, and teachers) in the interpersonal context. This repertoire acts as a mechanism through which children influence their environment by obtaining, removing, or avoiding desirable and undesirable outcomes in the social sphere. . . . The extent to which they are successful in obtaining desirable outcomes and avoiding or escaping undesirable ones without inflicting pain on others is the extent to which they are considered *socially skilled*. (Rinn & Markle, 1979, p. 108)

BACKGROUND INFORMATION

The development of social skills in children continues to be of major importance to educators and children alike. Educators are particularly interested in the topic based on research findings that suggest a strong relationship between social competence in childhood and social, academic, and psychological functioning. Children have an interest in developing social skills because they are vital to their interpersonal success as social beings (Edwards, 1995).

As we explore the significance of social skills attainment and social skills training programs for children, the importance attributed to the outcomes of both will become quite apparent. To assume that children will learn and practice all that they need to understand in developing responsible interpersonal relationships with others is to rely totally on wishful thinking and a gambler's mentality to beat such odds.

383

Social Skills Components

To truly understand what it takes to enhance the social skills development of another person requires a deeper perspective of social skills than offered by most superficial definitions on the topic. Michelson, Sugai, Wood, and Kazdin (1983) isolated the major components most central to understanding the complex nature of social skills. Their work has enhanced the assessment, treatment, and development of children's social behaviors with respect to the following points:

> Social skills are acquired primarily through learning (e.g., observation, modeling, rehearsal, and feedback).
> Social skills compromise specific and discrete verbal and nonverbal behaviors.
> Social skills entail both effective and appropriate initiation and responses.
> Social skills maximize social reinforcement (e.g., positive responses from one's social environment).
> Social skills are interactive by nature and entail both effective and appropriate responsiveness (e.g., reciprocity and timing of specific behaviors).
> Social skills performance is influenced by the characteristics of the environment (i.e., situational specificity). That is, such factors as age, sex, and status of the recipient affect one's social performance.
> Deficits and excesses in social performance can be specified and targeted for intervention. (p. 3)

Importance of Social Skills

A review of the literature, spanning numerous years of research, is very clear regarding the importance of social skills development and competency and their correlation with overall adjustment and later functioning in society. Children who lack social skills and the ability to use them effectively often fail to develop positively and mutually satisfying peer and adult relationships (Bullock, 1988). Children who are ill at ease with others and fail to initiate interaction with others in a positive manner often are neglected or rejected children, whereas children who are more socially competent, are generally happier individuals, have a more positive outlook on life, do better academically, and have fewer emotional problems than their socially less successful counterparts. The degree of difficulty that children experience in initiating and maintaining interactions with their peers often effects their degree of popularity with their peers.

Popular and Unpopular Children

Children, when polled about who the most popular children are among their peers, usually have little difficulty in naming them (Boulton & Smith, 1990). Popular children seem to share certain personality qualities and characteristics that lead to their liking. Chance (1989) has stated that, generally speaking, popular children

- are socially aggressive and outgoing (Dodge, Cole, Pettit, & Price, 1990);
- have a high energy level that they express in socially acceptable ways in group activity;
- perceive themselves in positive ways (Boivin & Begin, 1989);
- enthusiastically and actively participate in social events;
- are friendly and sociable in relation to others;
- are accepting, protective, and show concern for others;
- are cheerful, have a sense of humor, and are generally good natured; and
- are average to above average in intelligence and academic performance.

Generally speaking, popular children have acquired the skills of friendship. They are self-confident, independent, sensitive to the needs of others, good listeners, and agreeable. They share ideas and material things, take turns, are open to the suggestions of others, and generally practice connectiveness building strategies in their relationships with others (Bullock, 1988; Mehaffey & Sandberg, 1992; Rice, 1992; Stone, 1993).

Unpopular children are just as easily identifiable by their peers and teachers. They likewise share a variety of personality characteristics and behaviors that set them apart form the more popular. Generally speaking, the least popular children (Chance 1989; French, 1990; Rice, 1992; Rogosch & Newcomb, 1989)

- are self-centered and withdrawn;
- are anxious, fearful, and moody;
- are more likely to be emotionally disturbed (Altmann & Gotlib, 1988; Asarnow, 1988);
- are impulsive with poor emotional control (French, 1988);
- show a lack of sensitivity to others and to social situations;
- behave in inappropriate ways (Gelb & Jacobson, 1988);
- are different looking or unconventional in behavior; and
- are more likely to be of low intelligence (Rice, 1992).

Unpopular children often are categorized as the *unliked* and the *disliked*. Unliked children are socially invisible. They are unassertive, withdrawn, isolated, shy, passive, and lethargic (Coie & Dodge, 1988). Many of these children, as they get older, will become progressively more accepted by their peers (Younger & Piccinin, 1989); however, unassertive children do pay a price in the social arena. They tend to carry their lack of assertiveness into adulthood with many suffering from psychosomatic and psychological disturbances (Elliot & Gresham, 1987; Bullock, 1988; Mehaffey & Sandberg, 1992; Rice, 1992).

By contrast, disliked children are perceived as being overly aggressive by their peers and never do become fully accepted even as they mature in age. Disliked children are often uncooperative and disruptive. They exhibit social skill deficits in their ability to cooperate with others, make their needs known in socially acceptable ways, respond appropriately with peers, and make friends. More specifically, they behave in ways that are unpleasant and inappropriate in the context of the social environment in which they are living (Hazler, Hoover, & Oliver, 1993; Hoover & Hazler, 1991).

Disliked children often exhibit their dysfunctions openly in the form of verbal and physical assaults on others, teasing, provoking, quarreling, fighting, and violating or ignoring the rights of others (Oliver, Young, & LaSalle, 1994). According to Patterson, Reid, Jones, and Congber (1975), aggressive behavior has the potential of generating many negative side effects for the disliked child.

> The socialization process appears to be severely impeded for many aggressive children. Their behavioral adjustments are often immature and they do not seem to have learned the key social skills necessary for initiating and maintaining positive social relationships with others. Peer groups often reject, avoid, and/or punish aggressive children, thereby excluding them from positive learning experiences with others. Socially negative/aggressive children often have academic difficulties and may achieve at lower levels than their classmates. (p. 4)

Disliked children tend to evoke anger in their peers and outward rejection by the environment. They pay a high price for their social ineptness and skill deficiencies in the loss of friendships; reduced interpersonal contact with others; and feelings of anger, guilt, worthlessness, and frustration. If not corrected, aggressive children, in addition to their obvious lack of popularity, are also at higher risk for academic failure, adult alcoholism, antisocial behavior, and psychiatric disturbances (Coie & Dodge, 1983; Little, 1988; Mehaffey & Sandberg, 1992).

Social Skill Problem Areas

Elliot and Gresham (1987) have developed a conceptual classification system for understanding children's social problems. The four areas that they have identified are social skill deficits, social performance deficits, self-control social skill deficits, and self-control social performance deficits.

Social Skill Deficits. Children who are lacking the necessary social skills critical to interacting appropriately with others are effected by a social skills deficit problem. For example, children who do not know how to or are incapable of sharing ideas or material things with their peers would exemplify this deficit. This deficit can be remedied through direct instruction, modeling, behavioral rehearsal, and coaching.

Social Performance Deficits. Many children have learned how to perform various social skills and possess the capabilities to do so; however, some of these same children fail to perform certain social skills, and when they do, they execute them ineffectively. For example, Bill has learned all the prerequisite steps for giving compliments to others. Although he possesses the skills and is capable of delivering them, he does not apply what he knows with any degree of regularity in appropriate social settings. Children may fail to perform social skills because they are not motivated to do so or may not recognize or take advantage of the opportunities when they do exist. Once it has been determined that a performance deficit exists rather than a skill deficit, children can be cued properly and positively reinforced at appropriate times so as to increase performance of desired social skills.

Self-control Social Skill Deficits. Some children fail to learn appropriate social skills due to anxiety, fears, or phobias. Susan becomes very anxious when meeting new people. Because of the stress, she has been unable to learn the appropriate steps to introduce herself properly to others. Her social anxieties inhibit her social approach behaviors. Impulsivity is yet another form of emotional arousal that also can block the learning of needed social skills. Self-control social skill deficits are recognizable because of an accompanying emotional arousal response and a lack of knowledge or performance of the skill in question. Remediation of this problem can be addressed successfully using emotional arousal reduction techniques (e.g., desensitization or flooding) and self-control methods (e.g., thought stopping, self-talk, and relaxation).

Self-control Social Performance Deficits. These children have learned the appropriate social skills in question and are capable of performing them; however, skill performance is hindered by an emotional arousal response. Other social-control reasons for performance deficits that may accompany an emotional arousal response are limited opportunities to practices the behavior and a lack of positive reinforcement for doing so. Jim knows how to give classmates compliments but does so infrequently and with a lack of consistency because of social anxiety. Children with self-control social performance deficits are identified based on two criteria: (a) the presence of an emotional arousal response and (b) inadequate or inconsistent performance of the social skills in question. Self-control strategies similar to those addressed for self-control social skill deficits can be used to ameliorate this problem.

Social Skills Assessment

Numerous assessment methods exist that can be used to evaluate the social skills of children. Perhaps some of the more popular methods are (a) direct observation, (b) rating scales, (c) sociometric techniques, (d) self-report methods, (e) interviews, and (f) the use of role-play methods. Usually a combination of these methods is used in establishing a high degree of confidence in the results obtained.

Direct Observation.   Another term used to describe direct observation is naturalistic observation (Elliot & Gresham, 1987). This type of observation usually takes place in classroom and playground settings in which children are observed in the natural environment by more than one person. These observers are responsible for recording the frequency, duration, and quality of specified target social behaviors. Such observations provide a functional analysis of specified behaviors in the natural environment at the time of their occurrence.

Rating Scales.   Rating scales are commonly used by parents, teachers, and counselors in assessing the social skills of children. Although the validity and reliability of rating scales often are called into question, they do provide a gross screening measure for identifying children whose social skills are perceived to be deficient. A number of behavioral checklists and rating scales assessing children's social skills are available commercially but should be reviewed for their accuracy and stability in the identification of targeted social behaviors.

Sociometric Techniques.   The use of sociometric measures have proven to be useful sources of information in which children identify their peers as individuals with whom they would like to play, sit, or work. This method also may use a negative question in which children are asked to identify those children with whom they would like limited or no contact. The data are analyzed on a sociometric grid that identifies the number of choices and rejections received by each child and by whom. A class play technique can be used to provide additional data in which children pick their classmates for hypothetical parts in a class play. They are asked to select those children who could play the various parts most naturally representing 10 positive and 10 negative social-interpersonal characteristics. When the data are examined from both instruments, it is possible to identify children's sociometric status (e.g., star, neglectee, isolate, and rejectee) and probable causes (class play results) for their rankings.

Self-report Methods. When assessing children's perceptions of their social skills and deficits, self-report scales, checklists, and narratives provide useful information on social functioning. As with all self-report instruments, they are highly subjective and lack demonstrated external validity. Nevertheless, they do provide some degree of insight into how children perceive themselves socially. Used in conjunction with teacher rating scales, sociometric test results, and observations, self-report devices have their place in assessing children's social sense of self-worth and self-esteem.

Interviews. Children also can be interviewed regarding their social skill attainment, skill deficits, and social status. While time consuming, interviewing does provide more in-depth data than can be secured from self-report instruments. Children also can be presented with open-ended, hypothetical social situations and asked to respond how they would address each. The interview process provides insight into children's perceptions and reasoning skills in resolving interpersonal problems and social situations.

Role-play Methods. Role-play methods can be used in the same manner as interviews. Children are placed in hypothetical social situations and then are challenged to role-play the event to its conclusion. Children are asked to step outside of their roles at various points to "think out loud" as they process their dilemma. Role-playing, though time consuming, does allow for a functional analysis on how children respond to various social situations.

The value of social skills assessment does not come from utilizing one assessment device. All of the methods have their strengths and limitations; however, when used in combination with one another, they provide for a more accurate assessment of children's social skills.

Social Skills Training Methods

Social skills training programs are designed to teach children appropriate overt verbal and nonverbal behaviors that will enhance their social interactions with others. Elliott and Gresham (1987) have defined social skills as behaviors that will help children attain specific social outcomes such as peer group acceptance, positive judgments by significant others, academic competence, positive self-concept, and good psychological adjustment (Forman, 1993).

Social skills training has been applied generally to children with diverse behavior problems relating to social isolation, lack of assertiveness, and aggression. Essentially, social skills training is designed to remediate deficiencies in interpersonal functioning caused by inadequate learning, faulty socialization, lack of use, reliance on inappropriate behaviors, and interfering emotional disturbances (Ladd, 1984). Thus, social skills training can help children develop new behaviors, strengthen existing behaviors, and remediate skill and/or performance deficits.

Social skills training has enjoyed a long history of success dating back to 1941, the first documented effort at theory development in this area. Miller and Dollard (1941) are credited with reviewing existing theories on imitation and formulating their own theory using a behavioral perspective (Forman, 1993).

In 1942, Chittenden provided one of the earliest examples of social skills training techniques. Since that time, a variety of different strategies have been developed and used separately and in combination with one another in successfully teaching social skills. What follows is a brief discussion of each of the most widely used techniques. Later, a more in-depth discussion will address how many of these techniques can be used in combination to create a dynamic social skills training package.

The specific social skills techniques to be addressed are modeling, positive reinforcement, coaching, and practice and problem solving (Bullock, 1988; Cartledge & Melburn, 1986; Forman, 1993; Michelson et al., 1983; Ormrod, 1995).

Modeling.   Children can learn by observing the behaviors of others and imitating what they have observed. Models can be actual people demonstrating a desired social skill (i.e., live model); represented symbolically in which a person or character portrays a desired behavior on TV or other medium; and through verbal description and instruction on how to behave absent the use of live or symbolic models. Modeling has proven to be a very useful technique in teaching socially responsible behaviors; however, like most techniques, it has to be used with caution. Modeling works best when

- the model is competent;
- the model has prestige and power;

- the model behaves in stereotypical "gender-appropriate" ways;
- the model's behavior is relevant to the observer's situation; and
- the observer believes he or she is capable of executing the behaviors successfully. (Ormrod, 1995, pp. 148-150)

In addition to the points discussed, the four components of modeling (i.e., attention, retention, motor reproduction, and motivation) are essential for successful modeling (Bandura, 1969, 1973, 1977a, 1977b, 1986).

Attention. The facilitator must make sure that children pay particular attention to the model and to relevant aspects of the model's behavior.

Retention. Children must be taught a variety of methods to remember the behavior(s) they have observed. Memorization, memory codes, and visualizations are just a few methods that can enhance retention.

Motor reproduction. Children need plenty of opportunity to practice what they have learned and to receive corrective feedback in helping them duplicate the desired social skills.

Motivation. Children must want to demonstrate what they have learned. They will model behaviors only when they are motivated to do so. Positive reinforcement and related incentives (intrinsic and extrinsic) are necessary motivators. Children need to see and experience personal payoffs for them to be sufficiently driven to model the desired behavior(s).

Positive Reinforcement. A second social skills training technique is positive reinforcement, which refers to the process by which the frequency of behaviors are increased because they are followed by rewards or desired happenings. Food, praise, a smile, and personal success are examples of positive reinforcers. Positive reinforcement works best when

- reinforcers are perceived as a positive consequence by the recipient(s),
- reinforcers are administered immediately following the desired action (behaviors),
- reinforcers are applied frequently as the new behavior is developing (continuous reinforcement),
- reinforcers are applied intermittently after the behavior has been learned, and
- successive approximations of the desired behavior are rewarded.

When using positive reinforcement strategies, care must be given to identifying the precise behaviors to be reinforced. The successful use of positive reinforcement is contingent upon increasing the frequency of desired behaviors and withholding reinforcers for inappropriate behaviors.

Coaching and Practice. Coaching is a multidimensional process involving instruction, modeling, the giving of feedback, and positive reinforcement. When children are coached, they are given clear instructions of what to do, observe the behavior being demonstrated, are prompted through practice sessions, and receive feedback to reinforce correct responses and to improve performance. Practice sessions give children an opportunity to rehearse new behaviors in proper sequence under the watchful eye of a facilitator.

Problem Solving. This social skills strategy is designed to teach children how they can use their social skills to solve problems. The premise is that children often use effective social skills inappropriately or not at all because they failed to consider the consequences of their actions in view of desired outcomes. Although there are a variety of problem-solving strategies that can be taught, all of them encourage children to

- define their social problem,
- state the desired outcome,
- explore alternative solutions,
- select solutions that are compatible with the desired outcome,
- explore the consequences of each solution (helpful vs. hurtful),
- select and implement the most appropriate course of action, and
- evaluate the results.

Because teachers and parents cannot fully anticipate the future, it makes little sense to teach separate responses for every social situation that children are likely to encounter. Rather the teaching of problem solving makes more sense so that children can generate effective responses as they encounter new situations. We advocate the use of 3 R's Decision Making in helping children meet their social needs.

Social Skills Training Format

Regardless of the social skills training package used to teach social skills, the effective programs use many of the previously discussed techniques in combination to improve children's social interaction skills and promote more positive peer relationships. The following components used together in sequence provide a solid format for teaching children a variety of social skills (Forman, 1993; Mehaffey & Sandberg, 1992; Michelson, et al., 1983; Ormrod, 1995).

Rationale. Group facilitators must thoroughly research the social skill they wish to teach before teaching it. They must be able to define and describe the targeted behavior(s) and its importance in satisfying children's needs. What purpose does the social skill serve? How do children benefit from using this skill? What are the pitfalls to those who do not learn it? These questions and ones like them should be thoroughly studied. The rationale provides a documented accounting of the social skill and its value to children regarding improved social interactions and peer relationships.

Mini-lecture. With appropriate background information gleaned from developing a rationale, facilitators should prepare a mini-lecture (five minutes) to be delivered to the children. This mini-lecture is designed to highlight the usefulness and practicality of what they are about to learn in improving their peer relationships and social interactions. Children also need to understand the pitfalls they can encounter if they remain deficient in the attribute to be taught. The use of props, charts, and related visuals is encouraged to highlight the main points of the lecture.

Modeling and Imitation. During the modeling portion of training, children will observe the social skill to be learned. The model used can be live (people) or symbolic (portrayed in film or video tape). Following the demonstration of the social skill, children should be guided through the process of learning that skill in carefully planned and sequenced steps with appropriate feedback and positive reinforcement as needed.

When the children are able to imitate the desired social skill correctly, they should be given an opportunity to practice the social skill under simulated conditions. Guiding children through open-ended role-play situations of a social nature is an excellent way to reinforce how and when to use the social skill.

Discussion. Following each role-play situation, children can share their observations of the social skill being practiced. They can discuss what would happen in each role-play if the social skill was not used or used inappropriately. Children also can discuss the importance of the social skill in developing peer relationships.

Problem Solving. As children progress in their understanding and application of the social skill, they are ready to use what they know in solving social problems. We have encouraged the use of the 3 R's decision making/problem solving model presented in Chapter 2 of this text. Children can be given open-ended, social-problem situations to solve using the 3 R's approach. With practice and learning a variety of social skills, children will become adept at solving their own social problems.

Homework. Many social skills training programs use homework as a means of providing additional practice in applying the social skill. We advocate the

Support Groups for Children

use of homework and have built homework activities into every support group session.

Transfer of Training. Teaching social skills is of little value unless children know how, when, and where to apply what they have learned. We advocate the use of brainstorming sessions to help children generalize the use of social skills beyond their use in support group sessions. Likewise, children are encouraged to set personal goals in putting their social skills to practical use. The Keystone Learning Model helps to insure for the transfer of training to life situations outside the support group.

Paraphrasing the work of Goldstein, Sprafkin, Gershaw, and Klein (1980), Forman (1993) offered the following suggested practices in order to heighten the transfer of training:

- providing general principles concerning competent performance;
- extending learning over more trials than are necessary (over-learning);
- making the learning setting, models, and situations similar to what is experienced in real life;
- using multiple models, trainers, and rehearsal situations (stimulus variability); [and]
- setting up supplemental programs outside the structured learning setting to ensure that trainees are provided with reinforcement when they use newly learned social skills. (pp. 56-57)

Transfer of training also can be enhanced when children self-affirm themselves especially when environmental support is lacking.

CHILDREN'S NEEDS

All children have a need to self-manage and to feel good about themselves. Children, like adults, are social beings. They depend heavily on their social skills and interpersonal behaviors in adapting to life-changing events and situations.

Children lacking in social skills find it difficult to develop rewarding peer relationships and to achieve academic success. They are more likely to experience social isolation, rejection, and a general lack of happiness when compared with their more socially successful counterparts.

Children have a need to initiate and maintain positive social interactions that evolve from a set of learned and acquired behaviors. These behaviors provide children with the ability to achieve their needs and wants in nonviolent ways. They form the mechanism through which children learn to behave in ways valued by society while benefitting themselves and others regarding goal attainment. Children have a need

- to belong,
- to trust and be trusted,
- to develop lasting friendships,
- to communicate with others,
- to receive the approval of others,
- to understand the benefits of social skills, and
- to develop positive social skills that will result in social competence.

Each of the above needs can be categorized under one general need, the need to be connected to self, others, and the environment. Having social skills and the willingness to use them provides children with the personal power (an internal locus of control) to self-manage.

> Thus, the relationship between social competency and life adjust-ment appears to be powerful and intricate. This cumulative body of knowledge, as viewed through an interdisciplinary perspective, sup-ports the hypotheses that social skills in children are closely related to present and future social adaptation. Thus, there seems to be a strong scientific rationale supporting the need for preventative and remedial social skills training for children. (Michelson et al., 1983, p. 11)

STRENGTHS TO BE LEARNED

Throughout this chapter, we have made reference continually to the term *social skill*. *Social* is used to describe an interpersonal process, and *skill* im-plies a learned set of behaviors. Used together, *social skill* describes an interpersonal competency that should be taught in a very systematic way using appropriate learning principles and techniques as described in this chapter. In conjunction with the terms described, *strength* implies the acquisition and utili-zation of a skill. In other words, a skill becomes a personal strength once it has been learned and is being used.

As a result of participating in social skills support groups, children will have an opportunity to develop a number of social strengths. In the next few pages, we describe a variety of social skills that children can develop including those that are taught in the support group sessions that follow. The one unify-ing factor among all the social skills is the process used to teach them. That process, simply stated, consists of the following steps.

A   Rationale for facilitator

B   Mini-lecture (five minutes)

a   Introduce the social skill
b   Benefits of the social skill
c   Pitfalls for not learning the social skill

C   Model and Imitate

a   Use live or symbolic models
b   Identify and discuss skill steps
c   Children demonstrate and practice the social skill in groups
d   Children are coached and receive feedback
   1)   facilitator feedback
   2)   children feedback

D   Discussion

a   Review importance of the social skill
b   Review potential drawbacks if the social skill is not used

E   Problem Solving

a   Children are placed in activities and role-plays
b   Children use 3 R's Decision Making/Problem Solving
c   Role-plays and activities are discussed (feedback)

F   Homework

a   Open ended case situations are distributed
b   Assignment is reviewed
c   Assignment is role-played and discussed at next session

G   Transfer of Training

a   Discuss how and where the skill can be used (opportunity)
b   Observe the social skill in action
c   Set goal(s) to use the social skill outside of the group

The following social skills represent a sample of the vast array of behaviors children can learn that will improve their social interactions, promote positive peer relationships, and enhance their social acceptance by others.

Importance of Rules

Rules can help children live and work together. Rules, by design, exist to build connections between and among people. Rules provide guidelines for acceptable behavior and they work to the extent that people value and practice them. Rules exist to enhance personal communication (e.g., speak one at a time), facilitate cooperative play (e.g., take turns and share) and promote safety (e.g., wear seatbelts, walk [not run] down the hall). Rules exist to promote family harmony, provide guidelines for playing games, and establish daily living standards of right and wrong (e.g., ethically, morally, and legally). We need to help children explore the value of rules in helping people live together in harmony.

Giving Compliments

Another connectiveness building social skill is learning how, when, and where to give compliments and, equally important, how to receive them as well. Compliments tend to help people feel good about themselves. Most people enjoy receiving sincere compliments. People who readily pay others compliments also tend to be on the high receiving end as well. People who are used to giving compliments are positive people who remain focused in their search for the good in others. Children can really benefit socially by learning to give and receive compliments.

Sharing

Sharing is one of the most important social skills that children can develop. Helping children understand the value of "sharing" in working together is a necessary condition for survival and growth. Children should be challenged to examine the many ways in which they and others have benefited from sharing. They likewise need to learn the how, when, and where of sharing as well.

Taking Turns

Taking turns is a form of sharing. There are many instances when taking turns can be beneficial and an orderly way of building connections between oneself and others. Taking turns represents an orderly system in which many people can benefit from limited resources. Working out a system of taking turns in itself has value in bringing people closer together so that all can prosper. Children need to understand and practice the value of taking turns.

Constructive Feedback Skills

Being able to give and receive constructive feedback is an important social skill. Giving constructive feedback is beneficial to the message sender because it can help that person manage his or her frustrations or anger in response to the situation or event that prompted the feedback. Receiving constructive feedback can help the receiver understand the sender's concerns and can prompt a responsible interchange between the two parties, thereby strengthening the relationship. Children need to understand that constructive feedback should be delivered in a manner that will help the other person do better, not make matters worse.

Empathy Skills

"Empathy is the ability to relate accurately and honestly to another person's feelings and emotions" (Michelson et al., 1983, p. 123). Empathic people are able to connect in positive ways with other individuals through their caring and active listening responses. They truly are able to understand and relate to others' feelings.

Helping children share their feelings with others and, in turn, helping them appreciate how others feel is a connectiveness building experience. Empathic children make good friends because they enjoy helping others. They are sensitive to their friends' needs, are not quick to judge or negatively criticize them, and like bringing joy into the lives of others.

Empathic children know how to communicate personal interest in what their friends are feeling and experiencing. They likewise acknowledge those feelings and understandings via appropriate verbal and nonverbal feedback.

Asking for Assistance Skills

At one time or another, we have all experienced a need for personal assistance. Whether asking for directions, phone operator assistance, or solving a personal problem, requesting favors is an everyday common occurrence. Children especially have a need to develop this social skill because of their dependence on adults in addressing their needs and wants.

Far too many people are either embarrassed to ask for help or assume that others will somehow magically understand their needs and wants and fulfill them. Unfortunately, far too many needs and wants go unfulfilled. By learning to ask for assistance directly and politely, children can learn the value of assuming personal responsibility for their own happiness. Most people are willing to assist others in times of need; however, to receive that help, assistance first must be requested.

Conversation Skills

Knowing how to participate in conversation is a necessary and valuable asset. As with any social skill, the more children know about it the better they will become at using it. Conversation is a primary vehicle for the exchange of ideas and information. Whereas most people enjoy conversing with friends, there are many others who feel awkward and uncomfortable in the process. Their shyness and unrealistic expectations of how they should perform results in their avoiding social events and their own self-imposed isolation.

Children need to be taught how to engage effectively in conversation. More specifically, they must learn how to initiate, maintain, and terminate a conversation in a socially acceptable manner. For children, communication serves as the essential mechanism for their social, emotional, and intellectual development.

Some of the specific skills that children need to develop are listening, speaking one at a time, introducing oneself to another person, sharing ideas, maintaining eye contact and developing a variety of nonverbal behaviors that will facilitate connectiveness building (head nods, smiling, body positioning, etc.). Although this is just a partial list of things children can do to improve their communication skills, this list does represent a starting point from which to begin.

Nonverbal Social Skills

Learning to communicate with others is a critical social skill. Most people think in terms of using words to communicate but often lose sight of the importance that facial expressions, hand gestures, and body positioning play in communicating with others. When nonverbal cues and verbal language are congruent, the message quality is enhanced and more easily understood. Nonverbal cues, when used effectively, can convey affect and intensity. They can add depth and clarity to the message; however when nonverbal cues are used without recognition or purpose, they can effect the content and flow of the conversation in adverse ways. Inconsistencies between verbal and nonverbal messages are likely to result in misunderstandings, double messages, and confusion regarding the communication. Too often, children and adults are unaware of their daily habitual nonverbal gestures in social situations and may be doing themselves a disservice without even realizing it. Learning to use nonverbal communication skills effectively is essential for both children and adults. Children need to understand a variety of nonverbal cues and how to use them with purpose in their interactions with others.

Assertiveness Skills

Learning to be an effective communicator requires children to understand and protect their personal rights. Social skills training can help children differentiate among passive, aggressive, and assertive behaviors in standing up for their rights in a responsible manner. In order for children to be successful in this arena, they must learn how to

- identify their rights,
- understand the meaning of those rights,
- recognize when their rights have been violated, and
- protect their rights.

Social skills training can help children understand what it means to be treated fairly and respectfully. They likewise can learn to set personal limits regarding how they want to be treated by others. And lastly, they can be taught a variety of assertive behaviors to use when standing up for their rights.

Refusal Skills

Learning to say no can be difficult for children especially if they think their friendships will suffer. All children face difficult peer pressure regarding whether or not to defy parental rules, cheat on exams, tease other children, steal from others, take drugs, or participate in acts of vandalism. Children often are caught in a moral dilemma between knowing what is right and doing the right things especially when peer pressure is factored into the equation. Unfortunately, many children find themselves giving in to the demands of their peers even when they know what they are doing is wrong. These children often feel frustrated, disappointed in themselves, and resentful of the fact that others are taking advantage of them.

Children who learn to refuse the will of others in tactful and nonpunitive ways will experience a sense of personal power, confidence in themselves, and the courage to act in accordance with their values. They also will learn that personal freedom comes to those who are willing to take the risk of behaving responsibly.

Other social skills that children can learn are the following:

- decision making,
- conflict management,
- group interactions (games, sports, clubs),
- rules of etiquette,
- being helpful,
- apologizing,
- cooperating, and
- respecting others.

The more social skills children learn to use, the greater the likelihood will be that they will improve their social interactions with others and develop satisfying peer relationships. What we teach them today, they in turn will be able to pass on to others tomorrow. In so doing, these children will be making a better life not only for themselves but also for all humankind (Ciechalski & Schmidt, 1995; Maag, 1994).

MESSAGE TO FACILITATORS

Your social skills support group is designed to enhance interpersonal functioning in the children with whom you will be working. They will be developing new social behaviors, strengthening existing behaviors, and remediating skill and performance deficits.

Forman's (1993) 30-year literature review of social skill program research studies has revealed that children and adolescents do benefit from participating in social skills training groups. One study showed that children participating in a 10-session social skills group improved in their assertiveness; ability to interact with adults; and increased their empathy for others, popularity, and acceptance among their peers (Rose, 1986). Other studies have not only revealed an increase in peer acceptance but also a decrease in social anxiety, withdrawal from others, and aggressive behaviors when such behaviors were present prior to beginning the social skills training program (Brake & Gerler, 1994). Your social skills support group can make a positive difference in the lives of children as well.

What Social Skills to Teach

Deciding what social skills to teach is based on the purpose of your group. Some support group programs focus on a particular set of goals to be achieved. These ready made programs share the belief that all children can benefit from social skills training. They also believe that there are basic social skills that all children should possess. They operate on the belief that their primary purpose is preventive-developmental in orientation. Their primary focus is teaching new social behaviors and strengthening existing ones. They do recognize, however, that some children in their groups are experiencing skill and performance deficits that they do address even though this is not their primary mission.

Some social skill groups have more of a therapeutic mission. They provide a group counseling experience with a primary focus on remediating skill and performance deficits. They may teach some new social behaviors and strengthen existing ones, but their primary mission is one of remediation. Children participating in these groups have been selected based on some very specific needs that have been identified using a variety of assessment and diagnostic instruments to include rating scales, self-report devices, sociometry, behavioral interviews, diagnostic role-plays, and direct observation.

The focus and primary purpose of the social skills support group that follows meets our first description. Your support group should be preventative-developmental in focus and will include a few children who are experiencing some skill and performance deficits. The children in your group will benefit from group support and participation in discussions relating to friends and friendships.

Group Goals

As we have indicated, the primary reason for creating this social skills support group is preventative-developmental with some remediation of skill and performance deficits. The theme of the support group that follows is "Learning how to make friends." Relationship building while learning how to successfully respond to unwanted peer pressure, when it occurs, is often difficult for children to understand and practice. With this mission in mind, the support group goals are designed to help children

- develop a social sense of connectiveness among their peers (i.e., develop a physical and psychological climate that promotes relationship building);
- discuss their ideas, feelings, thoughts, and myths about what it means to be a friend and to have friends;

- discriminate between helpful and hurtful responses (verbal and non-verbal) in developing friendships and relationships;
- identify successful social skills that are based on Right, Reality, and Responsibility (3 R's choices) in making friends and getting along with others;
- recognize what 3 R's social skills they possess that work for them in getting along with others;
- recognize behaviors they are using that are not working and should be stopped;
- brainstorm a variety of ways in which children can make 3 R's connections with others;
- learn a variety of social skills (strengths) they can observe, model, and practice in enhancing their interpersonal relationships with others;
- understand and develop a variety of socially acceptable peer pressure techniques they can use to diffuse unwanted manipulative advances of others; and
- set goals and practice using positive attitudes, knowledge, and skills that will enhance their friendships and relationships with others.

Membership Selection

Since your support group is not focused on remediation, and is instead preventative-developmental in its orientation, you do not need to rely heavily on the use of assessment devices to identify children. Rather you can advertise your group to parents, community groups, teachers, and children. Those children who can benefit most from your support group are ones who

- have friends but would like to enhance their relationship building strengths;
- have experienced difficulty in making and/or maintaining peer relationships;
- have developed inappropriate social behaviors that are not working for them (e.g., fighting, teasing, withdrawn, etc.);
- have just moved into your community and are experiencing difficulty in making the adjustment; and
- have excellent social skills and would like to help other children improve their peer relationships.

As you identify group participants, be sure to maintain a balance in your membership. Choose some children who have developed effective social skills to serve as role models. Identify others who wish to be group helpers and have the ability and personality attributes to make such a contribution. Identify other children who may be socially withdrawn or aggressive. Try to achieve a good mix of children with varying needs to be addressed. Above all, be sure to select children who can benefit from a group experience as well as contribute to it. They should be motivated in their desire to make personal changes in themselves and to try new ways of behaving, thinking, and feeling. This commitment can be insured, in part, by making sure that every potential participant understands the group's purpose and his or her role in it before joining. You may want to prepare a contract that describes the commitment and require participants' signatures after you have explained everything they need to know about the group.

Techniques for Teaching

Although your social skills support group will not be devoted entirely to training, you will be teaching a variety of social skills. Our experience has been that the following techniques used in sequence provide the best results.

Instruction. Children need information about the skill to be learned. They need a description of the skill, how it is used, and the benefits that can be derived from its use. You may choose to have children observe the skill directly or through video representation. You should encourage children to discuss what you present in your mini-lecture (five minutes). You may want to outline the main points of your presentation on poster board as a reminder of what you have presented.

Modeling. Now that children understand the skill, it is helpful to model it in action, pointing out the specific cues they can identify in assessing a quality performance. You may want to develop a script involving yourself and another child demonstrating the skill. Role-playing scripts helps insure an accurate performance.

Rehearsal. Once children have had numerous opportunities to observe the skill, they are ready to rehearse the skill themselves. This also can be accomplished through scripted role-plays. With additional practice, the need for scripts will diminish.

Feedback. Children need to know how they are performing the skill. This can be accomplished through feedback. Your goal is to support children and build their confidence while striving to improve their performance. Feedback should be direct, concrete, and continuous. Feedback can be applied verbally or by videotaping the children performing the skill and using video playback to improve the performance.

Coaching. In many ways coaching is similar to feedback. Coaching, however, goes beyond feedback in that you are giving children advice and ideas to consider as they perform the skill. Social skill coaching is no different than the process followed in coaching athletes.

Social Rewards. Children not only respond well to feedback and coaching but also need to be rewarded for their efforts. A kind word, smile, or pat on the back are a few ways of expressing your assessment of their success. Social rewards work best when you describe what the child has done that is so deserving of your attention.

Assignment. Children need opportunities to practice and apply the newly learned social skill on their own. Assignments (homework) can serve a useful purpose in accomplishing this end. Children can be asked to observe evidence of the social skill being used outside of the group situation. For example, this assignment could extend to studying social relationships and situations portrayed on television programs or observed at the local shopping mall.

Children can be given open-ended social interaction situations in which they must describe how a particular social skill could facilitate the interpersonal dilemma. Other types of assignments might include using a newly learned social skill or using 3 R's problem solving to solve actual peer relationship problems at home, in school, or on the playground.

Try to make the assignments fun and relevant for children. The assignments portray life situations that have meaning for children. This is particularly important since your goal is to encourage children to use the social skills they have learned outside of the support group.

Social skills training programs do work. They can help children acquire a variety of social behaviors to increase their peer acceptance while decreasing inappropriate actions (e.g., anxiety, withdrawal, and aggression) that can destroy social contact. Have fun making a positive difference in helping children develop lasting friendships and successful identities.

Resources

Share with parents and/or guardians Figure 12.1 so that they will have suggestions on how they can help their children at home. In Figure 12.2 are provided lists of resources to be used with and by children in the Social Skills Training Group. The resource materials are grouped according to age of child.

SOCIAL SKILLS GUIDE
Tips for Caregivers

Your child soon will be participating in a Social Skills Support Group. The goal of this support group is to help children learn socially acceptable behaviors that will enable them to interact appropriately and responsibly with others in any given situation. Children who possess a variety of social skills and know how and when to use them are successful in developing satisfying relationships with others while attaining their personal goals. You can play an important role in teaching your child responsible social skills that will last a lifetime. We are happy to share with you some tips that you can use in helping your child become socially competent in relating well with others.

1. There are many social skills that children should learn. You first must identify what social skills your child already possesses. Then decide what skills he or she still needs that will enhance his or her relationships with others.
2. Here are a few important social skills that will benefit your child.

To gain attention from others in appropriate ways	To take turns
To ask others for help	To return things to their rightful place
To greet others	To compliment others
To introduce oneself to others	To ask others to play
To help others	To distinguish one's own property from others
To speak one at a time	To tell the truth and to accept consequences
To follow home and school rules	To tell right from wrong
To share	To say thank you, please, and may I
	To eat properly at the dinner table

3. Observe other people and children. What behaviors do they use that please you? Make a list of these behaviors and select those that you would like to teach your child.
4. Identify problem behaviors in your child. Help your child discard these behaviors and substitute them with more responsible social skills.

Problem	Social Skills
Your child interrupts others.	Teach your child to wait for pauses in a conversation before speaking.
Your child does not play games according to the rules.	Teach your child how to play games according to the rules.
Your child always finds fault with himself or herself.	Teach your child how to identify positive self-behaviors and to self-affirm those positive qualities.

Teach your child new social skills using the following steps.

Step 1. Identify the social skill you would like to teach.

Step 2. Explain to your child the purpose or the benefits that he or she will gain from learning this skill. You also may want to discuss the pitfalls that children may incur if they do not learn it. Your child needs to recognize the value of this social skill. You can use videotapes, stories, and live examples of children using this social skill to help motivate your child in wanting to learn this new behavior.

Step 3. Identify the skill components and steps (chain of behaviors) you need to teach your child to learn this social skill. One good way of identifying these steps is to observe what others do who have learned the social skill. For example, making friends is a complex social skill. What behaviors would a person display who has developed this skill. Brainstorm a list of these behaviors.

Step 4. After identifying the skill components, place them in the order of their occurrence.

Step 5. Model the behavior. Your child needs to see the social skill in action. Go through each step and explain the step as you perform it. You can either model the social skill yourself or use stories, movies, or live models that can demonstrate the social skill for you. You must go slowly, provide clear and detailed directions, provide repetition in demonstrating the skill, and use a variety of different models to teach the skill.

Step 6. Have your child rehearse each step as it is being taught. Your child can be taught to verbalize out loud what he or she is doing. You also can ask your child to mentally picture himself or herself going through the steps before actually doing it.

Step 7. Provide feedback. As each step is performed, let your child know how he or she is doing. Be very clear in giving the feedback. Let the child know what he or she is doing correctly and guide him or her in shaping each step.

Step 8. Have your child practice the steps in sequence. Be sure to provide feedback and lots of praise for doing a good job.

Step 9. Once your child learns a new social skill, help him or her identify all the different places and ways in which it can be used.

Step 10. Give your child a "homework" practice assignment. Have him or her use the new social skill in another setting. Discuss with your child how things went. Help your child continue to improve upon his or her ability to use the social skill.

Figure 12.1. Tips for Caregivers to be given to parents and/or guardians. Permission to photocopy is granted.

RESOURCES FOR CHILDREN
Social Skills: Friendship

Ages 3 to 7

Ackerman, K. (1990). *The tin heart.* New York: Atheneum Publishers. (best friend)

Blume, J. (1987). *Just as long as we're together.* New York: Orchard Books. (best friend, meaning of friendship)

Clifton, L. (1992). *Everett Anderson's friend.* New York: Henry Holt. (making new friends)

Graham, B. (1988). *Crusher is coming.* New York: Viking Penguin. (friendship, sibling rivalry)

Henkes, K. (1989). *Chester's way.* New York: Viking Penguin. (making friends)

Martin, A. (1992). *Rachel Parker, kindergarten show off.* New York: Holiday House. (feelings of jealousy and competitiveness)

Powell, R. (1990). *How to deal with friends.* Mahwah, NJ: Troll Books. (ways to get along with others)

Rogers, F. (1987). *Making friends.* New York: Putnam. (what it means to be a friend)

St. Germain, S. (1990). *The terrible fight.* Boston: Houghton Mifflin. (friendship, communication)

Stock, C. (1990). *Halloween monster.* New York: Bradbury Press. (best friend)

Ages 8 to 12

Adler, C. S. (1988). *Always and forever friends.* Boston: Clarion Books. (making friends, best friend)

Auch, M. J. (1989). *Glass slippers give you blisters.* New York: Holiday House. (school friendships)

Bates, A. (1991). *What's the opposite of best friend?* New York: Scholastic. (enduring friendships)

Buscaglia, L. (1988). *A memory for Tino.* New York: William Morrow. (friendship and compassion)

Chaiken, M. (1988). *Friends forever.* New York: HarperCollins. (value of friendship)

Gilson, J. (1988). *Double dog dare.* New York: Lothrop, Lee and Shepard Books. (meaning of friendship)

Hines, A. G. (1989). *Boys are yucko.* New York: Dutton Children's Books. (best friend)

Hurwitz, J. (1979). *Also applesauce.* New York: Puffin Books. (being different, having friends)

Singer, M. (1990). *Twenty ways to lose your best friend.* New York: Harper Collins. (meaning of friendship)

Talley, C. (1992). *Hana's year.* Shawnee Mission, KS: Marsh Media. (influence of friends)

Ages 12 and Up

Betancourt, J. (1990). *Valentine blues.* New York: Bantam, Doubleday, Dell. (keeping friends and belonging)

Brancato, R. F. (1984). *Facing up.* New York: Alfred A. Knopf. (best friend, death of friend)

Cassidy, S. (1987). *Me and Morton.* New York: Crowell Press. (meaning of friendship)

Cooney, C. B. (1988). *The girl who invented romance.* New York: Bantam, Doubleday, Dell. (best friend, boy-girl relationships)

Erlback, A. (1995). *The best friends book.* Minneapolis: Free Spirit Publishing. (real life stories about friendship)

Hodge, L. L. (1987). *A season of change.* Washington, D C: Kendall Green Publications. (boy-girl relationships)

Levi, D. F. (1988). *A very special friend.* Washington, D C: Kendall Green Publications. (making and keeping friends)

Roos, S. (1987). *The fair weather friends.* Mahwah, NJ: Troll Books. (friendship and growing up)

Smith, D. B. (1987). *Karate dancer.* New York: Putnam and Grossett Group. (making friends, best friend)

Zalben, J. B. (1984). *Here's looking at you, kid.* New York: Farriar, Strauss & Giroux. (meaning of friendship, love)

Figure 12.2. Resources for use with and by children in Social Skills Support Group.

SESSION I—MAKING CONNECTIONS

BRIEF OVERVIEW OF SESSION

This session will provide an introduction to the group process, involve children in a getting acquainted exercise, provide group ground rules, and set the stage for the sessions on social skills.

GOALS

1. To help children understand their reasons for involvement in the group.
2. To encourage children to begin to make connections with other members of the group.
3. To present group ground rules.

MATERIALS NEEDED

1. Large sheets of newsprint for each child
2. Chart paper or chalkboard
3. Markers or crayons
4. 3" × 5" card for each child

PROCEDURE

1. Introduce yourself and have each of the group members introduce himself or herself by first name. Talk about the fact that this is a group where we will begin to identify and develop social skills that will enable us to make better friendships.

2. Begin to set the stage for the group by inviting a brainstorming session on group rules. Write the rules on chart paper or on the chalkboard and post them for future reference. Examples of possible initial group ground rules may include the following:

   a What is said in the group, stays there (confidentiality).
   b No put-downs are allowed.
   c Only one person talks at a time.
   d It is important to attend all sessions.

Note: If children do not suggest these group rules, you as facilitator should bring them up as part of the brainstorming session.

3. Give each child a piece of newsprint and instruct him or her to write three things that he or she really enjoys doing. (Make sure they allow a good deal of space between each of the three items.)

4. When all children have identified their three items, tape all of the sheets on the bulletin board or chalkboard where they can easily be seen by all.

5. Encourage the children to make "connections" with other group members by initialing on each chart the common interests they have with other group members. Example:

Name: RHONDA
Interest: Watching "The Disney Channel"
Initials: K.D., R.S., S.C.

Interest: Playing soccer
Initials: J.B., P.L., K.D.

Interest: Reading science fiction
Initials: R.S.

6. Allow time for the children to share at least one item from their charts and to connect briefly with the others who initialed their sheet. Talk briefly about how friendships often develop as a result of common interests.

CLOSURE

To conclude this initial session, congratulate the children for following the ground rules and remind them that they may want to follow up on some of the common interests or connections they have become aware of in today's group.

HOMEWORK

For a homework assignment, give each child in the group a 3" × 5" card and ask that he or she write an answer to the question "What is a friend?" and bring it to next week's session.

SESSION II—WHAT IS A FRIEND?

BRIEF OVERVIEW OF SESSION

In this session, children will begin to identify the characteristics of friendship. In doing so, they also will begin to identify some things that some children do that destroy friendships.

GOALS

1. To encourage the children to develop a definition of friendship.
2. To provide the opportunity for children to discuss the ideas, feelings, thoughts, and myths about what it means to be friends and have friends.

MATERIALS NEEDED

1. 18" × 24" poster paper for each child
2. Crayons or markers
3. Chalkboard and chalk
4. Copies of "Friendship Do's and Don'ts" worksheet (Activity Sheet 12.1)

PROCEDURE

1. Begin the session by encouraging each group member to read his or her definition of a friend from the homework card. List the comments from the definitions on the chalkboard. Examples might include

- shares with others,
- invites you to his or her house,
- lets you play with his or her toys,
- smiles, and
- says nice things to everyone.

2. Allow time for the children to share experiences as to when someone has been a friend to them by doing one of the above mentioned things. Also discuss how the person reciprocated this friendly act.

3. Provide a piece of chart paper for each child and encourage him or her to develop a "Recipe for a Friend." (Or encourage each to work with a part-

ner.) Give some examples of the kinds of things that might be included in the recipe. Example:

½ C. of Kindness
2 C. of Sharing
¾ C. of Smiles
1 tsp. of Consideration
Mix all items together and bake up some good times.

4. Allow sufficient time for all children to complete their recipe and to share them with the group.

5. Place the "Recipes" on the bulletin board for future reference.

CLOSURE

Provide a few minutes at the conclusion of the session to encourage the children to remember to use the recipe items during the next week as they communicate with their friends.

HOMEWORK

Provide a copy of the "Friendship Do's and Don'ts" worksheet (Activity Sheet 12.1) for each child to complete and bring to the next session.

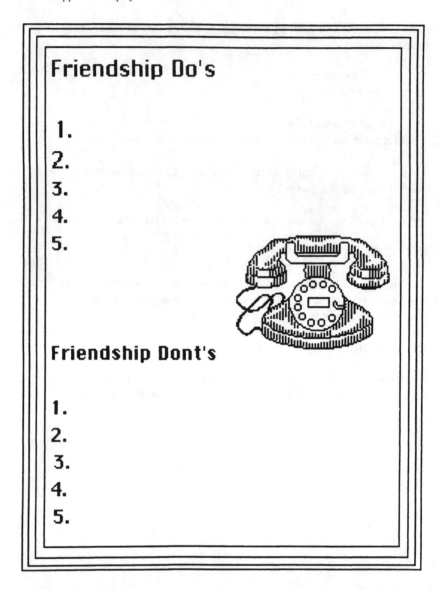

Activity Sheet 12.1.   Friendship Do's and Don'ts worksheet. Permission is granted to enlarge and photocopy for classroom use.

SESSION III—FRIENDSHIP DO'S AND DON'TS

BRIEF OVERVIEW OF SESSION

During this session, children will begin to identify some of the appropriate and inappropriate social skills that can either help or harm a friendship. They also will have an opportunity to practice some of the helpful situations through role-plays.

GOALS

1. To assist children in discriminating between helpful and hurtful responses (both verbal and nonverbal) that can help or hinder the development of relationships.
2. To help children recognize behaviors that are not working for them and that should be stopped.

MATERIALS NEEDED

1. "Friendship Do's and Don'ts" worksheets brought back by the children
2. Chalkboard and chalk

PROCEDURE

1. Compliment the children, as appropriate, on the completion of their homework assignment and encourage them to share the items they have listed under the do's and don'ts columns.

2. Begin to compile a master list of all of the suggested do's and don'ts from the assignments.

Friendship Do's	Friendship Don'ts
1. Sharing	1. Calling Names
2. Smiling	2. Hitting
3. Taking Turns	3. Being Selfish
4. Complimenting	4. Talking behind someone's back
5. Talking nicely with someone	5. Saying mean things
6. Inviting	

3. Talk briefly about each of the items on the lists and encourage the children to share experiences when they have done any of the listed items.

4. Invite the children to role-play some of the Friendship Do's as a way to practice for a real-life situation they may be facing. Provide as much time as possible and try to get all of the group members involved in the role-plays (if all are willing).

CLOSURE

Remind the children that today's session has provided them with many ideas for things they can do to develop friendships. Ask the children to think of the name of one person with whom they would like to develop a friendship in the future.

HOMEWORK

As a homework assignment, instruct the children to use at least three of the "Friendship Do's" in an attempt to develop a friendship with their chosen person.

SESSION IV—3 R'S FRIENDSHIP SKILLS

BRIEF OVERVIEW OF SESSION

In this session, children will begin to look at the 3 R's Decision Making model they have learned and apply it to positive social skill development.

GOALS

1. To assist children in identifying successful social skills that are based on Right, Reality, and Responsibility in making friends and getting along with others.
2. To help children recognize the 3 R's social skills they possess to help them in getting along with others.

MATERIALS NEEDED

1. Copies of the 3 R's Decision Making model shown in "3 R's Filters" handout (Activity Sheet 12.2)
2. Copies of "My 3 R's Strength" worksheet (Activity Sheet 12.3)
3. 5" × 8" cards with problem situations written on them

PROCEDURE

1. Briefly review the "Friendship Do's and Don'ts" from last session and allow time for the children to share experiences from their homework assignment. Ask the following questions: Was anyone successful in beginning a new friendship? Did anyone have difficulties? What kinds of difficulties? What were the good things that happened as a result of your homework?

2. Present the 3 R's model (Activity Sheet 12.2) and explain the filters of *Right, Reality,* and *Responsibility.*

3. Talk about how the filters can help one make good decisions about friendship.

4. Provide a few minutes for each child to identify at least one personal quality that would pass through the 3 R's filters and would be a good strength to use in developing friendships (Activity Sheet 12.3).

5. Present the following situations (or others of your choosing) as a way for children to decide if certain situations are good 3 R's things to do.

a   Mary wants to be friends with Jean so everyday she gives her a candy bar.
b   Jon is a good math student and would like to be friends with Charlie. He offers to help Charlie with his math homework.
c   Jennie heard Susie spreading a rumor about one of the other girls in the class. She shared the information with Lisa.
d   Pete has a really neat model car collection. He invites Joe over to his house to see it.

6. Provide adequate time for discussion of each of the situations.

CLOSURE

Bring closure to this session by reminding the children that the 3 R's Decision Making model can be very helpful to them in making and keeping friends if they filter their potential actions through each of the three filters as a way of determining if they are appropriate.

HOMEWORK

Ask children to think about the answer to the following unfinished sentences and be prepared to share their answers at the beginning of the next session.

I am a good friend because. . . .
One thing that keeps me from making more friends is. . . .

THE 3 R's FILTERS

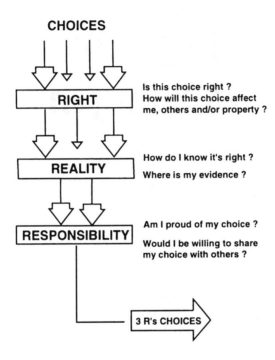

Activity Sheet 12.2.   3 R's Decision Making Model. Permission is granted to enlarge and photocopy for classroom use.

My 3 R's Strength

Activity Sheet 12.3. My 3 R's Strength worksheet. Permission is granted to enlarge and photocopy for classroom use.

SESSION V—MAKING AND KEEPING FRIENDS

BRIEF OVERVIEW OF SESSION

In this session, children will begin to put together all that they have learned in the four previous sessions and will identify personal qualities that can assist them in making new friends and keeping them.

GOALS

1. To assist children in recognizing a variety of ways in which they can develop connections with others.
2. To encourage children to utilize the strengths they have to enhance their interpersonal relationships with others.

MATERIALS NEEDED

1. Chart paper and markers for each group of two
2. Computer program for development of a poster (or use the "Keys to Friendship" worksheet [Activity Sheet 12.4] provided)

PROCEDURE

1. Begin the session by encouraging the children to share their comments from their homework assignment for unfinished sentences. Have each person describe a strength and a weaknesses he or she sees in himself or herself.

2. Ask the children to find a partner and begin to develop a list of "keys" for making and keeping friends. Remind them to use some of their newly learned social skills to work together cooperatively.

3. Allow time for the groups to share their "Keys" with others. Make a master list of "Keys," which may include but not be limited to the following:

a get involved in school activities,
b smile,
c be a good listener,
d share talking time with your friends,
e always call people by their name,
f be willing to start a conversation with others,
g spend time with people who have similar interests,

h   invite people to do things with you,
i   give honest compliments, and
j   invite people to come to your home (if you are allowed).

4. Encourage the children to create a personalized list of "Keys" that they will take home and post in an area that they will see often so that they can refer to the list on a regular basis. (If you have access to a computer lab where each child can create his or her own personalized chart, this would be a great way to allow the children to have some fun while creating their "Keys" chart. If not, the chart provided (Activity Sheet 12.4) is another option.

CLOSURE

Provide a few minutes at the conclusion of this session for the children to talk a bit about some of the skills they have learned and practiced to this point. Encourage them to talk about the ones that have worked best for them during the past few weeks.

HOMEWORK

Provide a sheet of paper for each child to write down a personal social skills goal for next session. This will prepare us for Session VI, "Goal Setting for Friendship."

Keys to Friendship

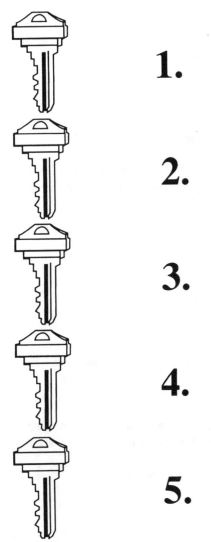

1.

2.

3.

4.

5.

Activity Sheet 12.4.   Keys to Friendship worksheet. Permission is granted to enlarge and photocopy for classroom use.

SESSION VI—GOAL SETTING FOR FRIENDSHIP

BRIEF OVERVIEW OF SESSION

In this session, children will set a specific goal that they wish to achieve in terms of their social skills. They also will learn a process by which to set and evaluate goals.

GOALS

1. To assist each child in the group in setting a personal goal that he or she wishes to achieve.
2. To encourage children to set goals and practice positive attitudes, knowledge, and skills that will enhance their friendships and relationships with others.

MATERIALS NEEDED

1. Sample "Goal Worksheet" (Activity Sheet 12.5) on chart paper for demonstration
2. Copy of "Goal Worksheet" for each child

PROCEDURE

1. Spend a few minutes discussing the "Keys to Friendship" activity from last session. Encourage the children to talk about where they placed their chart and to share any positive effects from the use of specific ideas from the chart.

2. Introduce the idea of goal setting as a means for helping one plan ways to enhance social skills and involvements. Demonstrate using the following sample:

Goal: To invite John to go to the movies next Saturday.

Things I need to do:

1. Ask dad if he will take us.
2. Make sure I have enough money.
3. Get the movie schedule so I know when it starts.
4. Call John and ask if he wants to go.
5. Have something else to do if John can't go.

Carry out the actions (check off each item when completed):

_____ Ask dad.
_____ Check money.
_____ Get schedule.
_____ Call John.

Follow through on the goal:

I called John and he said Yes! We went last Saturday.

Evaluate:

Was it a good goal?
Did I enjoy it?
Did John enjoy it?
Would I like to do something like this again?
Do John and I enjoy the same types of things?

3. Provide a "Goal Worksheet" (Activity Sheet 12.5) for each child and allow time for completion of the worksheet.

4. While children are working on their goal sheets, spend a bit of individual time with each child and discuss his or her personal goal.

CLOSURE

When the children have completed their goal sheets, an effective closure would be to provide a bit of time for them to share their goal plans if they wish to do so.

HOMEWORK

For homework, each child should be encouraged to carry out his or her goal plan.

Goal Worksheet

My Goal:

Things I Need to Do:

Carry Out My Actions:

Follow Through:

Evaluate:

Activity Sheet 12.5.   Goal Worksheet. Permission is granted to enlarge and photocopy for classroom use.

SESSION VII—PEER PRESSURE

BRIEF OVERVIEW OF SESSION

In this session, children will begin to discuss friendship in terms of peer pressure. They will identify areas of concern with which they have had to deal in friendships.

GOALS

1. To assist children in identifying areas of concern resulting from peer pressure.
2. To begin to work on potential skills for dealing with peer pressure.

MATERIALS NEEDED

1. Chart paper and markers
2. Copies of "Peer Pressure Cooker" worksheet (Activity Sheet 12.6)

PROCEDURE

1. Begin by reviewing the Goals Worksheet that the children developed last session.

    a   What have been your successes?
    b   What kinds of problems have you had?
    c   Did anyone complete their goal?
    d   What changes would you make for the future?

2. Remind the children that today we are going to talk about what happens when friends make requests of peers that we feel are wrong. Some kids will go along with such a request because they do not want to lose a friend. This is called *peer pressure.*

3. Provide a few moments for the children to talk about times when they have been in such a situation. List these situations on the chart:

    a   Friend wants to copy my homework.
    b   Friend wants you to smoke with him or her.
    c   Friend asks you to take something from the store.

4. Talk with the children about how one can refuse to do an inappropriate act and still, hopefully, maintain the friendship. Admit to the children that sometimes you may lose a friendship in this type of situation, but at that point, you have to ask if that person really is a "friend."

5. Present the following possible "refusal techniques."

a Say, "I don't want to do that."
b Just walk away.
c Make a joke, "You've got to be kidding. You know I wouldn't do that."
d Say, "I don't feel comfortable doing that."
e Say, "I'd rather not do that."

6. Ask for feedback from the children on their reactions to the refusal techniques. Provide some time for discussion, questions, concerns, and so forth.

CLOSURE

Remind the children that, while friendship is important, we do not want to be pressured by peers to do things that we do not want to do. We need to remember the 3 R's filter to help us make good friendship decisions.

HOMEWORK

Give a copy of the "Peer Pressure Cooker" worksheet (Activity Sheet 12.6) to each child and ask that the worksheet be completed for next session. Also suggest that the children try one of the "refusal" techniques during the upcoming week.

Peer Pressure Cooker

1. What happened?

2. How did I react?

3. What else could I have done?

Activity Sheet 12.6. Peer Pressure-Cooker worksheet. Permission is granted to enlarge and photocopy for classroom use.

SESSION VIII—PRACTICING REFUSAL SKILLS

BRIEF OVERVIEW OF SESSION

In this session, children will have an opportunity to practice the "refusal skills" introduced in the previous session. Through involvement in role-play, they will be able to rehearse the skills that they feel will work best for them.

GOALS

1. To continue identifying skills that will help children resist peer pressure.
2. To provide an opportunity for children to practice refusal skills.
3. To bring closure to the group experience.

MATERIALS NEEDED

1. 5" × 8" cards for role-play situations
2. Evaluation questionnaire for each child
3. Large chart with SOCIAL SKILLS written vertically down the left side.

PROCEDURE

1. Allow a few minutes for the children to share situations from their "Peer Pressure Cooker" worksheet. Encourage dialogue among the group members in regard to the "What else could I have done?" question.

2. Choose one or more of the situations and ask the children to role-play the situation using the refusal skills discussed during the previous group session. Compliment the children for their work in the role-plays.

3. Provide some additional situations for role-playing. You may use the ones provided below or tailor make some of your own.

   a. A friend asks you to watch his dog while his family is on vacation. You already have something planned for that week.
   b. You and a friend are in a music store and you see a tape that you would love to have. Your friend encourages you to steal it because "the owner will never miss it."
   c. You are at a friend's house watching TV. His mom has to go to the store and leaves the two of you there alone. After his mom goes, he brings out a bottle of Vodka and offers you a drink. (He says he'll put water in the bottle so no one will ever know any of it is missing)

d   Your best friend asks you to go to the movies but you are grounded and know you will not be allowed to go.
e   You worked hard on your homework and now your friend wants to copy it.
f   You are at a birthday party and someone there offers you drugs.

4. Talk with the children about the role-plays. Encourage them to discuss the kinds of things they did to keep from doing something they did not want to do. Remind them that being honest and saying "no" is much better than "going along with the crowd" when they know something is wrong.

5. Remind the children that the skills they have learned in the group will help them make and keep friends.

CLOSURE

As a way to bring closure to the group, show the children the chart with the words *social skills* on it. Ask them to think of sentences or phrases beginning with each of the letters to remind them of some of the skills they have learned.

S—smile often
O—offer to help someone
C—courtesy is always important
I—interest in what others have to say
A—always take turns with others
L—listen when someone else is talking

S—share time and talents with others
K—kindness is important
I—invite someone to play with you
L—loyalty is a special friendship quality
L—lucky are those who have good friends
S—success is achieved by those who try

At the conclusion of the activity, pass out the evaluations and provide time for children to complete them.

HOMEWORK

Because this is the final session in the social skills unit, the only homework assignment will be to use the skills they have learned on a regular basis and to check back to let the facilitator know how they are doing.

EVALUATION

1. Do you feel that participation in the Social Skills group was helpful to you? Why or why not?

2. What part of the group did you like best?

3. What part of the group did you like least?

4. If you had a friend who needed to identify some more positive Social Skills, would you recommend that he or she join this group or one like it? Why or why not?

5. Did you attend all eight group sessions?

_____ Yes _____ No

If no, how many did you attend? _____

6. Comments, suggestions, etc.:

REFERENCES

Altmann, E. D., & Gottlieb, I. H. (1988). The social behavior of depressed children: An observational study. *Journal of Abnormal Child Psychology, 16,* 29–44.

Asarnow, J. R. (1988). Peer status and social competence in child psychiatric inpatients: A comparison of children with depressive, externalizing, and concurrent depressive and externalizing disorders. *Journal of Abnormal Child Psychology, 16,* 151–162.

Bandura, A. (1969). *Principles of behavior modification.* New York: Holt, Rinehart, & Winston.

Bandura, A. (1973). *Aggression: A social learning analysis.* Englewood Cliffs, NJ: Prentice-Hall.

Bandura, A. (1977a). Self-efficacy: Toward a unifying theory of behavioral change. *Psychological Review, 84,* 191–215.

Bandura, A. (1977b). *Social learning theory.* Englewood Cliffs, NJ: Prentice-Hall.

Bandura, A. (1986). *Social foundations of thought and action: A social cognitive theory.* Englewood Cliffs, NJ: Prentice-Hall.

Boivin, M., & Begin, G. (1989). Peer status and self perceptions among early elementary school children: The case of the rejected children. *Child Development, 60,* 571–579.

Boulton, M. J., & Smith, P. K. (1990). Affective bias in children's perceptions of dominance relationships. *Child Development, 61,* 221–229.

Brake, K. J., & Gerler, E. R. (1994). Discovery: A program for fourth and fifth graders identified as discipline problems. *Elementary School Guidance & Counseling, 28*(3), 170–181.

Bullock, J. R. (1988). Encouraging the development of social competence in young children. *Early Childhood Development & Care, 37,* 47–54.

Cartledge, G., & Melburn, J. F. (1986). Steps in teaching social skills. In G.

Cartledge & J. F. Milburn (Eds.), *Teaching social skills to children: Innovative approaches* (2nd ed.) (pp. 3–180). New York: Pergamon Press.

Chance, P. (1989). Kids without friends. *Psychology Today, 23,* 29–31.

Chittenden, G. F. (1942). An experimental study in measuring and modifying assertive behavior in young children. *Monograph of the Society for Research in Child Development, 7,* 1–87.

Ciechalski, J. C., & Schmidt, M. W. (1995). The effects of social skills training on students with exceptionalities. *Elementary School Guidance & Counseling, 29*(3), 217–222.

Coie, J. D., & Dodge, K. A. (1988). Multiple sources of data on social behavior and social status in the school: A cross-age comparison. *Child Development, 59,* 815–829.

Dodge, K. A., Cole, J. D., Pettit, G. S., & Price, J. M. (1990). Peer status and aggression in boy's groups: Developmental and contextual analysis. *Child Development, 61,* 1289–1309.

Edwards, D. (1995). The school counselor's role in helping teachers and students belong. *Elementary School Guidance & Counseling, 29*(3), 191–197.

Elliot, S. N., & Gresham, F. M. (1987). Children's social skills: Assessment and classification practices. *Journal of Counseling and Development, 66,* 96–99.

Forman, S. G. (1993). *Coping skills interventions for children and adolescents.* San Francisco, CA: Jossey-Bass.

French, D. C. (1990). Heterogeneity of peer-rejected girls. *Child Development, 61,* 2028–2031.

French, D. C. (1988). Heterogeneity of peer-rejected boys: Aggressive and nonaggressive subtypes. *Child Development, 59,* 976–985.

Gelb, R., & Jacobson, J. L. (1988). Popular and unpopular children's interaction during cooperative and competitive peer group activities. *Journal of Abnormal Child Psychology, 16,* 247–261.

Goldstein, A. P., Sprafkin, R. P., Gershaw, N. J., & Klein, P. (1980). *Skill-streaming the adolescent: A structural learning approach to teaching prosocial skills.* Champaign, IL: Research Press.

Hazler, R. J., Hoover, J. H., & Oliver, R. (1993). What do kids say about bullying. *Education Digest, 58*(7), 16–20.

Hoover, J. H., & Hazler, R. J. (1991). Bullies and victims. *Elementary School Guidance & Counseling, 25*(3), 212–219.

Ladd, G. W. (1984). Social skills training with children: Issues in research and practice. *Clinical Psychology Review, 4,* 317–337.

Little, R. (1988, November). Skills for growing: A new K-5 program. *Principal,* 19–21.

Maag, J. W. (1994). Promoting social skills training in classrooms: Issues for school counselors. *The School Counselor, 42*(2), 100–113.

Mehaffey, J. I., & Sandberg, S. K. (1992). Conducting social skills training groups with elementary school children. *The School Counselor, 40,* 61–67.

Michelson, L., Sugai, D. P., Wood, R. P., & Kazdin, A. E. (1983). *Social skills assessment and training with children: An empirically based approach.* New York: Plenum.

Miller, N. E., & Dollard, J. (1941). *Social learning and imitation.* London: Oxford University Press.

Oliver, R. L., Young, T. A., LaSalle, S. M. (1994). Early lessons in bullying and victimization: The help and hindrances of children's literature. *The School Counselor, 42*(2), 137–146.

Ormrod, J. E. (1995). *Human learning* (2nd ed.). Englewood Cliffs, NJ: Prentice-Hall.

Patterson, G. R., Reid, J. G., Jones, R. R., & Congber, R. E. (1975). *A social learning approach to family intervention* (vol. 1). Eugene, OR: Castaglia.

Rice, F. P. (1992). *Human development: A life-span approach.* New York: Macmillan.

Rinn, R. C., & Markle, A. (1979). Modification of social skill deficits in children. In A. S. Bellack & M. Hersen (Eds.), *Research and practice in social skills training.* New York: Plenum.

Rogosch, F. A., & Newcomb, A. F. (1989). Children's perceptions of peer reputation and their social reputations among peers. *Child Development, 60,* 597–610.

Rose, S. R. (1986). Enhancing the social relationship skills of children: A comparative study of group approaches. *School Social Work Journal, 10,* 76–85.

Stone, S. J. (1993, Summer). Taking time to teach social skills. *Childhood Education,* 194–195.

Younger, A. J., & Piccinin, A. M. (1989). Children's recall of aggressive and withdrawn behavior: Recognition memory and likability judgments. *Child Development, 60,* 580–590.

Chapter **13**

STRESS MANAGEMENT

Stress management is a process that teaches children about the meaning of stress, how stress affects their lives, and how best to cope with the effects of stress.

BACKGROUND INFORMATION

The twentieth century has been a period of tremendous advances in modern medicine. Medical treatments and care are nothing short of common miracles by most people's standards when compared with where we were one hundred short years ago. Today, in many respects, the impossible has become possible. However, with all of our technological and scientific advances, there is a major void that modern medicine has been unable to address. Lay people and health professionals alike are recognizing that, despite medical advances, there is little that modern medicine can do to counteract the pathology caused by lifestyles gone awry.

Medical science now acknowledges the close link between lifestyle and modern medical problems. People's general knowledge, attitudes, and behaviors are closely linked with their health status. The concept of self-care as a pathway to disease prevention and wellness promotion is commonly accepted among the medical and lay communities. Despite all of the medical advances that can be cited, people can have a much greater and more significant impact on their own health and wellness than medicine can provide. For society's general health and wellness status to improve, however, people first must understand that they can make a difference in their own health promotion and disease prevention and then be taught what actions they can take to make that difference.

Stress is one lifestyle factor that is closely linked with people's health status. Stress is a normal part of life and living and is unavoidable. Children and adults alike are affected by stress on a daily basis. The amount of stress that children and adults experience varies from moment to moment and day to day. Stress affects people's lives in different ways. Some people have learned to cope with stress in responsible ways whereas others have created more stress in their lives in their attempts at self-management. Each person reacts differently to stress and exhibits varying levels of tolerance to it; however all people have their limits. When those stress tolerance limits are exceeded, the end result is often a loss of well being and eventual illness.

Most people do not understand the nature of stress, what causes it, how much they can tolerate, what they can do to lessen the effects of stress in their lives, and how they can increase their stress tolerance. Few people realize that they can learn to manage their life stresses and actually benefit from the energizing and motivating effects of optimal stress.

Those individuals most vulnerable to the effects of stress are children. Often they are placed in life situations not of their own choosing and are restricted in their options to act because of their dependency on adults and social systems that act in their behalf. These actions often run counter to children's needs and create additional stress for them. Consequently, they surpass their stress tolerance, which can result in illness and the development of coping behaviors that may be counterproductive and detrimental to their own and other's well being.

In this chapter, the nature of stress and its impact on children will be addressed. In particular, we will discuss the meaning of stress, signs of childhood stress, causes of childhood stress, the assessment of childhood stress, stress management methods, and stress prevention and wellness promotion.

DEFINITION OF STRESS

What would appear to be a simple task—defining the meaning of stress—is more complicated than one might imagine, as is evidenced in the professional literature (Aronson & Mascia, 1981; Forman, 1993; Romano, 1992). A review of the stress literature reveals three major definitions in use today:

(a) stimulus-based, (b) response-based, and (c) transactional (Forman, 1993; Romano, 1992). Each definition provides a unique perspective on stress, and taken collectively, they provide useful insights into the management of stress, which will be discussed later in this chapter.

Stimulus-based Definition

Stimulus-based definitions of stress focus on the impact that life situations have on people's well being. Stress is viewed as a strain on an individual caused by stimuli in the environment. Researchers ascribing to this understanding of stress have studied a variety of environmental events that either interrupt or disrupt normal activity and either are noxious or place excessive demands on people's lives (Holmes & Rake, 1967). Forman (1993) classified these events into three categories, namely major changes that affect large numbers of people's lives (e.g., disasters such as earthquakes, fires, floods); major changes affecting a few people (e.g., death of a loved one, divorce); and daily hassles (e.g., loneliness, failure of an exam, illness).

Compas (1987) further contributed to the stimulus-based definition by contending that internal events, in addition to external events, could likewise cause stress. Internal events such as disease, bodily changes in puberty, and handicapping conditions are life stressors. He further stated that stress could be considered chronic or acute. Chronic demands are environmental or internal events that continually pose threats or challenges to be addressed. Physical diseases, poverty, and family abuse are examples of chronic demands that cause stress. Acute stressors tend to disrupt existing and ongoing conditions. Parental divorce, death of a family member, and relocation (moving) are examples of acute demands.

According to the stimulus-based definition, any internal or environmental condition or event that affects children's lives would be viewed as a stress-producing experience. The amount of stress children experience would be equated with the number of events experienced in any given period of time. A major problem with the stimulus-based definition of stress is that it does not account for individual perceptions of internal and environmental events or variances in individual abilities to manage life stressors.

Response-based Definition

Rather than place the focus on the stressor in determining the presence of stress, the response-based research defines stress in terms of the presence of biological or psychological responses to a stressful situation. Selye (1974), a pioneer in stress related research, is one of the major proponents of this approach. He defined stress as the nonspecific biological reaction of the body to any environmental demand. Using this definition, any situation or condition, whether viewed as positive or negative by the person, that caused a physiological reaction would be viewed as a stress reaction. Thus Selye coined the terms eustress (good stress) and distress (bad stress) to account for this difference.

The biological changes within an individual are viewed as objective indicators of the presence of stress. When using the response-based definition of stress, the presence of stress in children is evidenced by their responses to internal and environmental events. Thus, children showing signs of depression, anxiety, headaches, and related disturbances would infer the presence of stress. The problem with the response-based definition, according to Forman (1993), is that a specific bodily response may not be an invariant indicator of stress.

Transactional Definition

Sometimes referred to as an interactional model, this approach, developed by Lazarus (1966), conceptualized stress in terms of a transaction between the person and the environment. According to this theory, the transaction consists of the person's perception of the stressor and its potential for personal risk, coupled with that person's perceived ability to cope with the situation. This approach emphasizes the importance of perception as an intervening variable in determining the significance of an event on a person's life.

The transactional definition of stress encompasses the two previous definitions but goes beyond both in taking into account the skills and abilities of the person involved in the transaction to mediate successfully the effects of a potential stressor. For example, Jim and Bob are to present book reports to their sixth grade class. Jim perceives the event as threatening because of past experiences in giving oral reports whereas Bob is looking forward to his presentation. Jim and Bob perceive the stressor (oral report) differently. Jim is anxiety ridden because he fears failure while Bob is hopeful that, with some preparation, he will do fine.

The transactional approach to stress emphasizes a three-phase process of threat, appraisal, and coping. First, Bill is confronted with a threat (e.g., an approaching dog); second, he appraises the situation (e.g., what is the likelihood that the dog will attack); and third, after interpreting the signs of perceived threat, he evaluates his personal coping strategies for responding to the stressful situation. Stress will increase if Bill believes that he is powerless in the face of this perceived threat; however, the presence of the dog may only present minimal anxiety if Bill believes that he has a workable plan (e.g., positive self-talk, deep breathing, and allowing the dog to approach him while he remains calm).

SIGNS OF CHILDHOOD STRESS

Signs of stress overload in children are often readily apparent under the watchful eyes of parents, teachers, and the school nurse. Adults working with children are apt to notice some of the following signs or symptoms indicative of possible stress effects (Elkind, 1981; Forbes, 1979; Sears & Milburn, 1990):

- regressing to infantile behaviors (e.g., bed wetting, thumb sucking, nail biting, crying, etc.);
- withdrawal from adults and peers, appearance of depression, quiet and noncommunicative behavior;
- loss of energy and motivation;
- inability to concentrate in school;
- marked behavioral changes, attention getting behaviors;
- irritable and unsettled for no apparent reasons;
- physical complaints (e.g., headache, stomachache, muscular pain, increased heart rate);
- difficulty relating with peers (aggressive);
- procrastination;
- boredom, loss of control feelings, hopelessness;
- anxiety about school;
- conflicts with teachers;
- excessive worrying about life events; and
- school attendance (prolonged absences).

Although the above list of stress signs is not all inclusive, it does provide an overview of the physical and psychological indicators of the possible presence of stress in children's lives; however, caution always must prevail when such signs are observed. Although they may be indicators of stress, causality cannot be implied. "That is, we can conclude that a number of childhood and adolescent conditions occur concurrently with stress although we cannot definitely state that these conditions are effects of or causes of stress, or that stress is a cause of or effect of the condition" (Forman, 1993, p. 10). Observing possible signs of childhood stress, however, should not be taken lightly. These observations should put teachers, parents, and all caring adults on alert encouraging them to focus their attention on probable causes for these changes.

Childhood Stressors

Stressors are life experiences, situations, or events that cause stress reactions. Many of the common stressors of children are school related. Elkind (1981) suggested that today's schools are very much achievement- and product-oriented emphasizing hurry and motivating children to grow up too fast. And while Elkind's statement may be considered historical by virtue of the calendar, it is very timely with regard to current school practices and pressures related to success and failure.

Erikson (1963), in response to his developmental stages, identified industry versus inferiority as being that period of time during a child's early school years (ages 6 to 11) when they learn the necessary skills that will enable them to become productive citizens. According to Erikson, the danger in this stage of development is that children who fail to receive encouragement, praise, and nurturance will not master the necessary skills and tools and are likely to develop a sense of inadequacy and inferiority.

Children, in their struggle to cope with the demands and expectations of others while at the same time trying to meet their own needs (often with limited abilities), are confronted constantly with stressors. Whereas the nature of these stressors will vary from child to child, there are some very common universal stressors that impact the lives of many children. Some examples of those stressors are the following (Forman, 1993; Henderson, Kelby, & Engebretson, 1992; Omizo, Omizo, & Suzuki, 1988; Sears & Milburn, 1990).

School Stressors

- anxiety about going to school
- changing schools
- conflict with peers
- bullies
- failing grades
- peer pressure
- not completing school work assignments
- fear of failure regarding exams
- parental pressures to achieve
- learning disabilities

Life Stressors

- child abuse, neglect, and family violence
- fear of school, community, and world violence
- childhood illness
- stress from parental depression or mental illness
- divorce of parents
- death of a parent, family member, or pet
- poverty
- discrimination
- catastrophic event (e.g., fire, flood, bombing)
- childhood fears (e.g., darkness, abandonment, teasing)
- drug and alcohol abuse in the home

The causes of stress (potential stressors) are related to experiencing change. How children perceive change (helpful vs. hurtful) and their ability to cope with it will have a profound effect on the physical and psychological duration and intensity of the stress they will experience. Researchers also appear to agree that life changes have a cumulative effect; that is, the more life changes that children experience in a given period of time will compound the effects of those stressful events, making coping more difficult than if the events had been spaced out over time.

The school environment in particular is a major source of stress for many children. The school places two major sets of demands on children. In the academic arena, children are pressured to master academic subject matter and to perform accordingly. They are likewise under stress to develop responsible interpersonal relationships with peers and teachers and to participate in class activities in a socially responsible manner. Environments that have high performance expectations and are controlled for excellence are fraught with stressors and children who are stressed. Is it any wonder then that children who experience undue stress outside of school (life stresses) find coping in school just another stress-producing environment that leaves them feeling powerless and hopeless? What appears to be gloom and doom for many children, however, can have a much happier ending, which this chapter will address in subsequent pages.

Assessing Childhood Stress

Although many more researchers are now studying stress in children than ever before, there is a scarcity of effective psychometric instruments designed to assess stress in children accurately (Matheny, Aycock, & McCarthy, 1993). In addition, most research on the measurement and identification of stress in children is based upon adult perception (Dickey & Henderson, 1989). Many of the current instruments designed to assess childhood stress in use today are adult modified instruments with new indices or scales specifically designed for children. Techniques for assessing childhood stress can be grouped in terms of five specific methods. They are as follows (Romer, 1993):

- detailed observation of a child's behavior,
- direct physiological assessment,
- rating of child stress by adults,
- child self-reports, and
- adult interview of a child.

Behavioral Observations.   Many researchers (Burts, Hart, Charlesworth, & Kirk, 1990; Feldbaum, Chrislenson, & O'Neal, 1990; Honig, 1986; Smith & Womack, 1987) believe that observing children's behavior can provide valuable information in identifying the presence of possible childhood stress. Through ongoing research studies, specific behaviors have been identified as valid and reliable indicators of stress in children's lives. They have been organized into observational checklists for more detailed and controlled behavioral assessments. The Classroom Child Stress Behavior Instrument (CCSBI) is one such assessment device (Burts, et al., 1990).

Behavioral observations of possible stress reactions in children require the observer to focus on such things as body language, emotional responses, and deviations from normative behavior patterns. Children who isolate themselves from group activity, avoid eye contact with adults and peers, pull away from physical contact, or flinch in response to noises may be exhibiting body language indicative of stress. Children who cry for no apparent reasons and who are either easily agitated or are prone to anger may be exhibiting emotional responses that are stress related. Outgoing children who gravitate toward shyness, changes in social interaction patterns and relationships, drop in grades, increased visits to the school health office, changes in appetite and sleep patterns, and personality changes represent shifts in common behavior patterns that also may be indicative of stress in children.

Other observable behavioral signs of stress in children are complaints of headaches; neck, shoulder, and back pain; constant rocking; constant playing with one's clothing; clinging behavior to caregivers (in young children); feeling sick; physical hostility or fighting; tremors or tics; nervous laughter; and nail biting (Burts et al., 1990). Adults who work with children need to fine tune their observational skills so that they can monitor behavior changes in children accurately. If childhood stress is present, the severity of that stress needs to be evaluated, the potential stressors identified, and a plan of action developed to facilitate stress relief.

Physiological Monitoring. Although physiological reactions within the body do correlate with stress and may indicate stress in children, such monitoring usually would be conducted by a medically trained health professional. Autonomic nervous system responses such as elevated blood pressure, elevated heart rate, increased respiration, dry mouth, muscle tension and decreased digestive track functioning are easily monitored in medical settings. The technology and training is readily available so that physiological monitoring could also be conducted in nonmedical settings, but few studies exist that currently promote this activity.

Children can be taught to engage in physiological self-monitoring activities for educational purposes in their understanding on how stress effects their bodies. Children in the upper elementary grades can learn to take their blood pressure, measure their own pulse rates, monitor the rhythmic quality of their breathing, and measure body temperature changes with thermometers and skin temperature changes with biodots (i.e., small plastic disks with adhesive backs that change color with temperature changes). By participating in stress monitoring activities, children can be taught to measure and compare physiological changes before and after stressful activities such as exercise.

Teachers, parents, and other adults in children's lives can be taught the importance of tracking stress-producing life events and changes in children's lives while watching for common indicators (behavioral and physiological) of stress. Many children will complain about physiological changes they experience. These complaints should be taken seriously and addressed accordingly.

Adult Ratings. Adult rating instruments are available for parents, teachers, and other child care providers. These instruments differ from behavioral observation checklists in that raters do not conduct direct observations of children but merely assess their perspective of child stress by checking life events that children have experienced over a specified period of time.

Coddington's (1972) Life Events Record provides "some of the best known measures of stress in school-age children" (Romer, 1993, p. 13). This instrument consists of four different scales covering four age groups from preschool to senior high. Coddington's scales give varying weights to a number of particular life events (by age group) as they impact on children's lives and the amount of stress they are expected to experience by event. The life events used were both positive and negative and were weighted by teachers, pediatricians, and mental health workers who were asked to rate each life event according to the amount of social adjustment that would be required in response to each event. From this information, readjustment ratings were computed and life change units assigned. "From the life changes of a sample of normal children, Coddington has obtained data that can be used to determine whether a child is experiencing events more stressful than is typical for his or her normal peers" (Forman, 1993, p. 5).

The use of adult rating scales can provide a gross measure of potential levels of child stress; however, they should be used with caution and only in conjunction with other assessment measures that collectively can give a more accurate assessment.

Self-reports.   Self-report is yet another method for assessing child stress. Such instruments commonly ask children to register their feelings about and to evaluate recent events in their lives. The collected data then is analyzed by adults using standardized inventory profiles developed by the researcher(s).

Self-report instruments work best when children understand the nature of stress, stressors, and stress reactions. With these understandings, children can play a significant role in identifying their own stressors and can assist in evaluating the severity of their reactions to stressful events.

Interviews.   As researchers have gained more confidence in child interviewing, they have gradually turned their attention to this important stress assessment process. Interviewing, like self-report, works best when children are knowledgeable about stress. This increases their ability to provide accurate information about what they consider to be stressful in their lives and how they cope with stress (Pryor-Brown, Cowen, Hightower, & Lotyczewski, 1986).

As with any assessment measure, professional ethical standards must prevail in their use. The same cautions that apply to general use of assessment data apply here as well. Users of stress assessment methods should neither rely on one method of assessment nor assume that behavioral and physiological changes are always stress related. Children should be assessed medically in response to noted changes before embarking on nonmedical stress management strategies.

STRESS MANAGEMENT

Stress is inescapable. It is a central condition of life itself. Stress either can be an energizer and a motivating force that adds excitement to life and living or it can become a life crippling destroyer. Whether children and adults benefit from stress or become controlled by it is a matter of their ability to manage life strains successfully and problematic events in ways that harness the harmful impact of stress.

Compas (1986) has noted in his studies the individual differences in children and adolescents that exist in their ability to cope with stressful life events. Some children seem to be more significantly impacted by stress related disorders than others. This difference may be, in part, explained by a range of varying coping capabilities that buffer the relationship between stressors and disorders (Forman, 1993).

Lazarus and Folkman (1984) have identified six major areas from which people draw in enhancing their coping capabilities.

Health and energy: People need energy to cope. Those individuals who are ill or tired do not have the energy reserves on which to draw in times of stress.

Positive beliefs: People who believe in themselves and their capabilities to manage their lives do better in coping with stress than do their more pessimistic counterparts.

Problem-solving skills: People who have problem-solving skills and use them effectively create systematic, reality-based plans that they can use to counteract stressful living conditions. Those people lacking in problem-solving skills become bystanders in life who rely on wishful thinking in managing stress.

Social skills: People who have the ability to communicate with others, and are adept at doing so, are socially accepted and socially effective in their relationships with others. They are able to use their social skills in ways that enhance connections with others thereby reducing the likelihood of interpersonal stress.

Social support: People who are able to derive support from others through effective networking capabilities are able to manage stressful life situations effectively. Those people lacking in networking capabilities tend to isolate themselves from others and have fewer contacts on whom to rely for support in times of stress.

Material resources: People who have access to money, goods, and services are able to utilize their resources in ways that enhance their control over life events. People lacking in such resources have fewer options and less freedom and often feel powerless in those situations where access to resources could bring some relief.

Children use the same social, psychological, physical and material resources in coping with stress. The major differences between adults and children are that children have fewer and less developed resources on which to
rely, lack in physical and psychological maturity, and do not exercise the same
level of control over their environment as do adults. Nonetheless, children can
be taught a variety of coping skills to mediate the effects of potential stressors
that impact on their mental and physical health and their social adjustment. They
can learn to deal with stress in a constructive manner by learning coping skills
that will help them alter physiological responses to stress, change their dysfunctional thinking, and make lifestyle adjustments that will help them to develop
healthy lifestyles.

The goal of teaching stress management practices to children is to provide
them with the personal and social coping resources that will enable them to live
healthy, energizing lives in managing the inevitable stressors that will challenge
their essence. Children's needs and the strengths they must develop in learning
to be successful stress managers follow.

CHILDREN'S NEEDS

Children have three basic needs that must be addressed if they are to manage stress in their lives successfully. They have a need for knowledge, self-
management strategies, and lifestyle practices that will enable them to take a
proactive stand in their own wellness promotion.

Knowledge

Children have a need to understand the nature of stress and that it is a
normal part of their daily lives. They need to understand both the positive and
negative implications of stress. They likewise need to understand the signs and
symptoms of stress and how stress effects them personally. Armed with this
knowledge, children have a need to understand the sources of stress and be
able to identify the stressors that elicit stress responses in them.

As children become more knowledgeable about stress, they will be able
to use that knowledge to plan courses of action that will reduce their susceptibility and increase their tolerance to stress. They will also learn how they
can promote their own wellness through developing a healthy mind, body, and
spirit.

Self-management Strategies

If children are to learn how to manage stress effectively, knowledge helps, but it does not go far enough. They have a need for coping strategies to counteract the physiological, cognitive, and behavioral effects of stress.

Physiological Effects and Strategies. Children can expect to experience bodily discomforts brought on by stress. In particular, an increased heart rate, stomach distress, muscular pain, and sleep-related problems represent some of the physiological effects they may experience.

Children have a need to feel connected to their own bodies in positive ways. This is difficult to accomplish if they feel uncomfortable in their own skin. Unfortunately, because the drive to seek bodily comfort is so strong, children may be tempted to use whatever works in neutralizing the stress response. Harmful coping strategies that children may model from parents, peers, and advertising are the self-prescribed use of "over the counter" medications, illicit drugs, and alcohol; the use of tobacco products; and the physical withdrawal from life itself in order to avoid stress producing situations.

Stress, left unchecked for long periods of time, can escalate into stress related disorders, such as ulcers, hypertension, headache pain, some forms of arthritis, and intestinal track disorders. A word of caution is in order here in that the relationship between health and stress is purely correlational with many medical authorities in disagreement as to the extent to which stress actually influences physical disorders. Children and adults also should be cautious in attributing physical complaints, such as the ones mentioned, to stress. Before any such conclusion can be drawn, a thorough physical evaluation conducted by a skilled health professional is a must.

Before stress is allowed to cause extreme physical discomfort, however, children have a need to manage physiological responses to stress in safe and healthy ways. Children can be taught diaphragmatic breathing, muscle relaxation training, imagery and visualization exercises, biofeedback training, and more specialized interventions (e.g., self-hypnosis, meditation, and autogenic training) when necessary (Romano, 1992).

Cognitive Effects and Strategies. There is a strong "mind and body connection" in relationship to health and wellness. The relationship between thoughts, feelings, and bodily responses has been well documented by researchers like Beck (1976), Ellis (1984), and Burns (1980). Children have a need to understand that their thoughts and beliefs do have a direct influence on their emotions, behavior, and body chemistry.

Maladaptive thinking can lead to emotional disturbances based on the frequency, intensity, and duration of those thoughts. Maladaptive thinking refers to thoughts and beliefs that cannot be substantiated by facts or evidence and lead to emotional disturbances and self-defeating behaviors in those who ascribe to them.

Ellis (1980) has indicated that there are three major irrational belief clusters under which all irrational beliefs can be categorized. They are as follows:

> I must do well and win approval for my performance or else I rate as a rotten person.
> Others must treat me considerately and kindly in precisely the way I want them to treat me; if they don't, society and the universe should severely blame, damn, and punish them for their inconsiderateness.
> Conditions under which I live must get arranged so that I can get practically everything I want quickly, and easily, and get virtually nothing that I don't want. (pp. 5-7)

Waters (1982) identified ten irrational beliefs that emerge in childhood and become quite problematic for those children that ascribe to them. These beliefs support the cluster theory proposed by Ellis.

> It's awful if others don't like me.
> I'm bad if I make mistakes.
> Everything should go my way; I should always get what I want.
> Things should come easy to me.
> The world should be fair and bad people must be punished.
> I shouldn't show my feelings.
> Adults should be perfect.
> There's only one right answer.
> I must win.
> I shouldn't have to wait for anyone. (p. 572)

These and other dysfunctional cognitions, if not corrected, can cause emotional and bodily stress. When such stress becomes excessive, it can create psychological disturbances that can lead to anxiety, depression, poor self-esteem, substance abuse, suicidal behavior, a loss of internal control, and poor school performance.

If children are to manage the potentially damaging side effects of dysfunctional thinking, they must be taught skills and techniques designed to interrupt and correct faulty thinking. Children have a need to learn coping skill interventions such as rational thinking, thought stopping, and self-instruction techniques.

These techniques, when used successfully, help children understand the connection between dysfunctional thinking and their stress levels. They likewise learn and appreciate the value of thought correction techniques and developing more self-enhancing thought patterns in managing their stress.

Behavioral Effects and Strategies. Children's behaviors can be a source of personal stress especially if those behaviors do not meet their needs in satisfying ways. When children engage in specific behaviors, they expect to reap personal benefits from their actions; however, this is not always the case. For example, children wanting the attention of their peers may engage in unacceptable attention-getting behaviors during math class. These behaviors then are met with punitive consequences administered by the teacher causing stress reactions in both the teacher and the acting-out children.

Other examples of child behaviors that can create physiological and psychological stress reactions in children are aggressive behaviors, shyness, poor time management, lack of assertiveness, lack of social skills, impulsive behaviors, and classroom disruptive behaviors. All of these behaviors can and often do generate stress-enhancing consequences for the children involved. Few children actively seek to create stress-filled lives, but their unacceptable and often unproductive behaviors do just that.

Children have a need to develop "constructive responses to potential stressors" (Forman, 1993, p. 129). They can learn to develop constructive coping behaviors through behavioral self-control training. This process requires children to "assess and evaluate their own behaviors, set goals, arrange their attainment, and reward themselves when they achieve goals" (Forman, p. 129).

Behavioral self-control training works best with children when they are assisted by teachers, counselors, and related behavioral specialists in this process. Through behavioral self-control training, children can decide if those behaviors in question are helping or hurting them to get what they want. Together, adult and child search for more responsible and productive behavioral substitutes. Using this process, shy children can be taught to be more assertive, aggressive children can be taught how to avoid and resolve conflict peacefully, impulsive children can be taught responsible decision-making strategies, and children lacking in effective social skills can be taught how to improve their social interactions with others.

Lifestyle Enhancement

While children have a need to responsibly manage the physiological, cognitive, and behavioral stressors in their lives, they have an equally compelling need to develop and maintain a healthy lifestyle. Children have a need to examine how they typically cope with common stressors in their lives and whether or not those methods are health enhancing or detracting. After all, the primary purpose of promoting lifestyle enhancement behaviors is to instill in young people a wellness mind-set. A mind-set that advocates physical, emotional, cognitive and spiritual fitness will increase children's resistance to the effects of stress and help them manage stress-producing situations effectively.

STRENGTHS TO BE LEARNED

If children are to cope successfully with stress, they must be able to continually monitor and change their behaviors and cognition in response to external and internal conditions that they perceive as being stressful (Lazarus & Folkman, 1984). In order to prepare them for such a challenge, we advocate the development of the following five psychoeducational strength categories:

- self-exploration and understanding strengths,
- physiological stress inhibitor strengths,
- cognitive stress inhibitor strengths,
- behavioral stress inhibitor strengths, and
- lifestyle enhancement strengths.

Self-exploration and Understanding

Before children can participate fully in managing life stressors, they must develop a knowledge base about stress and how that information relates to them. More specifically, children must be able to

- define the meaning of stress;
- identify observable signs of stress in others and in themselves (e.g., weight loss or gain, change in eating habits, acting out, wringing hands, etc.);
- identify symptoms (i.e., unpleasant feelings or sensations that correspond with physiological changes) and signs of stress in self and others (e.g, pains, tension, agitation, anxiety, breathing difficulty);
- identify internal and external stressors in themselves and others;
- understand what stressors are and what role they play in causing stress signs and symptoms;
- understand the nature of positive stress and negative stress; and
- understand the relationship between stress and illness and stress management and wellness.

Aronson and Mascia (1981) made effective use of a pickup truck analogy in helping people better understand how they respond to stress under varying structural and environmental conditions.

> A pickup truck is designed to perform certain functions. It has built-in load-carrying limits, speed capabilities, engine RPM limits, and terrain limits. It must be maintained properly and must get proper fuel. If the design limits are exceeded without appropriate accommodating design changes, the vehicle will not function properly and may be damaged. A one-ton pickup truck can carry one and one-half tons for a short distance at a slow speed over level ground, probably without damage. If the driver speeds on rough terrain with a heavy load, however, damage will probably result. If the truck has heavy-duty suspension installed, the load capacity may be doubled from one to two tons without damage on all reasonable road conditions and at all but excessive speeds. (p. 4)

Children in many ways are similar to pickup trucks. The load represents a child's accumulation of stressors, the design of the truck represents the child's stress tolerance, and the truck's suspension is equivalent to the sum of the child's internal and external support systems. Unlike the truck, children must determine their own stress tolerance capacity. Their stress tolerance capacity will change with age, the passage of time, and changing attitudes regarding life and living. Children, unlike trucks, also will have to develop their own support system (internal and external).

The ability to self-explore and understand the nature of stress is a strength that will help children determine the nature of their stress, how much they can tolerate, ways in which they can increase their stress tolerance, how they can reduce and avoid stress when possible, and what they can do to take care of themselves so that they can live a healthy and satisfying life.

Physiological Stress Inhibitor Strengths

Children can be taught the physiology of stress in support group settings or in general science classes. They can learn to identify their own physiological responses to stress using stethoscopes to monitor their heart rates, thermometer and stress cards to measure body and skin temperature changes, and sphygmomanometers to detect changes in blood pressure before and after stress related activities (exercise and timed events). Children also can monitor changes in their pulse rates, muscle tension, and breathing patterns as well.

Experimental activities designed to increase stress provide children with an opportunity to utilize simple biofeedback monitoring methods to note the relationship between mind and body and to observe the correlation between stress and physiological responses. Once children recognize these relationships, they can become acquainted with stress related disorders that sometimes occur over prolonged periods of unchecked stress.

Following a discussion about the physiology of stress, children can be taught a variety of specific strengths designed to inhibit the physiological effects of stress. Children can learn how to control such effects through diaphragmatic breathing, muscle relaxation training, imagery and visualization exercises, and biofeedback training.

Diaphragmatic Breathing. Children can be taught to breathe slowly and rhythmically from the stomach while lying on their backs on a carpeted floor as the trainer provides the cadence. Having the children take rapid, choppy, shallow breaths is a way of simulating stress related breathing. Panting like a dog is stressful. Children easily can compare and contrast the two ways of breathing and will recognize the value of monitoring and practicing diaphragmatic breathing during times of stress.

Muscle Relaxation Training. Children can learn muscle tension and relaxation exercises that will help them combat muscle tension during times of stress. Relaxation audiotapes for children are available for purchase as are written scripts that can be found in child counseling books. Muscle relaxation exercises usually last about 20 to 30 minutes. Before and after the training, facilitators should emphasize the importance of muscle relaxation exercises in inhibiting the stress response.

Imagery and Visualization Exercises. Children enjoy imagery and visualization exercises. They participate naturally in these exercises during play and have vivid imaginations that support this process. The purpose of these exercises is to teach children how they can use imagery and visualization to conjure up relaxing, stress-relieving images. Such exercises help them refocus and shift their attention to more calming and pleasant scenes. Children can be taught how to create their own visual safe place, practice imagery and visualization through a prepared script, or use fantasy (pretend) visualizations that melt away reality and enhance creativity.

Imagery and visualization exercises should be practiced in a quiet place with few distractions. Children are asked to close their eyes, breathe rhythmically, and listen to soft background music as they visualize what they hear in the prepared script as it is read to them. Since imagery and visualization are designed to reduce the physiological effects of stress, facilitators must use care in selecting scripts that do not create stress for some children. Children who fear the water probably would not fare well with ocean scenes.

As with relaxation, children need to understand the purpose of imagery and visualization and how they can practice such exercises anywhere and at any time when they experience physiological responses to stress.

Biofeedback Training. Although most school districts and community agencies are unlikely to have access to sophisticated biofeedback instruments, nearly everyone can secure thermometers, body weight scales, mirrors, pulse sensors, blood pressure cuffs, and stethoscopes. These instruments, and ones like them, are designed to measure internal and external body activity. The purpose of biofeedback training is to sensitize children to physiological and bodily changes that occur during stress.

Children can be taught to alter physiological responses to stress by using muscle relaxation, rhythmic breathing, and imagery. They can monitor physiological changes within themselves using available biofeedback devices noting their success in using physiological stress inhibitor strengths like the ones mentioned.

Cognitive Stress Inhibitor Strengths

Unfortunately, most children experiencing problems in living have not been taught the importance that their thoughts play in contributing to their disturbances. Children's thoughts and beliefs represent powerful forces in their lives. They determine practically everything that happens to them. In many ways, children's beliefs act like strong magnets, attracting them to life events and circumstances that harmonize with their most dominant thoughts.

Positive rational thoughts fuel the "I can" consciousness and the "I will" state of mind so necessary to success. Positive rational thoughts give children the internal power to think their way through the most challenging problems or life situations. Children who cultivate positive rational thoughts about themselves, their environment, and their future expect to win in life and generally do.

Rational thoughts, when evaluated, seem to possess some rather specific characteristics (Worzbyt, 1994). Consider the following statements:

Rational thoughts are factual in nature and are based on evidence.
Rational thoughts are reasonable, logical, and seem to be true.

Rational thoughts help children attain their wants.
Rational thoughts yield emotions that are manageable and productive.

Children who learn to think rationally are better able to manage their emotions, are less likely to suffer from excessive stress, and possess more energy and higher levels of self-confidence than do those children who are influenced by maladaptive thinking that leads to emotional disturbances and self-defeating behaviors.

Children must be taught how irrational thoughts contribute to stressful emotions. When children learn to recognize irrational thoughts as unreasonable demands that they place on themselves, they can learn to challenge these thoughts and improve their emotional well-being. Some basic thought enhancing strengths that children can be taught are cognitive restructuring, self-instruction training, problem solving, and thought stopping.

Cognitive Restructuring.   Children are taught to write down their upsetting thoughts in response to a particular life event. Then they are taught how to analyze their upsetting thoughts in response to that life event. Thoughts that cannot be substantiated by evidence are not reality based and must be challenged. With training and practice, children can learn how to challenge their irrational thoughts and replace them with more reality-oriented thoughts that ultimately will produce more reasonable, responsible, and manageable emotional responses.

For example, a child who believes that anything less than perfect is unacceptable (i.e., "all or nothing" thinking), is practicing irrational thinking. Where is the evidence that makes this a true statement? Statements that cannot be validated with evidence need to be changed to reflect the truth (evidence). Teaching children how to use basic cognitive restructuring techniques will assist them in achieving a state of emotional wellness.

Self-instruction Training.   Children often talk out loud to themselves correcting their behavior as they guide themselves through daily tasks. Self-instruction training teaches children how to guide and monitor their progress in difficult situations. When children experience signs of stress, for example, those signs can serve as cues in initiating coping statements designed to guide behavior and reduce stress. With practice children can be taught to anticipate stress and use self-instruction as a form of stress inoculation. Learning to rehearse and use coping statements as counters to self-defeating patterns of behavior can help children reduce and in some cases avoid counterproductive stress.

For example, Billy is afraid of dogs. When he sees a dog, he generally becomes very anxious. However, using self-instruction training, Billy has learned to prepare himself when in the presence of a dog. He tells himself, "Take it easy. You will be okay. Remain calm. Take a deep breath and wait for the dog to leave." Billy concentrates on what he wants to do and positively reinforces himself with each passing success. Although Billy is still afraid of dogs, he has learned not to panic and has learned to reduce his stress when around dogs. Children also can be taught to use positive visual imagery and deep rhythmic breathing to support self-instruction training.

Problem Solving. Children can learn to manage stress more effectively when they realize that they have multiple options to consider when solving a stress related dilemma. We recommend using the 3 R's method of problem solving in this book. Children are first taught to STOP and define their challenge. Then they THINK about their options. During this stage, they generate many ideas and filter each idea through the Right, Reality, and Responsibility filters in search of safe choices. Finally, the children GO with 3 R's choices that will help them solve their problems.

Children can use the 3 R's in addressing peer relationship problems, solving conflicts, reducing anger, and getting assignments done on time. Most dilemmas that children will face can be responded to more effectively through problem solving than through passive, nonresponsive, or dependent behaviors.

Thought Stopping. Thought stopping is used to interrupt an ongoing sequence of aversive thoughts. Disturbing thoughts, if left unchecked, can get out of control and take on a life of their own. Children can become possessed by such thoughts and feel powerless to escape from them. When this happens, such thoughts can produce unpleasant and potentially harmful stress reactions. Children can be taught verbal, visual, and aversive techniques to stop unwanted, counterproductive thoughts.

For example, Susan thinks about failing exams at school. Susan is always well prepared academically and seldom fails exams, yet she has invading thoughts of failure that cause her much anxiety before exams. Susan has learned to yell "STOP" to herself when those thoughts occur. She also wears a rubber band on her wrist. When a negative thought starts, she also snaps herself with the rubber band (aversive response). Susan also has taught herself visualization. When she yells "STOP" and snaps her wrist with the rubber band, she pictures herself taking her exam on the beach listening to and watching the waves slap the shore. The positive mental pictures replace the negative, controlling thoughts. Susan finds that thought stopping really works well for her. She feels less stress because she is in control.

Behavior Stress Inhibitor Strengths

Children need to develop a broad-based, behavioral repertoire on which they can rely when responding to potential stressors. Behavioral self-management training teaches children how to use behavioral modification techniques based on operant and respondent conditioning principles in addressing behavioral and emotional problems. They can be taught to recognize their own stress producing behaviors and how to modify or change them while achieving their personal goals.

Children, in learning how to develop behavioral strengths, are taught to assess and evaluate their own behaviors as to whether or not they are working for them and the degree of emotional and physiological stress they are incurring with their use. If their behaviors are creating excessive stress, they can learn to set new goals, change their behaviors, and rearrange their environment in a manner that will help them achieve their goals while successfully managing their stress levels.

There are a number of behaviors in which children might engage that have the potential for causing high levels of stress. For example, children lacking in time management skills will have difficulty in completing academic assignments and related tasks by their due dates. Children lacking in effective interpersonal (social) skills will have difficulty in making and keeping friends. Children who find it difficult to stay focused during academic instruction will not be able to perform required tasks as taught. Many children have learned unacceptable behaviors at home and from their peers that will get them into difficulty with adults and their age-mates. Examples of some of these behaviors are hitting other children, taking things that do not belong to them, tattling, swearing, teasing, lying, disobedience, cheating, carelessness in work, shyness and withdrawal, and avoidance behaviors. Of course this is only a partial list, but it does illustrate all too well that children do learn counterproductive behaviors that they think will help them attain their wants. What they discover, however, is that such is not the case. They often fall short of their goals and experience unwanted stress in the process.

Most children do not set out to fall short of their goals or to create stress in their lives, but it does happen. Nevertheless, children can be taught a variety of behaviors that will help them succeed personally, socially, academically, and physically. They likewise can be taught how to change counterproductive behaviors using the same behavior modification principles.

Personal behaviors: Children who develop positive manners, effective communication skills, and acceptable personality characteristics (e.g., honesty, courage, kindness, humor, responsibility, respect) will possess and be able to execute behaviors that will help them attain their goals with manageable stress.

Social behaviors: Children who possess and use appropriate social behaviors such as sharing, taking turns, helping others, giving compliments, resolving conflicts peacefully, and managing anger successfully will be able to achieve a variety of social outcomes that will benefit themselves and others while managing acceptable stress levels.

Academic behaviors: Children who learn to take notes, follow directions, set goals, and develop effective study skills will possess behaviors that will benefit them academically while maintaining acceptable stress levels.

Physical behaviors: Children who receive plenty of rest, eat healthy foods, exercise regularly, and take needed fun breaks possess and employ healthy physical behaviors that are also effective stress inhibitors.

While we have provided only a sample of behaviors with each heading (personal, social, academic, and physical), the illustrations are significant reminders that children can benefit from learning a variety of behavioral strengths that will help them achieve their goals and manage their stress. Behavioral strategies, when used in combination with the other techniques cited in this chapter, provide a comprehensive approach to helping children successfully confront stressors through their life span.

Lifestyle Enhancement

While stress is a fact of life, the manner in which children learn to deal with it is a choice. Children can learn to be reactive beings or proactive. They can choose to live stress producing lifestyles and develop a defensive posture to stress management, or they can assume a proactive stance by learning how to live healthy lives.

A wellness lifestyle approach reinforces the point that health is more than the absence of pain or illness. Rather wellness may be defined as "the process and state of a quest for maximum human functioning that involves the mind, body, and spirit" (Archer, Probert, & Gage, 1987, p. 311). The goal of wellness from a developmental perspective is to increase personal growth and keep people moving in a positive self-enhancing direction. The belief is that healthy people tend to make healthy choices and decisions that enhance their life circumstances (Myers, 1992). They enhance their potential for living more fully and vigorously.

Children who strive to live a wellness lifestyle will learn the values of becoming the best that they can be regardless of their own personal limitations. Developing a health oriented lifestyle does not require children to be in perfect health to participate. What it does require is teaching children how to self-evaluate, make necessary life adjustments, and establish goals that will enhance their state of wellness (Worzbyt & O'Rourke, 1989).

"Wellness is a full integration of physical, mental, emotional, social, and spiritual well being—a complex interaction of the factors that lead to a quality life" (Hafen, Thygerson, & Frandsen, 1988, p. 2). Ardell (1982) identified five specific elements that, if followed, can take children to a proactive level in the management of life stressors. Those five areas are self-responsibility, nutritional fitness, physical fitness, stress awareness and management, and environmental sensitivity.

Self-responsibility: Children must learn the importance of their role in acquiring knowledge, skills, and self-confidence in participating in self-enhancement practices in relationship to the four remaining areas.

Nutritional fitness: Children need to develop sound eating habits, reduce their fat and sugar intake, understand the relationship between food intake and wellness, and recognize that food consumption for the purpose of managing stress is an unhealthy lifestyle behavior.

Physical fitness: Children need to understand the relationship between being physically fit and wellness. They likewise need to understand that physical fitness, like nutritional awareness, is a lifestyle practice that will enhance their total well being in addition to helping them manage stress in their lives. Physical activities that promote cardiovascular fitness, flexibility, strength, and endurance need to be encouraged.

Stress awareness and management: Healthy individuals are able to manage most life stressors successfully. They practice stress management behaviors on a daily basis rather than react to stress when it reaches unhealthy levels. They understand the value of stress and know how to use it positively as an energizer.

Environmental sensitivity: Children need to recognize and practice those behaviors that will reduce, if not eliminate, some environmental stressors while looking for ways to improve the quality of their environment through lifestyle practices that will enhance the health status of all people.

Self-responsibility, nutritional fitness, physical fitness, stress management, and environmental sensitivity represent lifestyle elements that can be addressed in child support groups, in the home, and throughout the entire school curriculum. A lifestyle management emphasis will go a long way toward promoting a lifestyle mind-set that will result in responsible behavioral changes. The quality of children's lives will be enhanced and they will have an opportunity to shape a brighter future for themselves and those with whom they share the planet.

MESSAGE TO FACILITATORS

As we have emphasized throughout this chapter, stress is a part of daily life. Children will encounter a variety of stressful situations at home, in school, and in their communities. All of the support group topics presented in this book represent stressful life experiences that children are facing. Each support group is designed to help children understand and cope more successfully and responsibly with the topic in question. In many ways, these support groups are stress management groups in that they help children achieve their goals while learning to control stress rather than having it control them.

What then is the purpose of a separate support group on stress management? In many ways this question has been answered for us. Most children do not understand the nature of stress and demonstrate their inability to handle potentially stressful situations responsibly (Forman, 1993). When this happens and children find themselves unable to cope with the stress, the resultant effects can be emotional, behavioral, and/or physical health problems. Seldom do we deliberately teach children purposeful stress reduction and coping strategies designed to bring about responsible and positive outcomes to potentially stressful situations. The literature supports this contention based on the paucity of support groups that exist to help children respond to stressors and stressful situations.

Therefore, the purpose of the stress management support group is not to duplicate services addressed in the other support groups but to provide an educational perspective on stress and how to manage it.

Group Selection

Because all children experience stress and few understand how to cope with it in a responsible and effective manner, all children are potential candidates for this support group. This having been said, you will want to select children for this group who are functioning rather effectively in their environment. Your participants should reflect children who are experiencing minor effects from stress so that they can benefit from an educational group experience with other children who are experiencing a diversity of stressors and mild stress reactions. In this way, children can learn about the nature of stress from each other and share a variety of coping strategies as well as learning new ways to cope.

Children who are experiencing high levels of stress in response to very specific life situations addressed by other support groups discussed in this book should join these groups first. Once they are able to sufficiently manage their needs as a result of having participated in a specific group reflecting their unique needs, an educational support group on stress management could be very beneficial.

Before any children are selected as participants in a stress management support group, be sure to clear their participation with their caregivers. (Also distribute Figure 13.1 to caregivers.) Children who are referred to you for possible inclusion in a stress management group because of stress related signs and symptoms should be cleared medically through contact with caregivers before any decisions are made regarding their placement (e.g., support groups or medical referral).

Group Process

As we have indicated, the stress management support group that follows is educationally focused. The group is designed to help children learn about stress, how it effects their lives, and how they can deal with stress in a healthy and constructive way.

Your goal will be to help children develop a general belief in themselves that they can have control over how they manage their lives in relationship to stress. Children who have confidence in themselves and the necessary stress management strategies to self-manage are more effective in coping with potentially stressful situations that those children who feel powerless to control their own destiny (Krause, 1987).

The children in your support group will benefit from their experience by your helping them

- understand the nature of stress (its benefits and dangers);
- understand that stress is a normal part of their daily lives and that all people experience the effects of it;

- understand the relationship between stress and wellness and stress and illness;
- understand that they can learn responsible and effective ways to cope successfully with stress;
- identify the signs and symptoms of stress in their lives;
- identify the stressors in their lives;
- learn and practice a variety of stress management coping strategies that will lessen the effects of stress; and
- develop and practice healthy lifestyle changes that will increase their tolerance to stress.

As children participate in your support group, they will have an opportunity to share the stressors in their lives and the coping strategies they have used. Help children understand that not all stress coping strategies are helpful. Many strategies that young people use can be harmful to their own health and can effect the well being of others as well. You can help children explore some of these counterproductive behaviors and why people use them. Consuming alcohol, smoking cigarettes, and using smokeless tobacco, over-the-counter medications, and illicit drugs represent harmful methods by which some people attempt to manage stress in their lives.

We encourage you to use the 3 R's Decision Making model (chapter 2) to help children discriminate between helpful and hurtful stress management coping strategies. Work with the children in your group to develop a variety of helpful and safe stress coping strategies. Be sure to reinforce the positive use of these strategies when children indicate their use.

When children share non 3 R's coping strategies, be sure to address the danger in using them, but do so in nonpunitive ways. For example, you might say "Some people do use this method or practice to reduce stress in their lives; however, we know that this practice could be harmful to people who use it. There are safer methods that can help you manage stress. Let's look at some (those ideas)." Using this approach, you are not criticizing the child or the person; rather, you are focusing on the method and indicating that there are other options with fewer potentially harmful side effects.

Before you conclude your stress management group sessions, you should emphasize how living a healthy lifestyle can increase their tolerance to stress. Explore a variety of wellness oriented practices that they can learn in relationship to nutrition, exercise, getting enough rest, and other self-care practices that can strengthen their resistance to stress.

We also have provided you with much information on stress and stress reduction practices in this chapter. Feel free to explore some of these ideas with your children if time permits.

Have fun working with your stress management group. Remember that your goal is to help children understand stress and ways that they can better manage it in their lives. Do not get too technical unless they are ready for it. Help them see the value of fun, humor, music, deep breathing, counting to 10, sharing feelings, seeking social support from others, and viewing life events from a different perspective as valuable 3 R's methods for managing stress.

Resources

Share Figure 13.1 with parents/guardians of group members so that caregivers will have suggestions for helping with Stress Management at home. In Figure 13.2 are provided lists of resources to be used with and by children in the Stress Management Support Group. The resource materials are grouped according to age of child.

STRESS MANAGEMENT GUIDE
Tips for Caregivers

Your child soon will be participating in a Stress Management Support Group. The goal of this support group is to help children understand the nature of stress, learn how stress affects their lives, and develop healthy ways to manage life stressing situations and experiences. We are happy to share with you some tips that you can use in helping your child cope effectively with stress. We have found that children who believe they can exercise some personal control over their own lives, experience fewer harmful effects from stress, and are more optimistic about their future than children who perceive themselves to be powerless victims of their environment. The following suggestions will help your child handle stress.

1. Learn to recognize common signs of stress in your child.

headaches	physical pain (neck, back, shoulder, stomach)
eating problems	
excessive crying	stomach upset
dry throat or mouth	shortness of breath
depression	general irritability
sleep problems	anger

2. Learn to recognize events or situations that cause stress in your child's life (e.g., schoolwork-related stressors; peer relationship stressors; relationships with teachers and adults; family events; personal injury; noise levels; loss of time; loss of comfort; death of a family member, pet, or friend; and discipline by adults). Children who experience fear and uncertainty concerning their own ability to achieve their wants will experience stress.

3. Help your child learn a few strategies in coping with stress.

   Talk: Encourage your child to talk about his or her fears and uncertainties.

   Help: Encourage your child to ask for help when feeling stressed.

Figure 13.1. Tips for Caregivers to be given to parents and/or guardians. Permission to photocopy is granted.

Break: When your child is experiencing stress overload, encourage taking ample breaks. Getting away even for a little while can help.

Breaths: When feeling tense, teach your child to take deep breaths.

Exercise: Have your child take a walk, run, or do something physical to reduce tension.

Support: Have your child seek support from family members, friends, and teachers.

Relax: Have your child make a list of fun and relaxing things to do to relieve stress (e.g., take a warm bath, read a book, listen to music, draw, or color).

Action: Help your child take direct action when feeling stressed. For example, if your child is having trouble solving a math problem, go to the teacher with questions for help.

Redefine: Sometimes children will experience stress because of the way they view a situation. Helping your child view the situation differently can help. For example, Susan may think that she has no friends because she was not invited to a classmate's birthday party. Have your child make a list of her classmates and check off those who are friends. You also could help her make a list of all the possible reasons why she might not have received an invitation that has nothing to do with friendship.

Accept: Help your child accept the fact that this event or situation can not be changed. Acceptance can reduce stress. For example, helping Steven accept that he cannot reunite his divorcing parents takes away the pressure to accomplish something that cannot be done.

You can teach your child to manage personal stress in a healthy manner; however, you will need to remember that practice and repetition are the keys to success in developing these and related coping strategies.

Stress can be beneficial when it helps you feel alive and energizes you and moves you to action; however, when stress controls your life instead of you controlling it, then the effects of stress can be harmful. Help your child understand that stress is a part of life and that it can be a friend but, when it starts to feel uncomfortable, action needs to be taken.

You also can help your child increase his or her stress tolerance by developing a healthy lifestyle that includes good nutrition, plenty of exercise, rest, fun, and social relationships.

Figure 13.1. (*Continued*) Tips for Caregivers to be given to parents and/or guardians. Permission to photocopy is granted.

RESOURCES FOR CHILDREN
Stress Management

Ages 3 to 7

Carlson, N. (1990). *Take time to relax.* New York: Puffin Books. (relaxing and relieving stress)

Hallinan, P. K. (1990). *Easy does it.* Center City, MN: Hazelden. (learning about stress)

Ages 8 to 12

Moser, A. (1988). *Don't pop your cork on Mondays: The children's antistress book.* Kansas City, MO: Landmark Editions. (causes and effect of stress)

O'Neill, C. (1993). *Relax.* King of Prussia, PA: Childswork/Childsplay. (causes and symptoms of stress)

Ages 12 and Up

Crutsinger, C. (1987). *Teenage connection.* Carollton, TX: Brainworks. (stress management through effective communication)

Elchoness, M. (1989). *Why can't anyone hear me: A guide for surviving adolescence.* Ventura, CA: Monroe Press. (stories about dealing with stress and other issues)

Fleming, M. (1993). *Take charge of your life.* Minneapolis: Johnson Institute. (coping with stress and avoiding chemicals)

Hipp, E. (1987). *Fighting invisible tigers: A stress management guide for teens.* Minneapolis, MN: Free Spirit Publishing. (dealing with stress)

Kranyik, M. (1985). *Growing up is . . . coping with adult problems when you're still a kid.* Whitehall, VA: Betterway Publications. (dealing with all types of stress)

Powell, S. J., & Brady, L. (1985). *Will the real me please stand up?* Allen, TX: Argus Communications. (self-discovery and dealing with stress)

Vedral, J. (1986). *My parents are driving me crazy.* New York: Ballantine Books. (stress management for dealing with parents)

Figure 13.2.   Resources for use with and by children in Stress Management Support Group.

SESSION I—MY STRESSORS AND HOW I COPE

BRIEF OVERVIEW OF SESSION

This session will provide an introduction to the group process, involve children in a getting acquainted exercise where they identify some personal stressors and coping mechanisms, provide group ground rules, and set the stage for the sessions on stress management.

GOALS

1. To help children understand their reasons for involvement in the group.
2. To encourage children to begin making connections with other members of the group.
3. To present group ground rules.
4. To provide an opportunity for children to begin to identify some of their own stressors and ways they cope with their stress.

MATERIALS NEEDED

1. Large sheets of newsprint for each child
2. Chart paper or chalkboard
3. Markers or crayons

PROCEDURE

1. Introduce yourself and have each of the group members introduce himself or herself by first name. Talk about the fact this is a group where we will begin to identify and develop stress management techniques that will enable us to more effectively cope with our stressors.

2. Begin to set the stage for the group by inviting a brainstorming session on group rules. (Write the rules on chart paper or on the chalkboard and post them for future reference). Examples of possible initial group ground rules may include

   a What is said in the group, stays there (confidentiality).
   b No put-downs are allowed.
   c Only one person talks at a time.
   d It is important to attend all sessions.

Note: If children do not suggest these group rules, you as facilitator should bring them up as part of the brainstorming session.

3. Give each child a piece of newsprint with instruction to make a list of his or her current stressors—things that cause them grief or worry.

4. When all children have identified their stressors, ask them to pair up with a partner and discuss their stressors. Also ask them to identify any areas that they have in common.

5. Allow time for each pair to share their list with the entire group and encourage the children to make "connections" with other group members in terms of common stressors.

6. At this point, ask the children to change focus and identify their favorite coping mechanisms.

7. Again have them pair up with a different partner and identify common "copers."

8. Complete the session by having each group member share a favorite coping mechanism with the group.

CLOSURE

To conclude the initial session, congratulate the children for the following ground rules and remind them that they have begun to identify some of their causes of stress and ways to cope with these stressors. In the next seven sessions, we will be discussing many ways they can identify and deal with stress in their life.

HOMEWORK

For a homework assignment, ask each child to choose one coping strategy learned today and try it as a new and different way to deal with stress. We will briefly discuss the results of this experiment at the beginning of next week's session.

SESSION II—MY ATTITUDES TOWARD STRESS

BRIEF OVERVIEW OF SESSION

In this session, children will have an opportunity to look critically at their own attitudes toward stress and to contrast and compare them with the attitudes of others in the group.

GOALS

1. To help children become aware of their personal attitudes and beliefs related to stress.
2. To begin to determine which attitudes need to be rethought.
3. To continue to promote group bonding and interaction.

MATERIALS NEEDED

1. Large signs with the words AGREE, DISAGREE and NEUTRAL printed on them
2. "Stress Attitude Survey" (Activity Sheet 13.1) for each group member
3. Chart paper and markers
4. 3" × 5" card for each child

PROCEDURE

1. Begin by providing a few minutes for the children to identify and discuss the coping skills they experimented with for their homework assignment. Encourage them to talk about the positives and negatives of the techniques they used and whether they would choose to use them in the future. Remind them that what is considered a good technique by one person may not work for another because we are all unique.

2. Give a copy of the Stress Attitude Survey to each group member and allow 3 to 5 minutes for completion.

3. Display the signs in the room (placed far enough apart so that differing opinions will be readily apparent).

4. Tell the children we are going to "Take A Stand" on the survey issues by physically moving to the sign that denotes their attitude on the particular

item as it is read. (Read each of the items on the survey and encourage the children to move to the appropriate sign.)

5. Encourage discussion of reasons for each position—those who AGREE should be ready to discuss what they see as the positives of the statement, those who DISAGREE should be able to identify the negatives of the statement, and those who are NEUTRAL should be able to identify the pros and cons that make a position difficult for them. As the items are presented, list them on the chart paper, or have the children list them in their "position" groups. (Because this process may be a bit time consuming, it may be necessary to choose just three or four of the issues for discussion rather than dealing with all of them.)

CLOSURE

As a way to bring a smooth closure to this session, the facilitator should provide a brief summary of the group's attitudes and remind group members that personal attitudes and beliefs play an important role in our responses to stressors in our lives.

HOMEWORK

In preparation for next session, provide a 3" × 5" card for each child to list five of the most important stressors in his or her life during the next week. These will be used as the basis for solving the "Mystery of Stress" next week.

STRESS ATTITUDE SURVEY

Please give your opinions as to whether you AGREE (A), DISAGREE (D), or are NEUTRAL (N) to the following statements.

_____ 1. My thoughts cause much of my stress.

_____ 2. My family is my greatest source of stress.

_____ 3. The best way to manage stress is to learn to relax.

_____ 4. Listening to music is a good way to manage stress.

_____ 5. Some stress is good for everyone.

_____ 6. Stress can be harmful to your physical and mental health.

_____ 7. What is stressful for me may not be for you.

_____ 8. Some people have no stress in their life.

_____ 9. Even little things can cause stress.

_____ 10. I can choose how I respond to stress.

Activity Sheet 13.1.   Stress Attitude Survey. Permission is granted to enlarge and photocopy for classroom use.

SESSION III—THE "MYSTERY" OF STRESS

BRIEF OVERVIEW OF SESSION

In this session, the children will begin to look at all of the questions one needs to consider in solving the "mystery of stress." They will be introduced to the 5WH process and, in a fun format, the children will learn to analyze the situational factors and identify patterns involved in causing their personal stress.

GOALS

1. To assist the children in identifying current stressors in their life.
2. To help children analyze and identify patterns that are apparent in their stress causing situations.

MATERIALS NEEDED

1. 3" × 5" cards from homework assignment
2. Copies of the "Mystery of Stress" worksheet (Activity Sheet 13.2)
3. The 5WH process on chart paper or the chalkboard (see procedure #1)

PROCEDURE

1. Invite the children to share one item from their homework assignment. Choose one of the stressors and begin to evaluate it in terms of the 5WH process (i.e., What, When, Where, Why, Who, and How) using the following questions? It may be helpful to have this on a chart that could be used for future reference as the children participate in the activity.

WHAT (Describe the situation, what caused it, and the result.)
WHEN (Tell about the time of day. What happened before the event and what happened right after?)
WHERE (Give the location of the event.)
WHY (Give the explanation of the reasons for the stress.)
WHO (Who were the persons involved?)
HOW (What was the "trigger" for the stress event?)

2. After you have modeled the process, give each child a copy of the "Mystery of Stress" worksheet (Activity Sheet 13.2) and provide time for the children to evaluate their five stressors using the 5WH process.

3. Encourage the children to share observations from the activity by discussing the following questions:

a   Now that you have gathered some facts, what are your "hunches" about the cause of your stress events?
b   What other things do you need to investigate to gain an even clearer picture of your stress?
c   What can you do to relieve your stressors?

4. Again have children compare and contrast the stress causes within the group and the similarities that are apparent.

CLOSURE

Take a few moments to remind children that they have, indeed, begun to unravel the "Mystery of Stress." When one knows what one's stress "triggers" are, one can begin to deal with them through self-talk, relaxation, and other stress reducers that we will be discussing in future group sessions.

HOMEWORK

In preparation for next session, ask the children to think about developing a plan for handling stress emergencies. Each child should come to next session prepared to identify at least one way to deal with their "emergency" stress.

Solve the MYSTERY

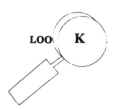

STRESSORS:
1.
2.
3.
4.
5.

LOOK

STRESSOR#	WHAT	WHEN	WHERE	WHY	WHO	HOW

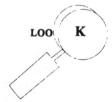

COMMON
ELEMENTS:
1.
2.
3.
4.

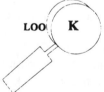

Activity Sheet 13.2.   Mystery of Stress worksheet. Permission is granted to enlarge and photocopy for classroom use.

SESSION IV—THE ABC'S OF STRESS MANAGEMENT

BRIEF OVERVIEW OF SESSION

In this session, children will have an opportunity to develop a personalized emergency plan for stress based upon A (Act), B (Breathe), and C (Clear). This plan is to be used for those acute stressors with which children often deal on a regular basis.

GOALS

1. To assist children in identifying options for dealing with emergency stressful situations.
2. To encourage each child to develop a personal plan for managing stress in emergency situations.

MATERIALS NEEDED

1. Copy of the handout about the "ABC's of Stress Management" (Activity Sheet 13.3) for each child
2. 3" × 5" card for homework assignment
3. Chart with the ABC's for introduction of the model

PROCEDURE

1. Introduce the idea that all of us have day-to-day stressors that we deal with on a regular basis; however, there are those "emergency" types of stressors that are more acute and make us feel overwhelmed. (Give examples such as a big exam, father or mother with an alcohol problem, etc.) At these times, we may feel a sense of being out of control and need to quickly regain our sense of being back in control. The ABC's of emergency stress management will provide a way for us to do that.

2. Present the ABC model using a chart. The model should contain the following information:

ACT—Do something! Call a friend; write down your feelings in a journal or on a piece of paper. The important thing is to get the feelings out and get on with other things.
BREATHE—Close your eyes and take a deep breath. Allow time for all

of your muscles to relax as you breathe in and out and visualize a pleasant scene or event.

CLEAR—Get away from the situation; do not hang around and wait for the stress to get worse! Do something altogether different. Usually you will be able to deal with the stressor.

3. Provide a copy of the worksheet to each of the children as a reminder to try to deal with those emergency stressors. Encourage them to hang it in their room or in a place where it will be easily accessible when they need it.

4. Take time for a few examples of how having one's own emergency plan for stress can be helpful. Allow the children to identify some things that they can do for each of the ABC's.

CLOSURE

To bring closure to this session, allow a few minutes for the children to practice each of the three steps and role-play a stress reducer.

HOMEWORK

Give a 3" × 5" card to all group members and ask them to create their own ABC actions that they can use in a stress emergency (and to try them during the next week in those emergency stress situations). Remind them that we will spend a few moments next session in discussion of the successes of their plan.

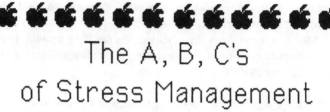

The A, B, C's
of Stress Management

A – Act – Do something! Call a
friend or write down your feelings in
a journal or on a piece of paper.

B–Breathe – Close your eyes and take
a deep breath. Allow time for all of
your muscles to relax as you breathe
in and out and visualize a pleasant
scene or event.

C– Clear – Get away from the
situation. Don't hang around and
wait for the stress to get worse!

Activity Sheet 13.3.   The ABC's of Stress Management. Permission is granted
to enlarge and photocopy for classroom use.

SESSION V—STRESS RECESS

BRIEF OVERVIEW OF SESSION

This session will provide an opportunity for children to work together to brainstorm some favorite stress reducers that can be used at various points in the day to provide a "recess" from stress.

GOALS

1. To enable children to affirm their own personal coping strategies.
2. To generate a list of ideas for reducing stress and relieving tension.
3. To encourage children to utilize their own personal stress recesses.

MATERIALS NEEDED

1. Chart paper and markers for each small group
2. 3" × 5" cards (5 for each child)

PROCEDURE

1. Spend a few moments discussing with the group the success of their ABC Stress Management plans. Provide an opportunity for sharing from group members who wish to do so. Reinforce them for their work in trying to live a more relaxing life.

2. Ask children to pair up with a partner and to begin to identify some quick stress reducers that they can use to relieve tension and provide some stress recesses throughout the day. (Remind them that the ideas should take no more than 2 to 5 minutes.) It may be helpful to provide a few examples such as getting a glass of juice or milk, taking a brief walk, doing jumping jacks, deep breathing, playing a favorite song, calling a friend to say "hi," etc.

3. Provide chart paper and markers for the groups to list their ideas in brainstorm fashion, getting as many ideas as possible down on paper.

4. Bring everyone back to the group for sharing of ideas from the charts.

5. Encourage all children to choose the five ideas that they feel will work best for them and write them on their cards.

6. Place all of the cards in a container and select one for a group stress "recess." (Even if it is not possible to do, children can pantomime the action.). If the time permits, do several of the brief activities to show the children how the idea can work for them.

7. Work with the children to make a list of the "top 20" stress recesses (and distribute to all group members at a later time).

CLOSURE

Remind the children that there are many things we can do to reduce stress briefly in our lives. When we allow these things to become a habit, we can lead more stress-free lives.

HOMEWORK

Encourage the children to choose at least one of the stress recesses for use every day (or several times a day) during the next week. We will talk about the effectiveness of this technique next session.

SESSION VI—STRESS SHIELD

BRIEF OVERVIEW OF SESSION

This session will provide children with an opportunity to begin to identify some of the personal qualities, life skills, and coping skills that will help them develop their own "shield from stress."

GOALS

1. To assist children in identifying qualities that will help shield them from life stressors.
2. To provide an opportunity for each child to make a personal stress shield.

MATERIALS NEEDED

1. "Stress Shield" worksheet (Activity Sheet 13.4) for each child
2. Crayons or markers

PROCEDURE

1. Spend a few moments of time for children to talk about their successes (or failures) of the Stress Recess technique. Allow for sharing of ideas and experiences.

2. Give a copy of the "Stress Shield" worksheet (Activity Sheet 13.4) to each child. Encourage him or her to think about the kinds of "built in shields" against stress that are already present in his or her life.

3. Remind the children that our "stress shields" come in many areas, but that some of the most common are in the areas of Attitudes, Life Experiences, School and Family Supports, and Personal Habits. Briefly describe each of the four areas as follows:

> **Attitudes**—beliefs that you have that help you view things in a positive manner.
> **Life Experiences**—experiences you have had that have taught you to manage stress.
> **School and Family Supports**—people in your life who are nurturing and caring.
> **Personal Habits**—things you do that help you release tension.

4. Provide time for each child to complete a "stress shield," identifying in each of the four areas the things that will shield him or her from life stressors.

5. Encourage the children to share their "shields" with the group. Place the completed shields on the bulletin board (or encourage the children to take them home and display them in an area that will remind them of their shields against stress).

CLOSURE

As a means of bringing closure to this activity, ask the children to name the area of their shield that they feel has the strongest influence in helping them deal with stress. Compare the differences among group members and remind them that this is another indication that each individual is different and unique.

HOMEWORK

As a homework assignment, encourage each child to share his or her "Stress Shield" with someone who is special in his or her life, and talk with that person about the positive ways he or she has learned to deal with stress in the past six sessions.

Stress Shield

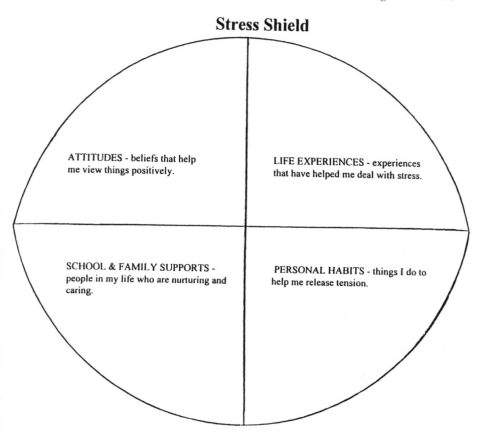

Activity Sheet 13.4. Stress Shield worksheet. Permission is granted to enlarge and photocopy for classroom use.

SESSION VII—STRESS MANAGEMENT
FROM THE EXPERTS!

BRIEF OVERVIEW OF SESSION

In this session, children will work in small groups to develop an oral presentation on the best methods of coping with stress. They will utilize what they have learned in the previous sessions as the basis for their presentations.

GOALS

1. To assist children in realizing how much they have learned about coping with stress.
2. To provide a review of stress management strategies.
3. To encourage children to utilize their creativity in sharing what they have learned with others.

MATERIALS NEEDED

1. Chart easel and markers
2. Video camera
3. TV and VCR (for viewing)

PROCEDURE

1. Spend a brief time discussing their homework assignments from their "Stress Shields." What was the reaction of the person with whom you shared your shield?

2. Encourage the children to think of all of the fine coping skills they have learned during the past six weeks. Tell them that since they have now become "stress reduction experts," they are going to develop video presentations on the "10 Best Ways to Cope with Stress." They will be divided into two groups, and each group will have 15 minutes to come up with their "10 best" list. The groups will then be videotaped as they present their lists.

3. Divide the group into two subgroups and provide chart paper and markers for their list. Allow them to work on their own to develop their list and decide how they will present it. (Remind them that everyone who wants to be a part of the video presentation should be included in some way, but no one should be forced to be videotaped if he or she does not wish to be.)

4. Play some relaxing music in the background to let the children know that they may have some background music for their videos if they wish.

5. Videotape the presentations, and then provide time for the children to view the videotapes.

6. Congratulate them on their presentations.

CLOSURE

Discuss with the children ways they can utilize the programs they have just developed to help others who also may be dealing with stress. Provide time for them to brainstorm ways they feel the videos could be used to help others. Some possibilities may include

1. Have them shown in classrooms.
2. Put them in the library for personal loan.
3. Make teachers aware of their potential for classroom use.

HOMEWORK

Inform the children that, since next week will be the final week for their group, we will be developing a group banner to identify "Positive Ways to Deal with Stress." In preparation for the activity, encourage them to begin collecting a variety of materials that they will use in developing their banner (e.g., pictures from magazines, crepe paper streamers, etc.). (Again remind them that they will be working in the same subgroups as they did for the video.)

SESSION VIII—STRESS BANNER

BRIEF OVERVIEW OF SESSION

In this session, children will have the opportunity to put what they have learned about stress management into a banner that will hang in the group room (or in a hallway) as a creative reminder of all the positive ways they have learned to deal with stress.

GOALS

1. To review all of the stress management techniques we have learned in the group.
2. To provide a creative way to serve as a reminder of group progress.
3. To end the sessions in a positive manner.
4. To provide time for the children to evaluate their group experience.

MATERIALS NEEDED

1. Large (mural-sized) paper for each subgroup
2. A variety of art materials and media
3. Old magazines
4. Scissors
5. Glue or paste
6. Evaluation forms and pencils

PROCEDURE

1. Talk briefly with the children about the materials they have brought for their banner. Remind them that this will be a fun and relaxing way to conclude our group on stress management.

2. Provide sufficient working time and adequate space for the two groups to spread out and work on their banner.

3. When the groups have completed their banners, allow time for sharing and discussion. Display the banners in the group room (or in an adjacent hallway) with the title "Positive Ways to Deal with Stress" lettered above.

4. Bring the whole group back together and talk briefly of your feelings about closure. Encourage the children to share their feelings as well.

5. Allow time for the children to affirm each other by sharing one thing they liked about every other person in the group.

CLOSURE

Provide a few minutes for the children to complete the evaluations and allow for any final comments about the group.

HOMEWORK

Because this is the final group session and there is no official homework, encourage the children to remember and use all of the stress management coping strategies they have learned during the group. Also remind them of your availability in the event that they need to talk further with you about any issues with which they may be dealing.

EVALUATION

1. Do you feel that participation in the Stress Management group was helpful to you? Why or why not?

2. What part of the group did you like best?

3. What part of the group did you like least?

4. If you had a friend who needed to identify some more positive Stress Management skills, would you recommend that he or she join this group or one like it? Why or why not?

5. Did you attend all eight group sessions?

_____ Yes   _____ No

If no, how many did you attend? _____

6. Comments, suggestions, etc.:

REFERENCES

Archer, J., Probert, B. S., & Gage, L. (1987). College students' attitudes toward wellness. *Journal of College Student Personnel, 28*(4), 311–317.

Ardell, D. B. (1982). *14 days to a wellness lifestyle.* Mill Valley, CA: Whatever Publishing.

Aronson, S., & Mascia, M. F. (1981). *The stress management workbook: An action plan for taking control of your life and health.* New York: Appleton, Century, Crofts.

Beck, A. (1976). *Cognitive therapy and emotional disorders.* New York: International Universities Press.

Burns, D. D. (1980). *Feeling good: The new mood therapy.* New York: The New American Library.

Burts, D. C., Hart, C. H., Charlesworth, R., & Kirk, L. (1990). A comparison of frequencies of stress behaviors observed in kindergarten children in classrooms with developmentally appropriate versus developmentally inappropriate instructional practices. *Early Childhood Research Quarterly, 5,* 407–423.

Coddington, R. D. (1972). The significance of life events as etiological factors in the disease of children: A survey of professionals. *Journal of Psychosomatic Research, 16,* 7–18.

Compas, B. E. (1987). Coping with stress during childhood and adolescence. *Psychology Bulletin, 101,* 393–403.

Dickey, J. P., & Henderson, P. (1989). What young children say about stress and coping in school. *Health Education, 20*(1), 14–17.

Elkind, D. (1981). *The hurried child: Growing up too fast too soon.* Reading, MA: Addison-Wesley.

Ellis, A. (1980). An overview of the clinical theory of rational-emotive therapy. In R. Grieger & J. Boyd (Eds.), *Rational-emotive therapy: A skills-based approach* (pp. 1–31). New York: Van Nostrand Reinhold.

Ellis, A. (1984). *Rational-emotive therapy and cognitive behavior therapy.* New York: Springer.

Erikson, E. (1963). *Childhood and society* (2nd ed.). New York: W. W. Norton.

Feldbaum, C. L., Christenson, R. E., & O'Neal, E. C. (1980). An observational study of the assimilation of the newcomer to the school. *Child Development, 51,* 497–507.

Forbes, R. (1979). *Corporate stress: How to manage stress on the job and make it work for you.* New York: Doubleday.

Forman, S. G. (1993). *Coping skills interventions for children and adolescents.* San Francisco, CA: Jossey-Bass.

Hafen, B. Q., Thygerson, A. L., & Frandsen, K. J. (1988). *Behavioral guidelines for health and wellness.* Englewood, CO: Morton Publishing.

Henderson, P. A., Kelby, T. J., & Engebretson, K. M. (1992). Effects of a stress-control program on children's locus of control, self-concept, and coping behavior. *The School Counselor, 40,* 125–130.

Holmes, T. H., & Rake, R. H. (1967). The social readjustment rating scale. *Journal of Psychosomatic Research, 11,* 213–218.

Honig, A. S. (1986). Stress and coping in children—Part 2. *Young Children, 41*(5), 47–59.

Krause, N. (1987). Chronic strain, locus of control, and distress in older children. *Psychology and Aging, 2*(4), 375–382.

Lazarus, R. S., & Folkman, S. (1984). *Stress, appraisal and coping.* New York: Springer.

Lazarus, R. S. (1966). *Psychological stress and the coping process.* New York: McGraw-Hill.

Matheny, K. B., Aycock, D. W., & McCarthy, C. J. (1993). Stress in school-aged children and youth. *Educational Psychology Review, 5*(2), 109–134.

Myers, J. E. (1992). Wellness, prevention, development: The cornerstone of the profession. *Journal of Counseling & Development, 71*(2), 136–139.

Omizo, M. M., Omizo, S. A., & Suzuki, L. A. (1988). Children and stressors: An exploratory study of stressors and symptoms. *The School Counselor, 35,* 267–274.

Pryor-Brown, L., Cowen, E. L., Hightower, A. D., & Lotyczewski, B. S. (1986). Demographic differences among children in judging and experiencing specific stressful life events. *Journal of Special Education, 20*(3), 339–346.

Romano, J. L. (1992). Psychoeducational interventions for stress management and well-being. *Journal of Counseling and Development, 71,* 199–202.

Romer, G. H. (1993). *Assessing stress in children: A literature review.* Knoxville: University of Tennessee. (ERIC Document Reproduction Service No. ED 365 704)

Sears, S. J., & Milburn, J. (1990). School-aged stress. In L. E. Arnold (Ed.), *Childhood stress: Wiley series in child and adolescent mental health* (pp. 223–246). New York: Wiley.

Selye, H. (1974). *Stress without distress.* Philadelphia, PA: Lippencott.

Smith, M. S., & Womack, W. M. (1987). Stress management techniques in childhood and adolescence. *Clinical Pediatrics, 26,* 581–585.

Waters, V. (1982). Therapies for children: Rational emotive therapy. In C. R. Reynolds & T. B. Gutkin (Eds.), *Handbook of school psychology* (pp. 570–579). New York: Wiley.

Worzbyt, J. C. (1994). *Beating the odds* (2nd Ed.) Altoona, PA: RJS Films.

Worzbyt, J. C., & O'Rourke, K. (1989). *Elementary school counseling: A blueprint for today & tomorrow.* Muncie, IN: Accelerated Development.

Chapter 14

DIVERSITY GROUPS

The differences that exist between and among people represent factors of human diversity. Diversity and uniqueness are synonymous in that they reflect those qualities that contribute to our humanness and give us our identity.

BACKGROUND INFORMATION

Children live in a world of human diversity and those differences are reflected in their very being. As human beings, children are first members of a world culture, then a geographical culture, a national culture, a regional culture, and lastly members of a racial-ethnic culture according to Clemmont E. Vontress (Lee, 1994). All children in this respect are multicultural, which accounts for differences in language, skin color, race, religion, dress, physical ability, customs, beliefs, and behaviors.

While diversity is a fact of life, for many children it is also a source of anger, pain, and loneliness. Children are often quick to recognize individual differences in themselves and others. In their quest to be accepted, some children find themselves the object of cruel teasing and physical abuse because they do not "fit in." They are shunned by their peers because they are overweight, lack athletic ability, look different, or are handicapped in some respect. These differences somehow make them unacceptable in the eyes of their peers.

Some children will voluntarily separate themselves from their peers because they devalue themselves. They make comparisons with others in terms of their physical attractiveness, quality and style of clothing, academic ability, and popularity. Wanting to be like their peers, these children focus on their differences, perceiving them to be quality defects that make them "damaged goods."

Much of the violence and cruelty in our society can be attributed to issues of diversity. Since the beginning of time, wars have been fought between groups and nations unwilling or incapable of achieving peaceful solutions regarding their differences. On a smaller scale, hate crimes, racial unrest, and acts of violence against the elderly and the mentally and physically handicapped are experienced in nearly every community in the United States. Unfortunately, many of these violent acts are perpetrated by children and adolescents who feel justified in striking out against those who are different from themselves. Diversity is here to stay as is violence unless adults can help children develop a different perspective on human differences, a perspective that teaches children the value of diversity among people.

WHY VALUE DIVERSITY?

Children must learn to value diversity at a very basic level because diversity is synonymous with self. A child's sense of self emerges from within and manifests itself in terms of how that child feels about himself or herself. Children cannot learn to value and appreciate others until they can cherish and love themselves for their unique qualities. How children view and feel about themselves influences their every action, interaction, and reaction (Drew, 1987; Rosenberg, 1992).

At a slightly higher level of involvement, children must learn to value diversity in developing personal relationships with others. Children who value and are at peace with themselves are able to relate to others more effectively than children who perceive themselves to be unworthy and inadequate. Children who appreciate and value their own unique qualities are more compassionate, caring, accepting, and tolerant of those who are different from themselves. They place a higher value on communicating effectively, resolving conflicts peacefully, and solving problems collaboratively than their less self-actualized counterparts.

At a higher level still, children must learn to value diversity because they are expected to interact with larger and more diverse groups than those of the family, neighborhood, organizations, and religious groups. Children, as they grow and develop in their appreciation of self and others, will be expected to participate in school, community, state, national, hemispheric, and global populations. As their spheres of influence enlarge, children will face ever increasing dimensions of diversity. They will experience greater numbers of people and more complex interpersonal situations and interactions.

If children are to advocate on behalf of caring and compassion, stand up against bias and prejudice, cherish human dignity, and bring out the best in themselves and others, they must learn to value diversity in themselves and others. Their well being and the survival of the human race rests with their ability and determination to confront and reconcile their own conflicts and failings and to embrace diversity as the pathway to self-actualization (James, Moore, & Gregerson, 1995).

WHAT CHILDREN ARE LEARNING

Despite the fact that children have a right to understand diversity and adults have the responsibility to promote its value, this goal is not being accomplished. While adults can help children develop an understanding and acceptance of diversity in people, they first must become aware of stereotyping and prejudicial subtleties that effect children's perceptions of diversity (Bauer, 1992). Stereotyping and prejudices effecting racial, religious, gender, and ethnic perceptions often times go unnoticed and therefore unchallenged. The end result is that children learn exactly what they are taught.

Television, toys, books, other forms of mass media, and language perpetuate stereotypes. For example, the villain in movies and children's cartoons is often portrayed as dark skinned, dressed in black, and speaks with an accent or dialect. In addition, the villain also may be depicted as handicapped (e.g., eye patch, pegged leg, hook), physically unattractive, not to be trusted, and mean. In contrast, the hero is usually lighter skinned, has blond or light colored hair, is physically powerful, attractive, articulate, speaks with no dialect or accent, and is rarely handicapped. Over time, children are conditioned to equate the villain's characteristics, singularly and collectively, with fear, a lack of trust, and negativity. Consequently, people with physical and mental handicaps, dark skin, and those who speak with accents and dress in native clothing are viewed as being suspect. Is it any wonder then that those stereotypical and biased characteristics ascribed to villains will, in time, become attached to people who are different in the eyes of children and adults? Such stereotypes and prejudices also can be quite confusing to children who are approached by people who are likely to do them harm but look and act like the hero.

Our language also contributes to confusing messages about people in the eyes of children. For example, angle food cake is white while devil's food cake is black. We use words like black days, black deeds, and black thoughts to describe negativity, darkness, and evil. In contrast, white is often associated with goodness, purity, cleanliness, and peacefulness.

In this country, we support freedom of religion; however Christianity, even with separation of church and state, is given more attention (e.g., paid public holidays—Christmas and Easter vacations) than other recognized religions (e.g., Judaism, Islam, Hinduism, Buddhism, etc.). Children are given the impression that somehow Christianity is the popular and most universally accepted religion.

Most misconceptions regarding issues of diversity are often not recognized as misconceptions and are unintentionally passed on from person to person and generation to generation. While preventing children from being confronted by stereotyping and biases is largely unrealistic, adults have the responsibility to challenge the portrayal of stereotypical and biased images of diversity regardless of what form they may take. As adults become more aware of their own biases and prejudices, challenging them as they emerge, they will be less likely to pass them on to others.

HOW CAN ADULTS MAKE A DIFFERENCE?

McCracken (1993) has identified four basic commitments that adults must take to heart as they challenge children to grasp realities of race and culture in society.

Commitment #1

Identify and examine how society—through its major institutions [such as] schools, health and welfare systems, government, and media—perpetuates racism and oppression in very obscure yet systematic ways.

By accepting that our society discriminates against and stereotypes people, adults can better understand the harsh realities that confront children's lives and can therefore be more effective in communicating responsible, reality-based messages to children.

Commitment #2

Examine how we as individuals participate in our own oppression and the oppression of others by unconsciously minimizing the oppressive relations of the larger society. This commitment, on behalf of children, requires adults to acknowledge and take personal responsibility for their own beliefs and actions.

Commitment #3

Truly understand what culture means to a group of people, understand how culture is a source of group power and strength, and examine how to allow groups to retain their cultural integrity while they gain the skills to function in the larger society.

Looking at our own lives and then attempting to put ourselves in other's shoes are good ways to consider how to meet these three interwoven challenges.

Commitment #4

Use our power to change the oppressive systems that exist in our society. Inequities have been perpetrated, at one time or another, on nearly every group of people who call themselves Americans (McCracken, 1993, pp. 7–12).

McCracken (1993) has stated that only through self-examination can we root out the prejudices, biases, and stereotypes that we have learned, practiced, and intentionally or inadvertently passed on to children. Children are the sum total of their experiences. They are affected by TV programs, movies, holiday celebrations, and statements made by friends, strangers, teachers, parents, and their peers.

Many adults harbor biases against males, females, people of color, people of low socioeconomic status, children with different abilities, the handicapped, and the list goes on (Curry & Johnson, 1990). McCracken's four commitments are designed to help adults overcome the tendency to harbor demeaning attitudes about some differences while placing a positive value on others.

Children are curious about each other. They want to explore commonalities, differences, and cultural heritages. They can and should learn about themselves and their peers while practicing the values that have made this country strong. Diversity should be explored in a democratic climate that reveres respect for others, free speech, truth, justice, trust, and harmony. When these conditions are present, children can gain a new perspective about themselves and others, a new perspective that will enable them to value diversity and make wise decisions that will protect and honor its existence (Hendrick, 1992; Perry

& Fraser, 1993). If we can produce safe and psychologically secure environments for children while exploring diversity, perhaps then we can control the tension, violence, and oppression that seem to characterize the national and international scene when issues of diversity are addressed.

LEARNING TO VALUE DIVERSITY

According to Pederson (1988) and Wittmer (1992), the valuing of diversity can be taught to others and that every effort should be made to do so through education. A model showing great promise in the teaching of diversity is ASK. In this program "A" stands for awareness of self and others, "S" is for sensitivity and skills, and "K" signifies knowledge about cultures different from our own. The ASK Model is designed to empower young people regardless of race, gender, religion, or creed to work together, care for each other, and achieve mutual understanding—conditions that are necessary if a society of diverse populations and groups like our own is to flourish.

By the year 2056, according to Wittmer (1992), the "average" United States citizen will trace his or her descent to Africa, Asia, the Hispanic countries, and/ or the Pacific islands. Far fewer people will point to White Europe in documenting their heritage. By the year 2000, 43% of the people in the United States will be people of color. In 1990, over 30% of public school students were either African American or Hispanic and by the year 2075, African Americans, Alaskan Natives, American Natives, Hispanic Americans, and Asian Americans will be the statistical majority in the United States (Locke, 1992).

Awareness

Pederson (1988) has indicated that awareness represents the beginning of change. Culture is within each person and is the sum total of what that person has experienced from which his or her internal identity emerges. Culture provides children with a personal orientation from which to think, decide, and act. Culture itself is difficult to define, as noted by Kroeber and Kluckholm (1952) who found over 150 different definitions. They, however, described culture as representing those things that a stranger needs to know to behave appropriately in a specific setting. Thus, culture can be described as a set of subsystems relating to geography, nationality, ethnicity, and, for some people, gender, religion, sexuality, handicap, and the aged. Culture represents a distinct network of traits located within each child that develop, change, and influence how that child sees and relates to himself or herself and others.

Because culture is a complex and dynamic set of conditions, children and adults can know some of the core elements that effect their attitudes, beliefs, feelings, and actions, but they can only know themselves in part. Although adults can observe some of the elements of a child's culture, other aspects cannot be assessed so easily. If adults are to enhance children's understanding of diversity, they must help them account for the many ways that culture influences their perceptions of self and others. If children are to make rational and responsible life decisions, they must develop an awareness of culture including their own prejudices, biases, and stereotypical thinking.

Knowledge

As children become more aware of themselves, others, their biases, their prejudices, and the stereotypes that negatively affect people's lives, and begin to see value in diversity, they will be motivated to increase their knowledge concerning all aspects of human diversity. In many instances, children will have serious gaps in their knowledge, limited information from which to draw understanding, and inaccuracies and faulty assumptions that will need to be corrected. Children need accurate information and facts and the opportunity to correct misconceptions concerning diversity so that they can develop personal empathy, caring, and understanding of those who are different from themselves.

Before children can be effective communicators and peacemakers, they must have the knowledge and cognitive understandings to appreciate other people's values, current problems, lifestyles, and actions. Only by understanding other people's perceptions can children appreciate their reality in search of common ground on which to build a relationship.

Sensitivity and Skills

Children can learn to develop a sense of personal awareness and acquire the necessary knowledge concerning a broad range of diversities; however, neither of these stages can prepare children to interact with others in a proactive way unless they also possess the sensitivity and skills necessary to do so (Grevious, 1993). Children need to develop a sense of caring and to find meaning and purpose in life that supports cooperation, harmonious living, and the acceptance of all people regardless of their differences (Kohn, 1991).

Children need to develop their sensitivity in relationship to others. This process begins when children learn to connect with their own humanness (i.e., feelings, thoughts, values, behaviors) and to identify with their own needs for survival, safety, security, love, belonging, self-esteem, and self-actualization. When children realize that they share the same needs with all members of the human race, they will shift their attention from looking at what makes people different from each other to examining the similarities that all people share in common with each other.

Children, who learn to accept themselves and recognize that they share many things in common with people who are different from themselves, are capable of developing relationships that promote freedom, hope, and fulfillment. Children and adults tend to build connections more readily with others in the absence of fear and threat and in the presence of positive regard and acceptance. To focus purely on diversity in relationship building can generate suspicion and fear; however, when the focus shifts to understanding human similarities, the door opens for relationship building and subsequent exploration and appreciation for what makes people different from each other.

An Existential Perspective

A central purpose of diversity training is to help children develop spiritual wellness, "a continuing search for meaning and purpose in life; an appreciation for depth of life, the expanse of the universe, and the natural forces which operate, a personal belief system" (Myers, 1990, p. 11). Children are spiritual beings with a natural curiosity and drive to seek meaning and purpose in human existence.

There are four basic questions, the answers to which can help children tap into their spiritual dimension as they seek to find meaning in diversity. These four questions are

1. What do you want to be?
2. What do you want to do?
3. What do you want to have?
4. What do you want to give?

In many ways, these four questions are addressed in Buscaglia's (1982) book, *The Fall of Freddie the Leaf.* This book is about the meaning of life and Freddie's (leaf) drive to understand life and his purpose for being. Freddie learns that he is one of hundreds of leaves on a tree and that all of the leaves are different but that they share many things in common as well. When Freddie discovers that he has a purpose, his life changes and begins to take on meaning. He realizes that his purpose is to provide shade, a place for children to play, and a place for the old people to gather, picnic, and talk of times past.

Children need to discover their purpose in life. While that purpose will change and grow, it must have a beginning. Adults can begin by helping children explore what they want to be. A list like the following is likely to emerge.

I want to be

- happy,
- liked by others,
- safe,
- friendly,
- helpful,
- caring,
- a peace maker,
- cooperative,
- trusted,
- courageous,
- healthy, and
- responsible.

As children explore all that they want to be, they are creating a reason for being. They are exploring their purpose. The second question, "What do you want to do?" indicates that children must learn specific behaviors in order to achieve each of their wants. If children want to be helpful, they must understand not only the meaning of helpful but also how they can become helpful through their actions and deeds.

When children succeed in developing their wants, they will have developed a variety of assets that will enhance their ability to connect with others. They will have responded to the third question, "What do you want to have?" because assets become personal possessions that never can be *taken away* but can be *given away* to others. Children's search for purpose and meaning in life is based on what they have to give to others, and what they have to pass on to people they meet and ultimately to the next generation.

Diversity training helps children see that they have a purpose in life that extends beyond their own personal gain. Their purpose is to care for themselves, others, and the planet. "Because without caring, human beings cannot thrive, communities become violent battlegrounds, the American democratic experiment must ultimately fail, and the planet will not be able to support life" (Lipsitz, 1995, p. 665).

CHILDREN'S NEEDS

If children are to value diversity, their lives must be shaped by environments that value caring, cooperation, collaboration, love and acceptance, and a sense of morality that places human existence and essence above competition, personal gain, and violence. Children must be given time and rewarded for acts of caring, kindness, and compassion, little of which is being practiced in any planned way in the public schools (Bosworth, 1995).

If diversity groups are to be successful, they must address children's needs in the following six areas:

- understanding self,
- understanding others,
- understanding conflict,
- understanding peace,
- creating a vision, and
- committing to that vision.

Understanding Self

Children have a need to understand and value themselves. They have a need to identify with their net worth and to develop fully functioning selves. They have a need to engage in self-caring activities and behaviors of a self-esteem enhancing nature, treating themselves with kindness and basic goodness. None of these needs can be met unless children's physiological needs have been met, they feel safe and secure, and feel loved and experience a sense of belonging. Adults and children are not likely to invest in themselves unless others have first invested in them. Children learn to care by being cared for, they learn to love by being loved, and they learn to treat others with kindness and respect if they have received similar treatment.

Children have a need to understand who they want to be, what they want to do, what they want to have, and what they want to give or pass on to others. They have a need to explore what they like about themselves, their assets, their liabilities, faulty assumptions about themselves, and hurts that need to be addressed and resolved.

Self-exploration leads to self-understanding and is a life long process. An eight-week support group can help children self-explore and reach new levels of understanding about who they are and what they want to become. This process can be facilitated by helping children study well known people and community members who value themselves and who have developed personalities, attitudes, and values that they and others admire.

As children explore other people's lives and their own, they will recognize that they share similarities and differences in terms of nationality, religion, language, physical abilities, mental abilities, and interests. Teaching children to connect with all dimensions of themselves and to cherish those dimensions individually and collectively will ultimately lead to self-acceptance and internal peace.

Understanding Others

Mutual respect and trust are core issues that must be addressed if children of diversity are to connect with one another in peaceful and self-enhancing ways. Teaching children to understand and appreciate others begins with the creation of a teaching-learning environment that invites children to explore their commonalities, diversities, and shared heritages; however getting there can be a challenge for children who have spent the first five years of their lives in the company of people at home and in their communities who understand them. White and Siegal (1984) have described how children feel when they are thrust into a diverse environment like the public schools with children who differ from them.

> It is the somewhat pleasant, but scary destiny of small children to be faced constantly with the task of going to where they have never been before, of meeting and dealing with people they have never seen before, of doing things they have never done before. In a new environment, they have to arrive at emotional and social settlements before they begin to enter into problems and processes of intellectual problem solving. They have to ask, "Is it safe here?" "Can someone like me be here?" "Can I trust the people here?" "Can I trust myself to manage what I have to?" (White & Siegal, 1984, p. 253)

Children have a need to feel psychologically safe and secure and to have their physical needs met as well. Teaching-learning environments that support children's needs are also sensitive and responsive to issues of diversity. In teaching children to value diversity, they have a need for information concerning issues of diversity, interpersonal skills that can teach them how to connect with others in positive and peaceful ways, confidence building experiences that will provide them with the courage to risk, and opportunities to practice community building. Teaching cooperative learning, collaboration, love and acceptance, calmness, peaceful problem solving, conflict management, and community building are all places to begin in helping children understand and live peacefully with others.

According to Chaskin and Rauner (1995), researchers in the program on Youth and Caring sponsored by the Lilly Endowment, have found that "caring and connectedness have a positive impact on the lives of children that can protect against specific risk factors of stressful life events. It appears that the protective dimensions of caring transcend ethnic, class, geographical, and historical boundaries" (p. 669).

Understanding Conflict

Understanding self and others, while important in helping children appreciate all forms of diversity, does not prepare children to address inevitable and seemingly unresolvable diversity related conflicts. Children have a need to understand the nature of conflict, its pros and cons, causes of conflict, ways to avoid it, and how to manage it when it does occur.

With regard to diversity, children have a need to understand the meaning of bias, stereotyping, prejudice, and their impact on a multicultural society if left unchecked and allowed to run their course. Children have a need to examine examples of bias, stereotyping, and prejudice as they affect all forms of diversity, past and present. They need to understand the pain (physical and psychological) that various groups have had to endure because of oppressive systems. More important, children have a need to examine discriminatory and oppressive systems that deny people their human rights as guaranteed under the Constitution of the United States. Perhaps closer to home, children have a need to examine their own cognitions, emotions, and response tendencies toward various groups and to challenge those that are not based on Right, Reality, and Responsibility (3 R's).

Children can learn to be standard bearers for human rights and learn to solve diversity problems at home, in school, and in their communities. They can learn to be community builders, peacemakers, and conflict resolvers. But if they are to do their jobs effectively, children must have a full range of connectiveness building skills at their disposal. Understanding conflict, its causes, and how to manage it responsibly are addressed in Chapter 9, Conflict Management.

Understanding Peace and Caring

Children have a need to understand and practice the concepts of peace and caring (Kohn, 1991). They need time to think about these ideas and explore their meaning as they impact on their present day lives and what significance they would like to have them play in their future. According to Drew (1987), author of *Learning the Skills of Peacemaking*, people generally prefer to get along with each other and work out their differences peacefully. She believes that children prefer harmony but often do not know how to achieve it. Achieving harmony and creating and maintaining an atmosphere of acceptance and peace is possible, but it takes patience, persistence, and a plan.

The plan for achieving peace, whether at home, in school, or in the community, requires the following elements:

- cooperation,
- calmness,
- willingness to work out differences,
- ability to work collaboratively to solve problems,
- love and acceptance, [and]
- the ability to say, "I'm human. I've made a mistake. I'll try again." (Drew, 1987, p. iv)

Children have a need to learn and practice these elements individually and collectively in building a peaceful climate in a world of diversity.

The words of Drew are echoed in the research of Pittman and Cahill as reported by Chaskin and Rauner (1995). Pittman and Cahill of the Center for Youth Development and Policy Research of the Academy for Educational Development cited the following criteria as being central to caring environments. Caring environments

- create an atmosphere in which young people feel welcome;
- structure opportunities for the development of caring relationships with adults and peers;
- provide information, counseling, and expectations that enable young people to determine what it means to care for themselves and to care for a definable group; and
- provide opportunities, training, and expectations that encourage young people to contribute to the greater good through service, advocacy, and active problem solving on important issues. (p. 670)

Children need to understand the nature of peace and caring and how to achieve both so that they can actively choose between living in a world of diversity that promotes anger, violence, and conflict or one that strives for peace and harmony. We owe children that choice for our sake and theirs.

Creating a Vision

If children truly are to connect with the power of diversity and the possibilities that peace making and community building hold in preserving diversity as a strength, they must learn to dream and to envision the desirable out of which possibilities can emerge. Children need to be given the opportunity and challenged to envision a hopeful world in which to live. The future starts with today's dreams.

Children can be asked to think about and respond to questions such as the following that will help them begin connecting with a future that they can create:

What would the world be like if everyone got along with each other?
How would the world be different from the way it is now?
What can I do to help bring peace and cooperation into my home, school, and community?
How does a peaceful community look and act?
How do people relate to one another peacefully?
How do you want others to treat you?
How do you want to treat others?
What are some things you would see people doing to and for each other in a caring community?
What kind of home, classroom, school, and community do you want?
What are some things that you and your friends can start doing now to make peace?

As children focus on questions like these, they will recognize that peace and community building begin with their dreams. When children feel empowered, they will experience more freedom. They also will recognize that with freedom comes responsibility.

Committing to the Vision

Visions are meant to excite, motivate, and propel people into action. They become the catalyst that sparks activity. Children have a need to recognize that winners must turn their dreams into reality. Vision and commitment are the cornerstones to peace and community building. Children need to be taught how to create and realize their visions for the future. A vision unfulfilled is a dream, but a dream attained is reality. We must teach children the significance of commitment and inspire them to view life's problems as challenges with opportunity that can only be realized through action.

STRENGTHS TO BE LEARNED

Learning to value diversity is an ongoing experiential process in which children acquire the knowledge, attitudes, and strengths (skills) necessary to promote caring and cooperating among all people. While there are many strengths children can develop that will help them live in harmony in a world of diversity, we believe the following to be in most need of our attention:

- self-esteem management,
- social skill development,
- 3 R's Decision Making, and
- valuing.

Self-esteem Management

Before children can learn to value others, they first must learn to value themselves. Most children know the value of money, but they do not know how to equate value in themselves. Those things in life that children perceive to have worth, they cherish, respect, and protect. Unfortunately, some children place a higher value on their possessions than on themselves.

Children who value themselves learn to appreciate all of their qualities. They recognize what makes them unique and that being unique contributes to what makes them special and worthy of self-affirmation. Children need to be taught how to self-explore in relationship to themselves. By asking the question, "Who am I?" they can begin, with assistance from adults, to explore the many dimensions of the self (e.g., physical appearance, interests, abilities, personality characteristics, religion, ethnic background, etc.).

With self-exploration comes self-understanding. When children can tell others who they are from a multidimensional, multicultural perspective, they are able to recognize their assets. They can say "I am a person of worth because of who I am." Self-affirmation is a strength that children can use to build their self-esteem and to remind themselves continually that their value and worth is a measure of what is on the inside.

With self-understanding comes action. As children learn who they are, they recognize what they can be. By doing those things that please themselves and others, they are contributing to their own self-worth and passing on to others some of their own goodness. Adults need to help children understand that their purpose in life is to become the best that they can so that they may, in turn, help others accomplish the same. Chapter 11, Self-esteem Management, provides many useful ideas in helping children value themselves.

Social Skill Development

As children continue to participate in their self-exploration and understanding, they will be learning not only about what makes them unique but about what makes others unique as well. Children are alike and yet different in so many ways. Before children can appreciate others, they must learn to build connections of understanding. A great way to begin is to start with children's own experiences and insights regarding what they have in common with each other and how they differ. Building connections often starts with exploring commonalities. Children can be asked to identify some of the basic needs that all people share, needs being those things or conditions that people must have in order to live. As children explore Maslow's need hierarchy, they will soon realize that people who live in different geographic locations of the world, dress and speak differently, eat different foods, live in different shelters, and practice different religions, all share the same basic needs.

Racial, gender, cultural, religious, and handicap differences do exist and yet, despite those differences, a common ground of similarities provides a platform for mutual understanding. Even prior to development of specific social skills to build connections, helping children see that people all over the world are mutually interconnected, because of who they are on the inside, can go a long way in developing satisfying human relationships. Chapter 12, Social Skills Training, discusses a number of specific social skills that children can learn in developing satisfying interpersonal relationships with others.

3 R's Decision Making

As children develop their social skills and learn to value their interactions with others, they likewise will begin to appreciate and value the importance of caring, cooperation, community building and peacemaking. As important, however, children need to understand the nature of conflict and the fact that many conflicts evolve from perceived differences (i.e., racial, gender, cultural, religious, and handicap) between and among people. Some children and adults view perceived differences as threatening, which fuels the fires of distrust. Stereotyping and prejudice evolve out of misinformation, misunderstandings, and unsubstantiated assumptions that often cast aspersions against those who look and act differently from the majority.

If children are to value diversity and commit themselves to it, they must be prepared to address the complexities of conflict. They must be taught how to define and understand conflict, how to explore alternatives in conflict situations, and how to select alternatives that are based on Right, Reality, and Responsibility (Chapter 2). Three R's Decision Making provides children with an opportunity to clarify and courageously support their values (i.e., trust, courage, cooperation, kindness, and respect).

For additional information and strategies pertaining to cooperative learning and conflict management, refer to Chapter 9. Anger Management (Chapter 8) and Stress Management (Chapter 13) strategies also should be considered when helping children settle their differences peacefully. As children learn to affirm themselves and others, they will see the value of investing in and protecting their connections.

Valuing

Eyre and Eyre (1993), in their book, *Teaching Your Children Values*, outlined 12 values that they believe to be virtually universally accepted by most people. The values they selected are, by nature, designed to bring people together rather than polarize or drive them apart. They can help children build connections around standards that promote basic goodness, help children discern right from wrong in celebrating basic human dignity, and are values that have stood the test of time in terms of proven results. We have identified 12 values based on Right, Reality, and Responsibility that promote community building and peacemaking in a world of diversity.

Honesty. Teaching children to be truthful, trustworthy, and to behave with integrity are all virtues that promote honesty. Children who learn to be honest with themselves, others, and society enhance their ability to build strong connections with whom they interact.

Courage. Teaching children to stand up for their convictions even in the "face of fear" is an important character trait. Learning to overcome fear and to challenge adversity when it may not be the popular thing to do is a mark of boldness and personal strength. Children who learn to be courageous can make 3 R's decisions in support of diversity.

Caring. Children who value diversity are caring people who have learned the importance of protecting their rights and interests, the rights and interests of others, and who ultimately support the ongoing development of their social and civic communities (Chaskin & Rauner, 1995). Caring children are self-confident and hopeful children who choose to serve others, their community, and are committed to social justice and social obligation.

Self-reliance. Children who are self-reliant have been taught how to create, package, and market themselves in ways that foster individuality, uniqueness, responsibility, and commitment to excellence. Self-reliant children create their own essence and can be counted on to do their part in accepting personal challenges and the consequences of their actions.

Self-discipline. Children who possess self-discipline are able to maintain a sense of balance in their lives. They are able to exercise spontaneity without gravitating to extremes in their actions. They have developed an internal guidance system that helps them discern right from wrong. They have the ability to monitor their actions and to make 3 R's decisions in support of human decency and caring.

Dependability. Learning to be dependable is another of those values that help children develop a sense of connectiveness with others. When children recognize the value of being able to rely on the words and actions of others with consistency, they too will want to be known for their dependability. "I can count on you" are words that, when supported with actions, become the cement that establish strong relationships.

Loyalty. While a new automobile may be dependable because you can count on it to start, it is incapable of being loyal. Loyalty requires caring. Children who are loyal to others will stick by them. They will commit themselves to those that they love regardless of the circumstances they must face. Loyalty and dependability are values that when coupled together represent a significant human investment in the well-being of others.

Respect. If children are to truly value diversity in themselves and others, they must learn to value human life. Children must be taught how to care for themselves, their parents, elders, friends, and people they are meeting for the first time. Respect means honoring the rights of others; accepting differing beliefs; and practicing courtesy, politeness, and manners with all people.

Sensitivity. Children must be taught to feel deeply, to empathize sincerely, and to accept others unconditionally. Sensitive people are able to transcend from I to We. They are capable of recognizing other people's needs and find themselves wanting to support others just because they value giving and sharing.

Kindness. Children who have learned kindness are those who readily connect with others through their smiles, gentleness, quiet nature, and soft touch. They are warm people who have learned to radiate their warmth and share it with others. Kind people are peacemakers who understand the value of maintaining and building connections while responding to potential disruptions regarding issues of diversity. They do their best to remain cheerful, helpful, and hopeful even during times of adversity.

Justice. Children who have developed a sense of justice have learned to differentiate right from wrong. They are fair-minded individuals who rely on their internal guidance systems in making decisions based on Right, Reality, and Responsibility. They strive to protect their own rights and the rights of others and they readily and willingly accept the consequences of their actions. Justice is a value that protects diversity while holding people responsible for unjust acts that violate Constitutional freedoms.

Forgiveness. If children are to become peacemakers and caregivers, they also must learn the value of forgiveness. Often the only bridge between people in conflict is the willingness of one party to give up resentment, anger, and the desire to punish for acts of the past. Healing begins with a pardon and a willingness to forego punishing oneself and others and to show forgiveness. To do otherwise results in continued tension and pain, often with little understanding of what caused the dispute in the first place. Learning to forgive others for sins of the past is often the first step toward understanding and resolving differences. Learning to forgive is a value that can support and strengthen diversity.

Today's children are tomorrow's adults. If adults are to pass on the best of themselves to their children, they first must recognize the value of diversity and the freedom it provides in allowing people to cultivate their own unique identities. Without diversity there are no freedoms, human rights, or personal respect for self. We believe that diversity, once understood and valued by adults, will result in adults wanting to teach the various strengths outlined in this chapter to children.

MESSAGE TO FACILITATORS

As we have emphasized throughout this chapter, human diversity is a very broad topic and can be examined from a multitude of perspectives. Diversity speaks to all those differences that exist between and among people. We want children to recognize, understand, and appreciate those differences in the context of what makes themselves and others special and unique rather than emphasize differences from the perspective of separation.

Your goals must be to prepare children to lead productive and rewarding lives in a world of diversity. They must be taught that mutual respect and trust are the cornerstones of success and peace. When one child is diminished in any way, for whatever reason(s), all children are diminished. Your goal must be to help all children discern differences between stereotyped, prejudiced, and biased portrayals of diversity versus authentic presentations of differences among people. In order to accomplish this end, you must not only examine your own prejudices, biases, and stereotypes so as not to pass them on to others, but also carefully examine the resources that you select for use with your group to insure that they do not perpetuate misinformation.

Group Selection

Because the emphasis of Diversity Groups focuses on the exploration and understanding of all forms of diversity, a wide range of children can be selected for participation in these groups. The differences among children selected for your group will provide the source for activity and discussion. Your group membership might reflect physical, cultural, religious, racial, and ethnic differences. Children are encouraged to explore differences in dress, last names, personalities, languages, foods eaten, celebrations, interests, skills, thoughts, and feelings about themselves and others.

Children new to the school and community, visitors and permanent United States residents from different countries, and children adjusting to physical and mental challenges can enrich a group experience while helping children adjust to change and challenges in their lives.

Group Process

Diversity group involvement is designed to help children develop strong interpersonal relationships with all people. Children need to understand the nature of violence, hate crimes, racial conflicts, violations of human rights, and related conditions that threaten peaceful living among people. In contrast to those conditions that cause social unrest, children likewise need to understand and practice peacemaking, friendship building, cooperative learning, human advocacy, caring, positive discipline, acceptance, and conflict resolution (Perry, 1992).

As children learn to accept and value themselves, they will see the value in others as well. Peace and harmony are the rewards we seek in promoting family, classroom, community, and global understanding and cooperation in a world of diversity and change.

The goals of this Diversity Support Group are to

- assist children in accepting and understanding differences in themselves and others;
- help children appreciate and value themselves and others;
- teach children about stereotypes, prejudices, and biases and how they affect people's lives;
- encourage children to explore their own misinformation concerning issues of diversity;
- provide children with reality based information regarding human differences;
- help children explore a range of differences among themselves in addition to cultural differences;
- explore with children a variety of ways in which they can improve communication with their peers and others;
- provide children with experiential opportunities to explore and appreciate diversity in others (e.g., celebrations, foods, dress, beliefs, and disabilities);
- give children an opportunity to work together in building a sense of community amongst themselves;
- assist children in understanding and developing the qualities of peacemakers; and
- help children collaboratively create a "Declaration of Peace."

Our hope for you and your group is that everyone participating in your group sessions will leave the experience appreciating and valuing diversity in all its forms; having a greater awareness and empathy for all people; and possessing peacemaking skills they will use in support of unity, world peace, and a healthy, wellness oriented environment.

As you prepare to lead your Diversity Support Group, we offer the following suggestions:

1. **Discover who the children are who will be in your group.** Learning about your children's skills, abilities, interests, cultural and religious backgrounds, strengths, deficits, and beliefs about themselves and others will help you tailor your group experience to your children's needs.
2. **Familiarize yourself with television programs, advertisements, children's toys and games, news, and community issues of diversity.** Being prepared to counter socially prevailing stereotypes, biases, and prejudices, if they arise in group discussion, will help you respond in a positive and caring manner with accurate information. Your goal must be to provide children with truthful information while maintaining a trusting and self-esteem enhancing environment.

3. **When children raise questions regarding issues of diversity, answer honestly and with sensitivity.** Younger children, because they are curious about differences among themselves, are likely to ask questions regarding differences in skin color, language, dress, and ability. Older children may ask questions that speak to their lack of information or misinformation about disabilities, race, and ethnic differences. If you do not feel qualified to answer some questions or to comment on the accuracy of a child's comments, tell your group that they have asked an interesting question or have provided some information that you need time to check out. Let them know that you will provide accurate information at your next group session.

4. **Be sure to help children explore and value not only their differences but also their similarities.** Help your group understand that all people are alike in many ways. In particular, we all share common needs. Help your children explore such basic human needs as survival, safety, belonging, acceptance, love, etc. All people share similar feelings, thoughts, hopes, goals, events, and needs. In many ways those things that we share in common often represent the building blocks of trust and acceptance that cement connections among people. Once connected, people are more willing and interested to explore, accept, and value differences.

5. **Build on pride, self-esteem, and self-worth.** You want your group to strengthen their love for self and each other while learning about diversity. Teach your children the value of cooperation, sharing, respect, dignity, and the other values presented in this chapter in building connections and community. You want your children to be proud of themselves, their families, and their heritage. You also will want them to be able to distinguish pride from superiority in their quest to exercise self-discipline in support of trust, respect, and responsibility.

6. **Utilize activities and experiences that will provide children with the opportunity to love themselves and others in responsible ways.** Children need to make realistic connections between group activities and responsible actions they can take at home, in school, and in their communities to promote community and caring. Your goal must be to inspire children to explore, understand, and act on those opportunities that will promote diversity and freedom.

7. **Teach children nonviolent ways to settle their differences.** Help your children understand that much conflict and violence is expressed in the name of diversity. Unfortunately diversity is often blamed for destructive acts when the lack of information, self-discipline, and failure to use peaceful resolution skills are the real sources of unrest. Teach your

children conflict resolution and mediation skills. Teach them how to make 3 R's decisions in resolving differences peacefully.

8. **Help children become activists.** The ultimate success of diversity groups can be measured in the proactive activities that children promote and carry out. Help your children to identify ways in which they can exercise their freedom in responsible ways in promoting understanding and diversity in those areas where they can make a difference.

Have fun with your Diversity Support Group. Your group members will learn much from you and each other in their growing awareness of diversity. Likewise, they will learn the values of working together in cultivating their own uniqueness in a partnership that values investing in others.

Resources

Share with parents and/or guardians Figure 14.1 so that they will have suggestions on how they can help their children at home. In Figure 14.2 are provided lists of resources to be used with and by children in the Diversity Group. The resource materials are grouped according to age of child.

DIVERSITY GROUP GUIDE

Tips for Caregivers

Your child soon will be participating in a Diversity Support Group. The goal of this support group is to help children learn about themselves and others and to appreciate the value and worth of all people. Children will be taught the importance of respecting human differences and the power of cooperation, caring, kindness, and peacemaking.

We believe that you, too, can play a significant role at home in helping your children live in love and peace with themselves, family members, friends, and other members of the human race. As children learn to like themselves and what makes them unique and special, they will be more open to valuing those who are different from themselves (i.e., race, religion, ethnic background, gender, and physical and mental ability). The following tips are provided for your consideration and use.

1. Before you can help your children to appreciate differences in others, examine your own beliefs and behaviors toward those who are different. Your goal must be to pass on the best of yourself to your children not your own biases, stereotypes, and prejudices.

2. Become observant of biases, stereotyping, and prejudices conveyed through children's television programs, the movies, games and toys, advertisements, and interactions with others so that you can recognize and correct misinformation and inaccuracies when they occur. Use these teaching moments to help your children understand the destructive nature of groundless assumptions.

3. Your children are very curious people, especially toward those who are different from them. Welcome your children's questions even at times when you may be embarrassed for those who may have overheard your child's question. Children need accurate information to understand differences regarding clothing, skin color, physical and mental disabilities, and language. Your children will learn to treat others with courtesy, respect, and common decency by your example. They also will be less likely to perceive their questions to be out of the ordinary if you answer them openly and as a matter of fact.

4. Teach your children that teasing, name calling, violence, and other acts of disrespect toward people different from themselves (i.e., race, gender, disability, religion, ethnicity) is unacceptable.

5. Help your children understand that all people deserve respect and that discriminating practices, for whatever reasons, are hurtful and

destructive. When you observe discriminating behavior, have the courage to intervene; to do otherwise is to condone this practice.

6. Do whatever you can to expose your children to positive examples of diversity. There are many excellent children's books, movies, and ethnic festivals to visit that can teach children the value of human decency and diversity. When buying children's toys and games, be sure that the purchase of such materials do not foster stereotyping, biases, or prejudices.

7. Teach your children to look for the good in others. Help them to discover their own goodness and what they can do to pass it on to others. Teach your children the values of caring, kindness, cooperation, and peacemaking.

8. Help your children to understand that they share the same basic needs with all people. Every person needs food, water, clothing, and shelter. We all need to feel safe, to trust, to love and be loved, to feel worthwhile and to belong, to have positive self-esteem, and to enjoy the same human rights of life, liberty, and the pursuit of happiness.

9. If you live in an area close to a college or university, sponsor an international student. Invite this person to dinner or for an outing with your family. This is a great way to learn about different cultures.

10. Visit ethnic events, exhibits, museums, and help your child obtain a pen pal from a different country.

Remember, you have a very important role to play in teaching your children the value of diversity (differences) and respect. You can help your children increase understanding, nurture sensitivity, and foster acceptance regardless of differences.

As you teach your children the importance of caring, cooperation, and kindness, give them opportunities to practice these attributes. They can volunteer their services (e.g., reading, letter writing, lawn care, etc.) to the elderly, people with disabilities (i.e., physical and mental), and new people to the community. Provide your children with many opportunities to value people for who they are. Teach your children that all people, including themselves, are special people, and that, when special people develop friendships, their similarities and differences will help them to connect with each other in special ways. Help to make your children's lives special so that they can contribute their share of color and brightness to life's rainbow.

Figure 14.1. Tips for Caregivers to be given to parents and/or guardians. Permission to photocopy is granted.

RESOURCES FOR CHILDREN
Diversity Groups

Ages 3 to 7

Carlson, N. (1990). *Arnie and the new kid.* New York: Viking Penguin. (dependence on wheelchair)

Dahl, T. (1989). *The same but different.* New York: Viking Penguin. (human differences)

Escudie, R., & Wensell, U. (1988). *Paul and Sebastian.* Brooklyn: Kane/ Miller Book Publishers. (prejudice, human differences)

Gerard, L. W. (1989). *We adopted you, Benjamin Koo.* Morton Grove, IL: Albert Whitman, & Co. (interracial adoption)

Guthrie, D. W. (1988). *A rose for Abby.* Nashville: Abingdon Press. (poverty, compassion)

Hoffman, M. (1988). *My grandma has black hair.* New York: Dial Books for Young Readers. (human differences)

Mendez, P. (1989). *The black snowman.* New York: Scholastic. (African-American relationships)

Scholes, K. (1990). *Peace begins with you.* Boston: Little, Brown. (human differences, peace)

Sheehan, P. (1988). *Kylie's song.* Santa Barbara: Advocacy Press. (feeling different)

Wills, R. (1988). *Shy Charles.* New York: Dial Books for Young Readers. (human differences)

Ages 8 to 12

Aamundson, N. K. (1990). *Two short and one long.* Boston: Houghton Mifflin. (ethnic and racial prejudice)

Angel, A. (1988). *Real for sure sister.* Indianapolis, IN: Perspectives Press. (interracial adoption)

Ellis, S. (1990). *Next door neighbors.* New York: Margaret K. McElderry Books. (ethnic/racial prejudice)

Fine, A. (1989). *My war with goggle eyes.* Boston: Joy Street Books. (human differences)

Girion, B. (1990). *Indian summer.* New York: Scholastic. (ethnic/racial prejudice)

Howard, E. (1987). *Edith herself.* New York: Atheneum Publishers. (epilepsy)

Hurmence, B. (1988). *The nightwalker.* Boston: Clarion Books. (prejudice, social class, Native American)

Ruby, L. (1987). *Pig out inn.* Boston: Houghton Mifflin. (human differences)

Strachan, I. (1990). *The flawed glass.* Boston: Little Brown and Co. (disabilities)

Ages 12 and Up

Betancourt, J. (1990). *More than meets the eye.* New York: Bantam Doubleday Dell. (interracial boy/girl relationships)

Cannon, A. E. (1990). *The shadow brothers.* New York: Delacorte Press. (Native American relationships)

Cohen, B. (1987). *People like us.* New York: Bantam Doubleday Dell. (religious prejudice, Jewish)

Collier, J. L. (1988). *The Winchesters.* New York: Macmillan. (social class prejudice)

Corcoran, B. (1988). *The sky is falling.* New York: Atheneum Publishers. (accepting change, human differences)

Dixon, J. (1987). *The tempered wind.* New York: Atheneum Publishers. (prejudice toward handicapped)

Gorgon, S. (1990). *The middle of somewhere: A story of South Africa.* New York: Orchard Books. (apartheid, family relationships)

Maoris, W. D. (1987). *Crystal.* New York: Viking Penguin. (African American ethical values)

Radial, R. (1988). *Haunted journey.* New York: Atheneum Publishers. (Appalachia, family relationships)

Robinson, M.A. (1990). *A woman of her tribe.* New York: Charles Scribners Sons. (family identity, Native American)

Roos, S. (1987). *Thirteenth summer.* New York: Atheneum Publishers. (parental expectations)

Figure 14.2. Resources for use with and by children in Diversity Groups.

SESSION I—WHAT MAKES US SPECIAL?

BRIEF OVERVIEW OF SESSION

This session will provide an opportunity for children to begin to look at the myriad of things that make cultures, races, or people in general special. It also will serve as a way for the children to become acquainted with each other and to understand the purpose for the group.

GOALS

1. To help children understand their reasons for involvement in the group.
2. To encourage children to begin to make connections with other members of the group.
3. To present group ground rules.
4. To provide an opportunity for children to begin to accept and appreciate differences in others.

MATERIALS NEEDED

1. 12" × 18" sheet of paper for each child
2. Chart paper or chalkboard
3. Markers and crayons or chalk

PROCEDURE

1. Introduce yourself and have each of the group members introduce himself or herself by first name. Talk about the fact that this is a group where we will begin to identify, understand, accept, and appreciate differences in others.

2. Begin to set the stage for the group by inviting a brainstorming session on group rules. (Write the rules on chart paper or on the chalkboard and post them for future reference.) Examples of possible initial group ground rules may include the following:

    a   What is said in the group, stays there (confidentiality).
    b   No put-downs are allowed.
    c   Only one person talks at a time.
    d   It is important to attend all sessions.

Note: If children do not suggest these group rules, you as facilitator should bring them up as part of the brainstorming session.

3. Give each child a piece of drawing paper and crayons or markers to draw a picture of "something beautiful." (The facilitator should also draw a picture.)

4. When all children have drawn their pictures, ask them to pair up with a partner and discuss their picture. Encourage them to identify any similarities and differences in what they see as being "something beautiful."

5. Bring the pairs back into one large group and encourage each child to share a picture with the whole group. (If possible, place the pictures on a wall or bulletin board where all of them are visible at one time for comparison and contrast.)

6. Point out that the old saying "beauty is in the eye of the beholder" certainly applies here as group members have all identified "beauty" in their own way.

7. Relate this to differences in people as well by asking what makes each of them "beautiful." Ask them to think about some of the things that keep us from appreciating the "beauty" in others (e.g., racial and cultural stereotypes, lack of understanding, fear, etc.). You may need to explain the word "stereotype."

8. Complete the session by having the group members talk about what qualities of the group make them special. (Because this group is, hopefully, of diverse backgrounds, some of these qualities may be mentioned.) Remind them that, during the next eight weeks, we will be learning to accept and appreciate the differences in others.

CLOSURE

To conclude this initial session, congratulate the children for following the ground rules and remind them that they have begun to identify some of the things that make this a unique group. We will continue to develop that understanding in our future sessions.

HOMEWORK

For a homework assignment, ask each child to get their parents to help them identify at least one cultural stereotype they have heard.

SESSION II—STEREOTYPES

BRIEF OVERVIEW OF SESSION

In this session, children will have an opportunity to look at their own personal stereotypes as well as become aware of many common stereotypes that are held by people. They will also begin to discuss how each of us can do our part to try to eliminate stereotyping.

GOALS

1. To help children identify common stereotypes that many people currently hold.
2. To encourage children to evaluate their own personal stereotypes.
3. To discuss ways to overcome stereotyping behavior.

MATERIALS NEEDED

1. A variety of pictures for display (e.g., an elderly person, a business or professional person, an athlete, a punk rocker, a clergyperson, a small child, etc.)
2. Chart paper (at least 3 pieces)
3. Markers

PROCEDURE

1. Begin by directing children's attention to the pictures that you have placed around the room. Tell them that you are going to ask them some questions about these people and they will see how they view each of the persons. We will show our choices by voting for the person we feel fits the description.

2. Ask the following questions (and provide time for voting and discussion after each question):

    a Which one is the richest?
    b Which one is the friendliest?
    c Which one would you be afraid of?
    d Which one has the most friends?
    e Which one likes rock music?
    f Which one is the most successful?
    g Which one is the most religious?

3. Following the discussion, ask the children to think about their choices. Why did they choose as they did? Are these some of the stereotypes we hold?

4. Divide the children into small groups and have them list some of the other stereotypes we hold about specific cultures or races. Remind them that this was part of their homework assignment so they should be able to quickly identify many common stereotypes. Some of the following are examples of stereotypes that some people hold:

a African-Americans are good athletes.
b African-Americans are lazy.
c Jewish people are stingy.
d Irish people are all drinkers.
f Asians are smart.
g Italians are gangsters.

5. Ask the children to identify some of the stereotypes that they can refute. Talk about the fact that we should get to know people rather than stereotyping them.

6. Talk about some ways to get to know people better. Ask the children for suggestions.

CLOSURE

Bring closure to this session by reminding the children that the purpose of this group is to help us understand and appreciate diversity. We can do this by resisting stereotyping behavior and getting to know people before judging them.

HOMEWORK

For homework, each child should make a concerted effort to get to know someone who is different from him or her during the next week.

SESSION III—DIVERSITY IN PHYSICAL AND MENTAL CAPACITY

BRIEF OVERVIEW OF SESSION

In this session, children will begin to identify things other than culture that make us different. We will consider differences in physical and mental abilities and how they, too, can make people seem "different."

GOALS

1. To encourage children to identify differences other than culture that can be found in our school or community.
2. To assist children in beginning to identify ways in which they can promote better communication among all people.

MATERIALS NEEDED

1. Pictures of handicapped children
2. A braille book
3. Sign alphabet cards
4. If possible, a visitor from the local Easter Seal Society to talk with the children about handicaps

PROCEDURE

1. Begin by asking the children to share with the group their experiences from their "homework" assignment. What were some of the positives of their experience? Allow brief time for discussion from each group member.

2. Ask if any of the children had the opportunity to get to know someone who was different in a way other than culturally?

3. Discuss some other "differences" we encounter each day. Provide time for brainstorming the following differences:

a   handicaps,
b   differences in school abilities,
c   differences in athletic abilities, and
d   differences in beliefs.

4. Show the braille book, the signing alphabet, and pictures of handicapped children. Provide time for discussion of familiarity with any of these.

5. Introduce the resource person from Easter Seal and allow time for him or her to talk with the children. Be sure to save time for the children to ask questions.

6. Encourage discussion of how these children can develop a friendship with a child who is a client of the Easter Seal Society. What are some things you could do with a special needs child? (You may want to talk about volunteerism at this point. Such groups as Easter Seal and Special Olympics always are looking for willing volunteers.)

CLOSURE

Bring closure to this session by providing a little "thinking time" for each group member. Ask the children to discuss their feelings about today's discussion.

HOMEWORK

For homework, each child is to spend some time thinking about what it might be like to be blind, deaf, or confined to a wheelchair. Encourage group members to write down their thoughts on a piece of paper and bring it to the next group session.

SESSION IV—WALK A MILE IN MY SHOES

BRIEF OVERVIEW OF SESSION

During the course of this session, the children will have an opportunity to actually experience what it would be like to be blind, deaf, on crutches, or in a wheelchair. This will provide an experience in sensitivity to the challenges of others.

GOALS

1. To provide an opportunity for the children to experience life with a "temporary" disability.
2. To encourage the children to discuss their experience in light of what it would be like to have such a disability on a "permanent" basis.
3. To continue to provide opportunity to understand and appreciate diversity in people.

MATERIALS NEEDED

1. Wheelchair
2. Crutches
3. Earplugs
4. Slips of paper with the words "blind," "deaf," "on crutches," and "in a wheelchair" written on them

Note: There should be enough so that each group member has the opportunity to experience a "temporary disability."

PROCEDURE

1. Take a few moments for the children to share their homework assignment with the other group members. Allow a few moments for discussion and reactions from group members.

2. Tell the children that today they are going to have an opportunity to "walk in the shoes" of a disabled person during this group session.

3. Have each child draw the slip of paper that describes a disability. Take a few minutes to have children get the proper equipment for their disabilities. Then describe the tasks that they need to complete while they are "disabled":

a   Blind—write your name; fill a cup with water from a pitcher.

b   Deaf—make a telephone call; ask directions to the local mall.

c   On crutches—Climb stairs (be sure to have a spotter for safety); make a telephone call.

d   In a wheelchair—negotiate an uneven surface; go outside and up a ramp (again with a spotter).

4. Provide about 15 minutes for the children to "experience" their disability and complete their tasks.

5. Bring the group back together and allow time for discussion of the difficulties they experienced in attempting to complete their tasks.

a   What was hardest for you?

b   Did you ask for help (or did you want to)?

c   What would it be like to have this disability on a permanent rather than temporary basis?

d   What can you do to make life more pleasant for those who have these disabilities?

CLOSURE

Because this is a pretty emotional session and there are a lot of feelings about the experience, provide time for the children to discuss their feelings. End this session on a quiet note.

HOMEWORK

In order to go in a different direction next session, encourage the children to think about and begin to collect information on some celebrations different from those that they are familiar with. Next session, we will spend a bit of time talking about the winter celebrations of Christmas, Hanukkah, and Kwanza.

SESSION V—DIVERSITY IN CELEBRATIONS

BRIEF OVERVIEW OF SESSION

In this session, children will have an opportunity to learn more about ways others celebrate their beliefs. Three specific celebrations have been chosen— Christmas, Hanukkah, and Kwanza—but the facilitator may want to use others depending upon the resources and variety available in his or her area (e.g., Native American Celebrations, Asian Celebrations, Hindu Celebrations).

GOALS

1. To assist children in learning about belief celebrations different from their own.
2. To encourage understanding and appreciation of a variety of beliefs.
3. To involve the community in promoting celebration of diversity.

MATERIALS NEEDED

1. People resources—a Christian, a Jewish person, and an African-American who celebrates Kwanzaa—to discuss their celebrations with the children and answer questions
2. Materials that can be used to demonstrate the three celebrations (e.g. Menorah, Christmas tree, Kwanzaa celebration garb, etc.)
3. Copies of "To Thank You" worksheet (Activity Sheet 14.1)

PROCEDURE

1. Ask the children if they were able to gather information about any of the three celebration topics mentioned as last session's homework assignment. Provide a few minutes to allow for discussion and sharing of information.

2. Introduce the resource persons and provide time for them to give a brief overview and demonstration of their particular celebration. Build in time for children to ask questions. (Keep in mind that they probably will have the most questions about the celebrations they are least familiar with.)

3. Encourage the children to discuss the things they learned from this session and to compare how the celebration they are most familiar with is similar and different from the other two. This discussion could be in diads or triads if the facilitator wishes.

4. Suggest that the children each write a letter to one of the three resource persons to show their appreciation to that person for coming to the group to talk about their celebration. Make sure the letters are divided equally so that each presenter receives at least two letters. Provide a "To Thank You" worksheet (Activity Sheet 14.1) for each child in the group.

CLOSURE

Remind the children of the new learnings they have gained as a result of today's session. Suggest that they take some time this evening at home to share some of this information with their family.

HOMEWORK

In preparation for next session, ask each child to enlist the assistance of his or her parents in preparing some type of food that is typical of his or her culture. These foods will be sampled by the group at the next session. Children should also be ready to tell the group about the food and how it came to be an important staple of their culture or ethnic background.

TO THANK YOU

Activity Sheet 14.1.   To Thank You worksheet. Permission is granted to enlarge and photocopy for classroom use.

SESSION VI—A DIVERSITY FEAST

BRIEF OVERVIEW OF SESSION

In this session, the children will begin to have a very personal view of ethnic and cultural differences in regard to food choices. Each child will bring a sample of an ethnic food that is a custom of his or her culture. The group then will have a feast of ethnic foods.

GOALS

1. To assist children in gaining a greater understanding of ethnic and cultural differences in food.
2. To encourage children to taste each of the various foods in the feast.
3. To further promote appreciation and understanding of all people.

MATERIALS NEEDED

1. Ethnic foods prepared by each child's family
2. Recipe sheet (Activity Sheet 14.2 is an example.)
3. Eating utensils (paper plates, napkins, cups, knives, forks, spoons)
4. Table and tablecloth

PROCEDURE

1. Talk briefly with the children about last week's session on celebrations. Allow for discussion of family reactions and so forth.

2. Remind the children that, in today's session, we are going to actually have our own mini-celebration of our heritage by sharing foods of our culture with the others in the group.

3. Provide a few minutes for each group member to tell the others about the food he or she brought to share. Place all foods on the table in an attractive manner.

4. Pass out plates, napkins, and plastic utensils and encourage each child to taste each of the foods that have been shared. (Allow time for seconds if they wish to resample any of the items, and try to make the sharing a social event with friendly conversation among the group members.)

5. Allow time for some discussion of the foods.

a   How were they different?
b   What did you like about them?
c   Which was your favorite?
d   Were you hesitant to try any of the foods?

6. Talk about the fact that ethnic restaurants are very popular in the United States today and that many people are learning to appreciate foods of other cultures.

CLOSURE

Bring this session to a close by allowing the children to talk about their feelings about this session. How did you feel about bringing your own food? How did you feel about tasting the food of others?

HOMEWORK

Give each child a recipe sheet (Activity Sheet 14.2) take home and ask a parent to copy down the recipe for the food item brought to share with the group. We will use the recipe sheets to make a small "Diversity Feast Cookbook" for them to have as a keepsake.

CELEBRATE DIVERSITY THROUGH FOOD ! !

Recipe Name_____

Ingredients:

_____
_____
_____
_____
_____
_____
_____

Directions:

_____
_____
_____
_____
_____
_____
_____

History of the Recipe:

EXAMPLE: Handed down from my grandmother who came to Pennsylvania as a baby in 1904. It is a holiday favorite in Hungary, particularly at Easter.

_____
_____
_____
_____

Your Name _____

Activity Sheet 14.2.   Recipe sheet. Permission is granted to enlarge and photocopy for classroom use.

SESSION VII—LET'S CELEBRATE DIVERSITY

BRIEF OVERVIEW OF SESSION

In this session, children will have an opportunity to work together to create a mural or collage to show their understanding and appreciation of the value of all people.

GOALS

1. To provide an opportunity for the children to work together to develop a "Celebrate Diversity" collage or mural.
2. To further encourage getting to know and appreciate the value to others.
3. To take the material from their homework assignment and develop a small ethnic cookbook.

MATERIALS NEEDED

1. Mural paper
2. Old magazines
3. Scissors
4. Glue or paste
5. Paints or markers

PROCEDURE

1. Talk briefly with the children about their homework assignment. Collect the recipes so that they can be duplicated and assembled into a small cookbook for children to keep as a remembrance of the group.

2. Spend a few minutes talking about the value of all people in creating the world in which we live. Encourage discussion of the things that make everyone a special part of our life.

3. Explain to the children that today's session is going to be spent in the development of a mural that will attempt to show others the kinds of things we have been talking about in group. Generate ideas as to how the mural should be made, what it should contain, and so forth.

4. Discuss an appropriate title for the mural. Some possibilities include

We are Different—We are the Same,
Living in Harmony,
Everyone is Special, and
Appreciate the Contribution of All.

5. Provide time for the children to work together to create their mural. Remind them that it can be drawn, painted, done in the form of a collage, or a combination of all of the above. The important thing is that we get the message we have learned out to others and that the children work together as a group to add each person's special talent to the creation of the mural.

6. When the mural is completed, hang it in a place where it can be seen by many persons. Stress to the children that appreciating and understanding diversity can help us have a better and more peaceful world.

CLOSURE

Bring closure to this session by again encouraging children to talk about their feelings. How did you feel when you were doing the mural? Do you think you can help others to appreciate diversity? How would you do it?

HOMEWORK

As a homework assignment, ask the children to think about how they can utilize the information they have learned in this group to create a more peaceful community (e.g., school, world). Give each child a 3" × 5" card to write three possible solutions to achieve this goal.

SESSION VIII—CREATING A MORE PEACEFUL WORLD

BRIEF OVERVIEW OF SESSION

In this final group session, children will have the opportunity to develop a list of suggestions for creating a more peaceful world. They will develop a "Declaration of Peace," that can be shared with others in the home, school, or community. They will realize that the old adage "peace begins with me" can, indeed, become a reality.

GOALS

1. To encourage children to reiterate the need for accepting, understanding, and valuing all persons.
2. To continue building on the understanding that human differences make people unique and special.
3. To assist the children in identifying and describing the qualities of peacemakers.
4. To assist the children in collaboratively creating a "Declaration of Peace."
5. To bring closure to the group and to complete a group evaluation.

MATERIALS NEEDED

1. Copies of "Declaration of Peace" worksheet (Activity Sheet 14.3)
2. Brief stories of peacemakers to share with the group
3. Group evaluation for each child
4. Pencils and markers
5. Copies of "Diversity Feast Cookbook" for all

PROCEDURE

1. Distribute the "Diversity Feast Cookbook" and encourage the children to take them home and share with their families.

2. Briefly talk about their impressions as to who are some people who have made attempts to be peacemakers in our world. Some names that may come to mind include

Abraham Lincoln,
Martin Luther King,
Mother Theresa, and
Ghandi.

3. Discuss these briefly with the children and ask them what makes these people special peacemakers.

4. Provide time for children to share their homework suggestions for creating a more peaceful world. List these on one large sheet of poster paper as possibilities for creating a "Declaration of Peace."

5. Begin to work together as a group (or divide the children into groups of two) to identify three or four statements that can be used as a "Declaration of Peace." A sample of some possible statements could be

We believe that human beings are different in many ways, and that our differences make us unique and special. We also believe that we are all interconnected regardless of our differences and we need to affirm and appreciate others for their uniqueness. When we accept ourselves and others, we can create a more peaceful world.

6. Have each child copy the final statement on a "Declaration of Peace" worksheet (Activity Sheet 14.3) and share it with his or her family.

7. Encourage discussion of final statement and talk about how these children can work together to make the world a more peaceful place.

CLOSURE

Conclude this session by having each child tell every other group member something that is special or unique about himself or herself and why he or she was a special group member. Pass out the group evaluations and provide time for completion.

HOMEWORK

The homework assignment for this group is to take the appreciation and understanding of others that they have learned and share it with everyone they meet. Encourage the children to start now to make their classroom, community, and world a place where everyone is valued and appreciated.

Activity Sheet 14.3.   Declaration of Peace worksheet. Permission is granted to enlarge and photocopy for classroom use.

EVALUATION

1. Do you feel that participation in the Diversity group was helpful to you? Why or why not?

2. What part of the group did you like best?

3. What part of the group did you like least?

4. If you had a friend who needed to identify, understand, accept, and appreciate differences in people, would you recommend that he or she join this group or one like it? Why or why not?

5. Did you attend all eight group sessions?

_____ Yes _____ No

If no, how many did you attend? _____

6. Comments, suggestions, etc.:

REFERENCES

Bauer, K. L. (1992, May). Helping children appreciate our cultural soup. *PTA Today*, 5–6.

Bosworth, K. (1995). Caring for others and being cared for: Students talk caring in school. *Phi Delta Kappan, 76*(9), 686–693.

Buscaglia, L. (1982). *The fall of Freddie the leaf: A story for all ages.* New York: Holt, Rinehart & Winston.

Chaskin, R. J., & Rauner, D. M. (1995). Youth and caring: An introduction. *Phi Delta Kappan, 76*(9), 667–674.

Curry, N. E., & Johnson, C. N. (1990). *Beyond self-esteem: Developing a genuine sense of human value.* Washington, DC: NAEYC.

Drew, N. (1987). *Learning the skills of peacemaking.* Rolling Hills Estates, CA: Jalmar Press.

Eyre, L., & Eyre, R. (1993). *Teaching your children values.* New York: Simon & Schuster.

Grevious, S. A. (1993). *Ready-to-use multicultural activities for primary children.* New York: The Center for Applied Research.

Hendrick, J. (1992). Where does it all begin? Teaching the principles of democracy in the early years. *Young Children, 47*(3), 51–63.

James, W. H., Moore, D. D., Gregersen, M. M. (1995). Cultural diversity in elementary saps. *Student Assistance Journal, 8*(1), 12–16.

Kohn, A. (1991). Teaching children to care. *Phi Delta Kappan, 72*(7), 496–506.

Kroeber, A. L., & Kluckholm, C. (1952). *Culture: A critical review of concepts and definitions.* New York: Vintage Books.

Lee, C. C. (1994). Pioneers of multicultural counseling: A conversation with Clemmont E. Vontress. *Journal of Multicultural Counseling and Development, 22,* 66–78.

Lipsitz, J. (1995). Prologue: Why we should care about caring. *Phi Delta Kappan,* *76*(9), 665–666.

Locke, D. C. (1992). *Increasing multicultural understanding.* Newbury Park, CA: SAGE Publications.

McCracken, J. B. (1993). *Valuing diversity: The primary years.* Washington, DC: National Association for the Education of Young People.

Myers, J. E. (1990, May). Wellness throughout the lifespan. *Guidepost,* p. 11.

Pederson, P. (1988). *A handbook for developing multicultural awareness.* Alexandria, VA: American Association for Counseling and Development.

Perry, T., & Fraser, J. W. (1993). Reconstructing schools as multicultural democracies. *Rethinking Schools, 7*(3), 16–17, 31.

Perry, S. K. (1992, May). Activities for exploring diversity. *PTA Today,* 7–9.

Rosenburg, E. (1992, May). Teach our children well: Each person is special. *PTA Today,* 10–12.

White, S. H., & Siegal, A. W. (1984). Cognitive development in time and space. In B. Rogoff & J. Lave (Eds.), *Everyday cognition: Its development in social context* (pp. 238–277). Cambridge, MA: Harvard University Press.

Wittmer, J. (1992). *Valuing diversity and similarity: Bridging the gap through interpersonal skills.* Minneapolis: Educational Media Corporation.

INDEX

ABOUT THE AUTHORS

Dr. Kathleen O'Rourke is the Counseling Department Chairperson and Co-ordinator of Comprehensive Prevention/Intervention Services for the Altoona Area School District, Altoona, PA. Her experiences include 30 years as an educator, 18 of which she served as an elementary school counselor. During those years, Dr. O'Rourke has become very aware of the value of student support groups as a primary method of providing counseling services to children. Such groups provide an excellent vehicle for assisting children in becoming aware of the fact that they are not alone in dealing with the struggles of childhood. Support groups also provide a formal as well as an informal network for children who need to realize that others are caring, understanding, and supportive.

Prior to becoming involved in the administrative facet of counseling, Dr. O'Rourke was an elementary teacher and counselor, served as one of five pilot project counselors for the Pennsylvania Elementary School Developmental Guidance Project in the 1970s, coordinated a Career Education project for the Altoona Area Schools, and was involved in Dropout Prevention programs. She also has served as a state consultant to districts involved in implementing comprehensive elementary counseling programs.

In the professional arena, Dr. O'Rourke has been very active since the early 1970s and has assumed the following leadership roles: PSCA President, Board of Governors Chair, Career Education Taskforce Chair and Elementary School Chair, ASCA Northeast Regional Vice President, Credentialing Taskforce Chair, Publications Committee and Governing Board, College Board Regional Council, and PHEAA Advisory Committee. In conjunction with these leadership positions, she has presented workshops throughout the United States.

Dr. O'Rourke holds certification as a National Certified Counselor and a National Certified School Counselor. During her years as a counselor, she also has been recognized with numerous awards. Among them are the Altoona Area School District CARE Award, the Distinguished Dissertation Award from Epsilon Chapter of Phi Delta Kappa, the Pennsylvania Counseling Association Eminent Practitioner, the YWCA Woman Educator of the Year, and the Northeast Regional Center for Drug Free Schools and Communities Award.

In the local community, Dr. O'Rourke currently serves on the AASD Q-site and Training Team and the Strategic Planning Committee, was Board President of Big Brothers/Big Sisters of Blair County, and served on the Family Life Committee and Church Parish and Finance Councils. She also is involved in the advisory council of the Taylor Center for Womens Health Care and the Altoona Hospital Drug and Alcohol Council.

Dr. John C. Worzbyt is professor and coordinator of doctoral and school counseling certification studies in the Department of Counseling, Adult Education, and Student Affairs at Indiana University of Pennsylvania (IUP). He received his bachelor's degree from the State University of New York College at Oswego and his master's and doctoral degrees in counseling from the University of Rochester.

John has 30 years of experience in education, having worked as an elementary and middle school science teacher, elementary school counselor, and counselor educator. He is a nationally certified counselor and holds memberships in the American Counseling Association, the American School Counselor Association, and the Association for Counselor Education and Supervision.

In addition to fulfilling teaching and administrative responsibilities, John is a consultant to school districts, social service agencies, professional associations, mental health clinics, and hospitals. His areas of expertise are child counseling, self-esteem enhancement, developing human potential, and creating healthy working climates.

As author, John has written articles and book reviews in a number of counseling related journals and newsletters. He has published three monographs and coauthored three previous books on guidance topics.

John is a registrant of the National Distinguished Service Registry: Counseling and Development; is listed in Who's Who in the world, American Education, and the East; coauthored *Elementary School Counseling: A Blueprint for Today and Tomorrow*, which received the 1990 Writing and Research

Award from the American School Counselor Association; coauthored the United States Congressional Medal of Honor Society Youth Program, *Beating the Odds*; and is a recipient of the College of Education (IUP) Faculty Recognition Award for Outstanding Accomplishments as teacher-scholar.

For the past several years, John has been a keynote speaker and workshop presenter at national, regional, and state conferences on such topics as Up Your Enthusiasm, How to Get High on Life, The Human Side of Leadership, and Developing a Happier Healthier You. He continues to offer a variety of human potential and self-improvement workshops to various groups and organizations through his private consulting business.